OWEN HART
KING OF PRANKS

First paperback edition November 2019

ISBN: 978-1-7040-2765-4 (paperback)

Imprint: Independently published

Dedicated to my Mum
Thank you for everything

Chapters

i

Acknowledgements

First and foremost I'd like to thank my Mum. Not only did she have the pleasure of birthing me back in the eighties, she went on to encourage me to write this book. She also helped edit, correct spelling and argue with me over punctuation. If it's all wrong, blame her. I'd also like to thank my sister Christina for illustrating the book, Lauren Brookes AKA 'The Goober' for her love and support throughout the process, Elaine Catterall for proofreading in her free time, Sean Waltman for coming up with the concept and then not doing anything about it, every wrestler who wrote me back and anyone who promised to buy the book once it was finished.

It's only proper to thank the following for the years of work they've put into their resource websites so people like me can pretend to know what they're talking about: Dave Meltzer and Bryan Alvarez (*Wrestling Observer*), Graham Cawthorn (thehistoryofwwe.com), some Germans (cagematch.net) and especially whoever redesigned the WWE Network so all their shows now have chapters, cutting production time by at least six months.

Lastly I'd like to thank Owen Hart. You were a damn fun person to write about.

Introduction

I was not a fan of Owen Hart.

There, I've said it.

I've been watching WWF/WWE programming full-time from 1993 when I was 7 years old until I reached adult age. If I had been older (and had regular access to Sky television) I would have been watching wrestling even earlier. I absolutely loved it. I first learned of the existence of wrestling through various media appearances of 'Big Daddy' Shirley Crabtree. Despite British 'World of Sport' wrestling being taken off Channel 3 (ITV) in 1988, Big Daddy still frequently appeared on kid's television and fluff news pieces and had remained a household name well into the 1990s.

I first became aware of the World Wrestling Federation when my older sister Christina took me to my school one Sunday where they were holding a little fair to raise money for charity. Christina gave me 50p for the lucky dip, which amounted to an orange bucket filled with confetti and lame prizes. I rummaged round the bucket until I pulled out several stickers. I was expecting them to be Panini football stickers, which I was collecting at the time. Instead of stilted publicity shots of Alan Shearer, Dion Dublin or Peter Beardsley gawking back at me, I saw these muscle-bound aliens striking poses and looking colourfully menacing. Featured among the wrestling stickers I retrieved from the bucket was Hulk Hogan, the top half of Irwin R Schyster and bottom half of Bam Bam Bigelow. The IRS sticker beguiled me the most. "Who was he? Why was he wearing a shirt and tie? Was he so pale because he worked in an office?"

Shortly after becoming a wrestling fan based solely on owning one and two-halves of a wrestling sticker collection, I got my hands on a video tape of *SummerSlam 1993*. I loved the larger-than-life characters, I loved the entrance music, I loved the melodrama and the rivalries and I especially loved the big, hard-hitting moves. Shortly after this wrestling revelation, my even-older brother Christian's best friend Phil furnished me with multiple tapes of WWF events he had recorded off Sky Movies+ (Sky Sports didn't exist yet) over the course of 1991 and 1992. After watching these video tapes hundreds of times over I officially became a wrestling fanatic. Growing up in the Greater Manchester region of England, my favourite wrestler was, of course, 'British Bulldog' Davey Boy Smith. Number two was Bret Hart followed by 'Macho Man' Randy Savage at three.

In 1994, the main World Wrestling Federation storyline concerned the blood feud between WWF Champion Bret Hart and his jealous little brother Owen. Owen had come from the bottom of the card to defeat Bret at *WrestleMania X*, seemingly out of nowhere. I thought it was a total fluke. I figured Owen, who was one of the smallest wrestlers on the roster, was lucky to be in the WWF at all and I couldn't work out how he kept besting his much larger opponents. I couldn't fathom why Owen was being given a Championship match against Bret at the *SummerSlam 1994* pay-per-view over the likes of The Undertaker, Diesel, Lex Luger, Savage or any number of other more deserving candidates. When Owen became the WWF Tag Team Champion along with Yokozuna in 1995, I assumed Owen was the lucky one to be teaming with a wrestler who so much bigger and better than him.

Like many fans, I lost interest in wrestling somewhere in the mid 1990s, only to re-discover the WWF in 1998 at age 12, along with everybody else in my school. All-time classic acts such as Stone Cold Steve Austin, The Rock, The Undertaker, Mankind, D-Generation X, Sable and my personal favourite, Kane, were the Federation's top stars and it was a wonderful time to be a fan. The WWF developed what it called 'Attitude', featuring lots of gratuitous sex, violence, swearing and crazy stunts in a successful bid to overtake WCW and regain the top spot in the Monday Night Wrestling Wars. Owen was still part of the WWF roster at that point, and I still didn't understand why. In the year 1998, Owen went from: challenging WWF Champion Shawn Michaels to avenge Bret Hart's unceremonious ousting from the company, to being destroyed by Michaels' lackey Triple H, to joining black militant group the Nation of Domination, to being portrayed as a 'shoot' (real) fighter, to becoming the goofy superhero The Blue Blazer, to becoming the third wheel in the Jeff Jarrett and Debra McMichael double act. One year. It seems that I wasn't the only one who didn't understand what part Owen should play in the Attitude Era.

To me, Owen was part of the old guard still clinging on to the back of the unstoppable WWF juggernaut with other antiquated 'pro wrestlers', like Vader. Between WWF and WCW's booking philosophies, the two companies somehow made actual professional wrestling look passé in favour of chair shots, rambling interviews and gesticulating at one's own crotch. Owen still wore his trademark singlet like a 'wrestler' instead of jeans and a t-shirt. What was up with that? He wasn't cool like The Rock or The Godfather or Road Dogg. He wasn't an outlandish freak like Mankind, Kane or Goldust. He wasn't a bad ass like Steve Austin, The Undertaker or Ken Shamrock. He damn sure wasn't a 100lb woman with big, fake boobies like Sable, Sunny or Jacqueline. Owen was just a wrestler.

The thing is... Owen Hart was a *great* wrestler. It's just that the 12-year-old me never noticed.

Owen was a very good babyface (good guy) during his early career and a great heel (bad guy) in the World Wrestling Federation. He was one of the only wrestlers in the history of the business that mastered every style of pro wrestling from around the world. After turning pro in 1986, Owen spent considerable time in Europe, Mexico and Japan honing his craft and putting food on the table for his family, as well as touring North America almost non-stop for a dozen years. His interview skills also developed over time to where he was one of the better speakers in the business. Owen was one of the most valuable and treasured wrestlers on the WWF roster.

Owen died aged 34 on the 23rd of May 1999 at the WWF *Over the Edge* pay-per-view, emanating from Kemper Arena in Kansas City, Missouri. Owen, as his goofy superhero alter ego The Blue Blazer, was scheduled to wrestle The Godfather for the WWF Intercontinental Championship at that show. The plan was for Owen to rappel down from the arena's catwalk at high-speed before being suspended several feet above the ring. At that point, Owen was to pull a quick release chord on the front of his harness and perform a pratfall into the ring. What should have been a spectacular entrance turned to tragedy as the quick release snap shackle prematurely disengaged and Owen fell almost eighty feet to his death.

Owen had serious misgivings about the stunt all day, which he had done once before six months earlier, minus the pratfall and the quick release snap shackle required to perform it. WWF Chairman Vince McMahon was disappointed with the previous drop, believing it to be too slow and looking bad on television. On the day of *Over the Edge*, Owen let it be known to a number of co-workers how uncomfortable he was, lamenting that he just wanted to wrestle and cut interviews like he used to. While in catering early that day, the stunt riggers asked Owen to rehearse the drop, which he declined. Owen then went with fan/friend Treigh Lindstrom to a nearby Gold's Gym, telling WWF agents he'd be back by 2pm. Owen purposely stalled for time, ignoring his ringing mobile phone until Vince McMahon himself called. McMahon reportedly told Owen he had to be back at Kemper Arena in fifteen minutes flat or he was going to fire him.

Putting his family's financials before his own serious misgivings, Owen returned to the arena at 3:30pm and completed one trial run, which hadn't gone perfectly, before refusing to practice the stunt a second time. The original plan involved having Owen lowered to the ring accompanied by midget wrestler Max Mini, dressed as a miniature Blue Blazer. Max was to be dangled between the Blazer's legs with his own quick release snap shackle attached around Owen's beltline. Thanks to Owen's deliberate procrastination, mini-Blazer's involvement in the descent was scrapped that evening and pushed back to the following night on the WWF's *RAW is WAR* television show, inadvertently saving his life.

Before the pay-per-view went live, the normally cheerful, easy-going Owen displayed a rare bout of anger backstage when he tossed his harness vest across the locker room in front of several stunned wrestlers. Come show time, Owen, disguised in overalls and a baseball cap, hurriedly walked past hundreds of fans before clambering up to the catwalk. Owen changed into his Blue Blazer attire and was hooked into the harness. While there have been several theories of why the snap shackle prematurely opened, what *is* known for certain is that Owen never should have been up there in the first place, as the stunt was entirely unnecessary. The descent was not advertised ahead of time and Owen was *not* a trained stuntman. The Blazer's lowering from the ceiling was designed to spoof the Sting character from WCW; hardly a top priority storyline-wise, especially as Sting himself hadn't performed the stunt in months.

Joe Branham had been the WWF's go-to stunt coordinator for this type of affair for years and had worked with Owen on a previous stunt, as well as with The Undertaker and Shawn Michaels on similar descents. Branham insisted on using a locking carabiner, which was the industry standard and repeatedly refused the WWF's requests to use a quick release snap shackle. For the 10th of May *RAW is WAR*, Branham quoted the Federation $5,000 to coordinate a stunt which would see Owen lowered from the rafters. The WWF, who would go on to make $56 million profit that fiscal year, said $5,000 was too expensive. Branham feared for Owen's safety in case the WWF hired the cheapest bidder from the competitive world of stunt rigging. Branham told his assistant to offer the WWF a discounted rate of $2,000, but by then the skit had been written out of the *RAW is WAR* script entirely.

Shortly after Branham's failed negotiations, a stunt rigger called Bobby Talbert, who was not as qualified as he'd claimed to be, cold-called the WWF's Vice President of Event Operations, Steve Taylor. Talbert, whom almost nobody in the stunt work business had heard of, told Taylor he had worked for WCW many times overseeing Sting's various descents from the rafters and would work for cheap. Taylor informed WWF Head Writer Vince Russo, who similarly took Talbert at his word. Russo wrote, "The Blue Blazer descends from atop the arena," into *Over the Edge's* running sheet, with Talbert set to rig the stunt. Ellis Edwards, who was *actually* the main rigger for the Sting descents, later went on the record to vehemently dispute Talbert's claims. Edwards asserted that Talbert was only an assistant on three of the WCW-based stunts and was *never* the lead coordinator.

When it was time for his sensational entrance at *Over the Edge*, Owen was dangled over the catwalk in preparation for his descent. Edward Ellis later stated that even a small amount of movement or pressure could have been enough to inadvertently trigger the quick release mechanism the way Talbert had rigged it. While Owen was hovering over the ring, he started messing with his cape, which was trapped in the harness. Owen's heavy breathing (as he was afraid of heights and genuinely terrified) could have also possibly caused the harness to disengage.

The fall itself was not broadcast to the pay-per-view audience as a pre-recorded montage of The Blue Blazer was rolling at the time. The arena lights had also been darkened to focus on the jumbo video screen, meaning most of the live audiences didn't see it either. Just before the fatal impact, Owen grazed the head of referee Jimmy Korderas who was in the ring clearing out debris from the previous match. Korderas was lucky to escape with only a slight bump on the head. Owen landed chest-first onto one of the top rope turnbuckles, narrowly missing the ring post. Aside from severe injuries to his arm, Owen suffered a severed aorta and bled to death internally. There was nothing anyone could do to save him. Owen was pronounced dead at Truman Medical Centre thirty-three minutes later. Around an hour after the fall, lead announcer Jim Ross, who had only been informed of the news over his headset from Executive Producer Kevin Dunn seconds earlier, had the unfortunate duty to relay to the viewing audience that Owen Hart had died. The news of Owen's death had been kept secret from the live audience and many fans in attendance had no idea how grave the situation really was, or even if it was just part of a storyline.

In what is now almost universally viewed as an abhorrent decision by Vince McMahon, the pay-per-view event continued on as normal. The next night, the World Wrestling Federation's flagship show *RAW is WAR* became a two hour tribute to the life and career of Owen Hart. It almost didn't, as according to former Federation Head Writer Vince Russo, Kevin Dunn pitched Vince McMahon on presenting a regular episode of *RAW* and acting like Owen never existed. *RAW is Owen* featured basic wrestling matches with clean finishes interspersed with dozens of tribute videos from his peers. The episode remains the third most watched RAW in the show's twenty-five year plus history. Some saw *RAW is Owen* as a beautiful and cathartic tribute. Others saw it as an exercise indamage limitation. It was both.

The morning after *Over the Edge*, Owen's death was the talk of the school. After eventually piecing together what happened from snippets of information I'd gleaned throughout the day, I experienced a sadness that I'd never felt before after learning of a public figure's passing. The *RAW is Owen* tribute show put paid to my innocence as far as being a wrestling fan was concerned. I already knew wrestling was contrived, show-business, or whatever synonym you prefer to use for being 'not on the level', but watching Owen's co-workers break character and pour their hearts out on television over what a wonderful wrestler, mentor, family man and friend he was made me look at Owen, and the wrestling business, in a whole new light. Wrestling was simultaneously more real *and* more fantasy than I'd previously understood. I realised that if all of these wrestlers were describing Owen as a fantastic in-ring worker, then they must be right and I must have been wrong. My young mind also understood that a highly-regarded, deeply-loved man had died needlessly after being forced into an untenable situation for the sake of a ratings war that the WWF had long since won.

Shortly after Owen's passing changed my perception of the business, my first real exposure to the inner workings of wrestling came from the biography *Have a Nice Day: A Tale of Blood and Sweatsocks* by Mick Foley. After twenty years it remains a fascinating read, and it spurred me on to learn as much about wrestling's inner workings as I possibly could. In 1999 I saw the documentaries *Beyond the Mat*, *Wrestling with Shadows* and the famous episode of *Louis Theroux's Weird Weekends*, which was partially filmed at WCW's Power Plant training facility, to get a sense of how wrestling 'really' worked. Eventually I discovered wrestling news sites and the pop-up adverts that came with them. The more I learned about the inner machinations of pro wrestling, the more I also became a fan of Owen Hart's work.

By 2002, I'd stopped obsessively taping every episode of *WWF Smackdown!* on Sky One and by 2003 I'd pretty much given up on wrestling altogether. When the niche Wrestling Channel satellite station started broadcasting in the UK in 2004, I gave wrestling promotions TNA, ROH, NOAH and even local upstarts FWA a chance before admitting to myself I'd grown out of wrestling in favour of boxing, mixed martial arts and football. I still kept an eye on the wrestling news and even started watching WWE again when they revived the ECW brand in 2006, before giving up for good when it was clear that wrestling would never be as great as it once was. A combination of out-of-character (known in the business as 'shoot') interviews by wrestling personalities and the rise of the candid wrestling podcast in the early 2010s rekindled my interest in the inner workings of the genre. I even started a YouTube fan channel for *The Jim Cornette Experience* podcast a few years back called *Jim Cornette's Talking Sense*, which became a lucrative enterprise for all concerned during its relatively short existence.

Back in 2011 I watched an in-depth interview with Sean 'X-Pac' Waltman that stuck in my mind more than most. After discussing Owen Hart's predilection for pranks, Waltman added, "There's some... ribs about Owen that honestly have to be written about." A number of humorous Owen stories had indeed already been written about and spoken of by his contemporaries since his passing and fans seemed to enjoy hearing tales of his classic pranks. I thought it would make a great book, but almost ten years after the Waltman interview, no one had bothered to write one.

Why not me?

I mean sure, I had no writing experience whatsoever and I gave up a degree course in law because I couldn't remember a single thing I'd read; but less qualified people than I have gone on to write worldwide best sellers - Dan Brown, for example. In October 2018 I started researching names, listening to old radio interviews and podcasts, studying books and websites and contacting some of Owen's former co-workers for stories. Eventually I collated over one hundred separate Owen Hart rib stories and over the course of eight months spent nearly every day putting them all into book form.

I've also added biographical snippets at the beginning of every chapter detailing Owen's wrestling career to add some depth. Throughout the book, there are postscripts at the end of most of the stories that will contain fun asides and little-known facts that will hopefully augment the tales contained therein. For the casual and non-wrestling fans, I have included a glossary of 'insider' terms I've used throughout at the beginning of the book that all hardcore fans will automatically understand.

The aim of this book is to make people laugh and celebrate the legacy of Owen Hart as a human being rather than just a character on television. This book will also not dwell on Owen's untimely passing beyond this introduction. Should you wish to learn more about the extraordinary circumstances which led to Owen's tragic death and the bitter lawsuit that followed, I recommend picking up *Broken Harts: The Life and Death of Owen Hart* by Owen's widow Martha Hart.

I wrote to Martha, as well as Owen's siblings Bret and Diana Hart, informing them of the book project and offered to donate a portion of the book's proceeds to Martha's charity, *The Owen Hart Foundation*. None of them replied.

Hope you enjoy,

James Romero

Notes to reader

All stories contained in this book come from publicly accessible sources such as books, online articles, shoot interviews, etc, as well as personal interviews. I have been faithful to the original storyteller or storytellers' versions of events while eliminating falsehoods or misremembered facts as best I can. If all else fails, the old adage will get us through: "When truth becomes legend, print the legend."

Should you know of any additional rib stories (with sources), or spot glaring factual or spelling errors in this book, please email owenhartbook@gmail.com – I may have a second edition in me to write.

While the company is now known as WWE, the abbreviation WWF (for World Wrestling Federation) will be used throughout the book, which is what the WWE was called between March 1979 and May 2002. The World Wrestling Federation was forced to rename itself after losing their final legal appeal against the UK-based World Wildlife Fund charity over use of the WWF initials.

Glossary of Wrestling Terms

Glossary of professional wrestling terms (2019) Wikipedia. Available at https://en.wikipedia.org/wiki/Glossary_of_professional_wrestling_terms (Accessed Nov 14 2019.)

Agent/road agent (also known as a producer) - A management employee, often a former wrestler (though it can be a current wrestler), who helps wrestlers set up matches, plan storylines, give criticisms on matches, and relay instructions from the bookers.

Angle - A fictional storyline. An angle usually begins when one wrestler attacks another (physically or verbally), which results in revenge.

Babyface/face - A wrestler who is heroic, who is booked to be cheered by fans.

Blading - A wrestler intentionally cutting themselves to provoke bleeding.

Book/booker - To determine and schedule the events of a wrestling card. A booker can also be described as someone who recruits and hires talent to work in a particular promotion.

Bump - To fall on the mat or ground.

Burial/to bury/be buried - The worked lowering (relegation) of a wrestler's status in the eyes of the fans. The opposite of a push, it is the act of a promoter or booker causing a wrestler to lose popularity and credibility through means such as forcing them to lose in squash matches, losing continuously, allowing opponents to no-sell or kick out of said wrestler's finisher, or forcing them to participate in un-entertaining or degrading storylines.

Card - The lineup of the matches that will be staged at a given venue.

Carry - The act of one wrestler guiding a typically less experienced or skilled performer through a match.

Clean finish - A match ending without cheating, outside interference, or any type of controversy.

Dark match - A non-televised match at a televised show.

Draw - A wrestler or program that attracts the attention of the audience; someone fans are willing to pay to see.

Feud - A staged rivalry between multiple wrestlers or groups of wrestlers.

Gimmick - The character portrayed by a wrestler.

Gorilla position - The staging area just behind the curtain where wrestlers come out to the ring, named after Robert 'Gorilla Monsoon' Marella.

Hard camera - The main camera(s) that shoots the ring from the crowd.

Heat

1. Negative reactions (such as booing) from fans. When the heat is directed at a heel this is seen as a good thing, as it means fans are reacting in the desired way.

2. Real-life tension or bad feeling between two wrestlers, or a wrestler and the promotion.

Heel - A wrestler who is villainous, who is booked to be booed by fans.

House - The amount of money drawn at a particular event.

House show/live event - An untelevised event.

Independent promotion - A smaller wrestling company that operates at a local (rather than national) level and typically employs freelance wrestlers, as opposed to signing wrestlers to exclusive contracts.

Jobber - A wrestler who routinely loses in order to build the credibility of other wrestlers.

Kayfabe - The presentation of professional wrestling as being entirely legitimate or real.

Legit (legitimate)

1. Refers to real-life incidents or events that have not been booked or scripted and are therefore not part of the fictional and kayfabe presentation. It is often used to describe a genuine injury to a wrestler, as opposed to one scripted as part of a storyline.

2. Used to describe a wrestler who has a genuine background in another combat sport (typically boxing, other wrestling codes or mixed martial arts) and so has proven 'real' fighting skills.

Lucha libre - Mexican professional wrestling. Translates to 'free fight' and is sometimes shortened to simply *lucha*, the Mexican style of professional wrestling is characterized by high-flying aerial moves, coloured masks, and the rapid series of holds, strikes, and manoeuvres.

Main eventer - A wrestler who is seen as on the highest level in a promotion and typically headlines shows.

Manager - A performer (usually a non-wrestler) who is paired with one or more wrestlers in order to help them get over, often by acting as a mouthpiece or interfering in matches on their behalf.

Mark

1. A pejorative term for wrestling fans that enthusiastically believe or behave as though they believe professional wrestling is not staged, or loses sight of the staged nature of the business while supporting their favourite wrestlers.

2. Used by some industry insiders to describe a participant in the wrestling industry whom they think believes that any worked aspect of the industry is more important than the money they can earn.

Mid-carder - A wrestler who is seen as higher than a low-carder, but below a main eventer, typically performing in the middle of a show.

Money mark - Someone who founds or invests in a wrestling promotion mainly to associate with wrestlers, often wilfully or ignorantly disregarding financial risks a profit-focused investor would avoid.

No-sell - To show no reaction to an opponent's offensive moves; a way to demonstrate endurance, appear invulnerable to pain, legitimately undermine an opponent or to illustrate masochistic tendencies.

No-show - A wrestler or performer's unplanned absence from a show.

Over - Achieving the desired crowd reaction, with the audience buying into a performer or gimmick.

Pinfall - Holding a wrestler's shoulders to the mat for a three count, to win a fall.

Pop - A cheer or positive reaction from the crowd.

Programme - A series of matches in which the same wrestlers face each other, usually due to the two being scripted in a feud.

Promo - An in-character interview or monologue.

Push - The worked rising of a wrestler's status in the eyes of the fans.

Rib - A practical joke.

Ring psychology - The process of wrestling a match in such a way that the crowd becomes emotionally involved. Performing an engaging match requires acting skills and a good grasp of dramatic timing.

Run-in - The unexpected entry of a new wrestler(s) or returning wrestler in a match already in progress.

Screwjob - An unfair and controversial finish, often involving cheating or outside interference.

Second - A person accompanying, or 'seconding', a wrestler to a match.

Sell - To react to something in a way which makes it appear believable and legitimate to the audience.

Shoot - When a wrestler or personality deliberately goes off-script, either by making candid comments or remarks during an interview, breaking kayfabe, or legitimately attacking an opponent.

Sports entertainment - The term WWE uses to describe both its own product and professional wrestling as a whole.

Spot - Any planned action or series of actions in a match.

Spot show - An untelevised wrestling event sporadically held in a town that wasn't a regularly/weekly stop in a wrestling territory's touring schedule.

Squash - An extremely one-sided match.

Stiff - Using excessive force when executing a move, deliberately or accidentally.

Stretching - The act of causing physical harm to prospective professional wrestlers, usually by the means of submission holds.

Swerve - A sudden change in the direction of a storyline to surprise the fans. Often, it involves one wrestler turning on an ally in order to join a supposed mutual enemy.

Turn - A switch in alignment of a wrestler's character. Turns involve a wrestler going from face to heel or vice versa.

Valet - A person, usually an attractive female, who accompanies a male performer to the ring.

Vignette - Any piece of video footage featuring characters or events which is shown to the audience for the purposes of entertainment or edification.

Visual win - A pinfall/submission that the referee does not see, but the crowd does.

Work

1. (noun): Anything planned to happen, or a 'rationalised lie'; the opposite of shoot.

2. (verb): To methodically attack a single body part over the course of a match or an entire angle, setting up an appropriate finisher; 'to work over'.

3. (verb): To deceive or manipulate an audience in order to elicit a desired response.

Worker - Another term for professional wrestler.

CHAPTER 1

The Hart Family and Young Owen

❤ ❤

Owen James Hart was born on the 7th of May 1965, the last of twelve children born to parents Stu and Helen. Stu, square-jawed and as tough as nails, had an upbringing as rough as they come. Having grown up in the last vestiges of the Canadian Wild West, Stu survived crippling poverty, back-breaking farm work, harsh winters sleeping in a tent and the after effects of the 1929 stock market crash. After learning the grappling game in a local YMCA in Edmonton, Alberta, Stu carved out a career as an excellent amateur wrestler, winning national titles before being chosen to represent Canada at the third British Empire (now Commonwealth) Games in Melbourne, Australia. Unfortunately, the City of Edmonton couldn't afford to send him, so he didn't go. Stu also qualified for the 1940 and 1944 Olympics but both events were cancelled due to World War II.

After joining the Canadian Navy, Stu wound up coaching the baseball team, as well as putting on wrestling exhibitions to entertain the troops. While on leave in 1943, Stu was sitting in a New York café when he was approached by wrestling promoter Joseph 'Toots' Mondt.[1] Mondt gave Stu his business card and promised him work when he was available. When he was discharged in 1946, Stu took Toots up on his offer. The handsome Canadian made a huge impression on the New York professional wrestling scene. Due to his amateur pedigree, Stu held his own against the grizzled veterans of the territory, who loved to terrorize young wrestlers. That same year, Stu met his future wife while walking down Long Beach.

Helen, one of five sisters, was the daughter of 1912 Olympic long-distance runner Harry Smith. In Stu's eyes, the 22-year-old Helen bore a striking resemblance to Rita Hayworth and became besotted with her. Although he was good-looking and considerate, the genteel Helen didn't quite feel the same way about Stu. She hated wrestling and was looking for someone more refined. After much wearing down, courting and letters sent while on the road, Stu and Helen became an item. "The moment I met him I knew that he and I had nothing in common," said Helen. "Later on I realised that we'd be totally incompatible, so of course we got married. We were married in a blizzard and I've been snowed under ever since!" Early in their marriage, when Helen asked how much longer they were going to be involved in wrestling, Stu would reply, "Just a few years."

Stu and Helen soon moved to Edmonton, where Stu opened up his first territory, Klondike Wrestling, in 1948. Stu worked as a wrestler and booker and Helen helped with the administrative side, usually while pregnant. "She didn't do it nine-to-five," said Owen on his mother's business contributions, "she would do it from nine 'til midnight." Helen spent most of her time in her office managing the family business, bookkeeping and dealing with wrestlers. Her hatred of the wrestling business never dissipated and later in life her worst nightmare was realised. "I know my Mum never wanted us to become wrestlers," said Owen "and she *certainly* did not want my sisters marrying wrestlers. Both of those nightmares came true. We're all wrestlers in some form or another and my sisters all married wrestlers." What Helen craved the most was a nice, normal existence, which she would never have again after marrying Stu. "[Helen] would tell me she was waiting to wake up from this god awful nightmare surrounded by wrestlers and boys," confirmed third Hart kid Keith.

Stu bought the Calgary territory in May 1951 and a few months later purchased a twenty-one room mansion sitting on thirty acres of land overlooking Calgary. The mansion would come to be known as 'Hart House.' Among its many features, Hart House had a basement that Stu converted into a gym, complete with weights and a 300 square foot wrestling mat. The basement would be nicknamed 'The Dungeon' and would go down in legend as the place where many wrestlers were tested, up to and beyond, their limits by Stu's torturous wrestling seminars. "It wasn't at all strange to look out the window of your room and watch some guy in nothing but wrestling trunks howling and running from the basement in the snow," recalled eldest child Smith. Grown mens' screams ringing through the mansion were accepted as completely normal. It wouldn't just be prospective grapplers who would be dragged down to the Dungeon for a dose of humility; he would stretch his kids too. "[Stu] would take you down there and methodically just wrestle with you [and] put you in submission holds," said Owen. "He always knew what he was doing but [I wondered] am I gonna get out of here alive? He was like a sheepherder, you gotta get all the kids in line and everybody behaved themselves and I think it worked."

"It wasn't meant to humiliate you," added tenth Hart kid Ross. "That's how you learned if you were meant to be doing this." If the Hart kids were quiet, they were allowed to sit in the corner and witness stretching sessions first-hand. Owen went down to the basement in the early 1980s to make an audio recording of one such drubbing. Stu, who was coiled around some poor unfortunate, berated his prey in his distinctive, often imitated, cadence. "C'man, have some gad-damn dignity. Be a man!" Those who survived received an offer to be trained as professional wrestlers but nobody was safe from being stretched by Stu. Everybody from wrestlers, kids, announcers, friends, daughters' boyfriends, sons' girlfriends, grandkids, strangers and even a car thief Stu gripped while he tried to steal one of his Cadillacs, had a degree of hurt put upon them by the Hart patriarch at one time or another.

Hart House was also home to a ridiculous number of ridiculous guests. Stu was big on charity and helping others in need and any transient wrestler who requested a bed for the night was usually welcome to stay over. All manner of giants, freaks, shooters and midgets roamed the house and its grounds on a continual basis. The yard was full of Cadillacs that dilapidated over the years, turning the grounds of Hart House into an automotive mausoleum. However, the most intriguing guests were the creatures that roamed in and around the mansion. Stu took in various farm animals and untold numbers of cats and dogs over the years but the most curious animal lodgers doubled as some of his most notable in-ring adversaries. Along with

3

cheetahs, wolves, attack dogs and Bengal tigers visiting the house on occasion, Terrible Ted, the wrestling bear, was kept in a cage under the porch on-and-off for years. "I remember watching my dad's powerful body with his perfect posture," recalled eleventh Hart kid and youngest daughter Diana, "leading the hulking 600-pound animal on a thick rope around our yard." Stu also allowed an alligator to stay at the house for a while but told everyone to keep it a secret from Helen as the 'gator was deemed a guest too extreme, even for Hart House.

The renamed Big Time Wrestling territory had some great years in the 1950s, featuring big name talent and performing shows across the Canadian Prairies, the Northern United States and even Alaska during the promotion's heyday. Back at Hart House, Stu assumed the role of both parents and was a strict disciplinarian when he had to be. According to daughter Diana, some of the kids not only received cuffs round the ears when they acted up but also one-on-one submission wrestling sessions in the Dungeon or even a head flushing in the toilet. When Heathcliff, one of the many cats roaming Hart House, took a whizz in the toaster, Stu took the 'bastard' cat by the scruff of the neck and gave him the swirly treatment too! At this point it should be stated that all the children had the greatest amount of love and respect for their father, including Owen. "I was intimidated by my Dad; I respected him. Just that fear of ever doing something wrong kept me from doing something wrong." Stu was also a pretty modern man, performing many of the tasks typically left to the mother at that time. "My Dad was the one who made my breakfast, the one that took me to school. Most of the time he was the one who made my lunch." Growing up destitute, Stu would be gravely offended if somebody didn't eat every scrap of food on their plate. There have long been accusations of Stu's lack of kitchen hygiene, mostly revolving around a supposed incident where he scooped up a dog poo with a spatula, then used the same spatula to cook eggs. Diana Hart refuted the story but did confirm that cats routinely slept in the salad bowls.

By the late '50s, Big Time Wrestling's business began to dip. The Boxing and Wrestling Commission started fining Big Time over violent content, causing Stu to tone down his television product. In 1960, Ted DiBiase's father, Iron Mike DiBiase, cut an inflammatory promo on the local audience. "If brains were dynamite, the people of Calgary wouldn't be able

4

to blow their nose," lambasted Mike. This line promptly saw Big Time Wrestling thrown off the airwaves. Stu then started co-promoting with Vancouver-based All Star Wrestling, which proved to be yet another money loser. Big Time experienced several ups and downs in the early '60s before going out of business in 1964.

By the time Owen was born in 1965, the family's finances were at an all-time low, but that didn't dampen enthusiasm over the arrival of Stu and Helen's final child. "This was the last baby and we all knew and we all were in awe of him," recounted ninth child Alison. Seventh child Georgia said, "[Owen] had a lot of attention and the older siblings gave him a lot of attention." Second child Bruce remembered being taken aback after learning his mother had given birth. Bruce found out about Owen's arrival from some kids at school who'd heard the news on the radio. "It sounds funny but I wasn't even aware she was pregnant." Helen had originally wanted an astonishing fifteen children but was mercifully told by her doctors that her tiny body couldn't handle any more pregnancies. All the Hart kids raced home from school to welcome the last sibling into the brood, with eighth child Bret leading the charge. "There was a bit of an obsession with Owen," said Bret. "Everybody was trying to pick him up and carry him around. He slept in the girls' room; he was the girls' project." Keith concurred, "He was the girls' tattletale; his allegiance was strictly with the girls."

When Owen turned three it was decreed that he would be moving in with the boys. "You could see everybody's eyes kinda look at Owen and you could see Owen swallow pretty hard," said Bret. "He just knew this was a big moment for him." Soon after, fifth kid Dean ended up rowing with sixth kid Ellie. When Helen came to break up the fight, Owen was asked who started it. Bret chuckled, "Right away Owen looked and he sized up the situation and went, 'Ellie started it!'" Keith was just as proud of Owen for making the smart decision. "He'd severed all the ties with the girls and he was one of the boys. It was like high-fives all around and we got the arm around Owen; he was the new team member!"

From a young age, Owen realised that his family was somewhat atypical. "My friends would say like, 'Wow! There's the Harts,'" Owen explained. "'They live in this big brick house mansion on the hill. As far as we know there's at least a dozen of 'em! Their Dad's this big, mean wrestler.'

We always had a very unique family." Bruce felt that the Harts were looked at more like 'The Addams Family' and 'The Beverly Hillbillies' by their neighbours. Owen often told reporters, "We thought we were rich but sometimes there wasn't even enough money for gas." Smith used to think of Owen as something of a mascot for the boys, who they would have fun dressing up. "We'd dress him up like a little punk in a black leather jacket and grease his hair down and stuff and get him to school like us." Owen was a bold kid, imbued with a sense of invulnerability instilled in him by his family. According to Smith, Owen was also a pretty tough customer, even at a young age. "He always had his fingernails worn down to nothing and scrapes and bruises and a black eye and stuff from little scraps and stuff. He wasn't a troublemaker at all but he was like Dean... he didn't take any crap from anybody and he didn't deserve any. That was the difference between [Owen and Dean], he didn't really ask for trouble but when somebody wanted to serve it to him he'd dish it right back."

Due to his hand-me-down clothes and 'fake wrestler' Dad, Owen received his fare share of tormenting at school just like the rest of the Hart kids endured at one time or another. When Owen fought and lost battles with kids much older than him, a bigger brother would step up to get revenge on his behalf, whether it was Bret forcing a bully to kiss to his knackered old Cadillac for calling it a 'shitmobile' or Dean screwing over a ruffian's parents by selling them a duff car. Even teachers got set straight on occasion when Owen was being mistreated. Former NWA Champion and family friend Harley Race humorously characterised Owen as, "An ornery little asshole," when he used to visit Calgary in the 1970s. Owen was never a troublemaker and according to his widow Martha, "Was practical, hard-working, strong and a decent man's man," just like his father. Keith Hart concurred, "I thought he was very humble, very much like my Dad for humility and very much like my Mother for his fine sense of humour. He didn't fall into the traps that the rest of us may have fallen into, maybe being a little headstrong and arrogant. Terrific guy!"

Although Owen would develop a predilection from pranking in his early teens, his penchant for ribs was evident at an early age. John 'JR' Foley, a Hitler 'tasche-sporting Scouser, was a manager and spokesperson for many heel wrestlers for Stampede Wrestling throughout the 1970s. One morning,

Foley was sat in the kitchen of Hart House waiting patiently for his pay cheque when Owen walked in with a bowl full of unidentified sweets. The devious Hart chewed away on a piece of carrot to con Foley into thinking he'd just tucked into the not-so-tasty confection and brought the bowl over. "Don't mind if I do," said Foley, before he shovelled a handful of what turned out to be pebble shaped cat treats called 'Sea Nips' into his mouth. "Owen was the master of the straight face," chuckled Bret. "His smile would never give anything away but when he got you, his blue eyes would always tell the truth."

Owen picked up the wrestling business almost by osmosis from his family and the great wrestlers who passed through Calgary, despite Stu not 'smartening him up' to the contrived nature of the pseudo-sport as a boy. A memory all of the Hart clan have is of Owen putting on wrestling matches he arranged between a stuffed monkey and Heathcliff the cross-eyed cat. "Owen had this little monkey with real hard plastic hands and feet and he'd whack that cat on the head a couple times and the cat knew it was game time," Bret said. "He'd have the cat in a headlock and all sorts of other moves. They were really, truly entertaining matches." Owen also learned fitness and gymnastics from a young age. Aside from being a wrestling training space, the Dungeon was also home to various pieces of (occasionally dangerous) gym apparatus, mostly cobbled together from assorted scraps by Stu. Along with Diana, Owen developed an interest in gymnastics before he hit his teenage years and was even coached by a girl from the Canadian gymnastics team who Bruce was dating. "He had great balance and technique," said Ross. Bret even caught Owen doing backflip drills off the top rope of the wrestling ring semi-permanently erected in the yard. "He'd get back on the ropes and he'd do it again and again and again," said Bret.

Owen's first real exposure to the crazy world of pro wrestling occurred when he was fourteen. In 1980, Owen travelled with Bruce and Keith to Honolulu, Hawaii for a wrestling gig set up by Dean, who had moved to the islands in the late 1970s.[2] Anyone of non-Polynesian heritage was automatically a heel and Bruce and Keith purposely riled the crowd up so badly that a riot broke out in the Blaze Dale Arena. As diminutive as he was compared to the gargantuan locals, Owen started throwing hands in defence of his older brothers. Owen grabbed the arm of a local gang-banger called

'Fast Eddie' to stop him from bottling Keith. Eddie immediately turned around and dropped Owen with a knuckle duster-assisted punch, giving him a big, black eye and a cut that required stitches. "It was crazy," Owen recalled. "I was in the middle of all these six-foot, three-hundred pound bodies... and the men were even bigger!"

In high school, Owen played American football, rugby and participated in track and field. At the encouragement of his father, Owen also joined the amateur wrestling programme. It was for amateur wrestling that Owen earned a scholarship for the University of Calgary. While he loved being able to tell his father he had won a wrestling scholarship, Owen never actually enjoyed the sport in any regard, "I was living my dad's dream of being an amateur wrestling Olympic champion. My Dad never made me amateur wrestle but it was encouraged and I hated it. I didn't like dieting, I didn't like being Owen Hart the famous Hart boy, but I always had this feeling of when I come home I wanna please my dad." Owen was going to University to learn and was determined to not fall into the trap of getting involved in pro wrestling like all his brothers had. "I think he was trying to break that mould," posited Bret's ex-wife Julie. "He didn't want to be a wrestler, he was 100% sure he just wanted to be a physical education teacher." Both Bruce and Keith worked as substitute teachers during their wrestling careers. Owen also considered becoming a fireman like his brother Keith, who got a job with the Calgary Fire Department along with brother-in-law BJ Annis and seemingly two thirds of the patrons of BJ's gym in the early '80s.

Truth be told, Owen had been actively involved in the wrestling business since he was five. Shortly after Owen was born, Stu got another chance to promote wrestling, thanks in large part to local sportscaster and long time wrestling commentator Ed Whalen. Ed managed to get Stu back in his old television slot on CFAC. Big Time Wrestling was revived and renamed Wildcat Wrestling shortly after Owen's birth. In 1967, the promotion was renamed again, this time to the more familiar Stampede Wrestling. Owen helped his father out by selling programmes and helping out however he could every Friday at Calgary's Victorian Pavilion. When he was eight, Owen started going on road trips with his brother Bruce. "He was always intuitive and perceptive and we shared many perspectives and great times on the road," Bruce fondly recalled. The Hawaii punch-up hadn't totally put Owen off eventually getting in the ring and neither had his fear of the terrifying wrestlers from his childhood, like Abdullah the Butcher.[3] When he was in his teens, Owen used to go in the dressing room and challenge some of the wrestlers to take him on right then and there. Former wrestler and current bounty hunter, 'Dr D' David Schultz, was one such opponent. "Every once in a while I'd hook [Owen]. Stu would walk in and of course Stu's famous saying was, 'It looks like you got that little bastard in a pretty tight situation there, David!'"

The 16-year-old Owen first crossed paths with his future wife Martha Patterson, a serious, 15-year-old gymnast, while travelling for a wrestling meet at her school. A month later, Martha and her wrestling-obsessed friend Odette went to the Friday night Stampede event at the Pavilion where Martha recognised the well-built, blonde-haired kid sitting at a table ringside and struck up a conversation. Martha now claims she put up with the wrestling shows just to see Owen but Bret maintains that Martha was a big fan of wrestling at the time. Being old-fashioned (some would say puritanical) Owen and Martha would hang out most Fridays for six months before even having their first proper date. They got on famously and had lots in common, not least that they both came from enormous families, their homes were treated like doss houses for any number of down-and-outs and strangers and they both hungered for a 'normal' life. "Owen wanted to have a very structured existence," said Martha, "an ordinary life." As the couple got more serious, Owen purposely spent more and more time away from the chaos of Hart House in favour of being with Martha's family or hanging out at Bret's place in Ramsey. Owen was already starting to get sick of the conversations and outright arguments that constantly revolved around wrestling. In later years, Owen would make his excuses and leave Hart House early whenever wrestling was brought up, which was almost always.

Martha's biggest fear was seeing Owen get sucked into the 'seedy, unsavoury environment'[4] of professional wrestling but it almost seemed inevitable. "[Owen] was just too good at it to not wrestle," claimed Alison. "Wrestling had already chosen him." Apart from height issue (standing around 5'8"-5'9") Owen had the looks and the ability and the rest of the Harts were salivating at the opportunity to get him in the ring. With practically no formal training, Owen filled in for an injured pro wrestler as a last-minute replacement in 1983 right after graduating high school. Combining his amateur wrestling credentials, high-flying gymnastic ability and natural gift for the sport, Owen was a huge success. Owen teamed with Stampede headliner and middleweight trailblazer 'Dynamite Kid' Tom Billington[5] and wore a mask to retain his amateur wrestling status, which was a common practice at the time. Shortly afterwards, Owen toured England, France and Germany for several months with brother Ross. Owen even made several appearances on the UK's wildly popular World of Sport Wrestling show, watched by millions every Saturday afternoon. Owen also occasionally donned a mask to wrestle at the annual wrestling shows at the Calgary Stampede festival or untelevised spot shows for fun and extra pocket money. "I don't remember anybody picking up the business so quickly," exclaimed Ross.

In 1984, Stu finally closed up the money pit that Stampede Wrestling had become, selling the territorial rights to the ever-expanding World Wrestling Federation, owned by Vince McMahon. Owen forgot about professional wrestling and concentrated on earning his degree in physical education. During the summer months he worked as an oilfield rigger and pipeline fitter. In 1986, Owen received a proposal to return to the ring. Instead of working back-breaking summer jobs out in the middle of nowhere, why didn't he wrestle during those months instead? Stampede reopened in late 1985 after McMahon hadn't lived up to his promises[6] and Bruce was now booking the promotion. "After my third year of university, my brother Bruce called me and said, 'We need a new Hart'," recalled Owen. "I was watching from the sidelines watching wrestling and said, 'Nah! I'm not gonna do that. I wanna be normal and be a fireman or a school teacher.'"

Eventually, Owen was swayed with the lure of finally making decent money and committed his services to Stampede for the 1986 summer season. Owen was a smash hit and the fans loved him. Owen's high-flying, acrobatic style was incredibly rare in the mid 1980s and he was only one of a handful of wrestlers who could backflip off the top rope. Along with his lineage, Owen also had a natural charisma that the fans gravitated to. He studied tapes of Japanese legend Satoru 'Tiger Mask' Sayama and was a huge fan of

Dynamite's work in Stampede before he left. Owen was on course to be the headliner Stampede desperately needed since Bret and Dynamite had been picked up by the WWF in 1984. His height wasn't an issue, as several years before, Stampede had taken the direction of featuring smaller, more talented workers instead of the lumbering oafs that populated much of the wrestling landscape at the time. Owen was so happy to be making decent money (CA$500 per week, later nearing CA$1000) he pushed back his final year of education to continue wrestling through to autumn 1987. Another reason Owen stuck with wrestling was because the University of Calgary had just dropped their amateur wrestling programme and his wrestling scholarship had been rescinded. Although in hindsight Owen felt he made the right decision financially, he still regretted not finishing his degree. "If I could do anything differently, it would have been [to dedicate] a couple more years to further my college and stuff, it would have been ideal."

Owen started off taking on all comers during his initial months as a pro, including: the Cuban Assassin, 'Honky Tonk' Wayne Farris, Kerry Brown, obligatory Russian Vladimir Kropoff and also tagging against the Viet Cong Express (played by Japanese wrestlers, obviously) with his sister Alison's husband Ben Bassarab. Owen's first major rivalry was with the heel stable Karachi Vice; a loathsome heel group of Pakistani terrorist sympathisers.[7] The group's leader, the 'Great' Gama Singh (Gadowar Singh) threw a fireball in Owen's face[8] and the crowd nearly rioted as the baby of the Hart family writhed around on the ring canvas in mock agony. Owen would frequently do battle with hairy 400lb blob and fellow Karachi Vice member Mike 'Makhan Singh' Shaw, who had recently become a 'born-again Pakistani' in a wacky on-screen ritual. The egregiousness of a white American sympathising with Middle-Eastern terrorists captured the ire of the fans and having him rival Owen proved to be a financial success for the promotion. The rookie Owen managed to get the very best out of Shaw in their matches and the two traded Stampede's top title, the North American Heavyweight Championship, between them five times from October 1986 to March 1988. In a later interview, Shaw rated the rookie Owen's mat skills highly, before adding, "Everybody looks at Bret as being the best wrestler [but] Bret and I could never have a good match. It just goes to show you, some guys mesh and some guys don't."

11

Some in the promotion grew jealous of Owen's rapid ascension, chalking it up to another example of a promoter's kid getting preferential treatment.[9] Others also felt that Owen came into the territory a little less humble than he could have been. "The first time I worked with Owen I didn't like him because I thought he was a spoiled brat," said 'Bad News' Allen Coage, who is one of the only wrestlers to ever go on record to say something negative about Owen. "Here's a kid that just got out of high school, he's wrestling and he never lost." Bad News had been one of Stampede's main event heels for years; he was a miserable human being and tough to do business with. When Owen started wrestling for Stampede full-time, Martha started attending the matches again. One particularly brutal match with Bad News had the still naive Martha ready to intervene on her boyfriend's behalf. "I didn't know that wrestling was fake and I even remember him wrestling Bad News Allen. They had this really bad brawl and I was ready to take my shoe off and throw it at Bad News Allen because he was hurting Owen and I just didn't know and Owen never told me." Any negative feelings towards Owen emanating from the locker room dissipated over time with his personality and wrestling ability winning over his detractors.

Bret had already suffered through his fair share of matches with Bad News when he was in Stampede and he hated facing him. Bret would have his comebacks cut short and he'd get far less offence in than he was otherwise accustomed to. When Bad News faced off with Owen in the rebooted Stampede promotion, the dynamic between them was much the same. Bret also accused Bad News of lacking charisma and wrestling psychology, only being able to work the hard-hitting, big move-trading Japanese style. As far as booking philosophy went, Bad News saw things a different way in regards to Owen, "If you want sympathy for the guy, you have him get in there and have everybody kick the crap out of him first," Allen claimed. "You can't have him coming in here beating up everybody; it's not going to sell. And it didn't and it started killing the houses. People said, 'This is bull.'" By late '87, Bret was riding high in the WWF with Jim 'The Anvil' Neidhart as part of The Hart Foundation tag team. He received a phone call from brother Ross asking him to put a good word into the WWF office to get Bad News out of the Stampede territory.[10]

Later in his tenure, Owen faced off against Karachi Vice associate 'Champaign' Gerry Morrow and the monstrous Jason the Terrible; a rip-off of Jason from *Friday the 13th* played by the 6'3" Karl Moffat. According to brothers Bret and Ross, Moffat was addicted to blading every night, which turned the stomachs of some audience members and proved detrimental to Stampede's bottom line. Owen himself had already bladed a few times but was uncomfortable with it and felt he was a good enough wrestler he didn't need to resort to the barbaric practice. Surprisingly, the nefarious Jason the Terrible ended up getting cheered by audiences. This necessitated a hasty babyface turn, which saw Jason team up with Owen on a number of occasions to fend off Stampede's resident band of evil doers. Owen frequently teamed up with Bruce Hart and hot young rookies Brian Pillman and Dynamite Kid clone Chris Benoit, who would go on to be one of Owen's toughest opponents in Japan as Pegasus Kid. Some of Owen's last matches in Stampede involved Johnny Smith, the storyline relative of Owen's future brother-in-law and pranking cohort, Davey Boy Smith. Johnny was reportedly such a nice man that when a Japanese fan presented him with a custom made ring jacket, Smith didn't have the heart to tell him he'd misspelled his name. Smith wore the jacket, with 'Jhonny Smith' emblazoned on the back, to the ring for the rest of his career.

It didn't take long for word to travel beyond Calgary regarding Owen's talents. He was invited to tour with New Japan Pro Wrestling regularly from August 1987 onwards, which was a big honour, as they invited only the cream of the crop of wrestling talent. Owen was named *Pro Wrestling Illustrated* 'Rookie of the Year' in '87, as well as 'Best Flying Wrestler' in both '87 and '88 by Dave Meltzer's *Wrestling Observer Newsletter*. In tribute to his young brother's abilities, Bruce Hart wrote, "For my money, Owen, in the late '80s and the Dynamite Kid, in the early '80s, were probably two of the most gifted and compelling workers I ever had the pleasure of watching and I've seen damn near every great and near-great star over the past thirty years." The World Wrestling Federation also had Owen on their radar. "There was this rumbling coming out of Calgary... the Hart you want is the baby," recalled WWE Executive Producer Bruce Prichard. "Owen is the worker, Owen is the one that's gonna be the star. At the time

Owen was doing a lot of high-flying things... long before it was in vogue to do."

After a number of mostly ignored WWF try-out matches while working for Stampede, Owen finally got the call he'd been waiting for when Bret managed to convince World Wrestling Federation Chairman, Vince McMahon, to take on Owen full-time in 1988. Stampede had been headlined by Owen for the past two years but his talent was too big for the small-time family promotion and Owen deserved the opportunity to make some real money while he was still young. "New York was where the money was - the WWF," said Bret. "That was the goal; to get him there and get him some money." Owen was also having disagreements with Bruce over some of his booking decisions and the time seemed right to get out before the business started coming between them. The running of Stampede had already started gobbling up what remained of Stu and Helens savings and Helen pleaded for Stu to consider folding the wrestling promotion he loved so much once and for all.[11]

---

[1]Mondt is one of the most influential people in professional wrestling history. In the 1920s, Mondt helped evolve pro wrestling from (mostly predetermined) mat-based snooze fests into what he termed 'Slam Bang Western-Style Wrestling', emphasising drama, larger-than-life characters and booking that kept audiences coming back for more. Mondt, Ed 'Strangler' Lewis and Billy Sandow formed the 'Gold Dust Trio' in the early 1920s, eventually spreading nation-wide. Mondt promoted in the North Eastern United States and in 1952 founded Capitol Wrestling with Jess McMahon. When Jess died in 1954, his son Vince McMahon Sr. replaced him. In 1963, Mondt and McMahon Sr. left pro wrestling governing body the National Wrestling Alliance and formed the World Wide Wrestling Federation, the precursor to today's WWE, owned by Vince McMahon Jr.

[2]Dean was helping local wrestling promoters Peter and Lia Maivia put on shows in Hawaii, sometimes performing referee duties too. Peter and Lia Maivia were the maternal grandparents of Dwayne 'The Rock'

Johnson, who had a good relationship with Dean when he was a little boy.

[3]Lawrence Shreve terrorised fans and wrestlers alike as Abdullah the Butcher; a 400lb, cleaver-brandishing, fork-wielding, shaven-headed black guy with deep scars on his forehead from decades of cutting himself to draw blood. "He used to scare me, man," said Scott 'Raven' Levy. "I was like, 'Ah! Wrestling's fake but that guy's out of his mind!'" Abby, as he was known to his friends, performed for over fifty years, never overstaying his welcome in any one territory. Abby had a bizarre ritual of wrapping his enormous wallet full of cash in a cloth secured with rubber bands, before hiding it in his baggy martial arts trousers before his matches. According to former wrestling manager Jim Cornette, the bizarre part came when Abby returned to the locker room. "When he came back from the ring and he took the butcher pants down and reached in and got the wallet out... [Abby] opened the wallet, pulled the money out and counted it... maybe he thought he was working with David Copperfield!" Abdullah the Butcher's 2011 WWE Hall of Fame induction was controversial because of Abby's over-reliance on brawling, weapons and bloodletting instead of wrestling. Abby also came under fire for allegedly infecting numerous workers with Hepatitis C when he bladed himself and bladed others *without* their consent. "[WWE] is a shameless organization to induct a bloodthirsty animal such as Abdullah the Butcher into their worthless and embarrassing Hall of Fame," fumed fellow WWE Hall of Famer, Wayne 'Superstar Billy Graham' Coleman.

[4]Stu Hart partially agreed with Martha's assessment of professional wrestling and, contrary to popular opinion, did not actively encourage his sons to become professional wrestlers. Bruce Hart stated, "I remember (Dallas-based wrestling family) the Von Erichs told me it was almost ordained or decreed by their father that they get into wrestling but my dad was probably disinclined for us. He saw the underbelly of it and a lot of the negative aspects, so we were probably discouraged." Stu originally mandated that any son of his getting into wrestling had to go to university first but the rule was ignored by some of the younger

Harts. Stu did however encourage his sons to take up amateur wrestling, with the hopes one of them could achieve his dream of making it to the Olympics.

[5]With the brutal travel schedule, freezing conditions, remote location and low pay-offs, box-office names were hardly tripping over themselves to call the Calgary territory looking for full-time work. With few exceptions, only certain categories of wrestler would work for Stampede: rookies on the way up, old-timers on the way down, foreign wrestlers looking to get a foothold in North America and those who were deemed 'undersized'. Bruce would go on foreign expeditions on the look-out for promising new talent to bring back to Calgary. Bruce's most significant discovery was in Cleethorpes, Lincolnshire during a six-week tour of the UK in 1978, where he witnessed Marc 'Rollerball' Rocco go head-to-head with British Welterweight Champion 'Dynamite Kid' Tom Billington. Bruce lured Dynamite to Calgary with the promise of, "A free car, a free apartment and $400 per week." British Promoter Max Crabtree's counteroffer of a pay rise from £12 per day to £13 per day was amazingly not enough to stop Billington from vacating his British and European titles and heading to Canada. Dynamite was such a revelation that Stampede created a brand new mid-heavyweight division, with Dynamite its first-ever champion.

[6]Stu Hart revived Stampede Wrestling in late 1985 with Bruce running the show, after folding the promotion over a year prior. When Vince McMahon purchased the rights to the Calgary territory, he agreed to take on Bret Hart, Davey Boy Smith, Dynamite Kid and Jim 'The Anvil' Neidhart as wrestlers and Bruce as a booking agent. McMahon would pay Stu $100,000 every year for ten years for the rights to run the Calgary territory and take over the Stampede television timeslot. Stu would also receive a percentage of the gate for any show the WWF ran in Calgary or Edmonton. Thanks to subpar live events the WWF booked in Calgary and an un-engaging television product called Maple Leaf Wrestling, the WWF was soon drawing less than 1,000 fans to their shows. Maple Leaf Wrestling was the WWF's Canada-exclusive hourly television show that ran from 1984-1986. It followed the same

format as the WWF's domestic programming, which consisted of one-sided 'squash' matches contested between a superstar and a tomato can, interspersed with geographically specific interviews hyping upcoming live events. The Stampede fans were used to hard-hitting, blood-letting, big-time matches playing out on their television screens weekly, which was not what the WWF was providing at that time. Aside from not drawing fans, McMahon was under financial hardship to the point that he was behind on payments to the TV stations that he paid to air his programming. McMahon gambled it all, even remortgaging his house, on the first *WrestleMania* event on the 31st of March 1985, which aired on closed circuit TV to arenas and movie theatres across the country.

[7]Karachi Vice was dreamed up by Owen and Bruce, with the name parodying the *Miami Vice* television show. Owen had been watching the news when he suggested turning Mike Shaw into a 'born-again Pakistani' parodying born-again Christians. They frequently did battle with the valiant Hart brothers, with crowds across Canada diplomatically registering their objections to Karachi Vice's existence with unsavoury chants like 'Paki shit' and 'go home, Paki!'

[8]The illusion of throwing a fireball is created by lighting up a few sheets of flash paper. Original 'Sheik' Ed Farhat was the fireball's most noted practitioner but Memphis-based Jerry 'The King' Lawler co-opted the spot many times, as did a host of others over the years. An embarrassing situation occurred at *WWF In Your House 14* in 1997 when Mick 'Mankind' Foley couldn't ignite the flash paper, leaving Mark 'The Undertaker' Calaway and William 'Paul Bearer' Moody fumbling around to improvise for minutes on end. Hulk Hogan's run-in with flash paper went even more wrong. In the middle of putting on one of the worst matches in history with Jim 'Ultimate Warrior' Hellwig at *WCW Halloween Havoc '98*, the only thing Hogan managed to burn was his own eyebrows off when the flash paper suffered a delayed reaction. Both farcical occurrences were broadcast live on pay-per-view and both times the live audience doubled over with laughter.

[9]The wrestling business is littered with promoters' kids getting preferential treatment. Some went on to live up to, or even outdo, their fathers' reputations in their home territory such as: Owen and Bret, Von Erich boys Kevin, David and Kerry, the Guerreros and Jeff Jarrett. Some wrestlers like Mike Graham, Dustin Runnels, Brian Lawler, Charlotte Flair and Greg Gagne had varying degrees of success but couldn't outshine their more famous fathers. Some wrestlers' pushes, like the ones David Flair, Erik Watts, George Gulas, Chris Von Erich and Mike Von Erich received, were so wholly undeserved that they ended up contributing to decreased ticket sales or even the outright collapse of their territory. Lanky, pigeon-chested, spectacularly talentless black hole of charisma George Gulas was the son of Tennessee promoter Nick Gulas. Nick doggedly booked George in his main events from his 1974 debut to the territories' closure in 1980, having him beat up everyone he wrestled. In 1978, George faced off against travelling NWA World Champion Harley Race. The match was so bad that the audience started booing the babyface George, provoking him to scuffle with some ringside fans. Legend has it that during the same match, Harley refused to react to some of George's languid, feeble-looking offence, prompting George to say in his thick, southern accent, "Daddy said sell! Daddy said sell!" When Nick closed his failing promotion and retired in 1980, George was also forced to retire because he sucked so powerfully nobody would hire him.

[10]After making some initial television appearances in January, the rechristened Bad News Brown started full-time with the WWF in February 1988 where he soon found himself in a programme with Bret Hart. Bret was due to be given a push as a singles wrestler but when he was paired with Bad News once again, his singles push was quickly aborted and Bret returned to the tag team ranks.

[11]Stu felt duty bound to keep Stampede around as long as Owen was putting in so much effort, as well as to provide jobs for several of his children. Shortly after Owen left for the World Wrestling Federation, Dynamite Kid and Davey Boy Smith, now known as The British Bulldogs, announced they were leaving the WWF to return to Stampede

as well as Japan. Dynamite, who had a mean streak a mile wide, had been tormenting Jacques Rougeau for a number of weeks in the WWF. Jacques got some well deserved revenge by sucker punching Dynamite's front teeth out aided by a concealed roll of quarters. The humiliated Dynamite left the WWF shortly after, taking Davey with him. When the Bulldogs returned to Stampede, Stu deposed Bruce as booker, handed the reins to Dynamite and carried on operating the territory for a little while longer.

Brian Pillman's ~~Bad~~ Horrendous Company

As told by various sources

With Stampede's revival in October 1985, added emphasis was put on smaller and more talented workers. In the '80s: Dynamite Kid, Davey Boy Smith, Chris Benoit, Gama Singh, Jushin Thunder Liger, Biff Wellington, Bruce Hart, Owen Hart and a host of other non-heavyweight grapplers called Stampede their home. Another of these promising up-and-comers from the revived territory was a first year rookie and former NFL Cincinnati Bengal, Brian Pillman.

Former Bengal's strength coach Kim Wood and wrestling journalist Dave Meltzer saw a budding pro wrestler in Pillman before he'd seen one in himself. With his eccentric, out-going personality, good looks and chiselled physique, he was a potential superstar in the making. The only attribute that could potentially hold Brian back from main event superstardom was his height. Most big-time wrestlers in the 1980s stood six feet tall or above; Brian stood around the 5'9" mark. Pillman, who played as a nose tackle during his football career, was also one of the shortest players in the NFL. Coupling the height issue with various injuries saw Brian prematurely cut from the Bengals, as well as being the last player axed from the Buffalo Bills before the start of the regular season. With little recourse, Pillman headed for the relative ignominy of the Canadian Football League, a league mostly populated with has-beens and never-was's, becoming a starting linebacker for the Calgary Stampeders in 1986.

After another ankle injury forced him back on the sidelines, Pillman decided to capitalise on his local celebrity and give wrestling a try. He trained in the art of professional wrestling in the storied Dungeon at Hart House for only two months before making his televised Stampede Wrestling debut. Brian was shoe-horned into the mix right away, involving himself in the business of Stampede's main event heel faction, Karachi Vice, before hooking up with Bruce Hart to form the babyface tag team, Bad Company.

Coming from the Wild West excesses of the NFL, Brian Pillman was more than happy diving into the sex, drugs and rock 'n' roll lifestyle that the 1980s wrestling scene provided. He was a known carouser and had groupies (known in the industry as 'ring rats') in every town Stampede visited. Pillman's lady admirers were all too eager to service the handsome young rookie making waves in the Stampede territory. Pillman even scored himself an impromptu blowjob in the back of the Stampede bus shortly after picking up a girl who'd broken down at the side of the road. This lascivious backseat act of debauchery was accompanied by a loud and exhaustive running commentary from Owen, Bruce and Chris Benoit, with the sole intent of winding up straight-laced former World's Strongest Man, Bill Kazmaier.[1]

With a penchant for the ladies and his rookie wrestler status, the future 'Flyin' Brian was a prime candidate for ribbing courtesy of Bruce and his pranking protégé, Owen. On several occasions, Bruce and Owen instructed Stampede's event coordinator Bob Johnson to book Pillman on inconvenient and nonsensical personal appearances, such as a 'say no to drugs' speech in front of a kindergarten class of four-year-olds. When Pillman grumbled about making these appearances (they were always booked for first thing in the morning or late at night), he'd get a well-timed phone call from 'Stu' (ably played by Owen or Bruce imitating their father's voice) reminding him of the importance of keeping toddlers away from street narcotics.

Another of these anti-drug presentations was sprung on Brian after a spot show in the middle of nowhere, British Colombia. Pillman, who'd organised a hot date with some girl an hour's drive away in Kelowna, was convinced by Bob Johnson, Bruce and Owen that they had to stop off on the way back so Brian could give another late night talk on the perils of crack-cocaine. At 10:30pm, they arrived at their destination, which turned out to be a local senior citizens centre. Despite the fact that most of the elderly residents were tucked up in bed, the Harts managed to convince the manager to allow Brian to stage an impromptu PSA because many of the residents were big wrestling fans. When the flustered Pillman began lecturing the room of bleary-eyed octogenarians on the scourge of drugs, Owen and Bruce slipped out of the building and drove off, leaving a transport-less Brian to find his own way back to Kelowna. With Pillman busy warning off the aging would-be addicts, Owen and Bruce headed to their hotel room to hatch one of their most legendary ribs.

After eventually hitchhiking his way back to Kelowna, the unhappy Pillman finally arrived at the hotel room he was sharing with the Hart brothers. His hot date was long gone, presumably concluding that Brian stood her up. He walked into the room and flicked the light switch - nothing. He flicked it several more times to no avail. This was phase one in Owen and Bruce's plan; they'd unscrewed all the light bulbs in the room to create maximum disorientation. Brian then fumbled his way across the pitch black room to try the bathroom light. Rather than finding a light switch that worked, Brian instead received a whack on the head and a thorough soaking from head to toe, courtesy of a bucket of water the Harts had precariously placed on top of the bathroom door. Wet through and in an even fouler mood, Brian splodged back across the dark hotel room where he saw an unexpected shape disturbing the lining of the bed covers. Maybe my date went to bed to wait for me and fell asleep? he may have reasoned to himself.

When Brian jumped on the bed to embrace the mysterious figure (he'd probably taken the bucket off of his head at this point but we can't be sure) what jumped out the bed was anything but. Instead of a scantily clad young woman welcoming him back from his journey, Brian was greeted by a huge, terrified dog that was inexplicably dressed like James Dean. The dog, spooked from its nap, bounded out of bed and ran straight out the door.

While Owen and Bruce were waiting patiently in their car for Brian to thumb his way back to Kelowna, they'd spotted a bedraggled, stray dog roaming the grounds of their hotel. The hound's long hair was wet and matted and the dog reportedly stank to high heaven. Instead of ignoring it or calling the local pound, Owen and Bruce hooked the dispossessed pooch up with some of their leftover pizza and then ushered it into the hotel room they were sharing with Brian. There, they dressed the dog up in Pillman's Bad Company wrestling attire; a black leather biker jacket, a bandana and snappy sunglasses, before tucking the mangy mutt into Brian's bed.

It was said that for months afterwards, a running joke between Bruce, Owen and Brian was to keep a look out on the streets of Kelowna for the dog dressed like Arthur 'The Fonz' Fonzarelli. The rumour that in lieu of being stood up, Pillman's hot date hooked up with his canine doppelganger instead has never been confirmed.

[1]Three-time World's Strongest Man, Bill Kazmaier, was a firm favourite among the Stampede crew to wind up while making the long drives between towns. Despite having an awesome physical presence, he was beyond hopeless as a wrestler and would arrogantly proclaim himself to be the WWF's next big star. He also despised drugs in a territory where most of the boys were recreationally using. During one drive, Brian Pillman and Ben Bassarab passed around a bag of white powder on the bus and started 'snorting' the contents with gusto, before handing the bag to young wrestler John Hindley for his first-ever taste. As John was poised to hoover up a line of bugle, Kazmaier screamed, "Don't do it Johnny, it's the devil!" The white substance in the bag was, of course, just baby powder and little Johnny wouldn't get hooked that day. Another prank designed to get at Kazmaier involved Ben Bassarab making racist remarks to black wrestler Gerry Morrow. The minibus was stopped on the side of the road and Bassarab and Morrow staged a bloody fight. As the former World's Strongest Man watched in utter terror, Owen, who was pretending to be asleep but actually in on the ruse, demanded to know who started the fracas. Without missing a beat, Brian Pillman said it was Kazmaier who was responsible. Kazmaier chased Pillman off the van and down the highway, with Pillman laughing at Kazmaier's inability to catch him. Even though the WWF roster was full of enormous, useless lugs at the time, Kazmaier only wrestled for the Federation once in 1986. Kazmaier would find a home in WCW for several months in 1991, carrying with him to the ring, a giant prop globe. While Kazmaier may have carried the weight of the world on his shoulders, none of his opponents could carry him to a decent match. Bill would leave wrestling for good in 1992.

Prank Phone Calls:
Bad News Allen

As told by Natalie Neidhart

Hart family patriarch Stu was in the kitchen of Hart House eating dinner with his family when the phone rang.[1] On the other end of the line was the top drawing heel for his Stampede wrestling promotion, the self-styled (and original) 'Ultimate Warrior', Bad News Allen.[2]   Allen was scheduled to wrestle in the main event on that night's big Stampede show but Bad News had a sudden change of heart and felt that he wasn't being sufficiently compensated for his efforts.   Over the phone, Bad News told Stu in no uncertain terms that unless he received more money up front, he wasn't going to turn up for his scheduled match.   "[The show] was a big deal and Bad News Brown was main-eventing it," recalled Stu's granddaughter, Natalie Neidhart.

While it's a comparatively routine occurrence in WWE today,[3] not delivering on an advertised main event in the territory days could have catastrophic consequences. The promoter would lose serious money handing out refunds and the failure to deliver the advertised main event would cost the promotion the trust of the fans, affecting future ticket sales in that town. Because most major wrestling markets in the territory days were running the same towns weekly, this could seriously affect a promotion's bottom line. After Bad News kept demanding more money and more outrageous concessions, Stu, who was growing more infuriated by the second, eventually told Allen, "WELL THEN IF YOU'RE NOT GOING TO COME TO MY SHOW THEN I DON'T CARE!" before slamming the phone receiver down in frustration with the uncompromising grappler.

Almost as soon as the heated exchange between two of the most feared men in wrestling history came to its natural conclusion, Bad News Allen wandered into the kitchen of Hart House as if the whole phone exchange had never happened.   "[Stu] was like, 'What do you want?' Bad News's like, 'What's *your* problem?' 'What's your problem?'" replied Stu.

Of course, it wasn't Bad News who'd placed the ransom call at all but a troublemaking Owen all along. The prank temporarily caused some genuine conflict between the two until Stu eventually worked out that the master impressionist had got him once again. "Nobody wants to be in a fight with Bad News Brown," laughed Natalie, "especially not in the middle of your kitchen with your family about ready to have your dinner! I'm glad they worked that out; that was all because of Owen."

[1]"Stu had two different phone numbers and two phones right beside each other in the stair well," explained family friend TJ Wilson. "At least one of them was listed... fans would call all day long and ask if Bret's there. It's like, 'No, you see he's the WWE Champion. If you can believe it he doesn't live with his father anymore. Smith still lives here, Bret does not live here!'"

[2]Before entering professional wrestling, 'Bad News' Allen Coage was an American judo star, achieving his 3rd dan black belt just five years after picking up the sport before earning a bronze medal at the 1976 Montreal Olympics in the heavyweight category. Not only was Coage a legitimate tough guy, he was an angry young man who, over the course of the next decade, developed into a seething middle-aged man who hated nearly everyone he came into contact with.

[3]In today's WWE culture, an advertised wrestler no-showing an event might disappoint but won't engender the same vitriolic reaction from fans. This is because for over thirty years, WWE has pushed the brand itself over any individual worker. Many WWE fans have been groomed to accept that 'card subject to change' is par for the course. This also leaves less power in the hands of wrestlers who may get too popular in WWE's eyes and be in a position to demand more concessions from the company. It also means that wrestlers have less chance of becoming box office attractions and, ultimately, WWE selling fewer tickets in the first place. One of WWE's first forays into intentional mis-advertising involved Davey Boy Smith and Dynamite Kid. Performing as The British Bulldogs, Smith and Dynamite were at the peak of their careers as WWF Tag Team Champions in 1986. On the 13th of December,

Dynamite suffered a devastating back injury (two ruptured discs and temporary paralysis), leaving only Davey Boy to defend the belts on the house show circuit. WWF made no announcement of this and continued promoting 'The British Bulldogs' on live events while pre-recorded Bulldogs matches were broadcast. For the next six weeks, Davey and a series of guest partners defended the Tag Team Titles in marquee matches. When there were no pre-recorded matches left to broadcast, the WWF scraped up a disintegrating Dynamite from hospital to drop the Tag Titles on television to Bret and Jim Neidhart.

Bulldog vs. Statue

As told by Jim Ross and Bret Hart

Back in the Stampede territory, Owen and Davey Boy Smith were travelling on the babyface bus[1] heading to the next town in the middle of the night. The Stampede territory covered most of the Canadian provinces of Alberta and Saskatchewan, which for many months of the year gets mighty cold. On this particular trip during an intense blizzard, the dilapidated bus's defroster had packed up and the driver couldn't see where he was going. The bus pulled up in a town square in the middle of nowhere so some of the wrestlers could pile out and scrape the ice off the windshield. Two of the wrestlers who stayed on the bus were Owen and Davey. Davey, according to speculation from Jim Ross, had consumed, "Too much strong Canadian ale," which caused him to drift off into a deep sleep. With Davey Boy completely knocked out, Owen figured this was the perfect time to catch him off-guard with a prank.

While other wrestlers were outside clearing the windscreen, Owen noticed a large statue near his side of the van. According to Bret, "[Owen] put the window down and asked the statue for directions and [began] pretending he was arguing with it." Owen's purposely loud conversation with the sculpture woke Davey Boy up. Davey, who still wasn't in the best frame of mind, asked Owen what was going on. Owen explained that he'd asked 'this guy' for directions and he was mouthing off to him. Without thinking, Davey leapt into action, jumped out of the van and marched into the blizzard straight up to the ten foot effigy. Davey proceeded to 'cut a promo' on the inanimate object for at least a minute before all the other wrestlers could take no more and fell about laughing. Davey, who finally realised how stupid he was looking gearing up for a fight with the inert sculpture, eventually calmed down and saw the funny side himself.

"Owen never missed an opportunity," recalled Bret. "He was always a guy who [would] pull the funniest pranks on you... sometimes just an opening of... one second where something can happen and Owen would jump on those kinds of moments. You'd find yourself arguing it out with the bell clerk or somebody at the airport and Owen would be snickering because he set the whole thing up. He never missed an opportunity to rib somebody."

[1]The wrestlers in Stampede travelled between destinations on two separate buses; one for the babyfaces and one for the heels. During Stampede's late 1950s heyday, Stu purchased a jet plane for $25,000 because destinations were so far apart, especially as Stampede ran shows as far away as Alaska at the time.

Stu Hart Statue

As told by Bret Hart

In another instance of mistaken identity involving enormous sculptures, many of the Hart Brothers, including Owen, Bret, Bruce and Wayne, as well as Stampede wrestling stalwarts like Brian Pillman, used to play the same rib on rookie wrestlers during their first loop in the territory and wrestling legends who occasionally ventured north for a payday.

The workers would be travelling west back to Calgary after a show when someone would ask the uninformed wrestler if they'd ever heard of a town called Drumheller. Drumheller, the self-styled 'Dinosaur Capital of The World' on account of its many significant fossil finds, is located in the Canada badlands sixty-five miles north east of Calgary. The other wrestlers would tell their gullible victim that Stu Hart was born in the little town and the locals had erected a statue in his honour for all the work he'd done for their community.

Not only was Stu Hart widely recognised in the area for his wrestling-based accomplishments, he'd helped raise money for more than thirty charities over the years, for which he was made a Member of the Order of Canada in 2000.[1] Stu having a statue constructed for him was not a far-fetched claim. Everyone on the bus would talk up Stu's accomplishments for the duration of the journey until they arrived at Drumheller. When their vehicle would cruise down into the Red Valley River, the mark, who would be expecting to see a statue of Stu, would be confronted by a thirty foot tall figure of a Tyrannosaurus Rex.[2]

Right on cue, over-exaggerated impersonations of Stu would tumble out of everyone's mouths, "Eh, c'mon, ya big bastard!" NWA Heavyweight Champion and native Albertan Gene Kiniski, who had been friends with Stu for decades, also fell for the rib; being taken in so completely he went to grab his camera to snap a photograph of the monument. After the big reveal, everybody, including the wrestler they'd suckered in with the story, would enjoy a good laugh at the harmless rib.

That would be until Jeff 'Brick Bronsky' Beltzner, who also fell for the light-hearted prank, relayed the story to Diana Hart and Davey Boy Smith. On this occasion, Owen, Bruce and Brian Pillman had been the ones to prank Bronsky, who'd taken the joke well. When Davey and Diana heard of the rib, they took great offence at what they saw as a slight on Stu, as did Dynamite Kid when Davey told him about it. Because Owen and Bruce were off-limits, the rookie Pillman became the target of brutal retaliatory hazing, courtesy of the Bulldogs.

[1]The Order of Canada is the country's second-highest civilian honour, recognising, "Outstanding achievement, dedication to the community and service to the nation." As of 2019, 4,640 Canadians have had this honour bestowed upon them.

[2]Drumheller now boasts an eighty-six foot green and yellow T-Rex installation that tourists can climb up and stand in the mouth of.

Prank Phone Calls:
Stu Hart

As told by Mark Henry and Bret Hart

No one would receive more prank phone calls from Owen than his father, Stu, who was getting on in years and was partially deaf. No matter how many calls were made, he never seemed to twig that it was Owen on the other line winding him up. "Owen used to ring his dad at least once a week," laughed 'World's Strongest Man' Mark Henry. "Owen was a master of disguises and voices." Owen's cast of characters was extensive, including the time he called Stu pretended to be legendary tough man Luther Lindsay, asking if he could have a ride to the next town. Stu was great friends with Lindsay and had such enormous respect for the man's wrestling ability he kept a picture of Lindsay in his wallet for over fifty years. Lindsay asking his close friend Stu for a lift wouldn't be unusual, except for the fact that he died in 1972.

Another role Owen would adopt for his father was of a nagging old crone trying to get money out of him. "I remember him getting my dad on the phone and impersonating an old woman, speaking in a low, low voice," said Bret. "My dad was hard of hearing and he'd be going, 'Speak up. Speak up for chrissakes!'" Owen would keep up the pretence until Stu agreed to donate money to the old woman's made up charity.

On one call that Mark Henry witnessed, Owen phoned Stu accusing him of being even more of a genetic stud than anyone had previously thought. Owen introduced himself to Stu as an advocate of sorts for a young man who was claiming to be Stu and Helen's ninth son. Between 1948 and 1965, Stu and Helen Hart pumped out no less than twelve children – eight boys and four girls. Helen gave the following explanation for her enormous brood, "Funny thing, every time Stu hangs his pants on the end of the bed I'm pregnant!"

Stu wasn't buying Owen's story and set the record straight. "No, I have [eight] sons and that's it." According to his wife Helen, Stu never fooled around so he knew that it was impossible he'd conceived a child outside of wedlock, but that didn't stop Owen from pushing further. "No, we did some DNA testing and you have a kid outside your home." Mark Henry bore witness to the Hart patriarch's reply. "Stu was like, 'THAT'S BULLSHIT!' Stu would go off and then [Owen] would be like, 'Nah, Dad, I'm just playing with you!'"

CHAPTER 2

The Sorry Saga of The Blue Blazer

♥ ♥

Fresh from university and in his rookie year as a full-time professional wrestler, Owen, at the behest of Bret, filled in for an injured wrestler at a World Wrestling Federation show. Owen appeared on several of WWF house shows in 1986 under his own name and as Owen James, dropping his surname so there were no comparisons to his then heel brother. Even after impressing the crowd teaming with S.D. 'Special Delivery' Jones against The Hart Foundation in September of that year, Owen wouldn't make another appearance for the WWF for another eighteen months. Bret and others gushed over Owen's performance to road agent Chief Jay Strongbow but according to Bret, "Chief was reluctant to put Owen over too strong [to Vince McMahon], even though all the boys raved about him." Chief's demeanour had soured ever since former wrestler, Pat Patterson, was chosen to be WWF's head booker instead him. When Bret pleaded his case to Vince directly, the boss flat out wasn't interested. Bret did get Owen another tryout match for the *WWF Wrestling Challenge* tapings in Rochester, NY on the 7th of October but he was completely over-shadowed that night thanks to the debuting Tom Magee, a 6'5" Greek god of a man who Vince openly declared to be his next WWF Champion. To make matters worse, the jobber that Owen was paired with that night didn't support him properly on one of his aerial manoeuvres and Owen ended up falling flat on his backside. Magee went on to amount to absolutely nothing in the business and Owen headed back to Stampede totally crestfallen.

After two years toiling away in the frozen tundra of the Stampede Territory, Owen finally landed a proper WWF try-out match under his own name on the 8th of March 1988 in Bristol, Tennessee. After an impressive couple of outings against Barry Horowitz and Hercules Hernandez, Bret went to Vince McMahon imploring him to book Owen full-time. As preposterous a notion as it sounds today, Vince initially balked at the idea of bringing him into the fold, believing Owen, who stood somewhere around 5'8"-5'9" and weighing 230 pounds, was too small for his travelling freak show of giants and monsters. In fact, the only stars on the WWF roster shorter than Owen at that time were the 5'6" James 'Koko B' Ware and his three foot long parrot, Frankie.

Unable to deny talent but with Vince stuck in his ways, a compromise was reached; when Owen was invited back in July of that year, he'd no-longer be introduced as the youngest Hart but as the masked, mysterious, high-flying Blue Blazer character. Owen had originally pitched the name 'American Eagle' but was turned down. The Blazer character was partially an idea Bret had for himself in case his WWF tenure didn't work out when he joined in 1984. If the World Wrestling Federation chewed up Bret and spat him out like so many of his contemporaries, Bret planned to go back to Japan under a mask as a new character; something akin to Japanese wrestling superhero Tiger Mask. With his spot in the company seemingly secure, Bret instead pitched the idea of bringing Owen in as a masked superhero to add some extra flavour to go along with his acrobatic move-set. It also transpired that in the back of McMahon's mind he'd wanted to create a gimmick based on the Mighty Mouse cartoon character, which he was a big fan of as a kid. Owen would debut his new character, initially identified as The Blue Angel[1] on the 8th of July 1988, defeating preliminary wrestler Terry Gibbs on a house show in Redding, California. The Blazer soon made appearances on the WWF's main syndicated shows, *Superstars of Wrestling* and *Wrestling Challenge*.

Instead of being portrayed as a cool, Marvel-esque superhero fans could get behind, The Blue Blazer character came across as a wimpy, do-gooder type that was completely unbelievable even by 1980s WWF standards. Some of the wrestlers would soon derisively refer to the character as the 'Blue Sports Coat'. Owen's promo skills, which would eventually blossom in the 1990s, were truly atrocious. Whether it was threatening to win all his matches with his 'great wrestling acrobatics' or telling kids not to try cigarettes in such a feeble manner that thousands of children started chain-smoking in protest (probably), it was clear Owen didn't have the over-the-top personality at that time to portray such a colourful character.

Then there was the costume, which was particularly risible. During a meeting between Bret and Vince, the boss talked up the new Blazer character, claiming he was going to let the art department handle the costume while he himself would come up with the name 'featuring a bird or a rocket'. While The Blue Blazer featured nothing bird-like in name, his costume sure did. In stark contrast to the WWF's slick marketing machine and high quality presentation, Owen's televised debut on the nationally syndicated *Wrestling Challenge* show saw him jog to the ring in a blue, sequinned masquerade mask that was sewn inside what appeared to be an un-plucked chicken. Complimenting the fowl headwear was a sequinned blue cape with a red eagle emblazoned on it, topped off with a white chicken feather fringe motif. On commentary, a quizzical Bobby 'The Brain' Heenan enquired if Koko B Ware's parrot had finally grown up and was making his wrestling debut, before adding, "We know one thing, [The Blue Blazer's] been in the hen house!" Vince's promise about getting the art department to create the costume turned out to be empty, so a friend of Owen's wife ended up making the Blazer costume on the cheap. Owen didn't dare change his attire out of politeness as he felt, "It would hurt Martha's feelings," if he got some proper gear made.

After the audience's initial laughter turned into silence, Owen won the tired television crowd over with flashy wrestling and a perfectly executed moonsault off the top rope (a backflip landing chest-first onto the opponent). While the moonsault is ubiquitous today, back in the 1980s few were doing the dangerous manoeuvre. Lanny Poffo was the only Federation wrestler regularly performing the move. Poffo's version looked like he couldn't squash a raspberry where as Owen's had real impact. At the end of the match, manager Heenan was openly suggesting the Blazer could become the newest member of his stable of wrestlers. Unfortunately, The Brain would never get around to managing The Blue Blazer, instead filling the Heenan Family's poultry quota by renaming his latest charge, Terry Taylor, 'The Red Rooster' a couple of weeks later.

After several months winning nearly every match over preliminary wrestlers such as Barry Horowitz, Steve Lombardi and Jose Estrada, Owen's big coming out party was supposed to occur on the WWF's second annual Thanksgiving pay-per-view extravaganza, *Survivor Series*.[2] Owen was booked to have a decent showing, hitting some of his biggest, most crowd-pleasing manoeuvres on 'Outlaw' Ron Bass and the Honky Tonk Man before facing off with Greg 'The Hammer' Valentine. Valentine immediately ran the ropes and charged at Owen, who leapfrogged him without issue. When Valentine charged a second time, Owen jumped in the air for a second leapfrog. Unfortunately, this time Valentine barely ducked and head-butted the Blazer right in the groin. Owen gamely no-sold the legitimate pain coursing through his body and continued wrestling before being eliminated by submission via Valentine's Figure Four Leg Lock finisher. No one, not even Bret, knew how badly the mistimed leapfrog had hurt Owen until long after the match. Over the course of the next few hours, one of Owen's testicles swelled to the size of a cabbage and there was a genuine fear that it would have to be surgically removed. After taking a month off to deflate his distended gonad, Owen, who had been gaining momentum before the injury, was shunted down to the bottom of the cards.

The Blue Blazer made a single appearance on the World Wrestling Federation's flagship series of infrequent NBC specials, *Saturday Night's Main Event*, on the 16th of February 1989. Owen's only hope to defeat his opponent for the evening, 'Million Dollar Man' Ted DiBiase, was to bore him into submission with his monotone pre-match interview. The colourless promo apparently didn't work and DiBiase dominated the majority of the contest before putting the Blazer away with a routine powerslam in just 3:57. The Blazer's only other appearance on pay-per-view would be at *WWF WrestleMania V* in Atlantic City on April Fool's Day. Owen was pitted against Curt 'Mr Perfect' Hennig in a match designed to put Perfect over strongly. In what would be retrospectively viewed as the in-ring meeting between wrestling's two greatest modern day ribbers, the duo put on a humdrum affair in front of mostly disinterested spectators.[3] Bret recalled that, "Curt was good enough to give Owen more than his fair share" of the match because he respected Owen's talents and the Hart family.

The reason why their bout didn't get a reaction from the audience was because *no* match got a reaction, save for the main event. Most of the people in attendance only came to see Hulk Hogan exact revenge on his former friend 'Macho Man' Randy Savage. A large number of those in attendance were either high-rolling punters who were gifted corporate ringside tickets or the regular casino crowd who checked out the show without intimately knowing the product, not unlike how Las Vegas tourists would check out *Blue Man Group*. Many of the genuine fans who showed up to Trump Plaza[4] were upset at the massive hike in ticket prices compared to *WrestleMania III*, which put a damper on the occasion.

As if Owen hadn't yet figured out that his career was going nowhere, his final months would see him paired up with his old 'friend' from Stampede, Bad News Allen. Allen, now known as Bad News Brown because he refused to sign over the 'Bad News Allen' name to the WWF, had arrived in the promotion a year earlier with the promise of becoming the Federation's first black Heavyweight Champion.[5] In an attempt to get him over as a legitimate contender for the WWF Title, Bad News was booked to defeat everyone he wrestled, usually after hitting his 'Ghetto Blaster' finishing manoeuvre and pinning them clean in the middle of the ring. A spring 1989 tour of the North East, California and Canada would see the languishing Blue Blazer become Bad News' latest victim.

On one particular match during this tour, Brown hit the Ghetto Blaster on The Blue Blazer and pinned him for the three count as the pre-arranged outcome dictated. As Brown was walking back to the dressing room, he heard an incongruous cheer from the crowd. Owen, showing no ill effects from the kick, jumped up from the ring canvas, climbed onto the ropes and hit a pose for the crowd. Bad News, whose finishing manoeuvre was 'knocking out' everyone including Hulk Hogan, felt that Owen wasn't properly selling his established finisher and told a backstage agent to remind Owen of his place in the pecking order. When the tour hit the Saddledome in his home town of Calgary (which was also Brown's adopted home), Owen successfully campaigned to win the match. Owen defeated Bad News via disqualification, which engendered more bad feelings between the two.

The next night in Edmonton, Owen once again campaigned to win but this time was unsuccessful. Bad News, who was still furious with Owen not selling the Ghetto Blaster properly from earlier in the tour, told referee Earl Hebner in no uncertain terms that, "If [Owen] jumps on those ropes tonight I'm going to kick the crap out of him." The match itself went down as usual, with Brown hitting his finisher and getting the three count to a chorus of boos from the crowd. Bad News then walked down the aisle way of Edmonton's Northlands Coliseum, through the entrance curtain and waited around the corner. Owen figured that the coast was clear and hopped up off the mat, jumped on the ropes and hit his pose to a huge roar from the crowd. According to Bad News, "I looked my head around [and said] 'Okay'. I walk back out, he's coming out the ring and I hit him. WHACK! Down he went and I start putting the boots to him. Earl's trying to grab me [saying] 'NO, ALLEN, YOU'RE GOING TO KILL HIM!'" After leaving Owen lying, Bad News said, "Let that be a lesson to you," before walking back to the locker room area. When Owen gathered his bearings and returned to the dressing room, he was confronted yet again by the Olympic bronze medallist, who further admonished the youngest Hart. "Let me tell you something you little punk, if it wasn't for your Dad you'd be selling programmes here! What is this nonsense? We all have to put everybody over. I had to put Bret over a million times [in Stampede]."

After the incident, Owen would last less than a month in the WWF, continuously losing to Bad News Brown before suffering the ultimate ignominy in the final match of his first Federation run; losing cleanly to bottom-of-the-rung preliminary wrestler Barry Horowitz. According to Bad News, "[Owen] told Vince [McMahon] he didn't come to the WWF to lose, so Vince started laughing. [Vince] said, 'I'll tell you what... this will be your last night, or you can finish your schedule out.'" Because it was obvious that if he stuck around any longer it would kill his career and partly on the advice of Bret, Owen made the bold choice to leave the WWF at the end of June 1989. Martha added, "It made [Owen] look at wrestling in a different light like, 'You know what? Maybe this isn't all it's cracked up to be. That maybe it's not worth taking so seriously.'" Martha also asserted in her book that undisclosed parties in the WWF were pressuring him to get on the steroids, which he steadfastly refused to do.[6]

The writing was already on the wall long before the encounter with Bad News. Earlier in the year a journalist from the San Francisco-based Fox affiliate *KTVU* wanted to profile Owen. Even by the late '80s boom period, the World Wrestling Federation and its top superstars like Hulk Hogan were not receiving a tonne of offers to participate in positive news pieces, especially in major markets like the Bay Area. According to the *Wrestling Observer's* Dave Meltzer, the WWF turned down the journalist's request to film a mini biography on Owen with the explanation that, "The Blue Blazer... is someone we are not looking to promote." When Cuban superstar Charles 'Konnan' Ashenoff was originally being courted by the WWF in '89, McMahon informed Konnan he would be taking The Blue Blazer's spot as, "[Owen] would only wrestle certain guys."

Owen spent the next two years rebuilding himself as a credible wrestler overseas, where he enjoyed success touring Japan, Mexico and Europe.

[1]According to Bruce Prichard, the character was always called The Blue Blazer and originally announced names such as 'The Blue Angel', 'The Blue Demon' and 'The Blue Laser' were all screw ups by ring announcers or otherwise lost in translation. The unfortunate mix-up with the names was possibly an omen for what turned out to be a miserable run and a wasted opportunity all round.

[2]Owen would be part of a traditional ten-man tag team elimination bout, teaming with fellow good guys: 'Jumpin' Jim Brunzell, Sam Houston, Brutus 'The Barber' Beefcake and The Ultimate Warrior against the bad guy team of: 'Outlaw' Ron Bass, 'Dangerous' Danny Davis, Greg 'The Hammer' Valentine, Bad News Brown and The Honky Tonk Man.

[3]Another of the reasons for the lack of crowd reaction was Trump Plaza itself. Bruce Prichard would later describe the Plaza as, "A dump and a half," and that the only positive about working there was that "it was close to the hotel... that was nice." The Convention Centre was a

cavernous barn of a place that was seemingly 5% usable space and 95% roof, causing what little noise the spectators bothered to make to evaporate into the atmosphere. On the plus side, Mr Perfect, acting cocky during his ring entrance, nearly fell over when he failed to anticipate an extra step on the entrance walkway.

[4]Trump Plaza was the informal name given to the Historic Atlantic City Convention Hall (now renamed Boardwalk Hall) as the show was sponsored by Donald Trump's casino. Trump himself paid a lot of money to bring *WrestleMania IV* to the venue in 1988, including shelling out for building decorations, as well as picking up the hotel tab for the cast and crew. Trump was also sat in the front row of ringside opposite the hard camera to lend the show some extra star power. Despite drawing around 17,000 paying fans, *WrestleMania IV* generated more money ($1.6 million) than *WrestleMania III* which hosted at least 78,000 fans thanks to a big hike in ticket prices. *WrestleMania IV* is arguably one of the worst *WrestleManias* in the brand's thirty-five year history thanks to the unsuitable venue, the casual audience and a tediously-booked tournament to crown a new WWF Champion. Despite the critical failure, the Federation returned the next year for *WrestleMania V.* The Convention Hall's layout and decorations were still in place from the previous year and Trump was still picking up most of the tab. Atlantic City was also located relatively near WWF's Connecticut headquarters and the prestige of emanating from a casino venue like a prize fight convinced McMahon to return. *WrestleMania V,* aside from the main event, would similarly be looked at as one of the weaker *WrestleManias* in history.

[5]In early 1989, Bad News Brown would unsuccessfully challenge World Wrestling Federation Champion Randy Savage in a series of 'Street Fight' gimmick matches, as well as face off against new champ Hulk Hogan later in the year. McMahon's promise of making Bad News his first black WWF Champion never materialised. Bad News was booked to lose to Jake 'The Snake' Roberts throughout July and August 1990, with his last match occurring at *SummerSlam* 1990, before leaving the WWF and the national wrestling scene for good.

[6]During an AOL Online chat in late 1995, Owen was unequivocal on his stance on performance-enhancing drugs. "Never used them, I never needed them, which should indicate how I feel. Let's face it, I am not going to be a giant no matter what they invent. So I rely on my wrestling ability, not bulging biceps. So I don't have to worry about organ damage or balding prematurely because of steroid use. So for any of those young wrestler wannabes who want to consider using steroids don't let your vanity ruin your health."

The Ultimate Rib

As told by Ross Hart and TJ Wilson

One of Owen Hart's travel buddies during the original Blazer run was Jim 'Ultimate Warrior' Hellwig. Warrior arrived in the World Wrestling Federation in June 1987 as the less awe-inspiringly named 'Dingo Warrior'. Both Warrior and Owen had a couple of things in common; they were both relative rookies in the business and wrestling was never the most important thing in their lives... and that's pretty much where the similarities end. Owen was a legitimate athlete, a talented professional wrestler and by all accounts a wonderful person. Conversely, Warrior was a former competition bodybuilder, who at that time was incapable of performing an entertaining match that went beyond three minutes, including the rambunctious entrance. Warrior was also a danger to himself and others in the ring, as well as acting like a world-class prima donna to his peers and office staff. What Warrior had over Owen was size, an incredible body, out-of-this-world charisma and a marketable presentation. Despite the youngest Hart's obvious talents, Owen would become a glorified jobber for the rest of his tenure, while Warrior rocketed to the top of the card, eventually dethroning Hulk Hogan and becoming the undisputed king of the WWF in 1990.[1]

Along with his in-ring talents, Owen brought his pranking expertise to the WWF, including his predilection for mimicry. Ross Hart recalled that, along with imitating people's voices, he could also convincingly impersonate animals. While Owen and Warrior were walking down the street one day they passed a snarling dog. Ross recalled, "If you were walking in the street and you passed a dog, he'd make these lunging noises like the dog was attacking you." Spotting his chance, Owen took a step behind Warrior and made canine attack noises so convincing that Warrior, who Bobby Heenan once characterised as being so jittery he made coffee nervous, leapt off the pavement into the road to avoid the fictitious mauling.

On another occasion, the wrestling equivalent of *The Odd Couple* arrived back at their hotel to find that the lobby was full of wrestling fans hoping to meet their heroes. The tetchy Warrior didn't want to deal with the throng of wrestling fanatics. He asked Owen to keep a low profile so they could slip past the fans to their room undetected. Because Warrior was wearing a baseball cap with the brim pulled down low to obscure his face and nobody in the United States knew what The Blue Blazer really looked like, the duo had a chance to make it through the lobby undetected... or they would have done if it weren't for Owen. With Warrior busy surveying the scene, Owen reached into his gear bag, put on his Blue Blazer mask and waited for the fans to notice him. The congregation of fans immediately recognised the Blazer mask and deduced that the giant bodybuilder he was stood behind *had* to be The Ultimate Warrior. Warrior was immediately mobbed by hordes of kids, autograph hunters, die-hards and weirdos.

[1]The Ultimate Warrior would remain champion for ten months before losing the WWF Title to Sgt Slaughter at *Royal Rumble 1991*. Warrior would be fired in August of that year when he 'held up' Vince McMahon over money. Warrior reportedly refused to go to the ring for his *SummerSlam* main event match until he was paid more for his *WrestleMania* bout, among other concessions. Vince McMahon agreed to every one of Warrior's demands just to get him into the ring. When Warrior walked back through the curtain, McMahon immediately fired him. Warrior made a surprise return eight months later at *WrestleMania VIII*, then was fired again that November, this time for importing human growth hormone from England when the WWF was trying to clean up their image after steroid investigations by the Federal Government. Davey Boy Smith was fired at the same time for the same reason, leaving the WWF without two of its top four babyfaces, speeding up the promotion's decline. McMahon also suspected the pair of supplying HGH to other wrestlers in order to beat new steroid tests, which was never proven or confirmed. According to Bruce Hart, a half-cut Davey Boy told WWF's Head of Talent Relations, JJ Dillon, that the recent Bret vs. Ric Flair Heavyweight Title match was a 'fooking abortion' and that *he* should be WWF Champion. Bruce suggested this interaction might have gone some way towards McMahon decision to fire him. Warrior would return to the WWF yet again in 1996 for a few months, until he was fired yet again, this time for missing dates.

Prank Phone Calls:
Hacksaw Jim Duggan 1

As told by George Steele, Bret Hart, Jim Duggan and Terry Taylor

Back in the days before smart phones, Google Maps and online check-ins, booking hotels and finding your way around an unfamiliar town was an altogether more primitive affair. Rooms needed to be booked by phone (or by just turning up to the hotel and requesting a room), credit card payments were authorised with a signature and endless forms had to be filled in at the check-in desk. During one such visit to a hotel in Dayton, Ohio, 'Hacksaw' Jim Duggan and his wife Debra were the first in a long line of WWF crew members to fill out the forms and head to their room, while other wrestlers, including Owen, Bret and George 'The Animal' Steele stood around waiting their turn.

Shortly after the Duggans got to their room, Jim made a phone call down to the front desk to inquire as to the whereabouts of the nearest gym. The well-mannered desk clerk who picked up the phone didn't know, so he lowered the phone, held his hand over the receiver and asked those around him if they could help. Owen, who was still hanging around the front desk, said he knew exactly where the gym was and beckoned to the man behind reception to hand over the phone. According to Bret, "Owen gets on the phone and of course, Jim thinks it's just someone on the front desk."

George Steele who also witnessed the phone conversation, vividly recalled what happened next. "When Hacksaw asked about the nearest gym, Owen asked Jim if he had a phone book in the room. Jim said he did but since he didn't know the town very well he did not know where the addresses were located. That's when Owen inquired if Duggan was one of the wrestlers who was staying in the hotel. When Jim said yes, Owen went on to talk about how stupid wrestlers were."[1] Owen would continue to purposely aggravate Hacksaw, saying in an aggressive manner, "Why don't you look it up yourself you lazy bastard! You wrestlers are so lazy, just look it up!" On the other end of the line, Jim was incensed and ready to combust when

Owen hit the go-home line. "If you wanna do something about it, come down here and I'll kick your ass!" The 6'3" Duggan was pushing close to 300 pounds in his prime and was well known in the business as a legitimately tough customer. Hacksaw was more than happy to oblige.

According to Bret and Steele's recollections, the receptionist heard what Owen said and was absolutely terrified of the unwarranted beating that he was about to receive. "[Hacksaw started] getting dressed and coming down to the lobby to straighten out this front desk guy," said Bret. "I remember Owen just hands the phone back to [the desk clerk]. The guy says, 'Don't do this to me' and Owen says, 'don't worry, just tell him it was me, Jim Powers!'" By the time a foaming Duggan stormed downstairs to confront the 'tough guy' who'd just given him an earful, Owen had already filled in his paperwork and headed off to his hotel room, leaving the clerk to lay the blame on Jim Powers. At the next show, Duggan snatched the innocent Powers in the locker room and shouted, "YOU DON'T RIB ME, POWERS!" among some other choice words in front of his co-workers.

Version two of this story, according to Duggan himself, was that Owen challenged him to a fight then slammed the phone down. Before Hacksaw left the room to go downstairs he received another call from the real desk clerk who apologised profusely for the previous call. When Duggan asked who made the call, the clerk asked Owen (who was still loitering at the front desk) for his name, to which he replied 'Jim Powers'.

Version three comes from Terry Taylor and differs so much from the first two versions that it might actually be a completely separate incident. Terry claimed Owen Hart was behind Jim in the queue to pay for the hotel. After he filled out the hotel forms, Duggan may have been overheard down the hallway that he was going to work out. While Owen was filling out his paperwork, the receptionist answered the ringing phone and said, "Hello, Mr Duggan... the nearest gym? One moment, please," and put the phone down. When the clerk went to the back room to find a copy of the Yellow Pages, Owen picked up the phone and said, "Mr Duggan? You're not going to the gym you fat slob! I can tell by looking at you, you haven't been in a month! You want me to tell you where the all-you-can-eat buffet is? Don't bother me, I'm busy!" Owen then slammed the phone down.

Jim rang back immediately. The front desk guy was still absent from his post, so Owen answered the phone. Duggan yelled, "WHO IS THIS? I'LL COME DOWN THERE AND I'LL..." before Owen interrupted with, "You couldn't beat anybody up you fat, old, out-of-shape, good-for-nothing, cross-eyed..." etc. When Duggan threatened to come down to the lobby, Owen said, "Good, I'll beat the crap outta ya!" Owen then filled out his paperwork and walked around the corner. The receptionist returned to the front desk with the yellow pages and saw the phone had been hung back up. Shortly afterwards, Hacksaw strode down the hallway, madder than a hornet and ready for a fight. The front desk guy told Jim he'd found a list of gyms before the Hacksaw cut him off with, "HOW DARE YOU TALK TO ME THAT WAY, I'LL PULL YOU OVER THAT DESK, I'LL KILL YOU," before turning around and seeing Owen laughing hysterically at him. Duggan then said, "OWEN, you got me again!" The guy at the front desk had no idea what just happened and everyone else went back to their room laughing about the confrontation. In this version at least, poor Jim Powers remained unmolested by Duggan.

[1]Steele, who was an educated man himself, defended Duggan's intelligence in his biography, stating that, "Duggan had in fact gotten his degree in applied plant biology at Southern Methodist University. He was definitely no dummy."

Snake vs. Bulldog

As told by Jake Roberts and Roddy Piper

Even when he wasn't technically the guilty party, Owen seemed to be able to encourage others to engage in pranks that they otherwise might not have committed. Back in 1988, Jake 'The Snake' Roberts (Aurelian Smith Jr) was riding high atop the cards in the World Wrestling Federation feuding with arrogant heel 'Ravishing' Rick Rude. Since his WWF debut in 1986, The Snake would bring an actual snake with him to the ring; a fully-grown boa constrictor named Damien.[1] After vanquishing a foe with his dreaded DDT finishing move, the then heel Jake would dump Damien on top of his defeated man as an added form of humiliation.

As macabre as Jake's act was, he soon became incredibly popular with fans, in no small part thanks to the snake. When Roberts was engaged in a bitter feud with ultimate babyface, Ricky 'The Dragon' Steamboat, Steamboat started bringing a 'dragon' (really a small, docile alligator) to the ring to combat Damien. Young fans, who were the WWF's target market at that time, were awed by the battle of the reptilian creatures and soon more wrestlers were being accompanied by animals for marketing purposes. Koko B Ware, who had previously wrestled as the 'Birdman' while flapping his arms in Bill Watts' UWF, joined the WWF in late 1986 with a parrot called Frankie as his mascot.[2] In 1987, The British Bulldogs were given an actual Bulldog, Matilda, to accompany them to the ring (and carry them in the promo department as Davey and Dynamite were woeful talkers).

By the late 1980s, Dynamite Kid Tom Billington was an even nastier piece of work than in previous years since returning from a severe back injury, which saw his booze consumption escalate to cope with the pain. Davey, who followed his older cousin Dynamite's lead, also had a reputation as a vicious bully at the time. One day Davey was sat in the locker room amusing himself by riling up Damien so he'd attack Jake in the ring. "I walked into the locker room one night and caught Davey Boy, who did not smoke, getting lit cigarettes from Dynamite and throwing them inside the snake bag," said Jake.

Because Davey had gone after Damien, Jake decided to go after their animal mascot Matilda. With Dynamite and Davey elsewhere, Jake, at the suggestion of Owen, fed Matilda a few treats that might not have agreed with the dog's delicate constitution. "You know those hot dogs at a wrestling show? Not the best thing to feed an animal. Especially seven or eight of them with chilli," said Jake. For dessert, Jake 'mistakenly' fed Matilda something other than a tasty dog biscuit. "It looked like chocolate to me but it may have been Ex-Lax!"

Not only did she have a little accident at ringside during that evening's television taping, Matilda felt doubly unwell by the time the Bulldogs took her to the hotel that night.[3] After Davey and Dynamite ignored Matilda's groans and headed to the hotel bar, Jake went to their room and started banging on their door. The ailing pooch was startled so badly she began defecating all over Davey and Dynamite's hotel room. Jake waited a short while for Matilda to calm down, then banged on the door again and again and again, causing the miserable bulldog to spray a brown riptide all over the place, including on the beds. Jake waited up so he could listen out for the Bulldog's reaction when they returned to their room. When Davey opened the door at two in the morning, he saw the malodorous devastation and went crazy. "Fookin' motherfookin' dog, you fookin' piece of shit, you!" While he self-admittedly wasn't much of a ribber, Jake, at the behest of Owen, felt fully justified in teaching the Bulldogs a lesson. "[Even with] the mean bullshit that some of the guys did [in those days] those two guys were the worst, man."

[1]'Damien' was actually numerous snakes that would be rotated every three weeks. A shocking amount of the WWF wrestlers suffered with ophidiophobia, the fear of snakes, including: Hulk Hogan, Andre the Giant, Rowdy Roddy Piper and Jake himself. Piper was so terrified of Damien that when Jake brought the boa constrictor towards him in a Charlotte, North Carolina locker room, Piper grabbed a gun from his suitcase and pointed it at Jake! "It was a 9mm semi-automatic [and] I was scared," laughed Roddy when Jake reminded of the incident.

[2]As part of the double act, Koko used to 'ask' Frankie the parrot, who was perched at ringside, for advice during matches. This goes some way to explaining why Koko didn't win all that often.

[3]The wrestlers were completely in charge of their animal mascots, including feeding them, cleaning them, transporting them and, as rumoured in the case of The British Bulldogs, giving Matilda steroids. "I don't know how many shots that dog may have received," speculated Roddy Piper, "but she could bench press about 550lbs!"

ROOM Nº 2

Prank Phone Calls:
Reg Park

As told by Bret Hart

Long before Owen was born, his father Stu Hart purchased the Calgary wrestling territory and shortly afterwards bought the famous mansion that would come to be known as 'Hart House' in 1951. Aspiring wrestlers from all over the world were physically tested in the Dungeon. Some would eventually thrive in the snake pit-like environment but most would escape with their tail between their legs, never to return. Back in the '50s heyday of Stampede, one of the many pretenders to try their hand at the grappling game was former (and future) Mr Universe winner, Reg Park. Park, from Leeds, England, was 6'1" with a world-class physique and movie star good looks. Despite all his attributes, Park somehow never made a dent in the wrestling ring[1] but ended up becoming good friends with Stu. "Reg would come up [to Calgary] at different times of year passing through," recalled Bret.

      Fast-forwarding several decades to the 2nd of April 1989 and *WrestleMania V* was being held in Atlantic City, New Jersey. Everybody was in town a day early in preparation for the biggest event in the WWF's calendar. Because both Bret and Owen would be on the show together for the first time, Bret decided to bring his father and his eldest daughter Jade along for the big weekend. Stu especially enjoyed the trip, having first visited the thriving seaside resort in the city's first boom period in the 1940s. "*WrestleMania V*, I brought my Dad down and he was in a big suite with me and [Jade] and he had a big, long nightshirt on. He was having a great time and it was his first *WrestleMania*. He was meeting different guys and wrestlers." Bret, Stu and Jade, who were all rooming together, were still half-asleep on the morning of the big show when the hotel room phone rang; it was Stu's old friend Reg Park calling for a chat. Bret handed the phone to his father, who greeted the Englishman with an enthusiastic, "How the hell are ya, Reg?"

The two old-timers shared pleasantries for a short while until the conversation abruptly took a turn towards the confrontational. According to Bret, "Next thing I know I'm just watching my Dad and he's starting to pace around the room and he's got the phone [in one hand] and he [was still in] his nightshirt. He was just waking up." Stu's jaw clenched, the veins in his legs began to swell and he started blinking rapidly with agitation as he listened to the bizarre diatribe from the normally easy-going Park. "Stu, you were always afraid of me. You never had the balls to try me, or I would have shoved your head up your ass!" threatened the mild-mannered former bodybuilder. Bret's young daughter Jade was getting upset seeing Grampy get so angry. "[Reg] wanted Stu to fight him in the lobby of the hotel!" Bret chuckled. "I just remember seeing my Dad's face while he was holding the phone. First he was, 'How the hell are ya, Reg?' Then a minute later it was, 'IF YOU WANTED TO TRY ME WHY DIDN'T YOU TRY ME?'"

Before Bret had chance to intervene and take the phone away from his flustered father, the spirit of the phone call adjusted again. "All of a sudden I remember [Stu] slammed the phone down and sat on the bed in his night shirt and was just shaking his head and he looked at me and goes, 'That lousy Owen, he got me!'" Of course, it was Owen all along. Owen had only met Reg a couple of times when the WWF was passing through his home town of Phoenix, Arizona, but that was all the face time Owen needed to do a serviceable impression of him. According to Bret, "Owen decided he'd call my Dad up from the lobby of the hotel and pretend he's Reg Park. I answered the phone 'cause it was my room and he fooled me... he *did* sound just like Reg Park." Owen continued to bait his father until he couldn't keep up the pretence anymore and burst out laughing, telling Stu, "It's me, Owen! I'm pulling your leg!"

Owen would employ the soft-spoken English accent many times over the next decade from hotel lobbies to wrestlers' rooms in ways to be detailed later on in this very tome.

[1]Reg Park did eventually make a contribution to the wrestling industry but not as an in-ring performer. In his later years, Park would become a maker and designer of some of the most iconic championship belts in

the wrestling business, including the 'Winged Eagle' belt, inarguably the greatest incarnation of all the WWE's Heavyweight Championship motifs. Aside from bodybuilding, Park is best remembered for appearing as Hercules in five Italian 'sword-and-sandal' adventure films from 1961-65, as well as being Arnold Schwarzenegger's inspiration and mentor.

"Waking Up The Blazer"
As told by Shane McMahon

As the son of WWF owner Vince McMahon, Shane was exposed to all aspects of the wrestling business behind the scenes, including pranks. In his pre-teen years, Shane was already a fixture of WWF locker rooms, keeping himself busy by either being helpful or being a nuisance to the wrestlers while his father went about his administrative duties. By the time he was 11 years old, Shane was already getting ribbed by some of the all-time greats. "[Don] Muraco... he would lock me in a locker... and the boys would blow cigarette smoke in there... and bang on the locker; things like that. I remember one time, Muraco put me in one of those big oil drum trash cans... and rolled me down the hallway and down a couple of steps!"

By the time Shane had reached his teenage years, he'd been taken under the wing of legendary party animals Muraco and 'Rowdy' Roddy Piper, among others. "I'm there with the kings of the frat house and once you're in the frat house you do what the frat boys do and you grow up in that element. By the time I got to college, everyone's like, 'Let's go out, let's do whatever,' and I'm like, 'This is boring!' I'd be catching a nap because I'd lived rock 'n' roll to the fullest extent." One of the many wrestling carousers Shane would befriend in his teenager years was Owen's brother Bret.

Shane was 18 by the time Owen was hired by the World Wrestling Federation in 1988 to perform as The Blue Blazer. Even though Owen was 23, prime partying age, he'd already made up his mind he wasn't going to be like the vast majority of wrestlers and drink every night in order to escape reality. One evening after one of the numerous shows the WWF held in Chicago's Rosemont Horizon,[1] the crew were downstairs in the hotel bar; all except for Owen, who'd checked in and gone straight to his room. After consuming a few adult beverages, Shane and Bret decided to punish Owen for being unsociable. "Bret and I were hanging out and we decided to go and 'wake up The Blazer' as Bret would say. So we went upstairs and we peaked in because Bret and Owen were sharing a room and then we tackled him!"

Owen didn't appreciate the late-night, 'Cato from *The Pink Panther*' ambushing and enacted revenge on his brother and the boss's kid before they woke up the next morning. "The next day, Bret's boots were missing [and] my stuff somehow wound up in the shower!" The old wrestling proverb, "You don't rib a ribber," has never been more apt.

[1]The WWF held at least 10 shows in the Rosemont Horizon in 1988 alone. Chicago is well known for having some of the rowdiest wrestling fans in North America and the Rosemont was a favourite stop for many performers, including Stone Cold Steve Austin.

Prank Phone Calls:
Iron Sheik

As told by Smith Hart and Ross Hart

Iranian native Hossein Khosrow Ali Vaziri, better known as The Iron Sheik, is one of the most outlandish individuals in and out of the ring in a business built on colourful characters. The decorated amateur wrestler was a bodyguard for the Shah of Iran before escaping the increasingly draconian Islamic regime and heading west for America. Sheik turned pro while helping coach the American Olympic wrestling team, eventually morphing into the ultra-nationalistic Iron Sheik character, complete with vaudevillian moustache, bald head, 'loaded' curly-toed boots and hilarious promos where he'd declare, "Iran number one" in broken English. Long after his physical prime, Sheik was still seen as a man to be feared by his peers, even well into his forties. Decades of hard training and bumping in hard rings, well as years of drug and alcohol abuse, had taken its toll physically and mentally on the ageing Iranian and his volatile temperament was well known in the locker room.

After a big show in Manchester, England, The Iron Sheik was in his hotel room unwinding when he received an unsolicited phone call. The professional-sounding British voice on the other line belonged to a sports journalist looking to write a biography of the man behind the handlebar moustache. The Iron Sheik was not interested as he was already in bed but the reporter buttered Sheiky-baby up by convincing him it would be a huge story that would be carried in all the newspapers.

Sheik soon relented as the sports reporter seemed to know his stuff concerning Sheik's amateur credentials. The reporter also stroked his ego about being a real world's champion, unlike the 'phony' Hulk Hogan. The journalist claimed that there were several people on hand in the lobby to make a front page story but there was a catch. "You gotta come down with... your boots and... the whole outfit. I'm going to have a picture of my kid

Camel Clutching you... I'm a prize-winning photographer and I've got a whole crew here."

The sleepy Sheik agreed and got dressed in all his regalia, including his medals, traditional Arab headdress and curly-toed boots and headed downstairs. When Sheik walked into the lobby, there was no one there to profile him. He looked all over before asking the check-in clerk where the journalists were waiting for him. The clerk obviously didn't know anything about any journalist, or why a middle-aged Iranian dressed like Ali Baba was asking him such a question. The perturbed Sheik headed up to his room, undid his boots, got into bed and tried to forget the whole thing.

Five minutes later, The Iron Sheik received a frantic call from the journalist. "Where are you, we're waiting, what's going on? My wife's here, I was getting the equipment... [but] we're all set now, come on down." Poor Sheik got dressed up once again to head downstairs where, of course, nobody was there once again. According to eldest Hart brother Smith, "The Sheik just looked around and scowled and didn't even bother asking the desk clerk; he knew it was Owen." Owen knew it was a job well done when he heard The Iron Sheik shuffle into his room and slam the door hard. Owen heard the door slam particularly clearly because he happened to be staying in the room next door and the walls were thin. This further explains the unfortunate timing of the phone calls that Sheiky received that night.

Another time in another hotel, The Iron Sheik was once again in his room drifting off to sleep when he received a phone call from Owen pretending to be a journalist looking to do a profile on the man from Tehran. This time Owen caught Sheik in a better mood and he was flattered at the idea of being profiled for a major publication. The telephone interview started innocently enough, with Owen quizzing Sheik about his early days growing up in Iran and his background in amateur wrestling, before discussing breaking into the professional ranks and working his way up the ladder of success.

Owen led him on for several minutes before letting Sheik know what he really thought of his amateur credentials. According to Jim Ross, "Owen started disrespecting him, telling the Sheik he wasn't that good of a wrestler." Anyone who has witnessed one of his extraordinary shoot interview outbursts over the past fifteen years can testify that The Iron Sheik is as hilarious as he is vulgar when riled up. Sheik immediately went on the attack, threatening the sports reporter in ways best left to the imagination. After jawing back and forth, the 'journalist' claimed he was in Sheik's hotel and challenged the proud Iranian to a showdown right there in the lobby.

The multi-time AAU silver medallist gladly accepted the challenge from who he thought was a combative reporter and, in a scene that would be repeated countless times over the years with various wrestlers, The Iron Sheik blustered into the hotel lobby in shorts and a t-shirt covering his ponderous belly ready to humble the phantom journalist. Sheik hunted high and low for the would-be biographer to the amusement of a number of wrestlers who were hanging around the lobby/bar area, including Owen. Owen had placed the phone call from the lobby in front of a number of WWF personnel and they all decided to stick around and watch the latest Iron Sheik meltdown, before observing him head back to his room empty-handed.

62

Prank Phone Calls: Mr Fuji

As told by Bret Hart, Jim Cornette and Mr Fuji

This wasn't the only time Owen would fool a dastardly foreign heel wrestler whose physical prime was in the rear-view mirror. Harold 'Mr Fuji' Fujiwara, a prototypical wrestling caricature of the evil Japanese, salt-throwing bad guy,[1] was considered one of the all-time connoisseurs of the rib. The most famous example of Fuji's brutal method of pranking supposedly involved killing a pet dog and feeding it to Billy White Wolfe (and possibly Skandor Akbar) as revenge for them allegedly stealing his furniture from a Hawaiian lock-up. Other examples of the Fuji rib include having the engine removed from a fellow wrestlers' rental car just to see his reaction (a prank that was rumoured to cost $1,000), urinating on Lex Luger's boot while in a busy restaurant, cancelling other wrestlers' flights without their knowledge, slipping laxatives in fellow workers' drinks (just before a match, if possible), nailing manager 'Classy' Freddy Blassie's clothes to the locker room ceiling and rigging an M-80 firecracker under Spiros Arion and SD Jones' car so it blew the bonnet off when they tried to turn the engine over, among many more!

Jim Cornette speculated why arguably the two greatest ribbers of their respective generations didn't start a pranking war. "I think Owen and Fuji were both smart enough to know not to rib each other. I think Owen had so much respect for his seniors in the business that he would not have tried that with Fuji. [Owen] probably would have put Fuji's over like crazy if Fuji had done it." Cornette also suggested that if the two were to have teamed up it may have created a cosmic disturbance so awesome as to cause the Earth to implode on itself.

Unbeknown to Jim (and probably most of the roster at the time), Owen had indeed got Fuji on at least one occasion but possibly didn't let it be widely known in case a prank war broke out between the two. The set up was the familiar routine of calling Fuji's room and putting on a fake voice.

According to Bret, Owen had several distinctive voices nailed down including, "An English guy... [and] he could do an East Indian kind of voice where he'd be kind of pushy on you." This time Owen pretended to be a petulant kid who was looking to start trouble.

The war of words escalated until the 'kid' challenged Fuji to a fight in the lobby. "Come down an' I'll kick yer ASS!" sneered the little punk. By this time, the once feared Mr Fuji was physically broken, having endured seven knee surgeries at a cost of $300,000 over the years, as well as being way north of 50 years old. Even with all these ailments, Fuji accepted the challenge and hobbled down to the lobby. When he finally arrived, he was confronted by Bret, who asked him why he was in his kimono, half asleep and looking to throw hands at 3am. "Some kid called me and told me to come down...he said he was gonna kick my ass!'"

[1]Fuji is best-remembered for his role as a manager, donning a tuxedo and bowler hat in a near-exact replica of 'Oddjob' from the 1964 James Bond film *Goldfinger*. Oddjob was played by Harold Sakata, who also happened to be a wrestler who performed as Tosh Togo. The Rock's grandfather Peter Maivia, British wrestlers 'Bomber' Pat Roach and Milton 'Mighty Chang' Reid and, more recently, Dave Bautista among numerous other wrestlers have all featured as henchmen in Bond films.

Paul Boesch's Uniforms

As told by Bruce Prichard

The city of Houston, Texas was a historical hotbed for professional wrestling since before World War I all the way to 1987. The territory (which only encompassed the city of Houston) had only two owners spanning those eight decades; Morris Sigel and Paul Boesch. Boesch was a hugely respected figure in his home town having earned numerous medals, including the Purple Heart, for his services to the United States army during World War II. After decades of successfully running shows in the city thanks to working agreements with other promotions, Boesch folded the territory in '87 after his working agreement with the World Wrestling Federation juggernaut quickly went south.[1] After Houston Wrestling folded, the WWF/E has run multiple shows in the city every year since, which is where Owen found himself when he was accosted by a wacky fan with an absurd gift for his father Stu.

Owen was staying at the Greenway Plaza Hotel along with other WWF crew members when the oddball fan approached him in the lobby and tried to hand Owen a sack of old clothes. The old clothes were some of Paul Boesch's army uniforms from the 1940s and the fan wanted to give them to Owen to hand them to his father Stu. Perhaps the hotel was closer than the fan's nearest charity clothing bank. As the story goes, Boesch was partially responsible for introducing Stu to his future wife Helen while he and Stu were wrestling in New York in 1946. Why Stu would want Boesch's old army uniforms in the first place was a mystery, especially when Hart House was cluttered enough as it was. Owen and the fan ended up arguing in the hotel lobby when Owen refused to take the uniforms and fly them 2,200 miles back to Calgary. When the heated confrontation escalated, the fan called the police claiming Owen, who didn't want the uniforms in the first place, had stolen them!

Owen travelled light on purpose so he could spend less time in airports and make connecting flights more easily. Owen wasn't about to accept a gift he'd have to lug around with him for days and check in at every airport, then present to Stu, who most likely wouldn't have appreciated the

65

sentiment anyway. When the police turned up to calm the situation down, Owen took the officers aside and explained that the fan was the one who started the kerfuffle. "The [fan]... just worked himself into a shoot and Owen just wanted to get the hell outta there," said WWE Producer Bruce Prichard. "[Owen] was trying to give the stuff back to the guy; 'I don't want your stinkin' uniform!'" The police thankfully believed Owen's side of the story and escorted the fan off the premises, despite the fan being the one who called the cops in the first place. "Owen got hot and just turned it right around on the guy and ended up basically getting the guy arrested [and] getting him thrown out of the hotel!"

[1]The working agreement between Boesch and Vince McMahon soured quickly when Houston TV aired the Randy Savage vs. Ricky Steamboat classic battle from *WrestleMania III* several weeks in a row to promote the rematch at the Sam Houston Coliseum. On the WWF's part, McMahon, who was providing Boesch with wrestlers for his territory, kept switching out who would be appearing. This forced Boesch to promote cards where half the wrestlers would be different than advertised. After Boesch, his nephew and McMahon disagreed on how Houston Wrestling should be handled, Paul decided to run one last show then retire. McMahon provided the talent for the show, overspent on special guests and threw a huge after party in Boesch's honour. According to Prichard, who was involved in negotiations, Boesch's nephew emotionally blackmailed McMahon on the day of the event so he and Paul could keep the entire gate for that night, after previously agreeing to a 70/30 split in WWF's favour. After hearing the nephew's request, McMahon, who'd spent many tens of thousands of dollars out of his own pocket to put on the show, stood up and remarked, "God damn, pal, you didn't even use Vaseline!"

Prank Phone Calls: The Pizza Prank

As told by Triple H, Bret Hart and Martha Hart

Many of Owen's crank calls were placed late at night when everyone else was asleep or just dozing off. He found it difficult enough to bed down while travelling on domestic loops but on foreign tours Owen's body clock would be screwed up to the point he'd barely sleep at all. To entertain himself in the wee small hours, Owen would ring up unsuspecting WWF employees from his room or the hotel lobby. One of his most well honed acts was the Indian pizza delivery guy. "I really think that Owen was a bit of an insomniac," posited Bret. "[He'd call at] like two in the morning, usually in Europe, and call you to tell you there was a free pizza compliments of the hotel."

Like any great salesman, Owen wouldn't let hurdles like being asleep or not feeling hungry get in the way of him forcing the unsolicited pizza onto the unwitting recipient. To end the call, the wrestler on the other line would invariably agree to have the pizza delivered to their room. That's when Owen would launch into phase two; the toppings. "Next thing I know I'd be arguing with the guy about how he wanted me to pick my toppings, what kind of toppings I wanted," said Bret. "So I start going through the toppings and then he'd start pushing more toppings on [me]." After angrily conferring over the minutia of the pizza for a number of minutes, Owen would hit his mark with the big go home line; the pizza was free but the toppings were extra! Fury would be elicited before Owen would give the game away and let the poor unfortunate get back to sleep. "You'd go through this charade the whole time," smiled Bret. "Anyway, that was Owen."

The incessant nit-pickery over unwanted cuisine was not limited to pizza. In another late night phone conversation with Paul 'Triple H' Levesque, Owen pretended to be a hotel employee confirming a breakfast order that was never placed. "He'd put on like an English accent, 'Hello,

Sir... you ordered your breakfast, just wondering if you wanted your eggs... poached or fried?'" Nobody could possibly care what fashion their eggs were going to be cooked in when they've just been startled awake by a ringing phone at 4am, especially when they never wanted breakfast in the first place. Triple H was no different, insisting he never placed the order but Owen would continue to press. "No sir, it says here on the order. Just wondering; fried or poached if you could just answer the question, please?"

By this time, Triple H had had enough, put the phone down and went back to bed. Shortly after, the phone would ring again. "Sorry sir, we got disconnected!" said Owen. The egg conundrum would be pushed further until Triple H agreed to have them poached just to end the conversation. That's when Owen would launch into an inquiry as to how Triple H would like his toast. "He'd just keep doing it until you lost your mind!" recalled Triple H. Owen's sister Diana similarly recalled Owen and Davey Boy Smith having a rollaway bed brought to an unknown wrestler's door at 1am because they supposedly ordered it. "It was hilarious and just made him fun to be around," laughed Triple H.

A separate rib, also involving pizza, comes from back in 1988, when Owen was rooming with another 'World's Strongest Man', former Olympic weightlifter-turned-wrestler Ken Patera. Unlike Owen, who was a young up-and-coming rookie working as The Blue Blazer, Patera's career was sharply on the decline after his release from prison. Patera returned to the WWF in 1987 after completing a two year stretch for his part in damaging a McDonald's restaurant and then beating up a number of the police officers who tried to arrest him.[1]

With Patera still downstairs in the hotel bar (Patera reportedly drank and smoked even during his competitive weightlifting days) Owen got hungry and ordered himself a pizza. Some time later, Patera came back to their shared room where on the spur of the moment Owen declared, "I'm hungry, let's order pizza." Owen picked up the room phone and pretended to dial the takeaway and placed his and Patera's order using a phone that wasn't connected to anyone. Owen then hung up and waited. Not five minutes later there was a knock at their door. The pizza delivery guy was standing in the doorway with a piping hot pie fresh from the oven. In a state of consternation, Patera stared at the delivery guy before asking him, "What did you do, brother, cook it in the car?"

Owen's widow Martha fondly remembered her husband's penchant for phone pranks. "There weren't many in the WWF who hadn't played victim to some sort of prank phone call, room service at 3am or a misguided directive from head office courtesy of Owen."

[1]In 1984, Ken Patera went to grab some food at the Waukesha, Wisconsin McDonald's restaurant after a show. It was past midnight and therefore past closing time but the McDonald's lights were still on, as a commercial was being filmed on the premises. Patera saw a tray of burgers through the window and begged an employee to sell him some as nowhere else was serving. After his request was denied, Patera launched a '30 pound field stone' through the McDonald's window and drove off (Patera still contends it was another would-be customer). Larry Zbyszko claimed after he threw the rock, Patera yelled, "NO ONE SCREWS OVER KEN PATERA! IF YOU WANNA DO ANYTHING ABOUT IT I'M AT THE HOLIDAY INN, ASSHOLES!" When a couple of cops came to arrest Patera at the hotel, his roommate Masa Saito answered the door. Saito was confused as he didn't speak much English and when the young female cop maced Patera, Saito and Patera dropped them both. Backup was called and numerous other police officers attempted to arrest them, with Saito and Patera destroying them too. "We had 'em all stacked up like kindling!" recalled Patera. In 1985, both wrestlers were sent down for two years apiece.

CHAPTER 3

The Wilderness Years

❤ ❤

Shortly before his return to Stampede, Owen finally married long-time girlfriend Martha Patterson at Hart House on the 1st of July 1989 in what Bret described as a 'plastic affair'. The wedding's atmosphere was permeated with tension throughout the day, as Dynamite Kid, who had been deteriorating mentally as well as physically,[1] recently had an altercation with Owen's best man Bruce Hart. Dynamite's version described wind-up merchant Bruce rubbing it in the Bulldogs' face that they were back to travelling in a rickety old van with a missing windshield while Bruce was being chauffeured around in a Buick by the ring announcer. A drunken Dynamite lamped Bruce hard, dislocating his jaw, before Davey head butted him in the mouth. Dynamite then found the Buick-driving ring announcer and smacked him for good measure. Bruce's version is mostly the same except that he claims he caught and reprimanded the Bulldogs for spiking his beer. Further tensions were caused by the fact that Martha didn't care for a number of the Hart siblings and they loathed Martha right back. "The wedding seemed to bring the worst out of everyone," recounted Martha.

After the honeymoon, Owen started back at Stampede in late July 1989 before embarking on another tour of Japan the next month. Stampede worked closely with New Japan Pro Wrestling thanks to the Calgary promotion's long-standing tradition of booking foreign talent. Many foreign workers first cut their teeth on North American soil in Calgary; many from Japan, Europe and Australasia. 1987 saw future Japanese middleweight greats Hiroshi Hase and Keiichi 'Jushin Thunder Liger' Yamada leave Stampede to head back to New Japan. Both raved about Owen's work to NJPW officials and, thanks to tape trading, positive coverage in Japanese wrestling magazines and Stampede's Japanese liaison Tokyo Joe, Owen Hart-o (as he was referred to) was already a star in Japan before he'd ever set foot in the country in August 1987.

Calgary was highly regarded among serious wrestling fans for its violent, hard-hitting style and several Hart brothers (including Bret, Bruce, Keith and Smith) had already toured the country. Local wrestling magazines started referring to Owen as the 'Calgary Genius', claiming he was the best wrestler of all the Harts, even though he only had one year as a full-time professional under his belt. In spite of the language barrier, Owen lived up to the hype with his smooth wrestling, flashy high-flying offence and natural connection with the crowd. Owen would win the prestigious IWGP Junior Heavyweight Title from his first big Japanese rival Hiroshi Hase; the first foreigner ever to do so. He also engaged in programmes with Yamada and Kuniaki Koboyashi while still wrestling for his father's promotion back home. Aside from winning the IWGP Title from Hase,[2] Owen also loved facing off against his old Stampede tag team partner Chris Benoit, who was making a serious name for himself in NJPW as Pegasus Kid. Martha discussed the difficulties Owen faced while out on the road, including the lack of amenities and comforts of home, as well as the graunching schedule. "He took several four-to-six week tours to Japan only to return to Calgary for Stampede Wrestling mentally and physically exhausted."

While only in his early 20s, Owen had already developed some of his famous idiosyncrasies that were out of the ordinary for travelling pro wrestlers. He didn't go out to the nightclubs carousing or drinking or getting pilled up. Owen preferred to stay in his room watching incomprehensible television programmes or reading a book, which added to his homesickness. "Sometimes he wouldn't even eat out with us," recalled 'Pitbull' Gary Wolfe. "He'd have his little grill with him and he'd set it up in his room and he would cook his own food just to save money." When he stayed at the Keio

71

Plaza Hotel in Tokyo, Owen struck up relationships with some of the fans who were hanging around in the lobby, even managing to convince some of them to do his laundry. Owen was also a fully realised prankster at this point in his life. According to Japanese wrestling journalist Fumi Saito, Owen was once invited to a Korean barbecue, where he amused himself by throwing frozen meat at other wrestlers' heads. In total, Owen would partake in eight gruelling tours with NJPW from 1987 to 1991 and two short tours with the World Wrestling Federation in 1992 (co-promoted with WAR) and 1994.

Back at Stampede things were going south at a rapid pace. The British Bulldogs returned to Calgary in December 1988 to give the promotion some desperately needed star power. With Dynamite taking over booking responsibilities, the Bulldogs tag team were split up. The heel Dynamite teamed with Davey's storyline cousin (or brother, depending on the source) Johnny Smith and Davey teamed up with Dynamite's spiritual successor Chris Benoit in response. Stampede commentator and Executive Producer, Ed Whalen, was opposed to the breakup and edited out a lot of relevant footage, muddling the storyline's presentation on television.

Dynamite's tenure as booker was short-lived and booking duties were soon handed back to Bruce. Dynamite's escalating drug and alcohol abuse was causing him to become more unpredictable and unreliable, his ideas weren't very good and he was often injured. During one of his last Stampede appearances, a worse for wear Dynamite headed to the ring with his boots around his neck. Dynamite got on the microphone and slurred out an invitation for Chris Benoit, whom he was feuding with, to come to the ring. Unbeknownst to the decision makers and Benoit himself, Dynamite abruptly announced his retirement and handed his boots over to Benoit, saying he was the only wrestler who could fill them.

By the time Owen came back, Stampede's roster was further depleted after a horrific crash almost claimed the lives of Davey Boy Smith, Chris Benoit, Koki 'Sumo Hara' Kitahara and Jason the Terrible. Ross Hart was speeding on the icy, mountainous roads of AB-93 towards the small town of Jasper, Alberta, when he lost control of the van. The van only managed to stay on the mountain because they crashed into a campervan travelling the opposite way. Benoit and Ross escaped relatively unscathed. Sumo Hara suffered a broken hip and Jason reinjured his leg after the van's spare tire came loose and struck his knee. The camper van driver ended up with a broken leg but the camper's passenger, a parrot that was riding shotgun, was unharmed. The most gravely injured was Davey, who was sat up front, not wearing a seatbelt. He'd reportedly just admonished Ross for driving too fast right before the van hydroplaned. Davey was thrown through the windshield twenty-five feet onto the ground, sustaining two herniated discs in his neck, a separated shoulder, numerous lacerations that required 135 stitches and vision impairment in his left eye. After everyone initially thought the unconscious Davey had been killed, paramedics eventually arrived on the scene and resuscitated him. After coming to, Davey immediately began the search for the chocolate ice cream cone he was eating just before the crash.

Aside from Jason and Davey being injured and Dynamite frequently going AWOL, superstar-in-the-making Brian Pillman had already left for World Championship Wrestling before Owen's return, reportedly because of Dynamite's treatment of him. Mike Shaw, who had been one of the best heels of the rebooted Stampede era, was taken out of the ring and placed on commentary before leaving for WCW as well. Upon his return, Owen was plugged into the injured Davey's spot in the Dynamite feud but then Dynamite quit the promotion a few days later. Stu's money woes were so dire in 1989 he'd paid him what Dynamite considered an insultingly low amount. "[I] told him I was finishing and handed [Stu] the cheques back," explained Dynamite. "Evidently, you need these [cheques] more than me."[3] Dynamite was lured back to wrestle Owen a couple more times at the Calgary Pavilion before he left Stampede for good. In their last match, Owen outwitted Dynamite and Johnny Smith in a no holds barred 'Street Fight' before rolling up Dynamite for the clean victory. "The Harts had their final moment of glory, the crowd got a fantastic match and Owen, bless him, proved what a good wrestler he had turned out to be," said Dynamite.

Owen challenged 'Lethal' Larry Cameron for the Stampede North American Title and frequently did battle with David 'Angel of Death' Sheldon in the promotion's final months before Stu finally had enough. Stu and Helen had lost a reported CA$1 million since Stampede was revived in 1985. If they carried on at that rate they'd soon be out on the street. "In the end, I don't think [Stu] was even interested in running it," insisted Keith

Hart, "except as a career for Bruce and some of the boys." Stu's promoter's licence expired at the end of 1989 and on the first week of January 1990, Stampede was officially closed. After more than forty years enveloped in a business she loathed, Helen was reportedly over the moon to be finally free from wrestling.

Now a free agent, Owen headed back to New Japan Pro Wrestling in January and made his Mexican debut shortly after, where he would once again perform as The Blue Blazer in several stints for the Universal Wrestling Association. Owen wrestled mostly in tag team matches before facing off against Mexican headliner El Canek on the 19th of May 1991 in a mask vs. mask *lucha de apuestas* (betting fight).[4] El Canek defeated The Blue Blazer in a relatively quick 6:45 to win the Blazer's mask with a spinning wheel kick followed by a senton splash. The unmasking of an opponent is usually treated as a huge deal in Mexico but UWA's presentation of this particular event lacked the usual pomp and circumstance. When the camera zoomed in to capture the critical moment of the Blazer's unmasking, a large-headed referee wandered into shot, completely obscuring Owen's face. The ring announcer then declared to the crowd that The Blue Blazer's real name was in fact "Owen Clarke."[5]

Owen did well to survive the Mexican Wild West, enduring two separate knife attacks from crazy fans during the short stopovers. While he incorporated some of the high-flying acrobatics prevalent in *lucha libre* into his own arsenal, Owen was less complementary about the phoniness of the overall Mexican wrestling style. "They do a lot of high-flying, entertaining things but it looks so choreographed." Owen continued, "I see these guys, they throw a guy into the ropes and they do a backflip and then clothesline the guy and it looks stupid. Why don't you just clothesline the guy?"

In April 1990, Owen received a phone call from a German promoter inviting him to wrestle for Otto Wanz' Catch Wrestling Association. It was a great honour for Owen to be asked to participate in the tent tours, especially as CWA favoured true heavyweights. Unlike almost every other wrestling promotion, the CWA operated in the same location for weeks at a time before packing up and moving to the next locale. The exhausting travel schedule was replaced with spending more time relaxing with Martha, who would end up accompanying Owen on the road for over a year. Martha not only described this period as the most normal year of their marriage but also, "The most exciting time of my life." Owen made around CA$450-600 per week on the tent tours, which was not very much considering that's about what he made when he first started out in Stampede. Over the course of 1990 and 1991, Owen and Martha lived in Germany and Austria for a total of nine months. "We'd do a tour for six weeks in the same cities, Austria, then we'd go to France for a week's vacation, then work for another six weeks, then go to Venice, Italy for a week's vacation," said Owen. "It gave me a lot of good memories."

The CWA used European professional wrestling rules, which included boxing-style rounds, best of three falls and a football-style carding system for fouls and misconduct; the latter of which Stampede implemented some years before.[6] A more curious tradition in CWA concerned all the wrestlers walking out in their costumes one by one to the ring at the beginning of the show, then walking back to the dressing room in the same order they walked in, just like in traditional sumo events. Oldest brother Smith nearly got himself arrested for having too much fun during these introductory parades in the late '70s. One time Smith walked to the ring like a robot and another time he put a rolled up towel down the front of his trunks. Then there was the big one... or at least the *other* big one. On the last night of the Catch tournament, Smith, who had been growing a bushy moustache throughout his stay... surely you can see where this one is going? Smith clipped the sides of the moustache into a nice, neat square, combed his hair to the side and rubbed it with black shoe polish. Then, in all his Fuhrer chic, Smith goose-stepped his way to the ring before giving out the obligatory Sieg Heil salute to the audience. "The entire arena, which had been buzzing with excitement over the impending matches, went totally silent," recalled an embarrassed Diana. Smith was lucky not to get thrown in *gefängnis*, as performing the Nazi salute in Germany carries a maximum sentence of three years imprisonment.

While still wrestling in Germany, Owen received a phone call from the offices of World Championship Wrestling in early 1991. WCW already pitched the freelancer about coming in to replace Tom Zenk as Brian Pillman's tag team partner the year before. Owen politely declined as he wasn't keen to work for legendary misery guts and malcontent Ole Anderson.

By 1991, 'American Dream' Dusty Rhodes had left the WWF and taken over as WCW booker. Once again, Owen was pitched the idea of tagging with Pillman under the name 'Wings', no doubt in tribute to the ultra hip, Paul McCartney-fronted adult contemporary soft rock combo, as well alluding to their high-flying acrobatics.

Owen debuted for WCW in March 1991, while also debuting a series of highly unflattering, short-legged neon leotards that seemed designed to accentuate his love handles and nothing more. On the road, Owen took on some low level talent, as well as tagging with 'Flyin' Brian Pillman against the WCW version of the Fabulous Freebirds, Michael 'Purely Sexy' Hayes and Jimmy 'Jam' Garvin. On WCW television, Owen faced no-name bums, once while tagging with all-time great Ricky Morton. During the Morton tag team match, a video promo played in the top left part of the screen featuring Pillman hyping Owen's aerial abilities. "Lemme tell you something about Owen Hart; he loves to fly just like I do. Look out, this is gonna be exciting!" Unfortunately, this was WCW and production always went wrong. The promo ran a second too long, which was just enough time for the audience to witness Pillman break character and wipe the smile off his face before walking out of shot. This would be the only on-screen association Owen and Pillman would have in WCW, as Pillman was still engaged in a rivalry with Sid Vicious (Sid Eudy)[7] and Owen quit the promotion after a month. WCW were reluctant to offer Owen a contract unless he moved to their home base of Atlanta, Georgia. Serious thought was given to moving down south to the point where Martha filled out an application for a green card, before the young couple decided to stay put in Calgary.

Owen made frequent appearances in Europe, Mexico and Japan for the next few months, before more deeply considering his future. Despite the hardship on his body, it's mostly accepted that Owen really enjoyed wrestling but didn't care for the politics and constant travel that came with the profession. Over the summer of '91, Owen decided to follow in big brother Keith's footsteps and apply to the Calgary Fire Department. "To get on with the fire department, you need to put together a resume working with high-pressure hoses, working at heights, stuff like that," explained Owen. "I went and got jobs like irrigation work, pipe lining, working laying sod where we had to spray this high-pressure peat moss on the ground. I even got a job working on roofs. It showed that I wasn't scared working at heights." Owen further bolstered his CV by taking courses at Mount Royal College, as well as courses in first aid, CPR and even a CB radio course. Stu and Helen were outraged at Martha for what they saw as her manipulating her husband into retiring from the wrestling business. While it was easy to see why Stu was upset, Helen's anger was somewhat bewildering considering her opinions of the profession. Unfortunately, Owen's decision to forgo his last year of university came back to bite him, as the Calgary Fire Department was deluged with so many applications they would only consider prospective candidates with a degree. Owen applied three times but was never even given the chance to take the aptitude test. Going back to university was also ruled out as Martha had fallen pregnant in June and the family needed the extra money.

Owen went back on the road with Martha and the unborn baby in tow, wrestling in Mexico, Germany and even returning to the UK for a couple of shots. Owen actually returned to the UK while working for Stampede in 1987. Billed as a sort of Wild West cowboy complete with Stetson, 'Bronco' Owen Hart tangled with the incredibly talented Marty Jones for Joint Promotions' vacant Mid-Heavyweight Championship on the 25th of April 1987. In what is now considered somewhat of a forgotten gem, the full twenty-minute classic was broadcast on ITV to millions of viewers. "He was a hell of a grafter," said Marty Jones, "someone who could work as a heel or a babyface, a good workman, like a carpenter." Owen also made a single appearance for Joel Goodheart's Tri-State Wrestling Alliance in Philadelphia; the prototype for the revolutionary promotion Extreme Championship Wrestling. Owen defeated New Japan stalwart Takayuki IIzuka on the 21st of September 1991. This was also the day Owen would meet his spirit animal in the cheapskate department, Mick Foley.

Germany wasn't all positivity, however. Dean Hart, who everyone called 'Biz' because he was always up to some business, died of Bright's disease on the 21st of September 1990 at the age of 36. Dean had been hit by a bus back in 1978, which had severely damaged his kidneys. Dean put off going to see a doctor for years. By the time he consulted a physician in 1989, his kidneys had already lost 95% function. When Dean died, Owen was in Germany and couldn't make it back for the funeral. When Owen and

Martha were stationed in Bremen, Germany for another tent tour in autumn 1991, the caravan they were forced to stay in was a squalid, rat-infested hell hole with no running water. Things were looking bleak by the end of '91, as aside from living in a fetid caravan, Owen had been struggling to get on Japanese tours as of late despite a number of stellar matches and successful appearances. A full-time job in Mexico also wasn't happening, as aside from the inherent danger, Owen had lost his Blue Blazer mask, which potentially devalued him in the eyes of the fans. Owen needed a break and it just so happened he received a phone call from Bret when things looked to be at their bleakest.

[1]Dynamite severely injured his back in a tag team match with Davey Boy Smith against Don Muraco and Bob Orton Jr. Years of steroid abuse and a high impact, hard bumping style took such a toll on Dynamite's body that he was wheelchair-bound by the late 1990s.

[2]Japanese people generally take wrestlers and wrestling far more seriously than most other countries, as evidenced by how many native wrestlers became successful politicians. Hiro Hase served as Minister of Education, Culture, Sports, Science and Technology from 2015-2016 and NJPW kingpin Antonio Inoki served two terms as a member of the Japanese House of Councillors. Even FMW death match specialist Atsushi Onita won a seat in the Japanese Diet before being ousted for having a threesome with a government employee and a porn star on government property.

[3]Dynamite described Stampede's mismanagement as a case of there being, "Too many chiefs and not enough Indians." Dynamite rang WCW booker Ric Flair asking for a job after leaving Stampede. Flair pretended that they weren't hiring any wrestlers but in all probability he just didn't want Dynamite and his bad attitude upsetting the locker room balance any more than it already was. WCW was already going downhill since Ted Turner purchased and renamed Jim Crockett's Mid-Atlantic territory in November 1988.

[4]Mask vs. mask matches are generally the culmination of a long feud, with the loser receiving a big pay-off to finally reveal their face to the world. *Luchadores* also commonly put their hair on the line against another wrestler's hair, mask or wrestling title. Owen considered allowing his head to be shaved for a pay-off before Martha put her foot down over the matter.

[5]This botched announcement would precede Michael 'Let's Get Ready to Rumble' Buffer announcing the world-famous Bret Hart as "Bret Clarke" on no less than two separate *WCW Monday Nitro* telecasts.

[6]A common ploy the more talented wrestlers performed in Europe was to get the babyface fined by the referee. The heel would continually cheat behind the referee's back, giving them an unfair advantage. Late into the match, the babyface would get so frustrated at the heel's dishonesty that they would break the rules themselves. This time, the referee would catch the foul and hand the babyface an on-the-spot fine. If used judiciously, if the babyface was over and if the fans bought the act, audience members would give the babyface money to pay the fine. The money from the audience would then be split between the wrestlers and the referee.

[7]In October 1991, Pillman and Sid had one of the most astonishing real-life confrontations in the history of wrestling. Sid had recently jumped to the World Wrestling Federation and, in a rare instance, both the WWF and WCW crews were in Atlanta at the same time. At the bar, Sid drunkenly boasted about how great the WWF was and how much more money he was making to WCW road agent Mike Graham. Sid then started berating Pillman, saying that the WWF would never book the 5'9" Pillman against a 6'8" superstar such as himself, referring to their WCW rivalry earlier in the year. Sid also laughably claimed Pillman, who was a great worker, couldn't work. This was especially rich as not only was Sid a horrible wrestler but he'd legitimately injured Pillman with an errant powerbomb at the *WCW WrestleWar* pay-per-view that February. After the seriously tough Pillman stepped up to Sid, Sid backed off, citing a bicep injury and left the bar. Feeling humiliated

that he was punked out by a man almost a foot shorter than him, Sid routed through his car for a weapon to attack Pillman with. A short while later, Sid was seen by numerous WCW personnel appearing in the doorway of the bar clutching onto a squeegee. "I know it was Mike Graham who took the squeegee away from Sid," said Barry Windham, who witnessed the incident. After Sid was disarmed, Graham politely, but firmly, offered to stick the squeegee up Sid's bottom unless he departed that instant. Sid's version of the story goes slightly differently. "My car was dead, a guy was giving me a boost and Pillman was out there. It just so happens [the squeegee] was on... the passenger seat. I grabbed it and said, 'Hey, motherfucker, you want me to whack you in the fuckin' head with this?' Of course, he didn't."

Hotel Fire Extinguisher

As told by Steve Blackman

Straight-laced martial artist turned Hart Dungeon graduate Steve Blackman[1] (going by the swanky moniker Steve R Blackman) took part in NJPW's *New Year Golden Series* at the beginning of 1988 and had the pleasure of staying in the same hotel as the King of Pranks. "Owen's the biggest ribber I've ever seen in my life. His picture should be in the dictionary next to the word rib 'cause there's nobody like him," said Blackman. While they were staying on the same floor of a hotel, Owen decided to rib the rookie wrestler but ended up ribbing everybody within breathing range, including himself. "We were in Japan and we're on the eighth or ninth floor [of our hotel] and Owen, screwing around, brought a fire extinguisher over and he was trying to shoot it underneath my door just to mess with me. The handle got stuck and the [extinguisher] kept venting its entire contents." Owen had used a carbon dioxide extinguisher, which displaces oxygen in the air, meaning not only did Blackman start choking on the cloud of white dust in the atmosphere but so did Owen, who was out in the hallway. "Owen goes running back to his room, I close the door to my room and it's taken my breath now. So I open my window, stick my head out and just as I stick my head out I look down. I mean as far as I can see, every room has a head sticking out the window. Every Japanese person in the hotel was gasping for air on that floor!"

After the extinguisher's tank finally emptied, Blackman composed himself and grabbed a towel to put over his face. He poked his head out of the door to see who the culprit was, which didn't take a Jessica Fletcher to work out. "I stuck my head back out into the hall and there was a mist across the floor and you could see Owen's footprints going all the way back down to the door right into his room. I called Owen's room and told him about the footprints and he sprinted down the hall, holding his breath and covering his eyes with a towel. He starts flailing this towel to try and cover his footprints and just as he shuts the door to his room, all the security guys came off the elevator!"

Hotel security tried to pin the blame on Blackman, which made no sense as it was his room that was filled with white powder and it was obvious he was the recipient of the rib. The wardens also tried to blame a random guest who had no idea what happened. According to Blackman, the guards didn't want to accuse Owen because he was already a New Japan fixture and they didn't want to pin the blame on him. "Although [Owen] wasn't doing it to people in the hotel, he was trying to rib me and he ended up ribbing everyone on the whole floor. That was a classic because you couldn't breathe up there for a while."

[1]Poor Steve Blackman was well on the way to making a decent living for himself in professional wrestling, being just days away from signing a deal with the World Wrestling Federation. He'd previously agreed to go on a three week tour of South Africa in May 1989 where he contracted malaria and dysentery, leaving him bed-ridden and close to death for two and a half years. It took almost six years before he was able to train normally again. Happily, Blackman finally made it to the WWF thanks to his old Stampede running buddy Brian Pillman putting a call into WWF's talent relations department. Blackman enjoyed five years with the WWF during the company's hottest period until retiring in 2002 due to a neck injury.

Feeling the Burn

As told by Scott Hall and Mark Henry

In between the brief and unsuccessful WCW characters 'Gator'[1] and 'The Diamond Studd',[2] 'Texas' Scott Hall headed to Germany in 1990 for the Otto Wanz' Catch Wrestling Association. Hall enjoyed some success in the CWA, reaching the finals of Catch Cup 1990 before losing to The Soultaker (best remembered as WWE's Godfather). With many of the finest wrestlers in the history of the business wrestling on CWA's tent tours over the years, Scott Hall found himself living in a static caravan next to none other than Owen Hart. The best part of the tent tours were that the wrestlers would perform at the same venue for weeks on end, eliminating the time-consuming and exhausting travel from town to town. This meant there was plenty of time to take life easy, go sight-seeing and stay fit.

As well as having plenty of time to hit the weights, Owen would go about amusing himself while at the gym. In between sets of bicep curls and Romanian dead lifts, Owen would fiddle around with the gym's thermostat in accordance with the weather that day. Hall reminisced that if it was a blisteringly hot day in July, Owen would sidle up to the gym's thermostat and crank it up to 'about 120' Fahrenheit, then casually observe everyone around him begin to liquefy. Conversely, if it was the middle of winter, Owen would turn the thermostat down as cold as it would go, refrigerating anyone who didn't get out of the gym in time. This particular prank had three benefits:

1 – It required no planning.
2 – It could be done in any gym (or anywhere with an accessible thermostat).
3 – It is, as Scott Hall described it, a 'time-delay rib', so Owen could be far away from the temperature controls, wait patiently and watch people slowly melt or freeze over the course of a given workout session.

When he wasn't governing internal weather cycles, Owen would find other ways to annoy health club patrons around the world. WWE Hall of Famer and another 'World's Strongest Man' Mark Henry vividly recalled one of the more ingenious ploys he witnessed in order to save a dollar. Owen, widely regarded as one of the thriftiest (i.e. cheapest) people in the history of wrestling, would pantomime dying of thirst. "We'd go to the gym, he's falling on the floor collapsing, saying he needs water," just so he could score a free Evian from concerned staff instead of buying one from the vending machine or drinking out of a communal fountain. "Every week it was something," recalled Henry.

[1]For those interested, 'Gator' Scott Hall's entire character revolved around introduction vignettes of him nudging alligators with a long stick to the strains of *When the Going Gets Tough, the Tough Get Going* by Billy Ocean. The gimmick was so well received that Hall was booked to lose nearly every match he wrestled and was gone from the promotion in less than five months. The WWF, it should be noted, blatantly stole the unsuccessful character two years later, saddling the re-introduced Steve Keirn as the tobacco-chewin' alligator-huntin' Skinner, in a move destined to generate zero interest from the dwindling WWF audience.

[2]While The Diamond Studd character was unexceptional, the gimmick was the blueprint for what became Hall's most memorable role as 'The Bad Guy' Razor Ramon; a pastiche of Al Pacino's cocaine kingpin Tony Montana from the film *Scarface*. Ramon debuted in the kiddy-friendly WWF in 1992 as an implied drug dealer who draped himself in gold chains, cruised around Miami in outrageous low riders and, in one introductory vignette, preposterously claimed to own a golf course.

Pranking Martha

As told by Martha Hart

Owen's production of pranks weren't limited to the road. On the rare days he was home, Owen would put Martha through the ringer, trying out material that wasn't feasible on the wrestlers he was touring with. While Owen was all too happy to escape the craziness of Hart House when he moved in with Martha, he was still fond of animals and had a couple of cats marauding around the house. As a boy, Owen was fond of wrestling Heathcliff the Cat through the conduit of a stuffed monkey. To set up another wrestling match between the feisty felines, Owen attached a slice of bacon around one of the cat's collars to see what would happen. Owen sat back in amusement as the non-bacon garnished cat chased the bacon'd cat all around the house, swiping away at the tasty treat.

If it wasn't the pitting of felines against each in a hostile showdown over salt-cured pork, Owen would be convincing strangers that Martha was a crazed stalker chasing after him. In one instance, the young couple were jogging by a river when Owen got out in front. He spotted a group of runners coming the opposite way and launched into a ridiculous routine to embarrass his wife. "Would you quit chasing me? I told you I don't want to go out with you!" he wailed. "All I could do was hang my head until they passed," declared Martha.

One evening early in their relationship, Owen was hanging around at Martha's house making a nuisance of himself. Martha, who had a big exam the next morning, ushered him out the house so she could get some sleep. When Martha opened the door to her bedroom, she saw a mysterious figure under the covers with a mop of hair peaking over the top. After a considerable amount of time standing in the doorway considering her next move, she plucked up the nerve to walk towards her bed and prod the lump under the sheets. When the jabbing failed to elicit any movement from the unwanted tenant, Martha yanked off the covers to discover her giant stuffed teddy underneath with a wig on it. At least this time it was just the oversized toy Martha's brother had won at the Stampede festival and not a stray dog dressed as Danny Zuko such as poor Brian Pillman experienced in his hotel bed in Kelowna.

Even Martha, who was somewhat of a prude, was forced to laugh at some of Owen's exploits, despite the fact she sometimes found his perpetual practical jokes irritating. "One day I told him very seriously that his jokes had to stop; they were driving me crazy. Wearing a somewhat mischievous grin, he said he'd really, really try. Alas, the hi-jinks continued."

Foot Fetish

As told by numerous sources

The most notorious wrestler in the history of the business for possessing an unhealthy fascination with footwear is, of course, Tony Atlas, but it's a little-known fact that Owen also had an obsession with wrestlers' boots and shoes. The only difference between Owen and Tony was that Owen's fascination with footwear revolved around playing pranks, whereas Tony's fascination involved an altogether different form of self-gratification.

While wrestling a rookie D'Lo Brown early in his singles career, Owen could feel the tension in D'Lo's body and decided to quell his anxiety by playing around with him on the canvas. "We're wrestling around and I'm like a board... and Owen's like, 'Relax, relax, relax!' So he's doing something, calling the match and he's like, 'Look over at... [referee] Timmy White.' I look over and Timmy's shoes are unlaced. Then he goes, 'Look down' and I look down and my boot's unlaced. 'How'd you do that?'" D'Lo instructed the referee to tuck his boot in as best he could. D'Lo's boot was falling off while he and Owen continued to mat wrestle. After another short round of ground-based grappling, the unflappable Owen regained the upper hand and motioned to D'Lo to look at the referee's shoes again. Owen said, "'Look over at Timmy and now his other shoe's unlaced. I look down and my other boot's unlaced. I'm like, 'How the hell is he doing this?' All you hear back is Owen going, 'Hehehehe!' He's just giggling!"

The relatively inexperienced D'Lo couldn't believe that Owen could muck around without any of the 15,000 fans noticing the footwear tampering, yet still put on a good match. "What am I worried about?" the now serene D'Lo said to himself while still on the mat. "Then [Owen] goes, 'Alright, now we can wrestle.' I'm like, 'Oh! He did all that just so we can wrestle?'" Owen let D'Lo back up and they went on to have a far-better match than they otherwise would have done had D'Lo's body remained in a state of rigor.

Referee Dave Hebner similarly remembered having his laces messed with during matches Owen was involved in. "I used to referee [and] have fun with him. He'd tie my shoe [laces] together when I went down for the count. He just loved to play and carry on."

When Owen wasn't undoing or tying shoelaces together, he was taking them out completely. "He would just take the laces out of one of your shoes," said Bruce Prichard. "Just one, he'd never take 'em both, just take one. Or cut the laces off right at the eyelets; you got laces but you can't tie 'em!"

Occasionally Owen would keep the laces intact but make sure that there was no way the rightful owner would be able enjoy their shoes with any degree of comfort. According to Prichard, Owen ribbed his brother Bret before a match one day by stealing his boots, putting them in the locker room shower cubicle and turning the water on. Shane Douglas similarly remembered one of Owen's shoe-based ribs that caused consternation for the wearer. "His deal was to put a padlock on your shoes when you were running late to catch a plane or something like that. Things like that, that were more a pain in the rear end than anything else."

In the early '90s while Owen was still making frequent overseas tours with New Japan Pro Wrestling, future ECW Tag Team Champion 'Pitbull #1' Gary Wolfe was one of the rookies receiving their first taste of Japanese pro wrestling, as well as locker room pranking culture. Wolfe, who was changing into his wrestling attire for that evening's contest, laced up his boots with no issues. It was only when he stood up and tried to walk to the ring that he realised something was up. "I go to walk and my boots were superglued to the floor so I couldn't move!" Poor Gary's music was playing over the venue's speakers and people were frantically yelling at him to get out to the ring. "I'm telling them, 'I can't! I can't! My boots are stuck!' So I end up taking my boots off and wrestling without my boots that night."

At least Gary could rip his boots off the locker room floor and have the soles replaced. Mark Henry didn't even get the luxury of being able to retrieve his footwear easily, as one day Owen managed to superglue The World's Strongest Man's wrestling boots to the locker room ceiling.

D'Lo Brown would go on to pay tribute to the King of Prank's positive influence on the locker room. "Owen was cool as hell. You could not be sad around Owen. If you were sad or mad, Owen would find a way to break you and make you laugh or giggle. You weren't allowed to be mad around him. It didn't matter what kind of day he was having, he wanted to make everyone else's day better."

Airport Pranks

As told by Reno Riggins, Sean Waltman and Tammy Sytch

The one element many wrestlers agree on that makes professional wrestling such a tough occupation is the insane travel schedule. For many years, the World Wrestling Federation's backbreaking tours would see wrestlers on the road for up to 300 days per year and the biggest stars would be away from home even more, owing to extracurricular activities such as promotional appearances. In the old territory system, most promotions ran shows at least six days a week. The travelling NWA World Champion would be on the road practically every day of the year. Ric Flair didn't even take a day off for the birth of his son Reid in 1989. Jim Crockett bought no less than two private jets in the mid 1980s, so the wrestlers could make all the far-flung shows when Mid-Atlantic was attempting to go national (as well as speed up the process of losing as much money as humanly possible).[1]

It's a given that due to the ridiculous amount of travel required, every successful wrestler is going to spend a lot of their time in airports and Owen was no different. It also meant that in the heady, pre-9/11 world of air travel, light-hearted jokes may have been inflicted once or twice by the King of Pranks. "We'd be like fuckin' miserable travelling, going through the airport," said Owen's frequent collaborator of high jinks, Sean Waltman. When the escalator was absolutely packed with road weary wrestlers clutching onto their bags, Owen would pounce. "Owen would hit that fuckin' emergency stop button while everybody was half way up the escalator: Ah! Classic!"

The World Wrestling Federation was booking more tours across the world in the 1990s on account of the depression of the wrestling business domestically. On the very last day of the WWF's 1994 summer tour of the Far East, the exhausted wrestlers touched down at Changi International Airport in Singapore. The weeklong tour had already started off on the wrong foot. The flight from the United States to Manila, Philippines a week earlier had been such an all-out free-for-all amongst the wrestlers, they were banned from flying with Cathy Pacific Airlines. As the WWF crew piled towards customs clearance, preliminary wrestler Reno Riggins couldn't find his passport. Riggins was freaking out, looking through his pockets and luggage when a sympathetic Owen offered to 'help' him look for it. Of course, the passport was found in the nick of time, due to the fact that Owen was the one who stole it in the first place.[2]

No one was immune to being ribbed at the airport, not even Owen. During the fateful, prank-laden tour of Germany in April 1996, Owen found himself getting pulled up by the check-in clerk for having too much luggage to take with him on-board. When on European tours, not only would the WWF spring for quality accommodation, the hotels would provide a slap-up breakfast for the WWF crew every morning. "It's *gratis*, that means you pay nothing," is what Owen would constantly say in a vaguely foreign accent as he piled more food onto his plate. One morning before a flight, Owen not only filled himself up with *gratis* breakfast, he filled up his travel bags too. "Owen took advantage of the free food and drink and filled his two duffel bags with pastries, bagels and a quart of orange juice in each bag," recalled Tammy 'Sunny' Sytch.

When all the wrestlers arrived at the airport's check-in desk later that day, Owen declared that his luggage was carry-on only. According to Sytch, Davey Boy Smith, who was stood behind Owen in the queue, knew Owen's bags were full of comestibles and decided to have a little fun. "I'm sorry ma'am but those bags are too big to carry on," said Davey as he peered over his brother-in-law's shoulder. Owen told the Bulldog to butt out but it was already too late. The check-in clerk's curiosity had been piqued and she took a closer look at Owen's duffel bags. "Oh, I'm sorry sir but they do look too big. I'll be happy to check them for you."

The 'King of Carry-On' was bristling as he handed over the duffel bags to be weighed on the check-in scale, as Owen never checked luggage if he could help it. Davey had got one over on his brother-in-law but no one knew how entertaining the rib would be until the jetlagged grapplers arrived at their next destination. All the WWF crew, including Tammy, were waiting at baggage claim when they saw Owen's luggage circle into view. "We all saw Owen's two little duffel bags leaking orange juice out of every seam and running down the belt!" laughed Sytch. "All of his clothes were stained with orange; his regular clothes and his gear."

[1]Jim Crockett Promotions managed to lose millions of dollars despite booming business for the majority of the territory's mid '80s heyday. The purchasing of jets, the pointless buying out of dying wrestling territories, signing wrestlers to huge contracts the company couldn't afford, storyline mismanagement, misguided attempts to go national and stiff competition from the WWF forced Jim Crockett Jr to sell his wrestling promotion to Ted Turner in on the 2nd of November 1988 for $9 million.

[2]At least Riggins got his passport returned to him. Randy Orton, who has a reputation for playing pranks, fingered the late Curt Hennig over the pilfering of Shawn 'Planet' Stasiak's personal property at an airport in 2002. "We were overseas somewhere and [Stasiak] had his camcorder, all of his electronics [and] all his gear [in his bag] and the bag came up missing. No one knew where it was. His passport was in there... and he ended up having to stay back in the country until he got a new passport. It was just a big ol' mess... *That* was funny!" Stasiak (real name Shawn Stipich) had scorching heat in the WWE locker room for not only being incredibly tightly-wound but for being so paranoid he left tape recorders running in his gear bag so he could listen to what fellow wrestlers were saying about him behind his back. WWF VP of Talent Relations Jim Ross fired Stasiak in front of the locker room after the discovery of a secret recording of Davey Boy Smith and Steve Blackman arguing during a road trip to Montreal in November 1999.

Rib in Japan

As told by Sean Waltman

For decades, the World Wrestling Federation had a history of loaning out talent to Japanese promotions. During the early 1990s, the WWF engaged in talent trade agreements with the short-lived Japanese SWS promotion,[1] as well as loaning talent to WAR and New Japan. By 1994, the WWF made the decision to promote shows on their own and booked several live events that May, all featuring Owen Hart. Owen was no stranger to Japan, having embarked on nine tours of the country from 1987 to 1992. As one of the WWF's top heel wrestlers, Owen would return to Japan one final time for a four-date tour of The Land of the Rising Sun.[2]

According to frequent travel and pranking partner Sean Waltman, the insomniac Owen would go to extreme lengths to get some sleep. "Owen and I, we would travel together and share a room and Owen would... put shades over his eyes and he would tape the curtains or put aluminium foil on the window to keep the sun out. He had that hard a time sleeping." Coupled with jetlag, Owen found snoozing even more difficult whilst touring the Far East and felt the need to keep himself busy. One of Owen's go-to ribs was to crank call WWF employees in their hotel rooms during the middle of the night and while the WWF was touring Japan, the phones never stopped ringing. "JJ [Dillon] was the Head of Talent Relations... JJ was over there with us [in Japan], kind of like a tour manager," recalled Waltman. "We made sure he didn't get one wink of sleep. Every fifteen minutes we called him. The next day, we were out swimming in the pool and [JJ] comes out all haggard looking."[3]

On the last night of the Japan tour, all the wrestlers and various other WWF employees, including Owen and Waltman, were relaxing in a bar after the final show in Sapporo. Bill Dunn, who briefly worked as a ring announcer at the time, had imbibed one too many pints of Kirin Ichiban and was becoming belligerent. "[Dunn] got drunk and cocked off to, I think, [road agent] Jack Lanza, or somebody you need to have respect for. That's all we needed." Owen and Waltman had their next target in their sights and went back to the hotel to exact some revenge on Lanza's behalf. Owen pulled the old trick of telling the front desk he'd lost his room key and gave Dunn's room number as his. Either that or Owen convinced a hotel employee to open Bill's room claiming that it was his, depending on who's telling the story.

Owen and Waltman gained access to the ring announcer's room, then went overboard metering out punishment. "We went in there, I was part of it and we took all his clothes... some people might think this is a dick move and yeah, in hindsight it was, but it was fuckin' funny to us at the time. We ran the tub [full of water] and dumped his clothes in the tub." They then ordered every single X-rated pay-per-view movie they could on Dunn's television, racking up an impressive debt. As the coup de grâce, Owen and Waltman removed all the light bulbs and hid them in a dresser drawer. The next morning, the tour buses were ready to head to the airport but the intoxicated announcer was nowhere to be found. "We're on our way to the airport and he's not down there for the fuckin' bus so it's like 'GOD DAMNIT, BILL, WHAT THE FUCK, HURRY UP!' He comes down; he's in like some buddies' borrowed t-shirt. I think he's got an ICOPRO[4] rag top sweatshirt that everyone used to have [and] some sweatpants and he's all dishevelled. He had to go home."

[1]The short-lived Super World of Sports (and its Godzilla mascot) debuted in 1990. The promotion was founded by eye glasses manufacturer Megane Super, who lured Genichiro Tenryu away from All Japan Pro Wrestling, then went on a spending spree. Big name wrestlers took the money and SWS signed a working agreement with the WWF in October 1990. SWS and the WWF co-promoted several cards and traded talent until SWS ceased touring in June 1992. The fledging Japanese promotion was drawing decent houses but Megane Super was hit hard by the Japanese recession and withdrew financial support.

[2]The WWF's four-stop tour of Japan was unsuccessful, drawing an average of only 3,325 paid.

[3]Sean Waltman would soon be glad he caused JJ Dillon such distress that night. On the 1st of September 1994, Waltman's wrestling mentor

and father figure Larry 'Boris Malenko' Simon passed away. Dillon had cold-heartedly refused to let Waltman go to Tampa to visit Malenko on his death bed. Dillon claimed the WWF really needed Waltman (who was usually working the opening match) to stay on the road. "I guess he felt he had to beat us down into submission," said Waltman years after the fact.

[4]ICOPRO (Integrated Conditioning Programme) was a line of bodybuilding supplements that tied in with McMahon's fledgling World Bodybuilding Federation. ICOPRO was promoted heavily on WWF programming but both the supplements and the WBF were total flops, costing the WWF millions of dollars. During a backstage meeting in 1992, all the wrestlers were given gift baskets full of ICOPRO before the supplement's creator, Dr Fred Hatfield, called Yokozuna fat during a company-wide meeting. Joe 'Curtis Axel' Hennig claimed ICOPRO gave him diarrhoea during a pee wee football game. Bret Hart said, "[It was] the worst stuff... I don't think it had any value to it at all!" Regarding the ICOPRO drops that users were directed to squirt under their tongue, Bruce Prichard recalled that they tasted like "bad black liquorice... I can't think of anything that tastes worse..."

CHAPTER 4

Baggy Trousers

♥ ♥

With Hulk Hogan, Ultimate Warrior and the rest of the 'roided-up superheroes of the 1980s and early 1990s fired, retired or wrestling for WCW (which was like a well-paid semi-retirement), 1993 and 1994 saw Vince McMahon roll the dice and elevate new and unproven talent in the hopes of creating a fresh batch of box office superstars. Bret Hart was the first wrestler McMahon gambled the future of his company on when he was booked to defeat Ric Flair for the World Wrestling Federation Championship in October 1992. Over the course of the next eight or so months, an influx of new faces were injected into the mix to replace the old guard, including: Yokozuna, Razor Ramon, Diesel, Jerry Lawler, The Steiner Brothers and Lex Luger, as well as returning stars such as: Bam Bam Bigelow, Mr Perfect, Mike Rotunda and Bob Backlund. The only proven main event box office attraction left in the World Wrestling Federation at this time was Macho Man Randy Savage. In the struggling McMahon's infinite wisdom, Savage was put on commentary duty and rarely allowed to compete, despite desperately wanting to continue his in-ring career and create new stars.[1]

Arguably the most unproven of the wrestlers elevated into a high-profile position within the company during this period was Owen Hart. Until 1994, Owen's only experience as a main event player was during his rookie years in his father's modest Stampede Wrestling territory. Owen was booked as a mid-level talent most everywhere else he wrestled except for the World Wrestling Federation where, as The Blue Blazer, he was portrayed as a high-flying tomato can with a chicken on his head. Bret had been pestering Vince McMahon to bring Owen back to the WWF on a regular basis since he left in 1989. "Bret was always a huge fan of Owen," said Bruce Prichard. "If Owen were to have a cheerleader in the business, his biggest cheerleader was his brother Bret." In early November 1991, Owen was still in Germany when he received a phone call from Bret. Bret told him the WWF was looking for new talent and very interested in him. Owen quickly flew to WWF headquarters in Stamford, Connecticut to negotiate a deal with McMahon. Owen then wrestled twice at the 12th of November *Wrestling Challenge* tapings before rejoining his five month pregnant wife back in Germany to finish his commitments with CWA.

Owen returned to the Federation full-time in December, performing under his birth name rather than The Blue Blazer or any other half-baked, whacky gimmick. Unfortunately, McMahon didn't have much in the way of interesting storylines for Owen, so they lobbed him in a tag team with his similarly directionless brother-in-law Jim 'The Anvil' Neidhart to form The New Foundation. The idea to pair Owen and Neidhart together was actually Bret's; Bret even came up with the team's name. After making a few television appearances defeating jobbers, The New Foundation had their coming out party two months later at January 1992's *Royal Rumble* pay-per-view. They defeated Mr Fuji's Orient Express in the opening match, which ended up being so good that it almost distracted the audience from their outfits.

The New Foundation's wrestling attire was truly hall of fame-worthy for how terrifically unsightly it was. The main accoutrements were billowing parachute pants so embarrassing that they caused MC Hammer to disavow himself from the parachuted trouser scene and shoot future music videos wearing only zebra-printed briefs, combat boots and mock-leather driving gloves.[2] Along with The New Foundation's grossly offensive trousers were their equally unfathomable jackets, that can be loosely described as sport coats augmented with unnecessary flaps. The entire outfit was a mishmash of eye-swallowingly intense, purples, greens, oranges and blues, topped off with large black-and-white checkerboard motifs anywhere they would fit, including the boots and matching headbands. They looked like a pair of flags.

Just as The New Foundation looked to be gaining traction in the Federation, The Anvil managed to get himself fired. A few weeks after their *Royal Rumble* triumph, Neidhart arrived at an arena to be confronted by agent Chief Jay Strongbow and several doctors (also known as the 'pecker checkers') to administer a drug test.[3] Neidhart knew he was going to flunk the test and pretended all day he couldn't force out a urine sample. He then refused point-blank to lose to his and Owen's opponents that night, The Beverly Brothers. McMahon became enraged, not only that he dodged the test and went against the proposed finish but also because Jim still owed him many thousands of dollars for bankrolling an earlier lawsuit against American Airlines.[4] At the 17th of February *WWF Superstars* taping, McMahon fired Neidhart. Immediately afterwards, the furious Anvil hunted out road agent Chief Jay Strongbow and launched a TV monitor at him. The monitor missed Chief but managed to hit a television director in the leg. Neidhart then stormed out of the arena, got in his hire car and sped away, never to return to the WWF again... for two years.

On the 5th of March 1992, Martha gave birth to their first child Oje, which had been Owen's childhood nickname. Despite pressure from the company to get back on the road, Owen made sure to be at Martha's bedside for the birth. Owen drove Martha and their new son home then raced to the airport to get back on the WWF's never-ending treadmill.

With Owen left alone and The New Foundation dead in the water, the timing was perfect to reinvigorate the youngest Hart with a better gimmick and possibly even a stylist. Instead, manager-cum-commentator Bobby Heenan suggested that Neidhart's spot be filled by professional 'jobber to the stars' Koko B Ware. Along with Koko's parrot mascot Frankie, the tag team would be rechristened High Energy. The stylist never emerged but the seamstress certainly did, as another outfit was made for Koko as well as a couple of sets of braces (featuring the ubiquitous checkerboard pattern, naturally) to hold up their enormous trousers. If their outfits were loud, their promotional interviews were even louder. Owen and Koko would blare out the most babyface-est babyface promos as boisterously as they could, while smiling and thumbs-upping all the way. With his powerful singing voice, Koko came across as legitimately exuberant, almost like an evangelical preacher. Next to Koko, Owen looked like the whitest white man there ever was, unconvincingly conveying to the camera that his energy was in fact high and his enthusiasm was genuine. The theme song changed too. Instead of The New Foundation's generic, industrial-sounding beat of metal clonking on metal, Owen and Koko burst through the entrance curtain to a song eerily similar to Cyndi Lauper's version of *Girls Just Wanna Have Fun*. No matter how immense the amount of energy they generated or how much they flapped their arms at Frankie the beleaguered parrot, Owen and Koko found themselves at the lower end of the card, more often than not losing to bigger-named tag teams. In the beginning of 1993, the phasing out of High Energy began as Owen and Koko wrestled more singles matches.

On the 8th of March 1993 *WWF Superstars* taping, Owen was booked for a big match as a single. Owen finally changed his outfit back to the baby blue-style singlet he wore in Japan, which was a definite improvement on the previous ensemble. Owen was booked to wrestle in the feature matchup against tattoo-headed monster Scott 'Bam Bam' Bigelow. Late into the contest, Owen slipped while jumping to the top rope and landed awkwardly on his left leg. It didn't look like a particularly bad landing but Owen managed to tear the anterior cruciate ligament in his left knee so severely he would spend two months on the sidelines. Owen had suffered a history of knee injuries in the WWF, including tweaking it in the first week of his Blue Blazer run and in the summer of 1992 as part of High Energy. Several years later, Bret expressed his admiration for Owen's ability to continue wrestling after the injury in '93. "It's a tribute to his courage that he can work at all. I'm not talking about a strained ligament or a torn cartilage, I'm talking about severed ligament. I don't know how he does it anymore."

Koko would soon be shipped off to Jerry Lawler's minor-league USWA promotion on a talent trade and High Energy was finished up once and for all.[5] "Owen Hart and I joked around a lot, we road together, we stayed at hotels together," Koko B Ware reminisced. "We had a great time together... What a great guy he was. God knows I miss him." At the behest of Martha, Owen applied for more regular jobs while he was back home recovering, to no avail.

While Owen was on the injured list, Bret 'Hitman' Hart's career went from strength to strength since losing to WWF Championship to Yokozuna in March. After Winning the *King of the Ring* tournament in June, Bret was blindsided by Jerry 'The King' Lawler to set up their *SummerSlam* match in August. Bret wound up getting legitimately hurt when a careless Lawler stiffed him in the back of the head with a prop sceptre. To heat up the rivalry further, Lawler would verbally (and physically) attack the entire Hart family to get to Bret. Shortly after *King of the Ring*, the semi-healed[6] Owen headed to Lawler's struggling Memphis-based USWA promotion to seek revenge. No matter what dastardly deeds Lawler performed on WWF television, The King was still beloved in his home territory and Owen was booed out of the building. Owen, who first began to refer to himself as the King of Harts in USWA, also made several appearances as a singles wrestler, winning the promotion's top championship from Papa Shango before dropping it three weeks later to Lawler.[7]

Back in the WWF, a warm-up match for the *SummerSlam* showdown between Bret and Lawler took place when The King faced off against Owen on the 25th of July 1993 episode of *Wrestling Challenge*. Owen dominated the match until he 'slipped on a banana peel' and missed a shoulder tackle into the corner, allowing Lawler to hit his patented piledriver finished manoeuvre before getting on the microphone boasting how easy it was to beat him. The next day during the 26th of July 1993 episode of *WWF RAW*, Bret Hart and Bam Bam Bigelow were in the middle of a match when Jerry Lawler went into the balcony area of the Manhattan Centre to confront Bret's parents, who were in attendance. Lawler got on the house microphone and bombarded the elderly Harts with some classic putdowns, encouraging Stu to put his false teeth in backwards and eat himself to death and claim that when Bret was born, "Stu tried to collect on his accident insurance." Bret eventually left the ring and chased Lawler away.

On the 2nd of August, Bret headed down to USWA to wrestle Lawler to a double disqualification in front of 3,200 fans at the Mid-South Coliseum. Two weeks later, Bret and Owen were roundly booed as they teamed up to defeat Lawler and Jeff Jarrett in the main event. The pair had great fun performing as bad guys and because Memphis was known for its bonkers concepts and phony-looking wrestling, the Harts got in on the action. They quoted *Deliverance* on the house mic, wiggled their posteriors at the crowd of 'hillbillies' and wound up their punches à la Dusty Rhodes. Reminiscing about teaming with Owen in USWA, Bret said, "Those two Memphis shows would end up being some of the most fun that Owen and I ever had in the ring together."

The *SummerSlam 1993* pay-per-view occurred the next day and Owen and Bruce Hart were placed at ringside to cheer on Bret. Lawler came out on crutches claiming he'd had a car wreck and hurt his knee and that his 'court-appointed jester' Matt 'Doink the Clown' Borne would replace him. Doink came out with two buckets, threatening the crowd with their contents. Doink threw the contents of the first bucket over some audience members, which turned out to only be confetti. When Doink launched the contents of the second bucket at Bruce, the bucket turned out to be full of ice cold water, which totally caught Bruce off-guard and left him fuming. According to Bret, "Owen had caught wind of the rib before the match and had warned Matt that if he got a drop on him he'd rib him back for the rest of his days." While Matt Borne enjoyed perpetrating a good rib, he knew not to get on the wrong side of The King of Pranks and made extra sure he stayed dry.

After Bret defeated Doink, a miraculously healed Lawler attacked Bret with his crutch, once again legitimately hurting him. Despite the sneak-attack, Bret vs. Lawler was ordered to take place as scheduled. The Hitman defeated The King with his *sasori-gatame* leg lock, which he repatriated as the Sharpshooter. The decision was then reversed after Bret refused to release Lawler from the hold for four minutes. Bret purposely cinched up on Lawler as a receipt for the sceptre and crutch shots and when referees and officials came to pry Bret off Lawler, some actually leaned their weight onto Bret to put even more excruciating pressure on the back of the self-proclaimed 'King of Wrestling.' After the match, Bret waited at Gorilla position to see how badly he'd hurt The King. Lawler was so incapacitated from the Sharpshooter that he had to crawl along the floor like an alligator all the way to the dressing room. Bret said, "Singer Aaron Neville, who was there to perform the national anthem before Lex's match, laughed, shook his head and said to me, 'You did a job on him, man!'"

Shortly after *SummerSlam*, Bret had a meeting with Vince McMahon regarding his contract and future with the company.[8] Not only did Bret let McMahon know how unhappy he was with his character's direction since losing the WWF Title at *WrestleMania IX* but he also informed the boss that Owen was similarly dissatisfied and that McMahon was at risk of losing them both if he didn't do something about it. "They used [Owen] in a steady succession of horseshit roles," fumed Bruce Hart. "High Energy with Koko B Ware, with Neidhart [and] with those checkerboard, ugly, lime green pants and all this other [stuff]; none of which did him justice. If they'd just let him be like [future WWE star] Daniel Bryan or something like that, he would have been phenomenal for them."

Little did McMahon know just how close they were to losing the future King of Harts. Owen was still sending out applications for more conventional jobs as late as the 24th of September when he applied for a job as a United States Customers officer. Once again, the application process proved to be a waste of time and Owen didn't hear anything back. On the 19th of October, McMahon, booker Pat Patterson and Bret sat in a Holiday Inn bar until the small hours discussing both his and Owen's future.

The next day at the *WWF Superstars* taping, McMahon, who previously told Bruce Prichard, "God-damnit pal, brothers don't fight," pitched a brother vs. brother angle leading to a big blow off match at *WrestleMania X* in Madison Square Garden. According to Bret, the only problem with the storyline was that the brother McMahon wanted was older brother Bruce. It was pitched that the jealous Bruce would challenge Bret to a match, which Bret would refuse. Owen would then accept the challenge only to be murdered by Bruce so badly Bret would have to come to his aid. Bret would then accept Bruce's challenge and defeat him, before moving on to battle Lex Luger for the WWF Championship at *King of the Ring 1994*. The plan made no sense. Not only was Owen in his physical prime and arguably the best wrestler in the Hart family, the WWF audience was already familiar with him. The story of the young brother feeling held down by his more successful older sibling was a narrative more people could relate to. Although Bruce needed the money, he was in his 40s, smaller, had a bad knee and simply wasn't as good as Owen. Bret insisted Owen be his opponent and the wheels were put into motion.

At *Survivor Series 1993*, Bret, Owen, Bruce and Keith Hart faced off against Shawn Michaels and his Knights in a traditional four-on-four elimination tag match.[9] Owen was showcased throughout the contest, beating two of the Knights before being pinned by Michaels after Owen accidentally collided with Bret on the apron. After being eliminated, Owen angrily stormed off to the dressing room before returning to the ring at the conclusion of the match. Owen shoved Bret and blamed him for being the only Hart brother eliminated. On the following episode of *RAW*, Owen walked out in full heel mode. Now in his classic black singlet, he was full of arrogance and personality. He stole Bret's patented wraparound sunglasses and Sharpshooter finishing manoeuvre, all the while proclaiming himself to be the number one wrestler in the Hart family. On the 11th of December 1993 edition of *Superstars*, Owen cut the most important promo of his life during a sit-down interview where he officially challenged his brother Bret to a match,

"I've been living in the shadow of you, Bret, all my life and I'm sick and tired of it. So Bret, there's only one way to solve this thing with me being [in] the shadow of you, the Hitman. That's right, why don't you go out and step up to the plate. You and me, face-to-face, one-on-one. I'm challenging you, Bret, my brother, to a fight, one-on-one, just to prove to everybody, my family, all my friends, the wrestling fans out there [and] to you, Vince [McMahon], that I can beat you, Bret. If you've got the guts, step up to the plate."

Bret responded one week later. "I know there's all kinds of people who'd love to see that. People love to see any type of controversial fight. A great fight is a great fight, people thrive on that and I've never ducked any kind of challenge, I've never backed away from anybody. I would wrestle anybody and I would like to live up to those words when I say I'm the best there is, the best there was and the best there ever will be and I take on anybody. But under no circumstances would I ever... absolutely, positively not ever step in the ring with my own brother under any circumstances. I won't do it. There's a point and this is as far as it will go. I will not fight my brother."

Both promos were far from the typical 'your ass is grass and I'm a lawnmower', hollow, shouty-style of interview. Owen's interview was calm and quiet with a bubbling undercurrent of a man with something to prove, whereas Bret came across as the worn out older brother with the weight of the world on his shoulders. Both interviews would be replayed to death on WWF television for weeks on end leading up to January's *Royal Rumble* pay-per-view.

[1]Savage presented an intricate two-year storyline feud to WWF decision-makers where he would face off against rising star Shawn Michaels. Michaels was a mid-card tag team wrestler with Marty Jannetty before turning heel and embarking on a singles career as the conceited Heartbreak Kid in 1992. According to his brother Lanny Poffo, Savage always wanted to eclipse his 1987 classic *WrestleMania III* match against Ricky 'The Dragon' Steamboat before retiring and believed the ultra-talented Michaels was the man to do it with. Savage's storyline plans were rejected with the following explanation from Vince McMahon. "Randy, we're having a youth movement now and the best thing you can do is stay with the microphone." The 42-year-old Macho Man took the rejection personally and immediately jumped to WCW in late 1994, where he enjoyed several more great years in the ring. Along with on-screen rival Ric Flair, Savage is credited with boosting WCW live attendance in 1996, six months before the New World Order took WCW to the next level.

[2]This is in reference to MC Hammer's banned version of his 1994 single *Pumps and a Bump*. The video was banned by MTV for being too sexually explicit and a second, fully-clothed version replaced the original. Both are widely available to watch on YouTube as of the time of writing.

[3]The WWF had periodically instituted tests for recreational drugs since the late '80s. Due to the Federal Government taking an interest in the World Wrestling Federation over allegations of steroid distribution, the WWF started drug testing all contracted wrestlers (and managers) for performance-enhancing drugs too, with the first tests being

administered in New Haven, Connecticut on the 13th of November 1991.

[4]Jim was charged with punching an air stewardess while on a US Air flight but was acquitted of all charges. Thanks to Vince McMahon bankrolling him, Neidhart successfully counter-sued US Air for $380,000. Without repaying McMahon, Neidhart managed to blow the whole lot in under three years.

[5]Owen actually made one more appearance as part of High Energy, standing as best he could on the ring apron as Koko did most of the work in a losing effort to The Headshrinkers.

[6]Owen rushed back to the ring way too early because his family couldn't live on the token $200 per week the WWF was paying him to sit at home and rehab his injury. There has never been a union or comprehensive health insurance in wrestling and before guaranteed contracts, wrestlers mostly had to fend for themselves if they were injured in the line of duty. For the rest of his career, Owen would wrestle in a knee brace and eliminate a lot of his high-flying acrobatics in favour of a more conservative, ground-based style. "I would say injury has helped in bringing me down to reality," Owen explained in 1995, "but high risk manoeuvres can be effective but very dangerous. I have learned that I can do technical wrestling on the mat and when necessary high risk moves can be successful."

[7]As the Papa Shango character, Charles Wright had recently been loaned to USWA by the WWF and was already upset with Lawler. Wright felt that putting the USWA Unified World Heavyweight Title on him was done only to appeal to the prominent black audience and temporarily left wrestling to tend bar back in Las Vegas.

[8]During contract talks, Bret would negotiate the rights to the 'Hitman' name, as well as the ability to pursue an acting career. This was considered a big win against the WWF's draconian contracts at the time. Remembering how he felt during those difficult negotiations, Bret wrote in his memoirs, "The thought crossed my mind that a victory

over Vince probably meant he'd fuck me somewhere down the road."
He was right.

[9]The Jerry Lawler vs. Hart family feud continued to build on television, so why did Shawn Michaels mysteriously take Lawler's place at the last minute? Two days prior, Lawler was arraigned over a statutory rape charge stemming from accusations made by a 13-year-old girl from Louisville in June 1993, as well as charges of sodomy and harassing a witness. Michaels took The King's place but Lawler's three masked Knights remained on the team... sort of. Terry Funk was scheduled to wrestle as one of the masked Knights but no-showed the event. The former NWA Champion didn't fancy the idea of losing clean just to be unmasked on pay-per-view, so he called up Vince and told him that he couldn't make the show because 'his horse was sick'. The statutory rape and sodomy charges were dropped on the 23rd of February 1994 in exchange for Lawler pleading guilty to harassing a witness. The King returned to World Wrestling Federation programming some five months after he was suspended to co-commentate *WrestleMania X* with McMahon.

George 'The Animal' Steele

As told by Harvey Wippleman and Bruce Prichard

George 'The Animal' Steele was one of the longest-tenured wrestlers in WWE history, wrestling for the WWWF over the summers before heading back to Michigan to be a teacher and coach of the football team.[1] When the wrestling boom hit in the mid 1980s, Steele would develop into one of the company's most enduring characters by acting and wrestling like an uncontrollable animal to the delight of the fans. By the late '80s, Steele was almost fifty years old, struggling to keep up and showing signs of ill health. Unbeknownst to him, he was suffering from Crohn's disease and was, according to Steele, 'slowly bleeding to death' internally. The condition would ultimately force him to retire from full-time wrestling. In 1988, Steele transitioned from performing in the ring to working behind the scenes as a road agent (now referred to as a producer). Road agents were responsible for making sure that: events ran smoothly; handing out finishes to matches; helping structure matches; giving out 'draws' (cash advances on a wrestler's pay); fining guys who were late and tattling on the boys to WWF head office.

According to Bruno 'Dr Harvey Wippleman' Lauer, Steele was one of the absolutely worst agents the WWF ever had. "He made a career out of shaving his head, painting his tongue green and chewing up turnbuckles, [while telling] guys like Shawn Michaels and Owen Hart what was wrong with their matches. To add insult to injury, he did it in the cockiest, most condescending way, imaginable." Opinions vary as to the effectiveness of most road agents but the consensus among the Federation employees at the time is that Wippleman's assessment of George's road agenting skills is fairly accurate.

On the 11th of April 1992, the Federation was in the middle of their annual post-*WrestleMania* tour of Europe. The WWF buses stopped off in Brussels and performers and staff were disembarking the bus single-file. The relative new-comer Wippleman[2] was part of the procession, with George Steele in front of him and Owen Hart behind. When all three were at the front of the coach and George was about to walk down the steps, Owen

108

reached past Harvey and shoved The Animal hard, causing him to fall down the steps and onto the floor. Owen reportedly turned round to Harvey and cried, "Poor George!" laying all the blame on the rookie manager. While no doubt a lot of the witnesses on the bus were happy to see Steele receive a little comeuppance, the incident created genuine animosity between Harvey and George, who had believed Owen's side of the story. According to Wippleman, the two would eventually become friendly with each other, before adding that, "He was [still] a lousy agent."

It was well known to many in the World Wrestling Federation that Steele had been fitted with a colostomy bag due to his Chron's disease. It was also well known among the boys that it could sometimes cause issues when going through airport security. Unfortunately for Steele, one of the wrestlers who caught wind (perhaps literally) of George's security hazard was Owen. According to Bruce Prichard, the crew arrived at an arena for a TV taping from an international destination. Owen made sure to arrive at the building early and, with a look of deadly seriousness, walked up to WWF Chairman Vince McMahon. Owen informed the boss that George Steele had been, "Stopped at the border and thrown in jail." "Oh my god, what the hell, what for?" the stunned McMahon inquired. "For smuggling shit across the border."

George was also known for carrying around an air freshener spray that was strong enough to disguise even the most putrid pongs emanating from his colostomy bag. According to Prichard, Owen told everybody in the locker room to be, "Sniffing around and move away from [George] like he stinks. He's going to look for his air freshener thing, he's not going to have it and he's going to become self-conscious because he smells and he can't spray the stuff." When enough wrestlers held their noses around him, George got self-conscious enough to give himself an extra spritz of the trusty masking agent. When he searched his bag for it, it had of course disappeared; Owen had stolen it.

Despite the constant ribbing, George dedicated several pages of his 2013 memoir *Animal* to his favourite Owen pranks, while mentioning Bret just once in between the names Blackjack Mulligan and The Islanders as people he shared a plane with. Even though he was a constant pain in the ricker, it was obvious that Owen was The Animal's preferred Hart brother.

109

[1]Jim 'George Steele' Myers would keep his regular teaching job and his summer wrestling job completely separate. Over the years, inquisitive students would bring to school a wrestling magazine carrying a photo of Steele and suggest that Mr Myers and The Animal were one and the same. George would simply reply, "Do you really think I'm that ugly?" When the World Wrestling Federation started expanding from a regional territory into a national powerhouse, Steele would find it harder and harder to conceal his wrestling alter ego. One day, at the beginning of American football practice, he lined up all of his students to give instructions. What greeted him in return was a sea of green tongues stuck out of every student's face, in tribute to the Animal's trademark gimmick. Mr Myers was officially found out and he gave up teaching soon after to wrestle full-time for the WWF, enjoying the most successful run of his career while in his late forties.

[2]Dr Harvey Wippleman made his WWF debut some nine months previously managing 'Big Bully' Buisick and Sid 'Justice' Eudy. Sid brought Wippleman to be his WWF mouthpiece after the pair struck up a friendship in the Knoxville territory back in 1987 when Wippleman was known as 'Downtown' Bruno and Sid as the masked 'Lord Humongous'. The wrestling world sure loved to 'borrow' ideas from the *Mad Max* films.

Mr Hughes Stealing Towels

As told by Diana Hart, Jim Cornette and Curtis Hughes

Mr Curtis Hughes has always been one of the more curious figures in 1990s professional wrestling. A carbon copy of Ray Traylor's 'Big Bubba Rogers' enforcer gimmick, right down to the sunglasses, trilby, shirt and tie. Hughes gained some mild notoriety as a heel during his short tenure in WCW. Hughes acted as Larry 'Lex Luger' Pfohl's bodyguard before embarking on a career of just sort of turning up in a promotion, wrestling badly while frowning or standing outside and frowning, then disappearing again without explanation. Billed at 6'5" and 330lbs, the size-conscious WWF hired him no less than three times between 1993 and 1999, before cutting their losses relatively quickly each time. His 1997 run seconding Hunter Hurst Helmsley lasted just six days.[1]

Back to 1993[2] and Curtis Hughes was working up a sweat by stinking up World Wrestling Federation rings across the country. Like practically every other wrestler, Hughes brought a towel from the hotel to use after a post-match shower (hopefully the sunglasses stayed on like they did when he wrestled). Mr Hughes was, unfortunately for him, also staying at the same hotel as Owen Hart. When Owen was hanging out in Hughes' hotel room, he saw him unpacking his bag. Owen happened to notice that Curtis' suitcase was full of hotel towels, coffee mugs, ashtrays and soap; all stolen from the establishment. When Owen returned to his own room, Mr Hughes received a phone call with a very angry voice on the other end. "This is the hotel manager. It has come to our attention you are stealing things from our hotel." When Hughes protested his innocence that he was going to bring the towel back, the manager not only wanted him out of the hotel but also threatened to phone the police *and* his boss. "We're calling Mr McMahon and we want him to know he has a thief in the company and you're a disgrace!"

After a tense back and forth, a deeply apologetic Mr Hughes managed to convince the hotel manager to let him stay, agreeing to talk about the situation further after a good night's sleep. When the next morning came and the wrestlers were heading out to the next destination, Owen, who watched from the lobby, laughed as he witnessed a contrite Mr Hughes walk into the manager's office with two cups of coffee, apologising profusely for taking the towels. In a later interview, Diana Hart imagined the hotel manager saying, "Gosh! That Mr. Hughes! What a nice guy, he brought me coffee this morning and was apologising for taking the towels,' and Mr Hughes never knew!" The funny thing is Mr Hughes legitimately *never* knew, as when he was confronted with the story in a shoot interview many years after the fact, he had no memory of the incident, theorising he must have been drunk that evening.

It seems that stories about Mr Hughes and hotel freebies are a recurring theme when people talk about the big man. Jim Cornette was full of praise when it came to Curtis' unique money saving habits. "They found him in a number of instances asleep in the hotel lobby on one of the couches. As a matter of fact, when he was the bodyguard of Lex Luger, he used to be able to 'heel' in to hotels instead of staying at the fucking Super 8 or wherever the underneath guys were staying. Luger and those guys got nice hotel rooms at top hotels. Mr Hughes would come in and tell the staff at the desk that he was Lex Luger's bodyguard and he was going to be there in the lobby just to make sure. He would sleep in the lobby for free in this beautiful four star hotel 'cause they thought he was supposed to be there instead of having to go rent his own room. He was a smart individual."

Although his unique approach to overnight stays was appreciated by those who liked to save their money, no one within ear shot of Luger's former bodyguard appreciated his loud snoring. Hughes recounted during his first WWF run that his snoring was so deafening on a flight that, as a rib, his sunglasses were super-glued to his face, shaving cream was sprayed in his hands and the t-shirt he was wearing was cut up to shreds. After interrogating several people on the plane, a little kid dimed out Mr Fuji, who in turn sold out the Steiner Brothers as co-conspirators. Mr Hughes said it was all in good fun, after revealing he got them back later that day by urinating in their bags and zipping them back up.

[1]Hughes also worked for ECW sporadically from 1993-1996, wrestling and body-guarding (and frowning) for Shane Douglas. Promotion

owner, Tod Gordon, who booked Hughes for some early ECW appearances, said, "Curtis Hughes; a great guy; just didn't get it." When asked to lose to Peter 'Taz' Senercia on an untelevised house show in front of 200 people, Curtis believed he was too big a star to lay down for the diminutive 'Human Suplex Machine,' citing that he, "Once beat Lex Luger!" It was explained to him that he hadn't really, in fact, beaten anybody, but when it came time for Taz to get the win, Hughes lifted one of his shoulders on the count of three. Hughes was not invited back to ECW for a long time.

[2]Diana Hart tried to claim in her woefully inaccurate (and libellous) book that the hotel towel rib occurred in 1986. Not only did Mr Hughes not debut for the WWF until 1993 (where Mr McMahon was his boss), he didn't even start wrestling until 1987, debuting in Bob Geigel's Kansas City territory before moving onto the AWA.

Chief Jay Strongbow

As told by Harvey Wippleman and John 'Bradshaw' Layfield

By the early 1990s, Luke Scarpa had been employed as a WWF agent for nearly a decade after retiring from a near forty year in-ring career. His most notable success during his wrestling days came when he portrayed Native American character Chief Jay Strongbow in the WWF for fifteen years. Chief would come to the ring in a headdress, throw tomahawk chops and make a comeback on his opponent by circling the ring with an Indian war dance (all the while not letting the fact he was of Italian descent bother him). Opinions differ wildly among wrestlers on whether he was a good agent or even if he was a good wrestler but no one was mistaking the gimmicky Chief for a legitimate master of the art of shoot fighting.

Back in the early '90s, Owen Hart and Koko B Ware (High Energy) were facing off against Ted DiBiase and Irwin R Shyster (Money Inc.) in a tag team match. During the bout, the babyface Owen got the upper hand on IRS. Owen started clapping his hands and stomping his foot on the ring canvas in an effort to encourage the crowd to cheer him on. According to former manager Harvey Wippleman, Chief called over the youngest Hart in the backstage area to have a word with him over his match conduct. "'Rocket!' said Chief. Rocket was Chief's nickname for Owen. 'If you were in a street fight, would you clap your hands and look at the people who were watching?' 'No, Chief,' replied Owen, in his usual humorous manner, 'I'd probably break out into an Indian war dance!'"

Several years later, the story of Owen's put down of Chief still made the rounds in the WWF locker room. John 'Bradshaw' Layfield, who joined the WWF full time at the beginning of 1996, remembered hearing the story, as well as Strongbow's reaction. "It took Chief some time to get over his anger, hilarious!"

Prank Phone Calls: Hacksaw Jim Duggan 2

As told by Jimmy Korderas, Bruce Prichard and Mick Foley

Duggan's first incident with hotel receptionists wouldn't be his last during his time with the World Wrestling Federation. Another classic Owen telephone prank was calling wrestlers up late at night, long after they'd settled in, pretending to be the hotel receptionist, claiming there was an issue with payment. According to Bruce Prichard, "[Owen] had Jim Duggan down at the front desk one time telling him that his credit card didn't go through and he had to come back down. Duggan would come down and [the receptionist] would say, 'Oh no, Sir, there's no problem with your credit card.'" Throughout the whole confusing encounter, Owen would be milling around the hotel lobby listening in to the conversation.

After he had been assured that there were no issues with payment, Duggan went back to his room to once again settle in for the evening and rest up for the next stop on the tour. After a short while, Owen got on the hotel's house phone and placed another call to the Hacksaw. "Sir, this is the front desk. Erm, either you need to come down here and fix this credit card thing or you're going to have to leave. [In fact] you just need to get out now, Sir." Owen, in his best soft-spoken English accent, was convincing enough that Duggan got dressed once again and flew down the stairs to the front desk to confront the oblivious clerk. "HEY, LISTEN TOUGH GUY! I CAME DOWN HERE JUST BEFORE AND YOU TOLD ME EVERYTHING [WAS FINE], I DON'T KNOW WHAT'S GOING ON!" Owen would always make sure to be far enough away from the scene of the crime that he wouldn't be suspected, finding a quiet spot in the lobby where he would be, "Sitting in the corner, laughing his ass off."

It's unknown if Owen ever confessed the crank call to Duggan but what is known is that ol' Hacksaw wasn't the only one to fall for the ruse. Mick Foley, who was the only wrestler on the WWF roster who was a match for Owen in regards to thriftiness, was settling into his room at the Toledo,

Ohio Red Roof Inn back in 1997. Mick was falling asleep when he received a call from the hotel manager. A soft-spoken Englishman introduced himself and enquired as to how he was doing that evening. "I could literally picture this guy with grey hair and glasses and a thick wool sweater," said Foley. The pleasant sounding Englishman informed the 'Hardcore Legend' that he had been charged too little for his room and the hotel was going to charge him extra to make up the difference, despite the fact that Mick had checked in hours earlier.

After debating the ethics and legalities of such a price hike, the manager asked if Foley was one of the wrestlers staying at the hotel. When Foley confirmed that he was, the manager insulted his profession by calling wrestling the dreaded f-word; 'fake'. When Mick admonished the manager for insulting his livelihood, he apologised, before reminding Mick why he'd called in the first place. "I'm afraid I'm still going to have to raise your rate," the manager declared. "WHAT?" Mick yelled. "Suddenly I heard laughter on the other end of the line. I knew I'd been had by the best. 'Owen,' I yelled, 'You prick!'"

Former WWE referee Jimmy Korderas was also a victim of a late night phone call from a mysterious voice asserting that there was a complication with payment. "The person on the other end said he was calling from the front desk claiming that there was a problem with my credit card." The man on the phone said that it needed to be handled in person and Korderas had to come to the front desk to sort it out. The groggy referee plodded down in shorts and a t-shirt and explained the situation to the check-in clerk. The befuddled clerk assured him no such call had been placed to him from the front desk and that his credit card payment seemed to be in order. It was only when Owen walked up to the desk and said that he'd also received a call did Korderas put two and two together. While Owen and Korderas were having a good laugh in the lobby, a steady procession of WWF employees lumbered down to the lobby to deal with similar fictitious payment issues. "I looked at Owen as he smiled like the Cheshire Cat in *Alice in Wonderland*. Apparently, he was a busy man."

"Poor Howard"

As told by Howard Finkel and Paul Bearer

Life-long Wrestling fanatic and company man Howard Finkel remains WWE's longest tenured labourer, having started ring announcing for the World Wide Wrestling Federation in the mid 1970s before becoming WWE's parent company Titan Sports, Inc.'s first employee on the 1st of April 1980. Over the years, 'The Fink' has assumed basically every single role in the company from: ring announcing, commentating, arranging arenas and travel schedules, talent scouting, booking talent voiceovers, working on the website, writing pop quizzes, keeping up with insider newsletters and even wrestling on occasion.[1] If the Honky Tonk Man is to be believed, Howard was also a keen hobbyist involving more dubious subject matter. "He has, from what I hear, one of the largest collections of triple X sex tapes of anybody in the world," claimed Honky.

However, there is only one post Howard occupied for the entirety of his forty-plus year run with the promotion; the unofficial position of company whipping boy. Poor Howard was bullied 24/7 by practically everybody in the company at one time or another. One of the more creative ribs The Fink endured was broadcast on the 10th of May 1993 episode of *WWF RAW*. Mr Perfect and Shawn Michaels started brawling outside the Manhattan Centre, culminating in Perfect throwing Michaels into a car door, then through the same car's windshield. The car was Howard's, it was brand new and the first he knew of his prized vehicle being used as a prop in the angle was as it was happening. Another on-screen rib involved The Fink eating raw sardines with The Bushwhackers for a backstage skit. "I stood there and watched them do cut after cut after cut of Howard Finkel eating sardines 'til he was sick," recalled the late manager William 'Paul Bearer' Moody. "I've seen him crying where they were treating him so bad he'd just sit and cry and if they'd done me the same way I'd probably [have] cried too, because they treated him like shit."

Howard was seemingly born to be pranked, so it was only a matter of time before the King of Pranks managed to catch out the WWF's greatest ever ring announcer. Owen and The Fink were driving from Seattle to Vancouver when they were stopped at the Canadian border. According to Howard, a border guard with a Napoleon complex recognised Owen from the television and decided to make an example out of him. "They thought they were going to hit the jackpot with us," recalled Howard. "They searched every nook and cranny of the rental car and found nothing. From there we moved on."

Even after being detained for a very long time, Owen and The Fink still arrived at the arena early that day. Every subsequent wrestler and WWF staff member who arrived at the arena then made a beeline for Howard. The enraged employees blamed him for being pulled over at the border crossing, which caused a chain reaction resulting in *all* the wrestlers' cars being pulled over and searched. "It was upsetting to have gotten stopped and now the guys are really stoking the fire, blaming me for what happened." Poor Howard was distraught over causing the boys so much aggravation, even though it wasn't his fault. It was only later that the Fink was let in on the secret that nobody else had been pulled over; Owen just told everybody to pretend they had been and to blame Howard for it. "One of these days, [Howard] is the kind of person that's finally gonna take an AK-47 and just wipe the whole place out!" Jim Cornette joked... hopefully.

---

[1]The Fink has been involved in several storylines over the years. In 1998, Jeff Jarrett and Southern Justice (the former Godwinns) shaved off Finkel's moustache and what was left of his shedding hair, which was rather humiliating. In 1999, Howard acted as a professional goober for the debuting Chris Jericho, culminating in Howard being lost to Faarooq and Bradshaw in a hand of poker, which was relatively humiliating. The classic on-screen humiliation long time WWF fans remember is when Howard took on fellow sissy Harvey Wippleman in a 'Tuxedo match' - The first person to be disrobed from their tuxedo is declared the loser. Jim Cornette said of the match, "I love Howard, he's a great guy; never wanted to see him in his underwear. I constantly did, never wanted to."

119

George Steele's Halliburton

As told by Bret Hart

Long time pro wrestler and (at the time) road agent George 'The Animal' Steele was a particular favourite target of The King of Pranks. Bret Hart once described Steele as 'one of the worst' road agents', a 'motherfucker' and 'not a good guy at all'. According to Bret, when The Animal was actively wrestling, he would do, "Lines of coke and party with everyone else," but when health problems forced him out of the ring and he was offered a backstage role with a considerable amount of power over the wrestlers, Bret described Steele's attitudinal transition as immediate. Steele apparently went from being one of the boys to becoming a 'stooge' for the office. "He was like one of the prisoners who turned into one of the guards," accused Bret.

An example of why the Hitman and The Animal didn't get along occurred during a turbulent time for the WWF in late 1992, just after Bret had won his first World Wrestling Federation Heavyweight Championship. He was giving his 'lousy little brother' Owen and John 'Berzerker' Nord a ride to Hersheypark Arena in Hershey, Pennsylvania. Bret was a popular travel buddy because he would pay for the rental of the car himself and wouldn't charge the other wrestlers trans (a nominal amount of money per mile). The trio were taking their time laughing, joking and stopping off to get coffee before arriving at the arena.

As soon as they walked into the backstage area they were confronted by a perturbed George Steele, who was angrily gesturing at his watch. He curtly informed the trio that they were two minutes late and that he would be using his authority as a backstage agent to fine all three guys $500 for the infraction. While Bret was making very good money as a headline attraction, Owen and Berzerker were living paycheque to paycheque on the lower end of the pay spectrum. $500 was no small chunk of change to lose, especially for being only two minutes late. While being WWF Champion carried a certain amount of stroke with the company, it didn't help Bret's argument because, in George's opinion, it was Bret's duty to set an example to the rest of the guys by turning up on time.

As revenge for this incident (and no doubt similar incidents since the green-tongued Animal took an agenting role in the late 1980s), Owen and Macho Man Randy Savage pilfered George's Halliburton suitcase.[1] With The Animal's back turned, Owen and Savage snuck the case out of Hersheypark Arena under a jacket to their rental car. About an hour into their trip to the next stop on the WWF's never-ending tour, Owen, Savage and the Halliburton were travelling on a bridge over a river. Somehow, the case jumped out of Owen's hands and plopped into the river below, with Mr Steele's passport, medication, airline tickets and colostomy bags all along for the plunge.

While it might seem like an ignominious end for the suitcase; in terms of wrestling history it can rest easy at the bottom of the river knowing that it met the same fate as various prized wrestling mementos over the years. The list of sunken grappling memorabilia includes: multiple championship belts that were thrown into rivers as part of storylines; Dick Slater's Mid-South TV Medallion and Al Snow.

The incident ultimately wouldn't deter Bret, who would go on to become legendary in wrestling locker rooms for turning up late to shows to the exasperation of the backstage agents and wrestlers in both WWF and WCW. This included Shawn Michaels and Triple H, who made sure to have their opinions heard by everyone within ear shot, adding more fuel to the fire of their real-life animosity.

[1]Halliburtons are expensive aluminium luggage suitcases that were somewhat of a travelling fashion statement for wrestlers at the time. Halliburtons still make appearances in WWE suspended above the ring during 'Money in the Bank ladder matches'.

Bumped from First-Class

As told by Smith Hart and Diana Hart

Even though Owen and Davey Boy Smith were brothers-in-law AND brothers-in-practical jokes, Owen used to constantly rib Davey because his reactions were priceless. Owen's sister and Davey's ex-wife, Diana Hart wrote, "Owen loved to pull the ribs on Davey because he would get so mad and yet would be unable to stop laughing."

After another tour across the United States, Bret and Owen arrived at New York's Niagra Falls airport to grab the last flight back home to Calgary. All was not well in the locker room that day thanks to Davey winding up the Hart brothers throughout the afternoon over catching the last flight out. "[Davey] got the agents to give him permission to go much earlier [in the show] so he could catch a much earlier flight," claimed Smith Hart. "He was gloating so much about it. He should have just quietly gone on early and had his match and left; but no. He was gloating about it and Owen thought, 'This deserves a rib.'" Owen punished Davey's hubris by grabbing his gear bag, shoving it into a locker and padlocking it shut while Davey was enjoying a post-match shower.

After he eventually managed to find a custodian with bolt cutters to retrieve his gear, Davey changed and headed off to the airport. Thanks to Owen, he'd missed the earlier flight to Calgary but arrived at the airport in plenty of time to hop on the last plane home. Bret and Owen, who were main-eventing the show, finished their match and tore out of the arena as quickly as they could. With a bit of luck and a lead foot, the brothers arrived at Niagara Falls International just before their gate closed, where they were greeted by a friendly female clerk. The clerk happened to be a big wrestling fan and, in exchange for some signed 8x10s, the helpful airport employee hooked the Harts up with free first-class seats. She also handheld Bret and Owen through security so they didn't miss their flight.

The relieved brothers were in their seats and taking in the luxury of first-class when they noticed that they were the only two in the cabin. They also noticed that the preposterously muscular Davey Boy (who was the size and shape of the Thwomp from the *Super Mario* franchise) was scrunched into his tiny econo-seat at the back of the plane. When Davey got up, he walked over to Owen in first-class, who told him that he'd have a word with the steward to see if Davey could get bumped. After all, there was plenty of room to spare. The Bulldog headed back to economy and waited to be called up.

Before the plane left the tarmac, Owen beckoned over the airline steward and told him that there was an English bodybuilder sat in economy who was a loser wannabe-wrestler that followed the WWF stars around. "He really believes he's a wrestler and is always trying to act like he is one of us," Owen informed the steward. "I don't mind him coming up and saying hi but can you make sure he takes his seat back in coach after a few minutes?" The flight attendant understood the predicament and offered to shoo the Bulldog away when Owen gave him the signal.

After takeoff, Owen walked over to the back of the plane and informed Davey that everything was sorted and he was allowed to come up front. Davey brought his luggage with him and settled into the first-class seat in front of Owen and Bret. The brothers chatted for a little while before Owen brought out a Japanese wrestling magazine. While Bulldog had his head buried in the magazine, Owen gave the steward the pre-arranged signal. The steward dutifully walked over and politely informed Davey that it was time he headed back to his seat. An incredulous Davey replied, "What are you talking about? I'm s'posed to be 'ere. I'm a wrestler." Davey gestured to Owen and Bret sitting behind him and informed the steward, "These are my brothers-in-law." When the steward looked to Owen for confirmation, Owen pointed to his temple and circled his finger around for the internationally recognised gesture that Davey was a mad as a March hare. Unmoved, the attendant nodded politely at Davey's protestations before reaffirming that he had to go back to his original seat. The flustered Bulldog packed up his belongings while cursing the steward under his breath and headed back to the confines of economy.

Later on, the lights had been dimmed and the plane was quiet. Owen went back to economy and told the Bulldog that he'd had a word with the steward and it was finally okay for him to join them in first-class. Davey, a little more wary than the first time, once again grabbed his luggage and traipsed up to the front of the plane. The brothers chatted for a brief while before Davey lay back and closed his eyes for a well earned dog-nap. With Davey sinking into a deep sleep, Owen once again caught the eye of the air steward and gave him the pre-arranged signal. The steward shook the Bulldog awake and told him to get back to his seat. Davey protested once again but knew it was hopeless.

As Davey grabbed his bag to make his second walk of shame back to economy, Owen could take no more and burst out laughing at the dejected 'Dog. After witnessing Owen crack up, Davey finally worked out that his forced relocations had been a big set up. In his thick Mancunian accent, Davey yelled, "FUCK YOU, FUCK YOU AND FUCK YOU!" while aggressively pointing to Owen, Bret and the stupefied steward who hadn't been let in on the joke, before storming off back to the relative honesty of his cramped economy seat.

CHAPTER 5

Brother vs. Brother

On the 1ˢᵗ of January 1994 edition of *WWF Superstars*, Bret and Owen appeared together claiming to have patched up their differences over the holidays. To keep the peace, Bret declared he was going to dedicate the rest of his career to teaming with Owen. When it was Owen's turn to speak, he subtly conveyed that he was the captain of the team and Bret would be 'hitched right behind' him as they took on The Quebecers for the WWF Tag Team Championships at the *Royal Rumble* three weeks later. When the match took place, The Quebecers injured Bret's knee so badly (in storyline) he couldn't get to Owen to make the tag. Referee Tim White eventually called for the bell, awarding the match to The Quebecers. Owen freaked out and had a massive temper tantrum at Bret before kicking him in his bad knee, cementing his status as a fully-fledged bad guy. When Owen returned to the back, interviewer Todd Pettengill demanded to know why he committed such a 'despicable act'. In response, Owen, who was nearly crying, cut the whiniest promo in the history of the business that today is best remembered for the flubbed go-home line.

"The biggest opportunity of my life. I had a chance Bret and you stripped it away from me. You took it away from me, Bret, because you were too selfish. All you had to do was just tag me. My hand was there, just tag me. I knew your leg was bad, I was aware of that; just tag me. But you're too selfish, you just wanna put your Sharpshooter on. I could've won the match, I don't need you with a bad leg doing it, Bret. You're too damn selfish and that's why you're sitting there with a bad leg and THAT's why I kicked your leg outta your leg..."

Later on in the *Royal Rumble* pay-per-view, Owen became the fifth entrant in the Rumble match,[1] yelling, "I'M ONLY IN IT FOR MYSELF!" as he jogged down the entrance way to a chorus of boos. Owen was eliminated quickly by Kevin 'Diesel' Nash, as the real story of the Royal Rumble was Bret entering at number twenty-seven with his 'bad knee.' Bret and Lex Luger would be named co-winners of the Rumble after both men went over the top rope onto the floor at the exact same time. One referee raised the hand of Luger and the other raised the hand of Bret. This was a clever move by the WWF, as they were actually gauging the fan's response to both wrestlers when their arms were raised. Luger, who had been pushed hard as Hulk Hogan's successor for the past six months, hadn't connected with the fans and received a lukewarm response. Bret however was by far the most popular wrestler in the company and the fans cheered him like crazy when he was declared the winner. Booking plans were changed and Bret was picked to win the WWF Championship at *WrestleMania X* from Yokozuna. The fan reaction at the *Royal Rumble* show forced McMahon to concede defeat over the Luger experiment.[2]

To sell fans on the supposed reality of the brother vs. brother rivalry, Bret insisted on maintaining kayfabe, just like the old days. This meant no more hanging out together in public, being seen in the same restaurant or even sitting near each other on a plane. "We [had] to go through this charade, twenty-four hours a day, of two brothers that have this intense rivalry with each other and a lot of hatred and bad feelings," explained Bret. Their mother Helen had a particularly difficult time watching her sons squabble on television, even though she knew it was work. "I broke down and cried. I felt so bad. You have to go on and say you can't stand Owen and he's spoiled and rotten and Owen has to say you're a conceited oaf?"

While trying to keep up the illusion that they were still at odds, Bret recalled a noteworthy encounter the brothers experienced while being detained at Calgary airport. "Owen said something to me and I kinda leaned back and said something back to him; 'Yeah, right,' or something like that. All of a sudden this woman customs officer comes barging out of her little office and goes, 'I caught ya! I knew that you guys talked, I knew you were friends!' And we both looked at each other and burst out laughing."

Keeping in line with 1993's Royal Rumble match stipulation, the winner of the '94 Rumble received a WWF Championship match at that year's *WrestleMania* on the 20th of March. Because Bret and Luger were declared co-winners, there would be a three-man round robin tournament. Bret would wrestle Owen in the opening match before competing for the WWF Championship in the main event against the winner of the Lex Luger vs. Yokozuna Title match. Both Bret and Owen put a huge amount of thought into their initial encounter, with Bret constructing a match that would highlight Owen's high-flying prowess, yet keep him a heel. Three days before *Mania*, Bret and Owen met at the Dungeon in Hart House, threw out the old match and constructed another from the ground up, which would focus on Owen's newly acquired mean streak.

WrestleMania X in Madison Square Garden was a grandiose affair befitting of its tenth anniversary. After the pre-show hype video paid tribute to *Wrestlemanias* past, the pyrotechnics had exploded and Little Richard finished his horrendous miming of the American national anthem, it was time for the first match of the show - Bret Hart vs. Owen Hart, brother vs. brother in front of over 18,000 fans in the world's most famous arena. Without describing every move in the match, Bret vs. Owen was an instant classic. Gone were Owen's high-flying manoeuvres in favour of solid, basic wrestling and liberal cheating. The sneering Owen used every short cut he could think of and triumphantly raised his arms whenever he bested his 'lousy' older brother on the mat. It was a closely contested bout and the audience cheered like crazy for the Hitman. "My *Wrestlemania X* match with Owen was a really special match we put together that day," remembered Bret. "Too many people today don't realize how hard it is to put together a match like that."

In what was a genuine upset, Owen countered a Bret Hart victory roll at the 20:00 mark to cleanly pin his older brother. The match is still considered one of the finest in World Wrestling Federation history, as well as the greatest opening match at a *WrestleMania* to date. Owen had proved to the fans and his peers that he was a main event calibre performer. After returning to the back, Owen, with his mouth covered in gross, white slobber, declared himself, "The best there is, the best there was and the best there ever will be," in mockery of Bret's catchphrase, before claiming that he gave Bret such a beating he had no chance to win the WWF Championship later on that night.

Later in the pay-per-view Lex Luger was screwed out of winning the WWF Championship after special guest referee Mr Perfect disqualified him,[3] setting up a Yokozuna vs. Bret Hart main event for the title, which happened to be a rematch of the main event from last year's *WrestleMania IX*. Bret defeated the 550lb Yokozuna to win the WWF Championship in just over 10:00, followed by all of the babyfaces in the locker room coming out to parade the Hitman around the ring in victory. Even guest ring announcer Burt Reynolds came out to celebrate Hart's big win! With the mood high, the festivities in full swing and the Hitman's music blaring over the house speakers, a rancorous Owen appeared in the walk way, shaking his head in disbelief before agent Tony Garea shooed him back through the curtain.

The family feud storyline was just beginning to heat up. Owen would appear on WWF television for the next several months boasting of his *WrestleMania* win over his brother, while on the untelevised house show circuit, Bret Hart vs. Owen Hart for the WWF Championship, headlined every card they appeared on in North America, as well as Japan and the post-*WrestleMania* European tour. While the main event money wasn't what it was in the glorious 1980s or what it would become from the late 1990s onwards, both Owen and Bret were making $7,000 to $10,000 per week and having a great time together in the ring. The money was even better considering that when Owen re-signed with the WWF in November 1991, he was earning $100,000 a year and near the bottom of the card.

The next big pay-per-view was the *King of the Ring 1994* tournament in June, which in storyline Owen was determined to win so he could accomplish everything Bret had achieved. In a tournament qualifying match, Owen pinned the now babyface Doink the Clown (subbing for an 'injured' Earthquake) after Jeff Jarrett attempted to kidnap Doink's Mini Me clown manager Dink (welcome to the dark days of the child friendly WWF). At *King of the Ring* (the first big show branding the WWF Superstars as 'The

129

New Generation'[4]) Owen would cleanly pin Tatanka in 8:00 to advance to the semi-finals where he would defeat an 'injured' 1-2-3 Kid in 3:37. Jim 'The Anvil' Neidhart also made his surprise return to the Federation accompanying Bret to the ring for his WWF Title defence against Diesel. Neidhart, who appeared to be a babyface, interfered in the match and got Bret disqualified, ensuring Bret remained Champion.[5] Neidhart then stormed off to the back, allowing Bret to be double-teamed by Diesel and Shawn Michaels.

In the *King of the Ring* tournament final, Owen faced off against friendly Cuban drug lord Razor Ramon. Late into the match, Ramon set Owen up for his Razor's Edge (crucifix powerbomb) finishing move but found himself being backdropped over the top rope to the floor, 'injuring' his knee. Neidhart came out once again to interfere, this time sneak-attacking Razor and throwing him into the ring. All that remained was for Owen to hit a top rope elbow and pin the former WWF Intercontinental Champion to become the 1994 King of the Ring. After the match, the devious Owen and Neidhart beat down Razor, while Bret Hart, who was watching in the back, refused to comment on the scenes that were unfolding. It turned out that Neidhart had only helped Bret retain the belt so Owen could challenge him for it at the following pay-per-view.

After the big win, Owen and Neidhart walked to the entrance way for the coronation. Owen sat on a prop throne, wore a giant purple cape and held a sceptre while failing to look regal. Owen then demanded respect from the fans, then forced interviewer Todd Pettengill down on one knee. Neidhart then plonked a giant, hideous crown with the classic WWF logo on his head to complete the inauguration. The King of Harts was born and Owen was heading to *SummerSlam* to take on his brother Bret for the World Wrestling Federation Championship.

On the 27th of June edition of *RAW*, Owen appeared on Jerry Lawler's 'King's Court' interview segment to officially challenge Bret for the World Wrestling Federation Championship; the dozens of title shots he received and lost on untelevised house shows were obviously never referenced. Owen's interviews, which were the weakest part of his game, noticeably improved once he turned heel and had the right motivation. The recalcitrant tone in Owen's voice and contemptible facial expressions helped create a fully-rounded character of the sneaky, jealous little brother. After Owen first turned heel, there were discussions to pair him with Jim Cornette as his mouthpiece but according to Bruce Prichard, "[Owen's] stuttering and stammering… made it real and that made you go, 'Oh! Fuck you Owen, you're not that good!'"

Throughout the summer, Bret and Owen continued wrestling each other on house shows, now including several sixty-minute 'Iron Man matches' where the competitor with the most falls on their opponent after sixty minutes would be declared the winner. Even Bruce Hart would make several appearances in Bret's corner to counteract Neidhart's interference leading up to the big *SummerSlam* 'Cage match.'

During the height of the brother vs. brother feud, Owen was riding to the next town with good friend Ronnie Gaffe when they were pulled over by a state trooper. Ronnie was nervous, having never been pulled over in his life. When Ronnie, who assumed he'd been pulled for speeding, wound down the window, the officer leaned into the car, looked at Owen and said, "You betrayed your brother!" "[Owen's] face was all red," recalled Ronnie. "[Owen] said, 'Yeah, I did'… Thankfully the trooper said, 'Don't worry. First of all, you don't mind signing an autograph for my son, do ya?' Then he says, 'Don't worry, I'm not giving ya a ticket!'"

SummerSlam 1994 took place at the brand new United Center in Chicago, Illinois and Bret vs. Owen in the cage for the World Wrestling Federation Championship would co-main event.[6] While the fifteen foot high steel cage was being constructed around the ring, commentators Vince McMahon and Jerry Lawler interviewed some of the Hart family, who weighed in with their opinions, including the returning Davey Boy Smith.[7] Davey hadn't been seen in the World Wrestling Federation since November 1992 when he, along with Ultimate Warrior, were fired for receiving growth hormone shipments by mail. The irony was that, despite the steroid testing still in full effect, the newly re-hired Davey looked even more bulked up than when he left.

It was announced that the only way to win the match was to escape the cage, which was different to most Cage matches where you could win by pin, submission or escaping the cage. There was also a no-blood policy instituted by the WWF as a reaction to lobbying from various citizens groups. Despite the limitations, the match was easily one of the greatest Cage matches in history, with the 23,000 strong Chicago crowd screaming for Bret throughout, as both men battled back and forth to escape. After nearly 33:00, Owen's legs got tangled up in the cage allowing Bret to escape and retain his WWF Championship once again, in what Bret and Owen were told would be their last match together. "We were both really, really happy working with each other," smiled Bret, "it was a lot of fun." As soon as Bret hit the ground, Jim Neidhart attacked Davey Boy and his wife Diana Hart, before he and Owen threw Bret back into the ring and viciously beat him down. Neidhart and Owen fended off some of the Hart brothers until a topless Davey recovered and ran the nefarious duo off, before striking some bodybuilder poses for the crowd. There were rumours circulating at the time that Bret wasn't happy with Davey Boy coming back to the company at all, as Bret saw Davey as competition for his main event spot.

Owen and Neidhart would team up to lose to Bret and a revolving list of partners including Razor Ramon, Macho Man Randy Savage and Davey Boy Smith on the house show circuit leading up to *Survivor Series 1994*, where WWF Champion Bret Hart was scheduled to take on former World Wide Wrestling Federation Champion Bob Backlund. Backlund returned to the Federation in 1992 as a sort of George Foreman-esque character (in spirit rather than appearance), looking to regain championship gold in his 40s. When he was young, the babyface Backlund held the WWWF Championship for 2,135 uninterrupted days,[8] but was put out to pasture in late 1983 in favour of the returning Hulk Hogan and a crop of new, far more exciting stars. Backlund kicked around the WWF undercard for a few more months before making some appearances in regional territories and Japan before pretty much retiring from the business in 1985.

Two years on and the Backlund experiment had flopped. Even though Bob was in tremendous shape and as strong as an ox, he was terrible in the ring and put on one woeful match after another. The vast majority of fans never saw Backlund in his prime and didn't much care for his act, which was a big problem for a white meat babyface. Decisions were made to turn the simplistic 'Howdy Doody' Backlund into a money-drawing heel.

The turn started slowly, with Bob challenging Bret to a Championship match on the 30th of July 1994 edition of *WWF Superstars*.

After Bret rolled Bob up for the surprise win, Bob rejected a consolation handshake and went crazy, locking Bret in his Crossface Chickenwing submission hold (a kind of half-hammerlock/half neck crank with the hands clasped together) before letting go and staring at his hands in disbelief at what he'd just done. Over the coming months, he'd continue to 'snap' and attack opponents. Backlund would also start to claim he was the rightful World Wrestling Federation Champion, as he'd never given up to The Iron Sheik's Camel Clutch submission in 1983 (his manager Arnold Skaaland threw in the towel). Bob's heel turn was complete and the rechristened 'Mr Backlund', who took to wearing three-piece suits complete with dickie bow, was now an out of touch mad man who hated 'The New Generation' of WWF stars and fans for having low morals. Mr Backlund also started using unnecessarily sesquipedalian words, usually incorrectly, during his outlandish interviews.

Before *Survivor Series*, Owen would receive one final shot at his brother for the World Wrestling Federation Championship on the debut edition of *WWF Action Zone*, which would replace the long-running *WWF All-American Wrestling* on the USA Network. Billed as the 'last ever match' between the two, the contest is considered a forgotten classic, with Davey coming to Bret's aid to help him overcome Jim Neidhart's interference and vanquish his little brother once and for all. It was amazing the match even took place, as Bret recently suffered a cracked pelvis during an untelevised match at the hands of Mr Backlund. What looked like a hard hitting encounter between the brothers was, as Bret described, "The most pain-free match I ever had." Bret even thanked Owen as he grapevined his legs to apply the Sharpshooter for the win. After Bret's victory, Mr Backlund officially challenged Bret to a WWF Championship match at the *Survivor Series* pay-per-view.

Come *Survivor Series*, an interesting set of rules were put in place for the Championship match. The only way to win was by submission via their seconds throwing in the towel, with Davey Boy Smith in Bret's corner and Owen in Mr Backlund's. The Backlund vs. Bret title match was 35:00 of mostly tedium; exchanging headlocks and pointless submission holds no fan believed to be match winner. Bret finally hit his sequence of moves culminating in the Sharpshooter but Owen clotheslined Bret from behind, breaking the hold. Davey chased after Owen until he managed to 'knock himself out' by head butting the metal ring steps when Owen dodged out of the way. While a 'concerned' Owen hovered over Davey's prone body, Bret turned his back on Backlund and yelled, "YOU SONOFABITCH!" at Owen before letting himself get caught in Bob's dreaded Crossface Chickenwing.

With Davey still 'knocked out', Owen handed the towel to Stu and Helen Hart who were sat at ringside and pleaded with them to end the match on Bret's behalf. Owen hilariously overacted and cried at his mother to end the contest for Bret's sake. When Helen was about to throw in the towel, Hart patriarch Stu took it away. After nearly nine minutes of Bret being locked in the legitimately agonising hold (even when put on in a working manner) Helen could take no more and threw in the towel. As soon as Mr Backlund was declared the winner in front of a dumbfounded crowd, Owen grabbed the towel as a souvenir and joyously sprinted to the back to a chorus of boos.

In the back, Owen explained why he so desperately wanted Bret to lose his WWF Title. "Bret, I could've beaten you before but you CHEATED! But now you're nothing, you're below me, you're down there in the gutter, Bret. You're not a champion anymore, you're a loo-serrr and I'm a King and Bret, you're a nobody!" Backlund would quickly prove to be the very definition of a transitional champion when he lost the belt three days later to McMahon's latest project, the near seven foot tall Diesel in Madison Square Garden in an eight second squash match.

After their critically lauded feud in 1994 wound down, both Owen and Bret would be pushed way down the card to make way for fresh blood in 1995. The following year would see Vince McMahon entrust: Diesel, Shawn Michaels, the returning Sid, King Mable and Davey Boy Smith to main event his pay-per-views over the course of 1995, with wildly varying degree of failure.

[1]Owen actually won a special non-televised Royal Rumble match five days before in Madison Square Garden on the 17th of January 1994. The final four were Owen Hart, Bret Hart, Shawn Michaels and Headshrinker Fatu. Michaels eliminated Bret, Owen eliminated

Michaels and then Owen eventually eliminated Fatu after interference from both Headshrinker Samu and Bret.

[2] *Royal Rumble 1994* would become a source of controversy over the aggressive promotion of their premium rate telephone service. The 900 line did gangbuster business during the pay-per-view, enticing fans to call so they could find out Bret's Royal Rumble status after the knee injury, as well as the order of entrants in the Rumble match. Advertising also suggested that fans could influence the outcome of the Rumble match by voting for the winner, which could've have been construed as fraud, as all booking decisions were likely made well ahead of time and fan voting would have no influence. Many years later, Jim Cornette quipped that, "Wrestling and phone sex [lines] lasted because people have to hear wrestling gossip and they have to jack off. That's the only two things [wrestling fans are] naturally programmed to do, apparently."

[3] Luger hit Yokozuna with his 'bionic' forearm, 'knocking out' Yokozuna. WWF storylines claimed surgeons inserted a metal bar of some sort into Luger's forearm after he legitimately broke it in 1992 courtesy of a motorcycle accident. Yoko's managers Jim Cornette and Mr Fuji attempted to distract Luger but ended up getting laid out after some phony looking strikes. When Luger went to pin Yokozuna, Mr Perfect ignored the 'All-American' and tended to the recumbent managers instead. When Luger grabbed Perfect's referee shirt, Perfect disqualified Luger and awarded the match to Yokozuna. Perfect made a couple of follow up television appearances explaining his actions before his real-life chronic back problems flared up. To explain his sudden absence, Mr Perfect was 'suspended indefinitely' from the WWF, aborting the Luger vs. Perfect feud before it ever got started.

[4] The New Generation advertising campaign debuted earlier that week on *WWF RAW* in response to WCW officially signing the 40-year-old Hulk Hogan to be their top star. The World Wrestling Federation marketing themselves as the youth promotion couldn't have come at a more inappropriate time, as the *King of the Ring* pay-per-view was guest-

commentated by clueless septuagenarian and NFL Hall of Famer Art 'how much does this guy weigh?' Donovan and was main evented by the returning 'Rowdy' Roddy Piper (also 40) facing off against Jerry 'The King' Lawler (44). Although Piper was in great shape, he'd slimmed down considerably and looked to have aged ten years in the space of two, just like Hulk Hogan had when he briefly returned to the WWF the year prior looking considerably leaner. Piper and Lawler put on a meandering affair with little crowd interest, lots of middle-aged brawling and a ref bump, before Piper picked up the win. To make matters worse, prior to the match Todd Pettengill interviewed Maryland Governor William Donald Schaeffer, who proclaimed his favourite WWF wrestler to be Hulk Hogan. Whoops!

[5] For booking reasons, WWE titles can only change hands via pinfall or submission (unless otherwise stipulated). This is so WWE (and most current American promotions that followed suit) can book a champion to lose matches to rivals and prospective contenders, theoretically giving more ways to advance a programme or to create new stars without the champion losing the belt. Disqualification, count-out and blood stoppage are all ways a champion can lose and remain the champion in a regular match. Most wrestling promotions in other countries such as Mexico and Japan don't have such odd rules governing title changes.

[6] The other main event, which went on last, was a preposterous Undertaker (the original, portrayed by Mark Calaway) vs. 'Undertaker' match (portrayed by Brian Lee). 'Taker hadn't been seen on television since January's *Royal Rumble* where he faced off against Yokozuna in a 'Casket match.' In May 1994, heel manager Ted DiBiase claimed to have bought the services of The Undertaker, the imposter version played by Brian Lee. 'Taker's manager Paul Bearer promised to bring the genuine article back to defeat DiBiase's 'Under-Faker' at *SummerSlam*. When the meeting of Undertakers finally took place, the match profoundly sucked and the fans hated it. The feud was originally going to be long-term but after negative fan reaction in the weeks leading up to the pay-per-view, the storyline was wrapped up that night, never to be revisited. Not even the hiring of Hollywood legend Leslie Neilson of

Police Squad and *Naked Gun* fame to 'solve the mystery of The Undertaker' could save the storyline, especially since poor Leslie's WWF scripted lines were so atrociously written they made *2001: A Space Travesty's* script look like *Citizen Kane* by comparison.

[7]According to Diana Hart, Davey Boy was being courted to return to WCW by no less than Hulk Hogan himself, who had officially signed with the company a couple of months prior. "I'll look after you Davey Boy, even if I have to pay you out of my own bank account," Hogan allegedly said. After his negative experiences with WCW the previous year, Davey firmly told Hogan that he had no interest in returning and re-signed with the WWF.

[8]Bob's unbroken Championship reign is only according to WWE's distorted version of history. Backlund lost the WWF Championship on the 30th of November 1979 (they dropped a 'W' in March that year) to Japanese legend Antonio Inoki in Tokushima, Japan. When the rematch in Tokyo a week later ended in a no-contest, Inoki vacated the title. Backlund then defeated Bobby Duncum in a 'Texas Death match' in Madison Square Garden on the 17th of December to somehow regain the vacant belt. The Title was held up again after a match with Greg 'The Hammer' Valentine on the 19th of October 1981. Backlund won the match but a dazed referee accidently handed the belt to Valentine. For some bizarre reason, this meant the belt was vacated and Backlund had to win it back the next month. Despite both incidents, WWE still recognises Backlund's five and a half year reign as uninterrupted. None of what is written above is recognised as 'canon' by WWE and none of it makes any logical sense but that's wrestling for you.

Sardines

As told by Sean Waltman and Diana Hart

At the height of the brother vs. brother feud, Owen would ramp up efforts to prank Bret, including one of the all-time classics Owen would become famous for pulling. "Owen used to fuck with Bret all the time," said former '1-2-3 Kid' Sean Waltman. "Bret used to get so mad because he thought Owen should show him a little more respect because he was the Champ." During a sparsely attended one-week tour of Canada in June '94, Owen decided to amuse the boys and show how much reverence he had for his brother and the position of 'Champ.' Before the audience were let in to the arena that evening, Owen secretly headed out to the ring early to hide an item under the apron in preparation for the evening's frivolities. Owen then made sure that his bags were pre-packed and left near the locker room door.

When it was main event time (Bret vs. Owen headlined nearly every house show they appeared on for a six-month period in 1994) the sibling rivals performed their usual routine match, which they'd been perfecting over the course of the spring. When it was time for Owen to be the aggressor, he made sure to beat Bret until he was face-down on the canvas. This is when Owen decided to strike. He quickly rolled out of the ring and reached for the item he'd hidden under the apron. The item happened to be a can of sardines, with the tin being pre-opened. Owen grabbed a handful of the oily fish and went back into the ring, where Bret was still laying face-down on the mat. Owen sat on Bret's lower back, reached under his jaw and clamped him in a rear chinlock submission. With Bret in a prone position, Owen started slathering a hand full of sardines all over Bret's face and inside his mouth. Owen then closed Bret's mouth shut by clasping his hands under his jaw and leaning back. When Bret realised that the salty taste of Owen's fingers wasn't from sweat but from raw fish, he broke character and bucked Owen off his back like an enraged bull.

After quickly regaining control of the match, Bret locked Owen in his Sharpshooter submission hold more snugly than usual as a small measure of revenge on his little brother. Owen submitted, then jumped up off the ring canvas and sprinted to the back, past a hoard of cackling road agents and Davey Boy Smith. Bret acknowledged the crowd then ran to the back to catch Owen. According to Waltman, who was riding with Owen that night, "[They] finished the match [and] we already had our shit packed. [We ran] out the door and we were gone before Bret got back."

Undertaker vs. Cucumbers

As told by Paul Bearer and Bruce Prichard

As revealed by long time manager and confidant Paul Bearer in an interview with Jim Cornette, The Undertaker has a deep-rooted disgust, if not outright phobia, of cucumbers. Rather than humorously offering some seedy, Freudian explanation, Paul claimed, rather vaguely, that the dawn of 'Taker's loathing stems from being forced to eat them as a child and his revulsion carried on through to adulthood.

Bearer and former 1990s WWF mainstay Brian 'Crush' Adams used to have great fun at Taker's expense, watching the 'Dead Man' flip out at the site of a cucumber mysteriously appearing in his gimmick open crown hat or in the fingers of his purple leather mortician-style gloves. Bruce Prichard remarked that, "Just a cucumber on top of his bag would freak him out." Owen was also allegedly responsible for slipping slices of cucumber inside The Undertaker's wrestling boots so he wouldn't feel them until they were squished up between his toes and soaking into his socks.

In another rib that has been attributed to The King of Pranks by Prichard, Owen was never one to let an opportunity like this pass him by and hatched a plan in the wrestlers' favourite after-show eatery, Waffle House. With some of the finer details lost to time, all that is known is that Owen slipped some cucumber in The Undertaker's iced tea. According to Prichard, the cucumber slices had been pushed to the bottom of the glass, "So that when 'Taker drank the tea and drunk it back, he didn't realise the cucumbers were in there until he was looking at it in his face!" By the time the Dead Man noticed that his iced tea had been contaminated by the grotesque gourd, it was too late. The man who had been nicknamed 'John Wayne' and 'Cool Hand Luke' for his unflappable demeanour placed an impromptu call for 'O'Rourke'. Bearer recalled, "I saw The Undertaker throw up all over Waffle House because there was a cucumber floating in his iced tea." Prichard concurred, "Yeah, 'Taker didn't like cucumbers. He didn't like that very much."

With a vein this rich in potential pranking, Owen wasn't about to stop after the Waffle House escapade. During a tag team match, which pitted Bret Hart and The Undertaker against Owen Hart and an unnamed partner (likely Davey Boy Smith or Yokozuna), Owen gave The Dead Man the same treatment he'd given Bret. With an eerily similar set up to the Bret Hart sardine fiasco, Owen had The Undertaker face down on the mat in a rear chinlock. When 'Taker was right where he was needed, Owen reached for a handful of cucumbers he'd stowed away into his singlet and smeared them in the Dead Man's face. In this time of crisis, 'Taker had two options:

1 - Break character and expose to the paying audience that the 'Man from the Dark Side' is afraid of cucumbers, or
2 - Lie there and take it, because it's a harmless vegetable.

The Undertaker, who treats his character and the business with the utmost professionalism, chose option one. He squirmed out of the headlock and escaped the ring to compose himself. Then he shot Owen a death stare and probably contemplated leaving the arena right then and there. Since depriving the paying fans their main event over cucumbers wasn't really an option, The Undertaker settled himself down, re-entered the ring and soldiered on with the bout.

In a world of rigid hierarchy, it didn't matter if you were jerking the curtain in the opening contest, the World Champion or even the boss; Owen was going to get you sooner or later. In what is probably no comfort to The Undertaker, all available records show that he and Bret Hart very likely won the match.

142

Rene Goulet Loses $100 in Vatican City

As told by Bret Hart

In the early to mid 1990s, the wrestling business in North America sank to a low not seen for decades. A combination of: Hulk Hogan's dwindling star power and subsequent 'retirement' from wrestling; a near-complete turnaround of on-screen talent; general fatigue with the product and various scandals (including a rumoured gay paedophile ring, rape accusations and systemic steroid distribution) put paid to the WWF's drawing power by the early 1990s.[1]

With domestic arena attendance in the toilet, Vince McMahon began exploiting the European market to boost the Federation's coffers.[2] The WWF had only been broadcasting regularly in Europe for a few years and European fans hadn't had time to get burnt out by American-style wrestling. In the UK for example, the WWF debuted in 1986 with sporadic broadcasts of WWF matches in the traditional ITV wrestling slot.[3] It should be noted that on the WWF's momentous debut broadcast, the UK's very own British Bulldogs would make an appearance, being billed from the mining towns of 'Leed' and 'Wigans' respectively by host and anglophile, 'Mean' Gene Okerlund.[4]

By the 1990s, the WWF roster would fly back and forth to Europe several times a year, traversing the continent from arena to arena via tour bus. While the WWF mostly toured the UK and Germany (sometimes for weeks on end) other countries including France, Switzerland and Italy would get the chance to see wrestling action too. When the Federation tour bus arrived in Rome it was decided to make a short detour to visit the 110 acre Vatican City, which is enclaved within the Italian capital.

When the WWF tour bus arrived at the Vatican, the religiously-sensitive Bret Hart instructed road agent 'Sergeant' Rene Goulet to remind the rest of the guys to, "Watch the swears and... be respectful," while visiting the location of the Holy See. Goulet concurred and asked the guys to tone down the language on the rationale that, "It was better to be safe than sorry." After disembarking the tour bus, the wrestlers quickly reached into their pockets to purchase religious baubles such as rosaries, crosses and other assorted ornaments from one of the many mobile vendors. In the inimitable words of George Carlin, "God loves you and he needs money!"

'Sarge' was next to purchase one of the saintly doodads, burying his nose in the merchandise tray in search of a souvenir. Goulet was so engrossed in his potential purchase that he wasn't paying attention when Owen reached behind him and snatched the $100 bill out of his hand. All the wrestlers were tightly grouped in front of the merchant and, when Goulet slowly realised the bill was gone, he accusatorially turned round to Bret and demanded he give it him back. When Bret revealed his hands were in front of him the entire time, Goulet started searching for the real culprit, who had already absconded from the scene.

Rene, whose nickname backstage was 'JP Morgan' because, "He still had the first dime he ever made," renounced his own request to tone down the swearing and screamed out a string of loud and vivid expletives. Owen, with the $100 bill in his possession, walked over to Men on a Mission's fat manager-cum-rapper Oscar. Owen handed Oscar the $100 bill with the explanation that Rene had instructed Owen to give it to him. Oblivious to the ruse, Oscar went straight to Sarge asking why he'd given him $100. This caused an impassioned confrontation between the two in front of the Apostolic Palace while a happy Owen took a step back to witness the awkward encounter unfold.

While Bret and Rene had both been (temporarily) mindful of swearing, personal camcorder footage of the trip suggests that none of the wrestlers considered it an affront to the almighty by turning up to the Mecca of Catholicism wearing Zubaz workout pants, L.A. Gears, sleeveless Powerhouse Gym t-shirts and bum bags full of Somas and Vicodin.

[1]WCW, by this time the only other national wrestling promotion left, was fairing even worse than the WWF, having managed to shoot themselves in the foot so many times as to leave only a bloody stump. When the debt-laden company was sold to Ted Turner in 1988, former Pizza Hut bigwig Jim Herd was soon installed as WCW's Executive Vice

President, despite having practically zero knowledge of the business. Terrible booking resulted in some of the stupidest wrestling characters known to man (The Ding Dongs, The Juicer, The Candyman, Oz, etc, etc, etc). Horrid storylines and the slashing of talent pay created a mass exodus of some of WCW's most talented players, including: Ric Flair, Jim Cornette's Midnight Express, Kevin Sullivan and The Road Warriors. By 1993, WCW live show attendance was at an all-time low, averaging a little over 300 fans per show.

[2] From 1992 to 1996, numerous overseas tours largely propped up the WWF's business. While domestic ticket sales continued to tumble during this time frame, arenas across the Atlantic were still selling out.

[3] The debuting WWF product would be another nail in the coffin of British wrestling on television. Muscled-up superheroes such as: Hulk Hogan, Randy Savage, Ultimate Warrior and Roddy Piper, coupled with the WWF's world-class television production, made Joint Promotions and All-Star Wrestling's primitive TV and its pasty, shapeless wrestlers come across as embarrassing by comparison. The washed-up, morbidly obese, middle-aged Shirley 'Big Daddy' Crabtree was still pushed as the headline attraction and no new superstars were ever built up to replace him. With the cancellation of the *World of Sport* programming block in 1985, fluctuating time slots, sagging ratings and the appointment of Greg Dyke (who hated wrestling) as London Weekend Television's Director of Programming in 1987, British wrestling was finally cancelled in 1988. Ironically, after wrestling was taken off television, live attendance increased dramatically and the UK touring wrestling scene prospered for several more years.

[4] It's Leeds and Wigan, in case you didn't know. Why Davey Boy Smith was billed from Leeds in the first place was always a mystery as he, like Dynamite, was born in Wigan, which is in the metropolitan county of Greater Manchester.

Oscar vs. 1-2-3 Kid

As told by Sean Waltman and Bret Hart

When Paul Neu left the dying Portland territory to head to WCW in 1991, he was repackaged into Fat Boys-style wrestling rapper PN News. Neu didn't impress as a wrestler and the gimmick was almost universally derided as whack. Not to be outdone, Vince McMahon in 1993 brought in no less than three lame hip hop aficionados in the guise of the overweight Bobby 'Mo' Horne and the 500lb human barrage balloon known as Nelson 'Mabel' Frazier.[1] Mo and Mable were bunged into baggy, multicoloured silk outfits and, together with professional rapper Oscar acting as their manager, formed the accidental championship winning[2] tag team of Men on a Mission.

Oscar's hiring was pure serendipity as he happened to be in Vegas when he spotted a bona fide WWF legend walked past. "I was at the craps table right before *WrestleMania IX* and I saw Randy Savage walking through the casino. I just went up and started rapping to him. Vince was there and they were blown away by what I did." Instead of smacking him the instant he invaded his personal sphere of influence, McMahon hired Oscar to rap during Men on a Mission's entrance, where he encouraged fans to raise their hands in the air while waving them with blatant disregard for the consequences.

During an overseas tour, Sean Waltman (at this time known as 1-2-3 Kid) was purposely annoying Oscar before a show, jostling around with him in a fairly playful way. "I was just fucking around with [Oscar] then Owen was stirring it up and Owen got it all stirred up to where... it got kinda physical." They went back and forth until the Kid escalated the encounter further by jumping on Oscar's back. At the behest of Owen, the Kid, who was likely less than 200lbs at that point, thought he'd easily take down the 300lb+ manager who, "Didn't have an athletic bone in his body." Bret, who was in the locker room at the time, saw everything go down. "Kid expected to manhandle Oscar and jumped right on his back but Oscar panicked, charging back and forth into the walls and knocking Kid silly!"

Recounting the brawl years later, Waltman still blamed Owen for escalating the fight. "It got kind of physical to the point where Owen stirred the pot so much that it turned into a shoot for Oscar. It was like, 'You motherfucker, Owen!'"

[1]While never confirmed, it is possible Mabel was named after the 'Mabel rib'. While there were many variations in different territories, the Calgary version of the prank was the most elaborate. Veterans of the territory would convince a rookie wrestler (Wrestler A, the mark) that a gorgeous girl called Mabel lived out in the sticks and was looking for a real man to pipe her while her husband was away. The catch was Mabel would only accept the most magnetic, red-blooded cocksman to get busy in the backwoods with and needed a second wrestler (Wrestler B, who was in on the rib) for her girlfriend. The rookie Wrestler A would accept the challenge, be driven out to some obscure locale in the middle of nowhere by Wrestler B and meet Mabel in a ramshackle farmhouse. Before the horizontal hula commenced, the crazed, shotgun-wielding husband would kick the door down and 'shoot Wrestler B dead'. Wrestler A would understandably run for his life and find his own way back through the frozen tundra back to civilisation. This is where Wrestler A would later learn that, thanks to blank bullets and ketchup for blood, his 'murdered' companion was alive and well.

[2]Men on a Mission were never actually slated to become WWF Tag Team Champions. During an untelevised house show in the Royal Albert Hall in London on the 29th of March 1994 against The Quebecers, Mabel fell onto Quebecer Pierre and Pierre just sort of forgot to kick out. The Quebecers won the titles back two days later in Sheffield. In a rare departure from kayfabe, the WWF acknowledged the title change on the 3rd of April 1994 episode of *All-American Wrestling*, instead of pretending it never happened, which was the usual way of handling such matters.

Bad Matches:
Owen Hart & Shawn
Michaels vs. Bret Hart &
Razor Ramon

As told by Bret Hart

"Those intentionally bad matches, done away from the camera eye, before the age of the internet, where road-weary wrestlers could forget all their problems and just enjoy the utter brilliance of a classic Hart stinker" - **Mick Foley**

In April 1994 the WWF headed to Israel for the third time in seven months. They'd gained enormous popularity in the country after Federation programming began airing over there in the early 1990s on Sports 5.[1] The first two day tour in October 1993 was completely sold out. The second two day tour in February 1994 was notable for many wrestlers' positive experiences touring Jerusalem. Bret and Owen were deeply moved when they visited the Wailing Wall and various WWF crew members visited The Dome of the Rock, the Dead Sea and the Via Dolorosa: the processional route Jesus supposedly walked while carrying the crucifix. The tour was also notable for the absence of Marty Jannetty, who had been fired once again the day prior.[2]

The WWF was back in Israel again less than two months later with another batch of shows. The second show of the three stop April tour took place in Holon and featured WWF Champion Bret Hart teaming with Razor Ramon against Shawn Michaels and Owen Hart in the main event. As Palestinian and Israeli children stood shoulder to shoulder to cheer on their heroes, Bret had a sense of foreboding the second Owen walked through the curtain. "[Owen] had a smirk on his face that he couldn't wipe off."

Owen went right on the offensive, as in offending lovers of serious professional wrestling. Owen started off by circling around the ring as if he were a dinosaur, lurching around with giant, arching steps. When Razor Ramon caught Owen in an armbar, Owen reacted as if the submission attempt was boring him, before lifting his free arm to his mouth and smoking an imaginary cigarette. When Razor attempted to continue the match standing, Owen once again refused to co-operate. "Razor tried to pick Owen up but Owen was flat on his back and went dead weight like a 220lb starfish," said Bret. "As hard as Razor tried over and over he couldn't budge Owen as Shawn and I nearly fell off the corners of the ring laughing." After refusing to get up for Ramon following the armbar attempt, Owen all of a sudden went from being disobliging to over-selling Razor's offence; boinging all around the ring, taking over exaggerated, phony-looking bumps. When Owen regained the upper hand, he put Ramon in a bear hug submission. In theory, a bear hug should look like you're squeezing the life out of your opponent. According to Bret, Owen's version of the submission move looked more like 'a romantic embrace'.

After cuddling The Bad Guy half to death, Owen started acting out of control and threw Razor outside to administer more punishment. While Razor was face down on the mat, Owen grabbed the ring announcer's microphone cord and wrapped it around Ramon's trachea. Unbeknownst to Razor, who was busy pantomiming being choked unconscious, Owen was doing far more than pretending to strangle him.

Razor had no idea that Owen was in fact tying him up like a calf in the rodeo 'from hoof to head' before returning to the ring, leaving the tethered Bad Guy futilely squirming on the floor. Sensing that the match was falling apart, Shawn Michaels managed to untie his trussed up opponent while making it look like he was attacking him. After he was finally unravelled, Razor made it to his corner to tag Bret in for the contest's finishing sequence. Bret hit his patented series of moves on his joyful brother before grapevining Owen's legs to apply the Sharpshooter. "Owen was laughing so hard I could barely turn him over!" laughed Bret. "It struck me at that moment that the crowd was having an even better time than we were."

As amusing a situation as it was for all concerned, the microphone cord spot proved effective and Bret banked the idea for a future match. The match turned out to be the *Survivor Series 1995* main event, which saw Bret defeat Diesel to become a three time WWF Champion. Bret did not credit Owen in any future victory speech.

[1]The WWF was not the first American wrestling promotion broadcast in Israel. That distinction curiously goes to Dallas-based World Class Championship Wrestling back in the 1980s. WCCW became one of the most popular English language shows in the entire country during its run. WWF was taken off Israeli television in 1995 by the government after claims wrestling caused an upsurge in school violence. WWE programming would return to Israel in the 2000s.

[2]Marty would earn the dubious distinction of becoming WWE's most fired wrestler ever, with a total of eight times from 1987 to 2006. While most reasons for his various firings are well known (being under the influence, starting bar fights, being under house arrest after attacking a police officer), the February 1994 dismissal has never been confirmed. Some theorise that it was something to do with the upcoming civil suit being brought by former wrestler Charles Austin. Austin was paralysed on the 11th of December 1990 *WWF Superstars* taping after incorrectly taking Jannetty's Rocker Dropper finisher. Austin, who had only been wrestling for a few months, insisted he had taken the move many times. When Jannetty hit the Rock Dropper, Austin jumped and rolled as if it were a DDT instead of taking a flat front bump. Austin spiked himself head first into the mat, breaking his neck instantly. Austin's lawyer originally asked the jury for $3.8 million in damages but ended up winning a staggering $26.7 million. Both Austin and Jannetty were found to be 5% culpable, with Titan Sports, Inc. shouldering 90% of the legal and financial responsibility. "All WWE... had to do [was] pay his hospital bills," said Jannetty. "[Austin] wasn't looking to make money until [the WWE] fucked him over."

Car Rides with Owen:
What Was That Noise?

As told by Savio Vega and Sean Morley

Juan Rivera was a stalwart of the World Wrestling Federation from 1993 to 1999, debuting as the masked ninja Kwang, before re-debuting in 1995 as proud Puerto Rican Savio Vega, complete with salsa entrance music and fiery Latino temperament. Back in 1994 and still wrestling as the onomatopoeically named ninja, Vega, along with Owen and brother-in-law Jim 'The Anvil' Neidhart, finished up at a show in Allentown, Pennsylvania and were driving to the next stop on the tour, which was located in a more mountainous region.

With Savio at the helm, the trio travelled down the highway through a forested area when they saw a deer on the edge of the road. Savio clocked the deer and pointed it out to the brothers-in-law. As the speeding car passed the deer there was an almighty THWACK! that apparently came from the bumper. "OH MY GOD YOU HIT THE DEER, YOU KILLED IT!" screamed Owen. The distraught Puerto Rican pulled the car over and walked back to where he thought the deer's prone body would be lying, but couldn't find it. He searched around the entire area looking for it to no avail; all the while Owen was in hysterics, yelling, "OH MY GOD, YOU HIT IT!"

After a short while observing Savio combing the area for the deer's corpse, Neidhart decided he'd had enough of the charade. Years later, the man from Puerto Rico still remembered being let in on the rib. "Jim 'The Anvil' Neidhart looked at me and said, 'Come on, Savio, you're gonna believe him?'" Only then did the penny drop. Savio hadn't clipped the deer at all. Owen, who had his arm hanging out of the window, waited until the car was parallel to the deer and smacked the car's roof, creating an enormous thud. "Owen was a funny guy," said Vega, "he was a funny, funny guy and I miss him."

This wouldn't be the only occasion a whack on a car roof caused undue aggravation. In 1998/99, Owen and Jeff Jarrett were teaming together on-screen and were great friends and travel buddies off-screen too. The second generation wrestlers were being driven by an unknown driver (most likely one of Owen's cadre of fans) out of an arena. As the car was driving up a ramp from the arena's underground car park, Owen reached through the open window and smacked the car's roof. When the driver looked to Owen for answers, Owen immediately pointed to some random guy who was standing overhead and accused him of launching a rock at the car.

The driver was understandably furious that his car may have been damaged and sought revenge. "The guy stops the car on the ramp, gets out of the car, runs up the ramp, runs around the rail and charges at the guy Owen pointed at," said Sean 'Val Venis' Morley, who witnessed the scene. Luckily, a policeman, who had seen Owen hit the car roof, managed to step between the driver and the innocent bystander. "A cop steps out in front of the driver and says, 'Whoa, this guy didn't throw any rock, the guy with the blonde hair in the car hit the roof of your car with his hand.'" The driver turned back round to the car, where the blonde-haired Owen turned round to the also-blonde Jarrett and sincerely asked, "Jeff, why did you hit the top of the car?"

Interview with a Prankster

As told by Diana Hart and Bob Holliday

In 1993, Owen's sister, Diana, befriended Christina Neal, a music journalist based in England. Over the next few years Christina started developing an interest in professional wrestling and asked Diana to contact Owen to see if he'd be interested in being interviewed for a piece. Owen obliged and scheduled the interview to coincide with a WWF tour of the UK and arranged for Christina to meet him in his hotel room. Christina arrived in his hotel room at the allotted time and waited patiently. Owen emerged from the bathroom dressed in a t-shirt, tight trunks and what appeared to be a barber's pole bulging out of his gentleman's region.

When wrestlers and fans compare the size of wrestlers' tallywhackers (which happens far more than it should) names such as: Robert Fuller, 2 Cold Scorpio, Lanny Poffo and Virgil are often cited as having some of the more remarkable utensils in the business. Owen's name is never brought up in such intimate debates but on this day the journalist would have been willing to rank the youngest Hart among the Johnny Holmes' of the world for sheer magnitude. Owen sat at the edge of the hotel bed, stone-faced and cross-legged and asked Christina to proceed with her questions. "Oh my God! Is he for real?" the journalist thought to herself, before launching into her questions, hoping her face wouldn't give away how uncomfortable the whole situation was making her. After the interview, Owen let the blushing journalist in on the joke. While he was in the bathroom, Owen rolled up a small bath towel and shoved it in the front of his trunks to see if she'd find it funny. Christina, relieved, laughed at the prank and the two stayed in contact after the outlandish encounter.

When Owen wasn't weirding out journalists he'd only just met, he was pretending to be one on the phone. Bob Holliday was the local WWF promoter for the Winnipeg area when he received a phone call from a journalist purporting to be from *Prairie Home Living Magazine*. Owen had been crank calling wrestlers pretending to be from the very-much fictitious periodical, hassling the unsuspecting grapplers for 'being uncooperative' over giving interviews. Holliday ended up receiving a barrage of complaints about wrestlers from the imaginary correspondent, even though the Winnipeg promoter had no authority to force the wrestlers to do interviews. "Everybody was in on it," said Holliday. "He had me going for two days in St. Albert and Saskatoon."

Holliday was also present for another classic Owen rib. The day after the hugely successful *WrestleMania XV* pay-per-view, the WWF broadcast *RAW is WAR* live from East Rutherford, New Jersey on the 29th of March 1999. Holliday witnessed Owen walk up to the room where all the WWF's computer tech guys were hanging out and slide the bolt on the door, locking them in and causing a big panic. Owen did this because... well, why wouldn't he?

CHAPTER 6

Life After Bret and Camp Cornette

♥ ♥

Heading into 1995, the original booking direction for Owen was to keep him teamed up with brother-in-law Jim Neidhart, with the nefarious duo eventually winning the WWF Tag Team Championships from The Smoking Gunns. Off-screen, the clean-cut Owen was a good babysitter for the hard-partying Neidhart but Jim still managed to get himself fired again in January 1995 after no-showing several live events over the Christmas period. With booking plans having to be rearranged, Owen and Bret continued to face off in one-on-one matches on the house show circuit, this time performing in the middle of the card instead of in the main events. They would have one more 'last time ever' televised one-on-one match on *RAW* on the 27th of March 1995, with Bret beating Owen by submission in a no disqualification match, officially ending their year long programme. Unsurprisingly, the *Action Zone* match, which was also billed as the 'last time ever' was not their last.

The brother vs. brother rivalry wouldn't be resolved completely until 1997 but Owen vs. Bret was no longer the main focal point of Federation programming. Bret was shunted down the card to the position of number three babyface behind new WWF Champion Diesel and soon-to-be babyface Shawn Michaels. Owen would be dropped even further down the pecking order than Bret. As an example of how far from the main event Owen would be booked, look no further than January 1995's Royal Rumble match. Owen would last a grand total of three seconds[1] before being eliminated by his brother-in-law and that year's runner-up Davey Boy Smith. On the bright side, Owen was probably over the moon to be paid pay-per-view money for so little work.

Heading toward the *WrestleMania XI* pay-per-view, Owen teased a mystery tag team partner to go head-to-head to challenge for the WWF Tag Team Championships held by The Smoking Gunns. Come the big day, Owen announced that his mystery partner had achieved what he'd always wanted to do; beat his brother Bret for the WWF Championship. The mystery partner would be the returning Yokozuna, along with managers Mr Fuji and Jim Cornette.

Yokozuna hadn't been seen in the WWF in four months and only had one tune-up match prior to his WWF return, losing to Genichiro Tenryu in Tokyo for the Japanese WAR promotion. During his four month period of inactivity, Yoko also managed to put on even more weight. The odd-couple tag team won the Tag Titles at the 10:00 mark, with Yoko doing more than his fair share of work while looking like he was about to keel over from exhaustion throughout.[2] The tag team would become the first two members of the WWF's latest heel stable, Camp Cornette, with the eponymous Jim as leader. Owen and Yokozuna successfully defended the WWF Tag Team Titles against 1-2-3 Kid and Bob Holly on *RAW* a couple of weeks later. Over the course of the next few months they would defend their belts against The Smoking Gunns, Razor Ramon and Savio Vega and the newly-dubbed Allied Powers; 'British Bulldog' Davey Boy Smith and 'The Total Package' Lex Luger.

Owen would take occasional breaks from tag team action to compete in the singles ranks during this time. On the 5th of June episode of *WWF RAW*, Owen and the British Bulldog had a great match to qualify for the *King of the Ring* tournament. Both of these all-time great workers were eliminated when the time limit expired, so neither advanced to the pay-per-view. The only big stars to make it to the quarter finals, Shawn Michaels and The Undertaker, were also quickly eliminated. This left only awful wrestlers and marginal stars to compete on what turned out to be one of the worst pay-per-view events in Federation history. The lack of star power cleared the way for 500lb human waterbed and in-ring liability Nelson 'Mable' Frazier Jr to take the crown and battle WWF Champion Diesel in the *SummerSlam* main event.[3]

Thanks to an invitation from Bret, Owen wrestled an untelevised tryout match with his old friend from Stampede Chris Benoit on the 7th of June *Wrestling Challenge* TV taping. At the time, Benoit was not only one of the best wrestlers in the world but also a free agent. Since his Stampede days, Benoit built his reputation in New Japan Pro Wrestling where he was a one-time IWGP Junior Heavyweight Champion, two-time Super Juniors tournament winner and one-time Super J-Cup winner. Benoit's only recent exposure in the United States was from his appearances in regional hardcore promotion Extreme Championship Wrestling. ECW was going through turmoil at the time both management and talent-wise. ECW, who had no idea Chris Benoit was trying out for the WWF, were potentially losing not only the 'Canadian Crippler' but also their former Heavyweight Champion Shane Douglas who was also present at the TV taping. Owen and Benoit put on the best match of the night by far and made a big impression on the crowd. The WWF made Benoit an offer which included time off to tour with New Japan. Benoit passed, not only because the money offer was too low but because at around 5'9", there was no way the WWF was going to give him a serious push. Benoit headed off to WCW later that year, where he was immediately put with Ric Flair and the revived Four Horsemen group.

At *In Your House 2* on the 23rd of July, Owen and Yokozuna scored a major upset when they successfully defended their tag team belts against number one contenders Lex Luger and Davey Boy Smith. Unbeknownst to the audience at the time, Davey was on the cusp of turning heel to set up a WWF Championship match against Diesel. Lex, whose Federation contract had long since expired, was preparing to jump to WCW shortly thereafter.

Owen's next major pay-per-view appearance was at *In Your House 3* on the 24th of September (he was left off the *SummerSlam* card). WWF Tag Team Champions Owen and Yokozuna squared off against WWF Heavyweight Champion Diesel and WWF Intercontinental Champion Shawn Michaels in the 'Triple Header' main event. In what was a unique stipulation for the WWF, whoever lost the fall would lose their belt to the match winner. At the beginning of the pay-per-view, it was announced that Owen Hart was not in the arena and manager Jim Cornette would have to find a replacement. It was touch and go whether Owen would even make the pay-per-view, as he was determined to be at Martha's bedside for the birth of their second child, Athena. "Athena was the apple of his eye," smiled Martha, "they were just so connected." After learning of the birth of Owen's daughter, Bret decided to get his own back and told everybody in the locker room that Owen had named his daughter after their father Stu. "It was kind of funny how mad he got when everybody kept congratulating him on the birth of his daughter Stuella," recalled Bret.

Fifteen minutes into the Yoko and Bulldog vs. Diesel and Michaels main event, Owen sprang out from the backstage area to attack Diesel, only to receive a Jackknife Powerbomb for his efforts. Despite being officially replaced in the match by the Bulldog, Owen was pinned and Diesel and Michaels were declared the new WWF Tag Team Champions. Owen had raced to catch the last flight out of Calgary to Michigan, arriving just in time to interfere in the main event. Owen was bed side for the birth of his daughter but the demanding WWF schedule forced him to leave the hospital soon after, leaving Martha to drive herself, their new baby and their 3½-year-old son Oje home on her own. "Obviously it wasn't his choice to leave but then, it wasn't his choice to be a wrestler either," said Martha. "That was just the way it was. It was tough on both of us."

The next day on *WWF RAW*, Jim Cornette's attorney Clarence Mason (Herman Stevens Jr in his WWF debut) got the match's decision reversed by WWF President Gorilla Monsoon and Owen and Yokozuna were once again declared Tag Team Champions. As a concession to the fans, Monsoon booked Owen and Yoko to defend the Titles that evening against The Smoking Gunns, a pair of kayfabe brothers working a bland cowboy gimmick. Commentator Jerry Lawler suggested that Billy and Bart Gunn were mentally scarred as children after the cancellation of the television show *Gunsmoke* before humorously speculating that Owen might have been late for his big pay-per-view match because his wife was giving birth (which, of course, was the real reason). The Smoking Gunns defeated Owen and Yoko clean in the middle of the ring, bringing to an end their several hour reign.

For the rest of the year, Owen would split his time tagging with Yoko and Camp Cornette's newest member, the British Bulldog, as well as wrestling in singles matches. "It was a unique contrast," recalled Owen when asked about Yokozuna in 1998. "The big, big monster and the littler high-flyer. So I wouldn't mind [teaming up], we got along real good. He was a nice guy and a fine, fine guy to tag up with."

Owen's most significant storyline of 1995 occurred on the 20th of November in Richmond, Virginia. Shawn Michaels was returning for his first singles bout since the 14th of October. In the early hours of that day, Michaels was legitimately beaten up so badly that the head injuries he received forced him out of action for several weeks. Shawn, Davey and Sean '1-2-3- Kid' Waltman were travelling from Binghamton, New York and headed to Syracuse for a show the next day. The trio loaded up on Soma painkillers and headed to Club 37. Their presence caused a stir at the club and when an obnoxious, half-cut Michaels cracked on to a young lady at the club, her overprotective ex-boyfriend Corporal Douglas Griffith took exception, leading to tensions escalating.

Shortly afterwards, the inebriated Davey, Waltman and a sober wrestling fan carried the passed out Michaels to the fan's car to get a lift to their hotel. Corporal Griffith, along with a couple of his military buddies (numbers vary on how many), followed the wrestlers outside and started causing trouble. After words and drunken punches were flailed, Griffiths yanked Michaels from the car, slammed the car door on his head and proceeded to put the boots to him while the intoxicated Waltman and Davey struggled to exit the vehicle to help. After the bouncers and the non-comatose wrestlers eventually got the upper hand on the jealous jarheads, Michaels was taken to hospital where he was treated for a concussion, cuts, bruises, swelling and a torn eyelid.[4]

Shawn's injuries would keep him out of the ring for a number of weeks. As the reigning WWF Intercontinental Champion (the second most important position in the promotion) and headliner of the WWF's domestic touring group (the other half of the roster was in Germany), the WWF decided to semi-acknowledge the real-life circumstances to explain his absence. The WWF claimed 'nine thugs' had taken Shawn out, which was a complete lie, but his very real concussion and recovery was acknowledged on WWF programming for weeks leading up to the Owen match.

On the 20th of November live *RAW*, Owen faced off against Shawn Michaels in the main event with both men putting on a wrestling clinic. Around eleven minutes into the encounter, Owen hit Michaels with his patented Enzuigiri kick to the back of Michaels' head. Shawn quickly fought back, gaining the upper-hand before clotheslining Owen out of the ring. Shawn hit a pose for the crowd, then all of a sudden grabbed his head and fell to the canvas, apparently from the Enzuigiri kick he had absorbed minutes earlier. Michaels had already returned to the house show circuit on the 3rd of November, competing in six-man tag team matches to take some of the workload off his shoulders and ease him back to full-time competition. In these untelevised matches, Michaels feigned dizziness in an effort to foreshadow his collapsing on *RAW*.

After Michaels passed out, the WWF went out of their way to convince viewers that the situation was no mere wrestling storyline. Instead of going after his downed opponent, Owen stood around confused, almost apologetic, before *RAW* went to commercial break. When *RAW* came back on air, Owen was gone and the ring was filled with EMTs and Federation officials. Vince McMahon, who almost never acknowledged his role as owner of the WWF on his television shows, left the commentary table to tend to Michaels in a bid to convince 'insider' fans that this was no mere storyline. The usually ubiquitous commentary was eliminated to heighten confusion. Michaels, who was having oxygen administered in the ring, was even taken to a real hospital for real scans. The true nature of the planned series of events was only known to the match participants, the commentators and The Kliq, who helped shape the storyline for maximum authenticity.[5] The angle was concocted for three reasons:

1 - Knocking out Michaels would give Owen's career a much needed shot in the arm.
2 - After being on the road for over a week, Michaels felt that he'd rushed back to the ring too soon and needed more time off.
3 - The WWF needed a hot storyline to counter *WCW Nitro's* main event, featuring a Hulk Hogan vs. Sting dream match.

Since WCW debuted *Nitro* in the exact same time slot as *WWF RAW* in September, the two companies had fought an all-out war for ratings supremacy. While *RAW* lost the ratings war the night of Shawn's passing out, *RAW* defeated *Nitro* in the ratings the week after, proving the effectiveness of the angle.

The next week on *RAW*, Jim Cornette and Owen Hart (who was clearly standing on a box to appear taller) expressed their pride in eliminating Shawn Michaels and challenged anybody on the roster to face Owen at the *In Your House 5* pay-per-view on the 17th of December. The challenge was accepted by Diesel, who had lost the WWF Championship to Bret Hart the month prior. After getting pinned at *Survivor Series '95*, the babyface Diesel had shown himself to be a poor sport and hit Bret with two Jackknife Powerbombs after the match, marking the starting point in his heel turn. At *IYH 5*, Diesel destroyed Owen for the most part, before shoving the referee down and hitting a second powerbomb on Owen. Owen technically won the match after Diesel was disqualified but the match further highlighted the fact that Owen was now firmly entrenched in the mid-card, having been a headliner the year before.

[1]Owen's elimination wouldn't even be a unique spot in the match, as Men on a Mission's Mo was *also* eliminated in three seconds, this time courtesy of King Kong Bundy.

[2]Rodney 'Yokozuna' Anoa'i's weight at the time of his 1992 WWF debut was under 500lbs. By 1996, Yoko ballooned to over 700lbs before topping 800lbs late in his life, making him the heaviest pro wrestler in the history of the business. The WWF eventually took Yoko off TV to send him to fat camp before reluctantly firing him in 1997. Soon after, New York's State Athletic Commission suspended Yoko's licence, making him practically unemployable (WCW made a serious play for him in early 1999 but nothing came of it). Yokozuna would spend the last few years of his life making sporadic appearances on the indies before dying in his sleep of a pulmonary oedema in Liverpool, England on the 23rd of October 2000. He was 34.

[3]Diesel vs. Mabel was pretty awful, as expected. Aside from Bret, Kevin 'Diesel' Nash had been handed one stinky opponent after another to work with since becoming WWF Champion. Nash received an elbow injury after landing badly courtesy of a Sid powerbomb in May. During the August *SummerSlam* match with Mabel, Diesel was lying face down on the mat when Mabel kicked his legs out and drove all his weight down in the small of Nash's back. Nash suffered torn abdominal muscles and nearly didn't finish the match. After hurting so many other wrestlers, this was Mabel's last chance to prove he could work safely. "They were going to fire him on the spot," said Nash. "Vince gave him his papers right there. I said 'Whoa, whoa, whoa! That ain't gonna happen. You ain't gonna fire him.'" Mabel was fired a few months later.

[4]The rest of Shawn's 'Kliq' had helped calm similar situations down before a fight broke out but Diesel, Razor and Helmsley were all in Germany at the time. The Kliq were upset at Davey for not helping more but not only was Davey inebriated, he was stuck in the backseat of the two-door car while Shawn was getting his head stoved in. Vince McMahon was not only furious that Shawn had made the wrestling business look weak, McMahon was upset that the babyface Michaels and heel Davey disregarded kayfabe and were out partying together when they were headlining shows against each other on that very loop. Davey and Michaels were also booked to be the main event the next evening. Michaels' ex-tag team partner Marty Jannetty took his place that night in Syracuse.

[5]Hospitals in the Richmond, Virginia area were bombarded with phone calls from Shawn Michaels fans wanting news on the condition of the Heartbreak Kid. Fans needn't have bothered blindly ringing around, as the World Wrestling Federation helpfully provided updates on Shawn's 'medical condition' on their premium rate 900 number. WWF ran weekly updates on Michaels, as well as playing a tribute video to his career set to a maudlin ditty entitled *Tell Me a Lie* sung by Fonda Feingold and produced by WWF in-house music impresario Jim

Johnston. Shawn of course, made a full recovery and returned to win the January '96 Royal Rumble match.

Hog Wild

As told by Jim Ross, Bret Hart, Jimmy Korderas, etc.

During the mid '90s wrestling depression, the World Wrestling Federation was under severe financial stress, losing $4.43 million during the 1994-95 fiscal year. WCW was buying up all available major and minor former WWF stars in an effort to compete and Vince McMahon was under pressure to generate extra revenue to remain in business. Along with the oft-mentioned overseas tours, McMahon's other successful money generating idea would be partly inspired by WCW's pay-per-view structure. When WCW announced they were stepping up to ten pay-per-view events for 1995 and raising the price to $27.50,[1] the WWF reacted by announcing monthly pay-per-view events. McMahon concocted a bunch of hare-brained schemes to lure fans into buying these shows, including giving away an *actual* house on the first *In Your House* event in May 1995[2] and promoting all manner of speciality matches, among other whacky concepts.

One of the most infamous of these speciality matches would occur on the 17th of December 1995 at *In Your House 5.*[3] On the undercard of the Bret Hart vs. British Bulldog main event, Connecticut blue blood Hunter Hearst Helmsley took on pig farmer Henry O Godwinn in a 'Hog Pen match'. The first (and last) of its kind, the wrestler to be thrown in the hog pen first would be declared the loser. To put on a hog pen match, the WWF needed a pen and, of course, some hogs. With the pen being built on the arena floor, the live pigs were loaded on to a delivery truck and were on route to Hersheypark arena.

When the pig truck arrived that afternoon, a WWF rep was there to greet the farmer and take the pigs off his hands. Since the pigpen wasn't fully constructed yet, the unnamed crew member needed to find temporary accommodation for the rented farm animals. That's when Owen and WWF's Director of Photography Steve Taylor happened to show up, claiming they knew exactly where the pigs needed to be housed. With Vince McMahon and all the agents behind closed doors for a production meeting, Owen confidently led Steve Taylor, the farmer and no less than eight fully grown pigs down the corridors of Hersheypark arena towards the pigpen in full view of the wrestlers and other WWF employees. The motley crew were nearly at the *In Your House* stage set when Owen happened on a particular door at the end of the hallway. Owen opened the door with one hand while surreptitiously holding up the other in such a way as to obscure the sign affixed to the front, then directed the farmer to leave his pigs inside the room. After all the pigs entered the makeshift accommodation, Owen shut the door, then considerately walked the farmer back to his truck.

Curiosity got the better of some who witnessed the pig procession march through the corridors and went to inspect which room they were locked away in. All who went up to the door immediately realised why Owen had gone to such lengths to conceal the sign taped to the door, which read 'Vince's Office.' Rumours quickly circulated backstage. Most who learned of the situation experienced two emotions. Former WWE referee Jimmy Korderas recounted, "Once it became evident, everyone was laughing and terrified at the same time. What if Vince thought that the crew had put them in there?"

While the crew were discussing whether to move the pigs into another room, the production meeting let out for lunch and McMahon made his way back to his office. No one tried to stop him as he opened the door to witness eight porcine occupants rooting around his personal possessions. "There was crap everywhere and pigs were knocking into his briefcase," said Bret, who witnessed the carnage left behind. "They knocked over all the furniture and crapped on the rug. It was just so funny."

Jim Ross, who was also in the production meeting, witnessed the pigs in the office and McMahon's reaction. "I had to do an interview with the winner [of the hog pen match]. Of course you know I'm going to be wearing the hog manure, so I wore bib overalls over my suit and a big ol' pair of knee high rubber boots like a farmer would wear. I had as many clothes on as I could get because I knew the pig manure was coming my way 'cause the heel Triple H was going over. I remember that Owen was directing traffic and by the time that Vince got there that office smelled like a barn; like a menagerie. There were more different kinds of animal manure in that office than you could ever imagine and I don't know how you'd ever get the smell out of it. It was just absolutely hilarious, though. That's what [Owen] did."[4]

Mercifully for Owen and the rest of his employees, Vince took the rib well. There was even a photo of McMahon published in *WWF Magazine* where he's seen laughing as he escorts the pigs out of his office, while clutching on to the dry-cleaned tuxedo he would be wearing on-camera that night. Many years after the incident, McMahon himself said "[Owen] would just think it was hilarious, as if I didn't know who it was. When you go to him, Owen didn't know anything; he had no idea. He'd give you that innocent look [and say], 'I don't know!' He was so good he could almost convince you that he really didn't have anything to do with it." In regards to Owen's targets when it came to pranks, Bruce Prichard succinctly summed up the youngest Hart's attitude. "Owen didn't give a shit; he did not discriminate when it came to ribs."

[1]WCW raising pay-per-view prices to $27.50 ($32.50 for same day orders) was to help offset Hulk Hogan's earth-shatteringly enormous contract, which included $300,000 per match, 65% of his merchandise sales and 25% of pay-per-view revenue above the WCW average.

[2]11-year-old Matthew Pomposelli was picked as the winner from a purported 340,000 applicants and was called live on the pay-per-view to be told the good news. Matthew took part in some vignettes wandering around his new house with The Bushwhackers and other wrestlers before selling the property just six months later for a cool $175,000, which went towards his university education.

[3]In the early years, most of the important storyline developments and title changes would be saved for the more established (and expensive) pay-per-view events. For example, the World Wrestling Federation Championship, which was frequently defended on these shows, only changed hands twice in the twenty-eight *In Your House* events. The first title switch was at *IYH 13: Final Four* in February 1997 after the WWF Title was made vacant and therefore someone *had* to win the belt in order to set up the *WrestleMania* event the next month. The only other title switch occurred at September 1998's *IYH: Breakdown* event where

Undertaker and Kane simultaneously pinned Steve Austin. Neither of the two victors actually won the belt. It was vacated and held up for two straight months during the Federation's hottest ever period.

[4]The other, mostly forgotten by-product of the hog pen match, was Paul 'Hunter Hearst Helmsley' Levesque getting physically scarred for life during the farcical encounter. Helmsley's back was sliced up in several places after Henry O Godwinn Irish-whipped him into the hog pen's metal gate, which had barb wire wrapped around it. The future Triple H was then military pressed into the pig slop, before Henry O threw globs of muck and pig winnits into his fresh wounds. When Triple H and Kevin Nash feuded in 2003, Nash discovered that Helmsley still had the scars across his back from the pig match eight years prior.

168

Car Rides with Owen: Driving Lex Luger Mad

As told by Lex Luger, Davey Boy Smith, etc.

Of all the stories collated for this book, the following rib stands out as the most rigorously planned and perfectly executed. Even though the prank was led by Davey Boy Smith, Owen had a hand in escalating the joke further, if not co-orchestrating the entire scenario.

One half of the Allied Powers and Davey's tag team partner, Lex Luger, had somewhat of a reputation as a fast driver and occasionally went over the speed limit, especially when racing to the next stop on a tour. "Fans always milled around [the arena] wanting autographs and Lex would take off as quickly as he could," explained former road agent George Steele.

During another interminable *WWF Wrestling Challenge* television taping in North Charleston, West Virginia,[1] Davey Boy decided to delight himself by squirting everyone around him with a water pistol. At one point, the Bulldog was mingling in amongst a group of wrestlers when he covertly sprayed a pair of plain clothes police officers who were stood a short distance away. Davey then quickly concealed the watery weapon out of view. When the group of wrestlers dispersed, the irritable officers walked up to Davey and Owen and asked if they knew who squirted them. Davey lied and told the drenched detectives that Lex Luger was the perpetrator. "We would like to get him," said one of the patrolmen. After some careful thought, the Bulldog told them that he and Owen would be travelling with Lex after the show and that Lex would be driving. That would be the perfect time to get revenge on 'The Total Package'.

After a successful night in the ring (the Allied Powers defeated Tatanka and King Kong Bundy, in case you were interested) Lex, Davey and Owen all piled into their rental car to drive to the next destination.[2] The plain clothes policemen closely followed them in their unmarked car as Lex exited the Charleston Civic Center car park and onto the I-64 Highway. Luger, who according to Davey was, "Notorious for driving through stop signs and red lights," was driving very courteously that evening, giving the policemen no reason to pull him over. To expedite the situation, Davey, who was sat in the front passenger seat, yanked hard on the steering wheel and jerked the car across the lanes of the highway. When Lex rebuked the Bulldog for his actions, Davey motioned to the unmarked cop car behind them claiming it was Shawn Michaels and he wanted to race him. Lex took on the challenge and sped up, giving the police probable cause to pull him over.

Lex had only driven a short distance before the policemen deployed their siren and pulled the 'All-American' over. The cops walked to the driver's side and demanded the jittery Luger's driving licence and registration. Lex, who really didn't want another speeding ticket, explained that they were wrestlers trying to escape the throng of autograph hunting fans surrounding the arena. After the officers walked back to their unmarked car to pretend to check on Lex's details, Bulldog yelled out in a quasi-American accent, "BLOW IT OUT YOUR ASS!" "Lex just about swallowed his tongue," recalled Owen's brother Bret. In varying versions of the story, Davey and/or Owen may have also yelled out, "FUCK YOU!" to the cops once or twice while they were checking Lex's details. The cops stormed back to the rent-a-car where a shell-shocked Luger vehemently protested his innocence with cries of, "It wasn't me! It wasn't me!" The cops turned to Owen who was sat in the back as innocent as a choir boy and asked him who shouted the obscenity. "Well Davey [and Owen are] going to own up to it that they cussed him," hoped Lex. "They [both] pointed at me. I'm looking at Owen and Davey and now I'm panicking. Now I know I'm going to jail for sure!"

The undercover policemen made Lex get out of the car and assume the position, with ten fingers on the fender and legs spread apart. One of the patrolmen was frisking Luger when they saw he had an unusual object concealed in the waistline of his sweatpants. The cop lifted Luger's shirt to inspect further before yelling, "HE'S GOT A GUN!" During the madness of getting pulled over, Davey managed to slip his water pistol into Luger's Zubaz workout pants. While Luger laid a red, white and blue egg at the thought of the policemen drawing their firearms on him, the Bulldog started to feel compassion and tried to put an end to the prank. When Davey got out of the car to call the off the crooked cops, Luger pleaded, "Davey, get back in the car, you're making things worse!"

At that point the jig was up and Davey, Owen and the undercover cops fell about laughing. So did Vince McMahon, who happened to be following the procession in his limo. The WWF owner watched from afar with glee as poor Lex was being traumatised on the side of the road. A number of fans also got to witness the charade due to the police pulling Lex's car over so close to the arena. With the benefit of hindsight, Lex paid tribute to both Owen and the British Bulldog. "[Davey] set the whole thing up, this elaborate thing involving the police officers... [And] I'm their buddy! So that's just one little thing they concocted on me travelling with them. Overall [they were] just incredibly hilarious."

[1]Davey Boy claimed the rib took place in Virginia and Lex Luger claimed it was Charleston, South Carolina. Neither location is possible as Luger, Davey and Owen all had to be on the same card, as well as Vince McMahon, who usually only turned up to televised tapings and occasionally to shows in the tri-state area. It is most likely the rib took place in North Charleston, West Virginia, where the WWF taped *Wrestling Challenge* on the 22nd of Feb 1995.

[2]While Owen was on-screen rivals with Davey and Luger, he and many of the wrestlers had given up on the notion of kayfabe by the mid '90s. Only a few years prior, on-screen rivals Jim Duggan and The Iron Sheik were arrested on the New Jersey Parkway when the police found cannabis and cocaine in their car. Any hopes of keeping the arrest a secret went out the window when the 28th of May 1987 edition of the New York Daily News ran the headline 'Boozing Bozos' with a picture of the wrestling rivals. WWF boss Vince McMahon was reportedly more upset that the adversaries were caught together in public than for the possession collar and summarily fired them. McMahon called a meeting at the 2nd of June *WWF Superstars* taping where he announced that Duggan and Sheik would never be seen in the WWF again, declaring, "This business is bigger than a six pack and a blow job!"

Both Duggan and Sheik were brought back to the company after a few months.

Prank Phone Calls:
First Call with Scott Hall

As told by Triple H

Unlike WWF domestic tours where wrestlers were responsible for their own travel arrangements,[1] on foreign tours, transport and accommodation was pre-arranged by the WWF. Two buses would be provided for the performers and staff, one for the baby faces and one for the heels, so on-screen rivals were kept apart in public to maintain the integrity of the business. Of course, arguments can be made that the WWF's booking of: wrestling clowns, Indians, evil taxmen, Puerto Rican ninjas and nuclear meltdown survivors caused more harm to professional wrestling's sporting legitimacy than the co-mingling of heroes and villains but that's a debate for another book.

On one of these never ending European loops, the wrestlers, including Scott 'Razor Ramon' Hall, made the traditional post-event pilgrimage to the hotel bar. Fellow Kliq[2] member Paul 'Hunter Hearst Helmsley' Levesque described his long time friend as a sullen and lugubrious figure, endlessly dragging his bottom along the ground and complaining about the World Wrestling Federation's tour schedule. Hall, who was likened by some of his comrades to Eeyore the Donkey, also had an established reputation for being notoriously late for the bus; being overly slow to get ready to set off to the next destination.

Weary from the rigours of the road, Hall left the hotel bar early and headed up to his room for a good night's rest. A couple of hours after he retired for the evening, a dishevelled Hall was witnessed by Helmsley (and the majority of the Federation crew who were still at the bar) running through the lobby heading towards the checkout desk with his bags half packed and looking a complete mess. Before Hall managed to hurriedly check out of the hotel, the self-described 'Man More Handsome Than Ten Movie Stars' turned round and bore witness to the congregation of WWF employees that were still convening around the bar. Hall grumbled to himself, "...Fucking Owen," before shambling back up to his hotel room, a defeated man.

Why Hall felt the need to evacuate the hotel shortly after arriving was due to a frantic phone call he received from road agent Sergeant Rene Goulet who, in his imitable French-Canadian accent, informed 'The Bad Guy' that he was late for the bus and holding everybody up. "RAZOR, WHAT DA FUCK, YA KNOW, COME ON, DE BUS, EVERY FUCKIN' DAY WE WAIT FOR YOU, EVERY DAY, COME ON, GODDAMNIT, YOU GODDA GET DOWN 'ERE, WE HOLD DE BUS FOR FIVE MINUTES BUT YOU GODDA COME NOW... *NOW!*"

Unfortunately for Razor 'The Moan' (as some had taken to calling him in the latter stages of his WWF tenure), the trouble with Rene Goulet's accent being imitable was that many wrestlers *actually* imitated him. This included Owen, who waited for a suitable period of time for The Bad Guy to fall asleep before calling up Hall's hotel room and rousting him out of bed with Rene's familiar French Canadian accent, claiming they were going to leave him in the middle of god knows where unless he was down in the lobby in five minutes flat. The fact that as soon as the dishevelled Ramon arrived in the lobby and immediately realised it was Owen who placed the crank call, suggests that this wasn't the first instance he had found himself being fooled by the King of Pranks.

[1]Aside from marquee talent savvy enough to negotiate first-class tickets and hotels into their contracts, WWE talent continue to pay for their own accommodation, rental cars, food and various other road expenses out of their own pocket. You know, because they're 'independent' contractors who aren't allowed to wrestle for any other company.

[2]The Kliq were an off-screen group of friends comprised of: Shawn Michaels, Kevin 'Diesel' Nash, Scott 'Razor Ramon' Hall, Sean '1-2-3 Kid' Waltman and later, Paul 'Triple H' Levesque. Others such as PJ 'Aldo Montoya' Polaco and Louis Spicolli (Louis Mucciolo Jr who portrayed Rad Radford in the WWF) were claimed to be ancillary members of the group. The Kliq were said to influence WWF booking decisions to benefit only themselves, bully certain members of the roster

and generally cause issues behind the scenes; leading to low locker room morale during the WWF's most fiscally discouraging years. Michaels, Hall and Nash originally asked Bret Hart to be their leader during an earlier tour of Germany but he declined. When Nash, Hall and Waltman left for WCW, all five Kliq members would flash the 'wolf hand' gesture on WWF and WCW television. This was their code acknowledging their real-life friendship across company lines. Louis Spicolli, who used the gesture in ECW after he was fired from the WWF, claimed shortly before his death that the Kliq had actually stolen the hand signal from Bret Hart.

Shane Douglas Tanning Salon

As told by Shane Douglas

By the mid 1990s, Troy 'Shane Douglas' Martin was the top heel in the upstart Extreme Championship Wrestling promotion. He'd won the promotion's top belt and developed a reputation as an excellent talker, memorably challenging WCW's Ric Flair to a showdown for months on end.[1] In spring 1995, Shane, in what he once described as, "The worst career decision that I made," entered into negotiations to return to the World Wrestling Federation.[2] Since Vince McMahon paid no attention to the wrestling world outside of his own company and never saw any of Douglas' dynamic ECW interviews, he set about creating a brand new character for the self-styled 'Franchise.'

Since practically every WWF wrestler in the mid '90s had to have an occupation-based gimmick,[3] McMahon delved into Shane's past and discovered that he'd previously worked as a teacher in Beaver, Pennsylvania. Shane Douglas was re-imagined as Dean Douglas, The Dean of Wrestling; a career-killing character that bore no resemblance to his previously successful persona. Out went the fantastic promos, foul language and intense Franchise character and in came the educationally pun-laden interviews, aqua-coloured singlet adorned with a giant exclamation mark, flowing gown and spankin' paddle identified as the 'Board of Education.'

Fast-forwarding to October, during yet another stop on yet another European tour, the wrestlers were staying in an unknown town in Eastern Germany. Douglas, along with Owen Hart and some other wrestlers, decided to kill some time and took a stroll from their hotel to a tanning salon a short distance away. When Shane had finished tanning, he headed to the reception area and asked the lady behind the desk if she'd seen Owen walk by. The receptionist confirmed that Owen had already finished and already left. As Shane exited the tanning salon into the car park, he saw Owen about hundred yards ahead of him surrounded by around fifty overenthusiastic, autograph-hunting German WWF fans.

Despite being a bad guy and having only appeared on WWF programming for a few months, the rabid wrestling fans were all eagerly waiting for 'The Dean of Wrestling' to come out of the salon. As soon as Shane poked his head out of the door, the WWF devotees made a beeline towards him, cheering all the way with autograph books and markers in hand. The last thing Shane saw before being engulfed by the crazed admirers was Owen with a big smile on his face, waving at him before jogging off back towards the safety of the hotel. Somehow, Owen had conveyed to the foreign group of die-hards that wrestling superstar and his *nicht gut, lausig bruder* Bret had just popped in for a tanning session: the fans fell for it.

What makes the situation curious is that Shane Douglas and Bret Hart look absolutely nothing like each other. Apart from being a similar height, the short-haired, bottle-blonde Douglas bore no resemblance to the long, dark, curly-haired Bret. Somehow, Owen overcame the sizeable language barrier to successfully employ the power of suggestion, deflecting the annoying super fans towards Douglas while he ran back to the hotel.

While Douglas, as well as the fans, was the recipient of a decent Owen rib, there was a silver lining to be found by the 'Smartest Man in Wrestling.' For the only time during his abysmal six month tenure, Shane knew what it felt like to actually be *over* with WWF fans, even if it was just for a few seconds. Douglas went on to lose every match on the German tour before sustaining a severe back injury and requesting, and receiving, a release from his WWF contract eighteen months earlier than stipulated.

[1]Douglas' constant burials of Flair on ECW television were to capitalise on legitimate bad blood between the two, stemming from their time together in WCW. Shane hoped to set up a series of box-office interpromotional ECW vs. WCW battles, which he would eventually win 2-1. After initially agreeing, Flair had a change of heart and plans for the feud ultimately fell through. Shane and Ric would eventually wrestle each other in the dying days of WCW.

[2]Before jumping to the WWF the first time, Shane Douglas wrestled in WCW as a neon-bedecked skateboarder (who never actually rode the skateboard) along with his tag team partner Johnny 'Ace' Laurinaitis,

forming The Dynamic Dudes. The duo quickly became the most hated tag team in WCW, which was a problem as they were booked to be the good guys. In August 1990, Shane threw away his skateboard, wayfarers and Day-Glo baseball cap for good and signed on with the WWF. Vince McMahon saw something in the young Douglas and set to work coming up with a modern rock 'n' roll gimmick for him to portray. Alas, 'Shane Bon Jovi' was never to be, as real-life tragedy befell his family. Douglas' dad was struck down by emphysema, which would ultimately kill him. Shane put his family first and gave up on a potentially lucrative WWF run so he could go home and care for his ailing father.

[3] WWF's litany of occupational gimmicks in the early to mid 1990s include: wrestling stockcar racers, hockey players, baseball players, repo men, tax men, moon men, magicians, models, mimes, clowns, cannibals, bull riders, bull fighters, bulls, sultans, kings, aristocrats, pirates, policemen, convicts, monks, soldiers, plumbers, dustmen, dentists, drug dealers, alligator hunters, undertakers, morticians, anti-Santas, hog farmers, rodeo cowboys, country music singers and, in the case of 'Portuguese Man O'War' Aldo Montoya, both a jellyfish *and* a facial jockstrap model. Even though it was never the intention, the amusing irony was that during one of the Federation's most fiscally turbulent periods, Vince McMahon had populated the WWF with wrestlers who apparently needed to work second jobs to make ends meet.

Turnbuckle Shots

As told by Scott Hall

During a run of untelevised live events in 'some nothing happening town up in Canada', Scott Hall recalled one of his fondest Owen memories. The 'nothing happening town' Hall referred to was Moncton, New Brunswick, Canada; the date was the 1st of September 1995 and Owen would be in the ring with one of his favourite rib victims, 'The Total Package' Lex Luger. The match would pit the team of Luger and Shawn Michaels against Yokozuna and Owen Hart for the WWF Tag Team Championships of the world in front of a paltry 2000 paying fans.[1]

During the main event match, Owen called for a spot where Luger would take the youngest Hart sibling into a neutral corner and ram his head into the soft, cushioned padding tied to the turnbuckle. Every wrestling fan on the planet knows that if a strike occurs in a corner of the ring, it is universal law for the crowd to count along with every blow until the magic number ten is reached - It is a tried-and-true theory that audiences cannot resist enumerating along with blows to the head. This night in Moncton would go a little differently but the set up for the spot would be the same. The 'All-American' Luger grabbed hold of the mulleted hair on the back of Owen's head and proceeded to drive his face into the turnbuckle for the devastating ten blows. Conventional wrestling wisdom would dictate that after the tenth turnbuckle shot, Owen would take a big back bump towards the centre of the ring while Lex howled and flexed his muscles to elicit a positive crowd reaction.

Instead of the back bump/pose/yelp on the tenth strike, Lex, at Owen's insistence, kept thrusting Owen's head into the corner padding. Ten headshots into the turnbuckle became fifteen, then twenty, then twenty-five and so on, with Owen not looking to slow down any time soon. Lex, who at some point during this omnibus of concussive blows figured that Owen required no further assistance, took his hand off the back of Owen's head and put them on his hips. Lex completely broke character and laughed uproariously, watching Owen drive the side of his own head into the

179

turnbuckle pad unaided. The probably exhausted audience diligently counted along until Owen had head-butted the turnbuckle pad *fifty* times, after which, Owen took a big bump into the middle of the ring and the match continued as normal.

Some could look at this incident as Owen 'killing the town' by exposing wrestling as show business, but Owen's friends unanimously never saw it that way. When the brutal WWF schedule took the wrestlers thousands of miles away from home where it was easy to succumb to loneliness, it was moments like this when Owen's humour was treasured the most by his compadres. In tribute to Owen, Hall said of his long-time friend that, "[Owen] made it fun and without that, the road is a tough place to be."

[1]This would actually be Lex Luger's penultimate match with the WWF as, three days later he appeared live at the Mall of America to interrupt the Ric Flair vs. Sting match and confront Hulk Hogan on the debut edition of *WCW Monday Nitro*. With Luger's main event WWF push eighteen months in the rear view mirror, the stale 'All-American' had been languishing in WWF's tag team division for the majority of 1995 with the British Bulldog as The Allied Powers. Luger actually gave his ninety day notice to the WWF in December 1994 and had been working on a week to week basis for months. Luger's good friend Steve 'Sting' Borden eventually convinced the sceptical WCW Vice President Eric Bischoff that hiring Lex was a good idea. After talking with Sting and Lex himself, Bischoff offered Luger a contract for less money than he was currently making to no-show his remaining WWF dates and debut on *Nitro*. Lex's tag partner Davey Boy had just turned heel and was being groomed to challenge Diesel for the WWF Title. The booking direction looked to have Lex and Davey feud, with Davey coming out on top. Luger, who would have likely been further devalued by losing to Davey, saw the writing on the Federation wall and took the WCW deal. While Owen pulled a decent rib on Luger that night in Moncton, it was Luger that pulled an all-time classic rib on Vince McMahon just 3 days later.

Messy Headlocks
and Halcion Days

As told by Shane Douglas, Duke Droese, Brian Blair, etc.

Another story recounted by the former 'Smartest Man in Wrestling' Shane Douglas occurred during a WWF Tag Team Championship encounter between reigning champions Owen Hart and Yokozuna vs. The Allied Powers. While the Dean of Wrestling was in the backstage area (presumably grading the night's matches on his chalkboard), he witnessed one of the more unusual occurrences in the history of the World Wrestling Federation; Owen bypassing the opportunity to rib Lex Luger in order to get to his brother-in-law instead.

During an untelevised house show match in 1995, Owen set up Davey Boy by giving him a flying mare and then, while Davey was belly down on the canvas, cinching in a front chinlock to immobilise his head. While the Bulldog pretended he was in great discomfort, Owen reached into his singlet and smeared his hand across the Bulldog's face. Instead of writhing around in mock agony, the Bulldog uncharacteristically and frantically started swatting away at his mouth. While he still had Davey Boy in a compromising position, Owen once again reached into his singlet and smeared his hand all over Bulldog's face, this time with several swipes in a series of motions that made no sense in the context of the match.

Only when the bout concluded and Bulldog returned to the backstage area, did everything make sense to the guys in the locker room. According to Douglas, Davey Boy, who was screaming, throwing things around and generally causing a big scene; was wearing, "A beard with all kinds of shit on his face," including "coffee grounds, ground-up bananas… and three or four other things." Douglas would go on to describe Owen as, "A great guy, funny as hell; if you think of a Gremlin that would be Owen to a T."

This wasn't the first time Owen had played this incredibly specific rib on The Allied Powers. Shortly before Douglas arrived in the company, the WWF held several shows in the Philippines in May '95. Mike 'Duke The Dumpster' Drose, who was working Mark 'Henry O Godwinn' Canterbury on the show, remembered watching Owen's pre-match preparations before he and Yokozuna squared off against The Allied Powers in the semi-main. "Owen packed his tights with a bunch of hot, rotted fruit that was left over," said Drose, "watermelons, things like that and also coffee grounds I think he had in there. He had this stuff packed in a certain place in his tights." During the match, Owen went through the familiar routine of getting Lex down onto the mat and applying a chinlock. When Luger was incapacitated, Owen reached into his tights, grabbed a fistful of the disgusting concoction and ground it into Lex's face to the crowd's bewilderment. "The crowd had no clue what was going on, they didn't know; it was the Philippines... they didn't even know how to react; they were just sitting there stunned!"

It's unknown if Bulldog ever got Owen back for the rotting food beard but the fact that he got so riled up over a harmless rib could be viewed as a bit rich considering the destructive pranks Davey had been co-responsible for back in the 1980s. In years past, Davey Boy, supposedly under the influence of his older cousin 'Dynamite Kid' Tom Billington, was responsible for some of the harshest ribs ever inflicted in the history of the wrestling business. These include such smash hits as: throwing syringes at the bare backside of Stampede wrestler Tom Nash (who was also forced to do a handstand); cutting up various wrestlers' clothing; hurting wrestlers on purpose and spiking unsuspecting peoples' drinks with the powerful sleeping drug Halcion, before interfering with their unconscious bodies.

Owen's drink was spiked by the Bulldogs in 1988 while he was out partying with Bret, Jim Neidhart, Dynamite and Davey Boy. Owen didn't hit the town with the boys very often, rarely got drunk and never touched recreational drugs. According to his sister Diana, Owen couldn't figure out why anyone would spend good money getting drunk just to suffer with a hangover the next morning. On this night however, Owen decided to show face and fit in with the rest of the guys for the special occasion, which was being held in a blues club in Chicago. When Owen's attention was diverted, one of the Bulldogs plopped a Halcion in his drink. Soon after, he was slurring, falling over, passing out and had to be carried back to his room.

Owen was the butt of the jokes for the next few days with the wrestlers needling him about not being able to handle his alcohol. Owen got off easily though when compared to Peter 'Outback Jack' Stilsbury, who famously received the Halcion treatment more than once.

Some of the wrestlers decided to set up a drinking contest after a WWF show in the bar of the San Francisco Holliday Inn after the incredibly unpopular Aussie[1] claimed he could out-drink any Englishman. Sitting at the bar with Outback was: Mr Fuji, Davey, Dynamite and 'Killer Bee' Brian Blair, who witnessed the rib in progress. "Every time [Jack] would get a beer, one of the Bulldogs would get Outback's attention and the other would drop a Halcion... into Outback's beer." After unwittingly powering down depressant-laced beer after beer, Blair told Dynamite to stop before he poisoned the big Aussie to death. "No, no, no, I'm just going to give him five or six," came Dynamite's reply. After Outback collapsed, Blair, fellow 'Bee' Jim Brunzell and The Bulldogs carried Jack to his room, where the immobilised Aussie (correctly) accused Dynamite of spiking his drink. Dynamite was so offended he urinated on Outback's head before leaving him to fend for himself.

After Outback scraped himself up off the floor, he picked up the phone and called who he thought was his girlfriend for a little phone sex, but somehow found himself talking dirty and masturbating down the phone to Stu Hart. Long after midnight, Jack left his room and lurched down to the busy hotel restaurant completely naked, save for some cowboy boots and his crocodile tooth-bedecked outback hat, and plonked himself on a stool at the counter. The hotel staff called the authorities, who unfortunately didn't arrive in time to stop the stupefied Outback relieving himself in the artificial plant garden in the middle of the restaurant. When the police arrived, they mercifully took the confused Aussie back to his room instead of arresting him. For good measure, Davey and Dynamite ripped off the crocodile head that adorned Outback's leather vest jacket he wore to the ring.

On an earlier occasion, Davey, Dynamite and Jack found themselves sharing a locker room in the suitably un-aroused Stu's Stampede territory. The Bulldogs invited him out for a drink where they once again drugged him unconscious. Davey and Dynamite took Outback to his room, shaved his head, spray-painted his body pink, superglued his hands to his face and then dumped him outside in the freezing cold Canadian snow.

There was yet another Outback Jack incident in May 1988. The WWF crew were on a commercial flight heading for the next destination when, yes, Outback Jack's drink was spiked with Halcion once again. Davey and Dynamite, in full view of the boys *and* non-WWF passengers, removed Jack's leather Outback hat and shaved off a big stripe of hair right down the middle of his head. According to Greg 'The Hammer' Valentine, who was on the plane watching the rib unfold, "They then put superglue on the hat and put it back on his head so he couldn't get it off." Jack was allegedly at baggage claim when he eventually managed to tear his hat off in what Valentine was informed was 'a horrible scene'. When Outback arrived at that evening's venue, agent Chief Jay Strongbow took one look at the ailing Aussie and refused to let him wrestle in his mangled state. At least this time somebody was punished for the barbarous prank. "You know who got fired? Outback Jack!" chirped Valentine. After the naked restaurant incident in 'Frisco and the Calgary freezer job, conventional wisdom suggests that Jack would have been wise to turn down the Bulldogs' offer to get the first round of drinks in.

[1]Very little is known about Outback outside of his brief wrestling career. He was discovered by WWF Vice President of Operations and former hockey player Jim Troy, who was responsible for setting up international television distribution. Because *Crocodile Dundee* was the hottest thing in pop culture, Troy convinced Vince McMahon to sign the big Australian to a deal and push his character hard on television, despite the fact he was a pretty darn terrible worker even by 1980s WWF standards. Unlike Mick 'Crocodile' Dundee, Outback Jack was anything but humble and easy-going. "He came in like he was bigger than Hogan; he is the new WWF man," said the Honky Tonk Man. "The Australian people and the English people just do not get along, never will... [but Outback] rubbed the American guys the wrong way too." He was terrible in the ring and all the wrestlers hated him but George 'The Animal' Steele had another theory on why he was canned

from the company. "He started dating one of the girls in the office. That was his demise: that was just a no-no."

186

"Vince, You've Got Something on Your Jacket"

As told by Davey Boy Smith, Paul Bearer, etc.

Brother-in-law, tag team partner and pranking co-hort Davey Boy Smith once said of Owen, "He'd rib anybody at anytime, anywhere." Even the boss himself wasn't immune to his practical jokes. On the 19th of December 1995, just two days after Vince's office was turned into a pig pen at *In Your House 5*, Owen decided the boss hadn't been ribbed quite enough. The scene of the next prank was Bethlehem, Pennsylvania during a *WWF Superstars* television taping. The taping had already got off on the wrong foot as Bethlehem was hit by a snow storm and attendance was a paltry 1,500 people. It was under these circumstances that Owen would once again prove that he, not Vince, was truly the man with 'balls the size of grapefruits'.

Vince McMahon, who was still living in the glorious era of wearing outrageous pastel coloured sport coats, was heading to ringside to commentate on the evenings' matches. William 'Paul Bearer' Moody recalled in a 2011 interview, "I see Owen go right behind Vince and put shaving cream all over his back while Vince was walking down the hall way for the show and Vince never knew it was there."

In a 1999 sit-down interview with Jim Ross, Davey Boy Smith distinctly recalled talking to McMahon in the hallway before he walked off in front of the live crowd. "Vince is just about to go out to do his entrance for commentating. I said, 'Vince, you've got shaving cream on you'." Knowing that the Bulldog was usually considered the second biggest ribber in the locker room (depending on whether 'Mr Perfect' Curt Hennig was with the company at the time), Vince dismissed Davey's genuine concern and grumbled, "Yeah, right!" before power-walking down the hall. It was only when road agent Chief Jay Strongbow stopped him and said, "Vince, you've got shaving cream on your jacket," did McMahon actually take it off and realise that his primary coloured blazer had zig-zag lines of shaving cream across the back. The Bulldog theorised that Vince's jacket probably cost him,

"$5000 or something," before adding, "Owen would not stop; it was like every day something new!"

McMahon was one of Owen's favoured targets, as was evident during an event in the late 1990s. At the Kiel Centre in St. Louis, Missouri, D'Lo Brown and Mark Henry witnessed McMahon go into full meltdown when he saw that someone had duct-taped his briefcase to a ceiling fan. As Henry recalled, "It was one of the most hilarious things I ever saw. You could hear Vince screaming and you knew nobody did that other than Owen. But Owen denied it and denied it and I think at the end even Vince laughed." D'Lo, who also witnessed the revolving case, said, "[Owen] was definitely the master of the practical joke. It didn't matter what mood you were in. He could make you laugh."

Allied Powers Press Slam Rib

As told by Lex Luger, Billy Gunn, Al Snow, Triple H, etc.

Aside from his awesome, bodybuilder physique, Luger was well known in the wrestling industry as being self-admittedly full of himself and had heat with many of his contemporaries because of his aloof attitude. It also didn't help that he wasn't a big fan of wrestling growing up and due to cosmetic reasons was treated (and paid) like a big star throughout his career.[1] Because of this, Luger would find himself a popular target to be taken down a peg or two. When he failed to fill the void of the departing Hulk Hogan in 1993, Luger was shunted down the card to make way for Bret Hart to become WWF Champion and company torchbearer. At the beginning of 1995, Luger and the similarly programme-less Davey Boy were shoved together in a makeshift team and dubbed The Allied Powers.

Lex and Davey got on famously. Both were obsessive bodybuilders and Lex would even stay at Davey's house when the WWF toured the UK. Despite Lex's friendship with Owen and Davey, 'The Total Package' still retained the ability to get under their skin simply with a snide remark. According to ring veteran Al Snow, there was one occasion where, "Lex made some smart ass remark to Owen about being a big star," which bothered the youngest Hart to the point where he decided it was payback time. Owen and Davey made it known to other wrestlers in the locker room that they were going to purposely make 'The Total Package' look like a total moron in front of that evening's audience.

While it likely wasn't a sell-out crowd on this particular night in 1995, it was most certainly standing room only for the wrestlers backstage. "Everybody was at the curtain 'cause they know Owen was notorious for driving Lex up the wall," recalled Monty 'Billy Gunn' Sopp, who was on the same card that night. "Literally, it was a curtain sell-out for the boys in the back. It was like little heads all up in the curtains [peaking through]."

Partway into the match, Owen called for Lex to give him one of his trademark power moves. "My big thing was I was supposed to be a strong man and so was Davey," said Luger, "that was part of our deal as The Allied

Powers. Owen called a press slam spot with me." A press slam is where Wrestler A grabs Wrestler B by the chest/neck and the crotch and presses them overhead with their arms fully extended, before dropping them back-first onto the mat. Davey Boy fondly remembered the incident. "We went into the spot and [Lex] threw Owen into the [ropes]. As soon as Lex went to press slam him, Owen hooked [Lex's] arm so he couldn't fully extend them." Instead of posting off Lex's shoulder to assist with the press slam attempt, Owen spider-monkey'd Lex's arm and went limp. This made it look like the wrestler who once bodyslammed the 568lb Yokozuna on the USS Intrepid[2] wasn't strong enough to press the 230lb Owen.

Completely dejected, Luger dropped Owen and made a quick tag to his Allied Power partner. When the brothers-in-law locked up, Owen whispered to Davey to perform the exact same press slam spot. Davey Irish-whipped Owen into the ropes to set up for the big press slam but this time Owen was more than cooperative, going up as light as a feather. Owen even allowed Davey to walk around the ring while performing shoulder presses 'four or five times' before slamming Owen to canvas. According to Davey's son Harry Smith, while Owen was in the corner in mock-agony, Davey turned round to Luger, flexed his muscles and shouted, "SEE LEX, I'M THE STRONGEST ONE IN THE TEEEAAM!"

"He double-crossed me!" recalled Luger years after the fact. "Davey turned towards me and Owen had a big smile on his face, laughing at me." Triple H, who was one of the heads peeking through the curtain, recounted that the whole charade was, "Just to make Lex look bad... Lex would get so mad."

When the Allied Powers got to the back after the match, Davey Boy continued to taunt the exasperated Luger, who was 'shaking' with frustration. According to Bruce Prichard, the Bulldog would continue to goad Lex backstage. "Davey Boy would go, 'Maybe you need to work out a little more, maybe a little fuckin' round the neck... you're getting weak. Fuck, I had no problem getting him up!'"

This wouldn't be the only time Owen would make Luger purposely look bad during a match. "Whenever Davey would get in the ring, Davey would hip toss him and Owen would just go flying," recalled Al Snow. "Davey would tag right out and Owen caught a hip toss from Lex and he

190

would just go over like a tonne of shit!" Not only was it fun to rib Luger, Owen was also teaching him a lesson while pricking the pomposity of 'The Total Package'. It takes two to tango and it takes two wrestlers cooperating to make each other look good no matter how much they hit the gym and how wonderful their bodies looks. Like everyone else, Luger only got to where he was thanks to the generosity of others.

[1]Thanks to his bodybuilder physique and 6'5" stature, Larry 'Lex Luger' Pfohl meandered right off the USWA football field and into the offices of Championship Wrestling from Florida. With no wrestling experience whatsoever, he was hired on the spot without 'paying his dues.' In general terms, paying dues in wrestling means: suffering through long days, low wages, hard matches and crappy conditions before working up the ladder of success. Those lucky enough to skip the low pay and poor treatment were generally resented by wrestlers who didn't have that option.

[2]To celebrate Independence Day on the 4th of July 1993, the World Wrestling Federation hosted the *Yokozuna Bodyslam Challenge* on the USS Intrepid aircraft carrier, which was docked in New York City. Various wrestlers and NFL, NBA and NHL stars attempted to slam the reigning WWF Champion to no avail. The then 'Narcissist' Lex Luger (a terrible nickname, even for a heel) was flown in via helicopter wearing a stars-n-stripes t-shirt to slam Yoko and reclaim the glory for the United States from its hated enemy, Japan... or Samoa, which was Rodney 'Yokozuna' Anoi'a's ethnicity... or San Francisco, where he was born and raised. By channelling the power of 'Murica, Lex slammed Yoko and turned babyface. Luger would then campaign across the nation for a shot at Yoko's WWF Title in a patriotically airbrushed coach dubbed the Lex Express.

Car Rides with Owen: Riding with Fans and Messing with Car Heaters

As told by Jeff Jarrett, Mick Foley, Bob Holly, Sean Waltman, etc.

It's no secret to those within the wrestling industry that Owen Hart was probably the thriftiest man in the history of the business. He preferred sleeping in flea-bitten motels and random fans' houses instead of the Marriott, so he could spend more money on his wife and kids. Owen and fellow skinflint Mick Foley would even keep each other in the loop with sweet deals on the road. "Owen and I didn't travel all the time together but when we had a deal [on a hotel room] that we knew of, we knew we'd share it with each other because we wouldn't ruin it! If you have a good deal the best way to ruin it is to tell the other [wrestlers] about it!" Owen and Mick also engaged in a 'who can spend the least amount of money in a week' competition. No one remembers who the victor was but the contest was won by a matter of pennies rather than dollars. "We took a lot of pride in the fact that we could stretch a dollar quite a way," said Mick. "At a certain point Abe Lincoln began screaming because I was pinching him too hard."

Owen and Mick also had a network of fans to drive them across the country in a bid to save money. While both Owen and Mick shared some of the same contacts, Owen's travel buddies were, on the whole, more peculiar, which gave him a perverse sense of enjoyment.[1] "He would ride with marks... when I'd ride with 'em, these marks would drive you crazy," recalled Sean Waltman. "Owen would just sit and take it; he would enjoy watching." Owen would also have fun at the expense of some of these fans, literally in some cases: Owen once managed to convince a fan to rent him a limo. Owen also 'pulled' the handbrake rib on his and Mick's mutual travel partner Ronnie Gaffe, with much the same outcome that Brian Christopher would experience in 1997.

When Owen and Jeff Jarrett were riding together, Owen constantly pulled pranks in an effort to alleviate some of the boredom during long journeys. "It's a hundred degrees outside in California and Owen would somehow, some way get the heat put on in that car and it would start getting hot," recalled Jarrett. "[I'd scream] 'OWEN, TURN THE HEAT OFF!' 'Oh, my bad!' said Owen. Just the little ribs, just the silly stuff." Later in his career when Owen was considered a senior member of the locker room, he would ride with younger wrestlers and pull the same car heater trick on them. "He'd get one of these young wrestlers in the car with him and he'd turn on the heat in the summertime," said Jarrett. "Owen was a veteran by this point, so these guys didn't want to show him any disrespect by saying anything." The poor rookie wrestler would feel obligated to drive around in the kiln-like environment, too afraid to ask for the heater to be turned off in case the veteran Owen took offence. Owen would wait to see how long the rookie could hold out before letting them in on the joke.

If Owen was irritating when the weather was hot, he was downright aggravating when it was cold. "He did this one night coming back from Edmonton [or] Calgary," said Jarrett. "I mean it was freezing and he was just thinking it'd be real funny that all of a sudden he'd [lower] all the windows in the back seat [where he was sat]; he would even rib himself. He'd put both windows down, it'd be freezing coming in and Owen would just start laughing and leave 'em down."

Probably the best rib Owen pulled in a car was when he, ring announcer Manny Garcia and Japanese wrestler Jinsei 'Hakushi' Shinzaki picked up a hitchhiker while riding down the highway in the middle of a summer heat wave. After squeezing the wayward commuter in the back of the car next to the muscle-bound grappler from the Orient, Owen, who was reclining in the passenger seat, decided to make things even more uncomfortable. He rolled up all the windows, turned off the car's air conditioning and blasted the heater on full. The hitchhiker, who barely spoke English, conveyed to Owen that he was too hot and asked him to turn the heater off. Owen denied the transient's request, claiming that Hakushi, who the hitchhiker was sat next to, didn't believe in the concept of air conditioning and had to remain hot because of his obscure religion. To make matters worse, Hakushi couldn't speak much English either and didn't

193

know what was going on but looked intimidating enough that the hitchhiker refused to argue the matter any further. "The poor bastard they picked up was sweating his ass off!" laughed Bob 'Hardcore' Holly.

After Owen and the rest of the desiccated passengers finally escaped the mobile sauna, Owen made it up to the hitchhiker for ribbing him the whole journey... sort of. According to Holly, "They brought [the hitchhiker] to the building. [Owen] got him into the show, got him in the back, met everybody, put him out in the front row in the arena and said they'd give him a ride to the next town." After the show, instead of taking the hitchhiker with them, Owen and friends drove off, leaving him stranded at the arena and wondering how the heck he was going to get a ride that late at night. "Oh, it was great, it was great!" hooted the normally Grinch-like Holly.

[1]Davey Boy Smith's son Harry proudly inherited Owen's weird fans once he got in the business, mostly because he got the same perverse pleasure out of hanging around them. When it comes to the legion of Owen disciples for Harry to poach, "The weirder, the better," asserted his cousin Natalie Neidhart. One of Owen's most well-known fans began stalking Harry and telling him about his disturbing sex life, which Harry derived great enjoyment from. Harry also once convinced Natalie, TJ Wilson and Chris Jericho to go to the same weirdo's house for a barbecue as a joke, which they all described as a harrowing experience, least of all because no food or drink had been provided. Jericho succinctly summed up Owen's logic for allowing these oddballs into his life. "Not only did [Owen] get a free home-cooked meal [and] free bed but [he] got free entertainment too!"

Early Entrance Music Ribs

As told by Sean Waltman, Ahmed Johnson, Mick Foley, etc.

For the longest time, the WWE would invite prospective wrestlers to audition for the company in the form of untelevised tryout matches. Fresh from stints wrestling for minor promotions Global Wrestling Federation and NWA Dallas, Tony 'Ahmed Johnson' Norris got his turn to impress Federation officials at a house show on the 15th of July 1995 in Houston, Texas. The former Dallas Cowboy linebacker[1] was unskilled, unwieldy and incredibly dangerous in the ring. He once even managed to give Owen a concussion with an axe kick to the back of his head in 1996. Then there were the promos - when Ahmed cut an interview he was so unintelligible he sounded like he had a mouthful of conference pear. Johnson would develop such a reputation for being mush-mouthed and incomprehensible that the in-joke among WWF producers would be to cry out, "GREAT GOOGILY-MOOGILY," whenever he spoke on television. Ahmed was also huge, charismatic and had a connection with the audience, which was exactly what Vince McMahon was looking for to bolster his thin roster.

Ahmed's opponent for the Houston tryout match was Puerto Rican mainstay, Rico Suave. According to Ahmed, he was making the most of his opportunity to impress WWF officials. "I'm sitting in the ring and I'm getting off with this guy and I'm having a helluva match. Fans are screaming, I'm doing stuff off the top rope... and all kinds of stuff and my music came on half way during the match." Entrance music playing during a match was, unsurprisingly, not standard practice for the WWF or any other promotion for that matter but because Ahmed had never wrestled in the big leagues, he assumed it was their way of telling him to end the match and get out of the ring. "I didn't know! I said oh, they're telling me to take it home 'cause they don't like the match or something," like he was at an awards ceremony and the winner's speech had overrun. Ahmed finished the match several minutes earlier than planned. "I told the guy, 'I'll shoot you in [the ropes], clothesline you and give you the Pearl River [Plunge], then pin you.'"

Ahmed got a nice ovation from the crowd before walking back through the curtain believing he'd done the right thing. Ahmed's agent for the match, Mike 'Irwin R Schyster' Rotunda, was none too pleased. According to Sean Waltman, "[the WWF] were trying to transition Mike Rotunda from in the ring to being an agent," with Ahmed's match being one of his first assignments. Rotunda walked up to Ahmed and, instead of congratulating him on a good matched, yelled, "WHO TURNED THAT FUCKING MUSIC ON?" IRS continued his foul-mouthed rant until he saw a couple of familiar faces walking out of the sound booth. Ahmed remembered the incident like it was yesterday. "[We] look at the booth [and] look who's coming out the sound booth; Owen and Davey!"

Waltman explained, "There was this telephone where you could talk to where the sound guy was and tell him, 'Okay, hit so and so's music, do this, do that.' Owen used to love fucking with those guys. Tony Norris/Ahmed Johnson was in the ring and he's having his match and right in the middle of the fuckin' match Owen picks up the phone to the sound guy and goes, 'Hit his music!' and they're like, 'what?' [Owen] goes, 'HIT HIS FUCKIN' MUSIC!' Boom! They hit [Ahmed's] music right in the middle of the match!"

Ahmed recalled Rotunda's reaction vividly when he saw Owen and Davey stroll out of the production room. "Mike Rotunda's like, 'I'M CALLING VINCE RIGHT NOW, YOU JUST FUCKED UP A GOOD MATCH, I'M CALLING VINCE!'" Of course, Owen and Davey denied everything, blaming each other with the classic, "I didn't do it, Davey did it. I didn't do it, Owen, you did it," panto routine that made it impossible to stay angry at them. "Mike Rotunda's really mild-mannered and if he wasn't the agent he would've been laughing, too!"[2] Waltman said. "Yeah, it was little things like that [that made it] great having Owen Hart in your locker room and on your roster. It was amazing. It was fucking amazing being friends with Owen Hart."

Ever since his first foray into the World Wrestling Federation, Owen was trying to get entrance music played at the wrong time. WWE's longest-tenured referee Mike Chioda[3] remembered Owen's penchant for audibly interrupting matches as early as 1988, when he was at the bottom of the pecking order wrestling as The Blue Blazer. "One of the funny stories I remember myself was before I was even refereeing, I was doing ring crew. I was [also] in charge of doing the music. I would be on headsets in the back and I left that position for maybe no more than, I wanna say, not even a minute." As soon as Chioda left his position, Owen would jab away at the stereo system until he played the wrong music at the wrong time just to ruin the match in progress and make himself laugh.

When Brian 'Road Dogg' James was performing as The Real Double J in 1996/1997, his entrance music was the Jim Johnston-penned country song *With My Baby Tonight,*[4] which he would sing along to live as he shucked and jived his way down to ringside. When the opening twang of *With My Baby Tonight* kicked in during his bouts however, the Dogg was left in little doubt as to who was to blame. "[Owen] would have the building hit your music or something in the middle of a match," said Road Dogg, "you'd just know that was friggin' Owen!"

On the 14th of June 1996, the WWF held a house show at the Denver Coliseum. Owen wrestled early on the card, losing to Savio Vega. Some time after the match, Owen decided to amuse himself (and maybe take his loss out on someone) by getting on a spare headset, pretending to be the local promoter and instructing the sound guy to play music during a match. On this occasion, not only did the operator refuse, he started arguing back. Owen and the sound guy went back and forth until Owen challenged him to a showdown. "Oh, yeah? Well come on down, tough guy, I won't be hard to find. I've got a big cowboy hat and a pair of cowboy boots that I'll stick right up your ass. Oh, yeah! Come on down, you bastard, so I can smash my big-ass belt buckle right over your head." Because Owen was preparing to do a run-in later on in the show, he probably hadn't even changed out of his wrestling singlet and was certainly not wearing a cowboy hat, cowboy boots or a 'big-ass belt buckle'. Who *was* wearing all these items, however, was the actual promoter for the Denver Coliseum; "A likeable but somewhat goofy-looking cowboy," as Mick Foley would describe him.[5] The 'goofy-looking cowboy' stood around the backstage area minding his own business and looking goofy the entire time without realising he was about to receive a smack in the mouth from a very angry sound man courtesy of Owen.

[1]Ahmed never played a regular season game

198

[2]Mike Rotunda wouldn't last as a WWF agent/producer. Rotunda was gone just a few weeks later after being lured to WCW with a new contract and the possibility of teaming with Ray 'Big Bubba Rogers' Traylor as the Certified Public Assassins. Rotunda was instead repackaged as Million Dollar Man rip-off character Michael Wallstreet. By week two he had been renamed 'VK' Wallstreet (as in Vincent Kennedy McMahon), then eventually re-renamed M Wallstreet. At least Tony Garea, who was fired to make way for Rotunda, was rehired when he left for WCW.

[3]Mike Chioda was promoted from ring crew to referee (who also did ring crew) in 1989. As of this writing, the 53-year-old Chioda has been a referee for thirty years having officiated some 15,000 matches and counting for the WWE.

[4]While *With My Baby Tonight* has a passing resemblance to *Take It Easy* by Eagles, at least it wasn't as obvious a 'tribute' as Razor Ramon's entrance theme was to *Those Shoes*, also by Eagles. WWF composer Jim Johnston must have been a big fan.

[5]By June 1996, WWF attendance was up but the 'goofy-looking cowboy' promoter had done such a poor job advertising the show that the WWF only drew 2,203 fans that night; far below the WWF average for the time period.

CHAPTER 7

The Mid-Card

♥ ♥

Spurred on by competition from WCW, the World Wrestling Federation made several changes to their booking manifesto in 1996. The WWF continued to debut new characters and mixed hints of edgier storylines in amongst the usual family friendly fare. Diesel was morphing into a foul-mouthed, middle-finger-gesturing, bitter anti-hero inhabiting the space between babyface and heel. The debuting Ahmed Johnson, for all his negatives as a worker, was actually a cool character fans could get behind. The Goldust character, which debuted in August 1995, was a homoerotic androgynous alien creature covered head-to-toe in gold, who fondled his opponents in an effort to gain the psychological advantage and enrage the working-class fan base.[1]

These were some of the better ideas the WWF came up with to get wrestling fans talking but for every step forward the Federation made, they took two steps back in other areas. At the end of 1995, manager Ted DiBiase debuted the anti-Santa, Xanta Claus (Jonathan Rechner, better known as Balls Mahoney) to steal kids' presents and beat up Savio Vega. That character was scrapped, unsurprisingly, just before Christmas. Ted DiBiase then introduced the WWF fans to his newest charge, Steve Austin, on the 8th of January 1996 edition of *RAW*. Austin, who'd been cutting some of the best promos in the business just weeks prior in ECW, was given DiBiase to talk on his behalf and was rechristened The Ringmaster. The name was terrible and Austin's dynamic personality was stripped away. Vince McMahon advertised evil dentists, bin men and scufflin' hillbillies with a straight face while WCW promoted huge names from the '80s and the most exciting, talented workers in the world on the undercard. For every successful character such as a Shawn Michaels or The Undertaker, there were three times as many failures blighting Federation rings.

Through it all, Owen was one of the consistent bright spots on World Wrestling Federation cards, despite no longer being featured in the main events. Owen competed in the first (and last) annual RAW Bowl match and defeated Marty Jannetty on television before making a decent showing at January's Royal Rumble match. Owen was co-eliminated by Diesel and eventual winner Shawn Michaels. Owen came back out to attack Michaels while he was brawling with the British Bulldog outside the ring.[2] This set up the anticipated rematch between Owen and Michaels at *In Your House 2* on the 18th of February. The two had a fantastic match, with Owen trying to land a second Enzuigiri kick to put Shawn out of action once and for all. After sixteen minutes, Michaels, who was on the fast track to becoming the WWF Champion at *WrestleMania XII*, hit Owen with his patented superkick and pinned him for the clean win. "[Owen] was great and by far the most talented of all the Harts," said Michaels in his first autobiography. "With Owen you could call things on the fly, change things up, experiment and basically do anything you wanted to do. He was a pure joy to work with."

In the lead up to *WrestleMania XII*, Owen, Bulldog and Vader triple-teamed Yokozuna on *RAW* until Ahmed Johnson and the now bible bashing Jake 'The Snake' Roberts[3] made the save, setting up a six-man tag team match at *'Mania* that did nobody any favours creatively speaking. Vader, who was well-known as a locker room malcontent, was especially upset being booked so low on the card, even though he would get the pin on Jake Roberts. Not only was Vader still recovering from surgery, he was supposed to be groomed for a main event run with new WWF Champion Shawn Michaels in the summer. As Vader and Yokozuna splintered off into their own issue, the now Slammy Award-winning Owen Hart (more on that later) and the Bulldog started teaming up more and more. Owen and Bulldog resolved their rivalry with Ahmed and Jake with a win at *In Your House 7*. Jim Cornette was probably happy not to be working with Jake any more. During an angle involving Jake, Cornette was supposed to have a 'heart attack' at the sight of the snake. After Cornette dropped to the canvas, Jake spontaneously dumped the enormous boa constrictor on the portly manager's prone body. Owen and Bulldog were laughing so hard at Cornette's unscheduled freak out they forgot to run away from the snake as scripted.

In another bid to drum up interest in the Middle-East, the WWF embarked on their first tour of the oil-rich nation of Kuwait. As a hook to drum up local interest, the WWF concocted a multi-day tournament for the inaugural Kuwaiti Cup – a prize equal to the Royal Samovar Trophy Davey Boy Smith won at *Battle at the Royal Albert Hall* for sheer worthlessness. Owen ended up reaching the semi-finals before being eliminated by tournament winner Ahmed Johnson.

When the WWF tour returned to the states in May, Owen had the 'pleasure' of being booked against his old roommate The Ultimate Warrior. Aside from working a few independent dates, releasing a bonkers workout video and opening a wrestling school in his hometown of Scotsdale, Arizona[4] no one had heard anything from the Warrior since being fired from the WWF in 1992. Warrior had made his return at *WrestleMania XII*, destroying Hunter Hearst Helmsley in 1:39 after no-selling his Pedigree finishing move.[5] Warrior received almost as much hype for his return as the Bret Hart vs. Shawn Michaels main event, with the WWF airing frenetic, epilepsy-inducing videos hyping Warrior's return for weeks leading up to the pay-per-view. Some of the Warrior footage purposely included him pinning WCW's Macho Man Randy Savage with one foot in 1991. Savage would go on to win the WCW World Title that April.

If Vader was a malcontent behind the scenes, Warrior was unbelievably combative, making numerous, ever more outrageous demands from Vince McMahon. In a Federation first, Warrior received WWF airtime to broadcast peculiar commercials for his wrestling school, as well as forcing the WWF to buy his *Warrior* comic books to give away to fans. Warrior hit the road once again, first destroying future title contender Vader, before moving on to Owen. Despite retaining his awesome physique, Warrior had lost any semblance of the speed, cardio or in-ring acumen he'd developed by his early '90s heyday. As great a worker as Owen was, even he couldn't drag a decent match out of him. During their fourth and final house show match in Madison Square Garden on the 19th of May, Warrior dropped Owen awkwardly, breaking Owen's wrist. Like a true pro, Owen never missed a day and incorporated his arm cast into matches, bonking wrestlers over the head with it while the referee's attention was diverted. For June's *King of the Ring 1996* pay-per-view, Owen was stuffed into a tuxedo and plonked at ringside to provide partisan colour commentary, before interfering on the Bulldog's behalf during his WWF Championship match against Shawn Michaels.

Around this time, Owen signed a five-year contract with the World Wrestling Federation. Owen was earning around $100,000 a year when he returned to the WWF in 1991, which ascended to $200,000 during his run with Bret. The new contact guaranteed Owen $250,000 per year plus roughly $50,000 per year in royalties. Vince McMahon had only offered 'opportunities' to his talent beforehand and could fire them any time he wished. With WCW slowly pulling ahead in the ratings war, McMahon started locking talent down in an effort to stop his company losing even more workers to the competition. While Owen only wanted to sign up for two years, McMahon refused to negotiate on the time frame. Owen relented and signed a contract that would see him work for the WWF until at least 2001. "I am content with WWF and I believe that there is more to wrestling than just money," said Owen months before he re-signed. "If you can maintain a good living and keep your dignity then I would prefer staying right where I am." With Owen finally enjoying some financial security, he and Martha started discussing the idea of having a third child and would eventually pick a plot to build their dream house on in 1998.

The taped edition of *RAW* on the 8th of July unconventionally opened with figurehead WWF President Gorilla Monsoon announcing the indefinite suspension of The Ultimate Warrior for missing house show dates.[6] The WWF had already invested air time promoting The Ultimate Warrior, Shawn Michaels and Ahmed Johnson against Camp Cornette in the *In Your House 9: International Incident* main event. As *RAW* was pre-taped, the Warrior vs. Owen main event was broadcast as scheduled and new interviews announcing Warrior's replacement had to be hurriedly shot with Michaels and Ahmed Johnson. Owen tried his absolute best with Warrior, idiot-proofing the match and selling well for Warrior's offence but it was no use. Warrior was exhausted and sluggish from the get-go and the crowd noise added in post-production couldn't hide the fact that the match was merely passable. Vader and the Bulldog mercifully ran in after eight minutes and tripled-teamed the Warrior to death for the disqualification.

Sycho Sid, who also had a reputation for being difficult to deal with, was announced as Warrior's replacement on house shows and the upcoming pay-per-view. At *IYH 9*, Owen managed to legitimately break Ahmed Johnson's nose with a wheel kick before Vader pinned Shawn Michaels for the surprise victory. The day after the pay-per-view, the WWF recorded a month's worth of *RAW* episodes. Owen competed in the battle royal to determine the number one contender for the WWF Championship,[7] before wrestling Shawn Michaels in a losing effort for the 12th of August episode.

On the 2nd of August, the WWF visited Montreal where Owen Hart squared off against former pro wrestler Ray Rougeau in a worked boxing match.[8] In 1996, Ray, who'd quit full-time wrestling in 1989, was working as a French-language commentator and backstage interviewer for the WWF. Ray was looking to make a one-off return to the ring and asked Federation owner Vince McMahon to book him in a match in his home town of Montreal. "I retired five months before my son was born," explained Ray, "so he never saw me in the ring." After Ray's original request of facing Shawn Michaels was turned down, Owen was chosen to box Ray in Montreal's brand new Molson Centre. The bout was set up during the WWF's previous visit to Montreal on the 12th of January, which was also the WWF's last show held at the old Montreal Forum before its closure. Owen and Bulldog would lose a tag team encounter to The Smoking Gunns that evening. Still smarting from their defeat, Owen attacked Ray Rougeau in front of 10,000 fans and Ray's father after Ray attempted to get an interview with the thwarted brothers-in-law.

Come the big fight, Ray was accompanied to the ring by local boxing hero Deano Clavet and his father Jacques Senior to square off against Owen, accompanied by Canadian boxing star George Chuvalo. After four rounds of sucker punches, stalling and heel tactics, Ray Rougeau defeated Owen in the fourth round via KO. Owen eventually scraped himself up off the mat and started berating his trainer Chuvalo, blaming him for the loss. Chuvalo, who had shared boxing rings with Muhammad Ali, 'Smokin' Joe Frazier and George Foreman, didn't take the rebuking kindly and knocked Owen out cold for a second time that night, to the audience's appreciation. Everything was pre-planned of course but Chuvalo's knockout punch didn't go as well as Ray's. "I only meant to graze him a little bit," explained Chuvalo. "I didn't want to hit him too hard but I miscued and hit him right in the chin. He was knocked out legit!"

After picking up a win at *SummerSlam* after striking Savio Vega with his cast, Owen faced off against his Camp Cornette teammate and brother-in-law 'British Bulldog' Davey Boy Smith. The two battled it out in a relatively courteous manner, with the crowd supporting the Bulldog and their manager Jim Cornette having an aneurism in the locker room over his wrestlers squaring off. Owen and Davey eventually battled their way to the commentary table, where Sunny ended up getting some of Jerry Lawler's Coca-Cola on her dress. With Sunny and the Bulldog arguing with each other, Owen snuck into the ring for the count-out victory. Davey ended up wearing Lawler's cup of Cola when Sunny threw it over him. After Cornette came down to ringside to calm down simmering tensions (and call Sunny 'a little slut') the match was made for the heel Owen and Davey to take on Sunny's also-heel team of The Smoking Gunns for the WWF Tag Team Titles.

At *In Your House 10: Mind Games*, four things involving Owen occurred:

1 - While Jim Cornette was recovering from his match with Shawn Michaels' manager/trainer Jose Lothario, diminutive lawyer Clarence Mason arrived

with legal papers. In his confused state, Cornette signed a legal letter which handed Owen and Bulldog's contracts over to Clarence.
2 - Owen's long healed wrist was now cast free thanks to Marc Mero stomping all over the cast on the *RAW* episode broadcast prior to *IYH 10*.
3 - Owen and Bulldog won the WWF Tag Team Titles from The Smoking Gunns.
4 - Owen and Davey, who were the two biggest pranksters in the company, pulled a storyline rib on Sunny.

The egotistical Sunny had recently taken to producing giant posters of herself from the rafters of the arena. When she pointed to the sky as the cue for her latest portrait to be unveiled, her once beautiful face now had glasses, a beard and a beehive painted on it and was signed, "To Bulldog & Owen, all my love, Sunny." The only difference between this rib and all the genuine ribs Owen had pulled over the years was that this one wasn't funny. Even Vince McMahon, who was sat at the commentary booth, couldn't be bothered to force out his famous 'yuck, yuck' laugh. Owen and Davey would remain WWF Tag Team Champions for eight months, defending the belts for the remainder of 1996 against: The Smoking Gunns, Shawn Michaels and Sycho Sid and The Godwinns.

The only televised singles match of 1996 between Owen Hart and his brother Bret occurred on the 25th of November episode of *RAW* in New Haven, Connecticut. While Owen had previously hinted that he and Bret had reconciled their differences, the truth was anything but, as the two brothers went at each other just like they'd done throughout 1994 and 1995. Bret had just returned to full-time touring after taking six months off following his *WrestleMania XII* loss to Shawn Michaels. Bret returned to TV on the 21st of October to legitimately and publicly turn down WCW's multi-million dollar offer to return to the WWF, to pay tribute to his nephew Matthew Annis[9] and to accept Stone Cold Steve Austin's challenge for a match at *Survivor Series 1996*. Bret refused point blank to tear up the contract WCW sent him during the interview, as McMahon had requested, as he felt WCW Vice President Eric Bischoff had been nothing but professional and honourable in their negotiations.

Bret defeated Austin at *Survivor Series* but the next night on *RAW*, Austin attacked Bret with a chair while he was locking in the Sharpshooter on Owen. When Austin clamped a folding chair on Bret's ankle in order to 'Pilmanize' it,[10] Davey Boy Smith ran to the ring in order to save Bret. While Owen and Bulldog argued (Owen wanted Austin to hurt Bret), Austin struck Bulldog with the chair. Owen, who was previously in favour of Austin's actions, chased Austin out of the ring and tended to the Bulldog. This angle turned out to be the very beginning of what would lead to the reunion of Bret, Owen and Davey and the inception of The Hart Foundation faction in March 1997. Bret would return the favour and rescue Davey Boy from a Sycho Sid powerbomb during a house show in London, England on the 28th of November.

For the next several months, Owen and Davey would argue among themselves during tag team matches, yet still retain the WWF Tag Team Titles because no other team in the Federation came close to them in terms of charisma, talent, ability or entertainment value.

[1]Androgynous and hyper gay characters were not a new concept to wrestling in 1995. One of the pioneers of the gender-bending role was proud Welshman 'Exotic' Adrian Street. Street, who stood at just 5'6", pranced around the ring with his hair in pigtails, wearing outrageous make-up. The 'Sadist in Sequins' enraged audiences in the UK and abroad before permanently taking his act to America in the early 1980s. 'Exoticos' have been a feature of Mexican wrestling since the 1940s. The WWF even had their own cross-dressing character in 'Adorable' Adrian Adonis in the mid 1980s. New York tough guy Adonis was reconfigured into a dress-wearing flower arranger in 1986, supposedly as punishment for gaining too much weight. The Goldust character took the sexually ambiguous character up several notches further than its predecessors. Dustin Runnels' first major angle as Goldust was professing his love for Scott 'Razor Ramon' Hall over a number of weeks. Hall personally disliked the Goldust character and didn't want to expose his young children to the unsavoury, hard to explain storyline as he saw it. McMahon refused to write Hall out of the angle and tensions boiled over during a European tour where Hall and Runnels

had a loud, drunken shouting match on a tour bus. By 1996, several WWF sponsors voiced their concerns to McMahon, who in turn reined in the more extreme aspects of Goldust's act, neutering the character considerably. Former WWF Head Writer Vince Russo said, "[Goldust] would have been an unbelievable World Champion... and just like that, the rug was pulled out from underneath all of us."

[2]The big story of the Rumble match was the debut of the newest member of Camp Cornette, Leon 'Vader' White. With Owen, Davey, Yokozuna and now Vader, the Camp Cornette faction was at full strength... for about eleven minutes. Vader attacked his former New Japan tag team partner Yokozuna, allowing Shawn Michaels to sneak up and eliminate them both. The next day on *RAW,* Vader, who needed shoulder surgery when he signed with the WWF, was 'suspended indefinitely' for viciously attacking WWF President Gorilla Monsoon. "I couldn't understand why they'd debut him in this big, hot angle, then suspended him so he could get shoulder surgery," said Vader's manager Jim Cornette. "[Vader] was assuming [the WWF] were going to leave him off [TV] most of that year to recuperate and he was surprised and shocked when they called him back after six weeks." Yokozuna remained a member of Camp Cornette for several more weeks until he attacked a castigating Cornette, causing Owen and the Bulldog to attack Yoko and boot him out of their group.

[3]Jake Roberts' battles with drink and drugs have been well documented. At the age of 40, Roberts reappeared in the WWF at the *Royal Rumble 1996* pay-per-view after a near four year hiatus from the promotion. Roberts quit the WWF in 1992 on the day of *WrestleMania VIII* after being passed up for the role of WWF booker in favour of the returning Pat Patterson. Roberts, who now looked like a haggard, 75-year-old panhandler, made his continuing sobriety and new-found Christianity part of his on-screen character. Many of the wrestlers doubted his sincerity as far as his faith and abstinence went and it didn't take too long for the Snake to once again succumb to the excesses of drink, drugs and women of easy virtue. Only in 2012 did Roberts manage to clean up his life when he moved in with fellow pro wrestler and yoga advocate

Diamond Dallas Page. Jake's journey back to health is documented in the 2015 documentary *The Resurrection of Jake The Snake*.

[4] *Warrior Workout 1* (number one in the one series anthology) was a twenty minute VHS tape advertised in the back of wrestling magazines for some obscene amount. The meat of the videotape consisted of ten minutes of intense workout footage accompanied by zero advice, before being replayed at double speed (dubbed 'Warrior Speed'). Warrior University aimed to train paying customers to wrestle (even though Warrior was a marginal worker at best) as well as teach his pupils the tenants of 'destrucity'. Destrucity was a word Warrior made up from the words destiny, truce and reality. Warrior advertised that his wrestling school wouldn't be a McDojo-style pop-up institution that people's took money and gave little in return. The school promptly closed its doors shortly after it opened when Warrior left the WWF in 1996, with no notable wrestlers ever being trained there. After meeting him for the first time at his Scotsdale gym in 1996, former WWF Producer Jim Cornette described Warrior as, "A raving lunatic living on the Planet Zambodia".

[5] "Probably one of the most unprofessional guys I've ever stepped in the ring with," was Triple H's assessment of The Ultimate Warrior several years after their infamous *WrestleMania* match. According to Bruce Prichard, the bout was supposed to go around twelve minutes until Warrior changed plans at the last second. "There were many discussions with Warrior... that night and afterwards. 'We don't do that here, things have changed and you can't go into business for yourself.'" In a 2016 interview, Triple H completely backtracked, saying that getting squashed by the Warrior was a pleasure. "Who can say that in their first *WrestleMania* ever, they got to step in the ring with one of the biggest icons in the business?" Triple H's opinion of The Ultimate Warrior seemed to take a dramatic u-turn after Warrior accepted a WWE Hall of Fame induction in 2014. Warrior (his legal name after changing it in 1993) passed away from a massive heart attack three days after the ceremony and has been practically canonised by the WWE ever since.

[6]"It is with great reluctance that I announce the indefinite suspension of The Ultimate Warrior. This suspension is a direct result of The Ultimate Warrior's failure to appear as advertised last weekend in Indianapolis, Detroit and Pittsburgh. This suspension will be immediately lifted, however, as soon as the Warrior posts an appearance bond (rumoured to be in excess of $100,000) to ensure WWF fans that he will appear where advertised... Despite the immense popularity of The Ultimate Warrior, no *one* wrestler is above answering to our loyal WWF fans." At the risk of this book turning into a Jim 'Ultimate Warrior' Hellwig biography, Warrior did indeed miss the weekend shows on the 28th, 29th and 30th of June. Warrior was supposedly furious that the WWF's booth at a trade show included Warrior's 'Always Believe' slogan without his permission. After no-showing the events, Warrior gave an unauthorised interview to Bob Ryder on a Prodigy chat, claiming he'd missed the shows because his father had just died. His father *had* actually just died... on the 30th. Supposedly, Hellwig hadn't seen his Dad since he was a young boy and couldn't have cared less for him. Warrior never returned to the WWF as an active wrestler.

[7]Ahmed Johnson won the battle royal but was attacked at the same *RAW* taping by the debuting Ron 'Faarooq Asad' Simmons, managed by Tammy 'Sunny' Sytch. Former WCW Champion Simmons was brought in to portray what Mick Foley termed a 'Black Spartacus', complete with an embarrassing powder-blue gladiator helmet. The gladiator gimmick was an unyielding misfire, as was Faarooq's surprise debut. When Faarooq sneak-attacked Ahmed Johnson during the *RAW* taping, Faarooq kicked Ahmed so hard in the midsection Ahmed suffered a lacerated kidney. Instead of Ahmed Johnson vs. Faarooq taking place at *SummerSlam*, Ahmed ended up in intensive care, spending five months on the injured list and vacating his newly won Intercontinental Championship.

[8]Montreal was once a hotbed for professional wrestling from the 1920s until the 1980s, with brothers Jacques Rougeau Senior and Johnny Rougeau being two of the Quebec territory's most beloved stars. The

then incumbent Montreal-based promotion, Lutte Internationale, was eventually swallowed up by the World Wrestling Federation's aggressive expansion in 1987. Jacques' sons Ray and Jacques Jr jumped to the WWF in 1986 to form The Fabulous Rougeaus tag team.

[9]Matthew Annis, younger brother of current indie wrestling star Teddy Hart (Teddy Annis) and Owen and Bret's nephew, died on the 13th of July 1996 at the age of 13 after contracting necrotizing fasciitis, commonly known as Flesh-Eating Disease. According to Bret, Matt most likely picked up the bacteria through a cut on his thumb while wrestling on the dirty canvas of the ring set up at Hart House. Paying tribute to his nephew, Davey Boy said of Matthew, "He was a remarkable kid. He loved wrestling and was going to go on in the family tradition." Owen said that Matthew's passing was, "Just wrong; such a healthy boy, it would drive me crazy to think that a week before [Matthew] was perfectly healthy, wrestling and the epitome of what a perfect young boy should be." While visiting him in the hospital, Owen told Matt he'd buy him a car if he managed to pull through. According to Matthew's friend TJ Wilson, "[Owen] paid for the funeral; every cent of it." Owen also paid for Matthew's parents to go to Hawaii over Christmas, as well as paying for TJ and Matthew's brother Teddy to fly to Vancouver for the *WWF In Your House 9* pay-per-view. As he made his way to the ring that evening, Owen mouthed to the camera, "We will never forget you, Matthew." TJ continued, "It just again showed his generosity and his heart and his compassion and really the type of person he was. Like I said, in and out of the ring, he was an absolute role model."

[10]Pillmanizing refers to the act of clamping an opponent's ankle in a folding chair and standing on it in an effort to 'break' the ankle. The process was named after Brian Pillman when Steve Austin 're-injured' Pillman's ankle via this method on the 27th of October 1996 edition of *WWF Superstars*. In reality, Pillman's ankle was still in total disrepair after he crashed his Hummer H1 that April. The Pillmanizing angle was created to write Brian off WWF television for several months so he could rehabilitate his pre-existing injury.

Jim Cornette-Stu Hart Phone Rib That Wasn't a Rib

As told by Jim Cornette, Bruce Prichard and Diana Hart

By 1996, Owen and Davey Boy's notorious reputation for playing pranks reached the point that their very presence would make those around them suspicious that a rib was in progress. No situation better illustrates the paranoia their mere existence would elicit than the time Owen and Davey went to behind-the-scenes agent, Jim Cornette, with a telephone claiming Owen's father Stu was on the line.

Back in April of that year, Davey Boy's wife Diana (who had made sporadic appearances on WWF television over the years) was brought into the Federation for a big storyline. On the 29th of April episode of *RAW*, Shawn Michaels and number one contender British Bulldog, his wife Diana and manager Jim Cornette were interviewed mid-ring by Vince McMahon. Cornette claimed WWF Champion Michaels had been sexually inappropriate with Diana backstage at the previous evening's pay-per-view, calling Michaels a 'sexual deviant' and a 'fornicator' who had attempted to 'de-flower' Davey's wife. Michaels rubbished the claims by telling Diana not to flatter herself, prompting Diana to slap the Heartbreak Kid. A big mêlée ensued between Michaels and the Bulldog to build interest for their Championship match at the upcoming *In Your House 8* pay-per-view.[1] Soon after, Cornette's storyline lawyer, Clarence Mason, drafted a restraining order against Michaels and sued him for 'attempted alienation of affection'.

Diana's father Stu watched the storyline unfold back in Calgary and was decidedly against it, worrying that people would confuse the on-screen portrayal of Diana for real life. At a subsequent show, Owen and Davey were sitting backstage where the premium rate WWF Superstar Line telephones were located, when Owen decided to give his father a quick ring. Stu picked up the phone and immediately launched into a tirade over the Diana angle and how their kids were being made fun of at school and wanted to speak to somebody in charge. Jim Cornette, one of several members on the WWF's booking committee, sat in a pre-tape room idly filling in paperwork when Owen and Davey shimmied around the corner holding what Cornette described as the Commissioner Gordon Bat-phone from the campy '60s *Batman* TV show. Jim was immediately suspicious. "Owen was not only noted for being a great ribber but he was also a master of telephone ribs," explained Cornette. "He'd tell them they have to come down and pay for their room because their payment hadn't gone through. He'd drive people insane."

Owen and Davey looked unusually happy as they handed the phone to Jim and informed him that Stu Hart was on the line. Jimmy, who already knew something was up, saw the phone cord trailing around the corner and at first assumed it wasn't plugged in. Fellow WWF Producer Bruce Prichard, who happened to do one of the best Stu Hart imitations in the company, was also conspicuous by his absence. Sensing all three were ganging up to prank him, Cornette picked up the phone. After a few brief pleasantries, Jim asked Stu why he was calling. Stu answered in his distinctive cadence that may or may not have been the inspiration for Triple H's lengthy heel promos in 1999.

"Well ehh, I just ehh you know I was watching the TV and ehh I just ehh wondered ehh what's going on with angle with ehh Diana and Davey and Shawn ehh. They're tryin' to make ehh Diana look like a ehh some kind ehh... whoo-urr." 'Whoo-urr' was Stu's unique take on the pronunciation of the word 'whore'. Stu continued, "It's just that ehh the kids are in school up here and ehh, all the other kids ehh, they're watching the show and ehh Diana ehh looks like some kinda whoo-urr." Cornette was now sure that Bruce Prichard was winding him up and decided to let Bruce know that he wasn't falling for it. "Well you know whose fault that is? It's all Bruce Prichard's fault. Bruce Prichard is one of those sexual deviants. Stu, he's a pervert. I mean he goes to those adult book stores, he goes to those peep shows where you have to mop the floor up afterwards." "I always thought that Bruce ehh was such a fine boy," continued Stu. "I know, Stu. I know how you feel I'm the same way, I wish we could have wrestling straight like it used to be but no, Bruce came up with this whole thing." "Well you know ehh, I don't mind 'em doing an angle but it's just that ehh they're making Diana look like ehh some kinda whoo-urr!"

After making further claims on Bruce's fetishism, Jim encouraged Stu to phone up WWF owner Vince McMahon to discuss the matter further, as well as insist Vince reprimand Bruce for allowing his sexual proclivities to seep into WWF storylines. "I may just have to do that ehh and call Vince 'cause I like Bruce but ehh you can't have Diana looking like a ehh whoo-urr!"

With the flabbergasted Owen and Davey witnessing the entire conversation unfold in front of them, Jim said his goodbyes to 'Stu' safe in the knowledge he hadn't fallen for the rib. "I hang the phone up and I look up and I go, 'Owen, who was that?' and just then, I swear to god, around the corner from the other side carrying papers, minding his own business and obviously oblivious to what the fuck is going on is Bruce Prichard! I looked up at Owen [and asked], 'Who was that?' He said, 'IT WAS STU!'" Prichard walked over to ask what was going on. "Bruce, I think I just told Stu that you're a fuckin' pervert!" was all Jim could offer.

According to Bruce himself, he picked up the phone and listened quietly as Stu admonished him for being a degenerate and for booking Diana to look like a whoo-urr. "That was a classic rib that was turned on me that wasn't even a rib," recalled Bruce. "That just kinda happened when Owen [was] around."

"Where Owen really shined was on the phone at the hotel in the middle of the night," laughed Cornette. "He'd jack guys up out of bed claiming he was the guy at the front desk and they had to come down and pay right then or he was gonna call the police... or asking them to help find a prowler that'd been seen around the breezeway of their area or whatever the fuck. That's when their talents really shone through but thankfully I was spared a lot of that except for the big one with the Bat-phone; it really *was* Stu. It was a double-reverse rib; they ribbed me because I thought because of their reputation that it couldn't possibly be Stu... and then it was!"

In 2001, Diana claimed that Stu was still upset over the angle years after the fact. "To this day my dad thinks that Jim Cornette and Bruce Pritchard are really warped guys who wanted a perverted, incestuous orgy to be portrayed on TV with his kids." Diana would act as Davey Boy's valet until June's *King of the Ring* pay-per-view, where Shawn Michaels beat Davey clean and the storyline was dropped completely. At least Stu got his wish and Diana was never portrayed as a whoo-urr on WWF television ever again.

[1]The *In Your House 8: Beware of Dog* pay-per-view was an utter catastrophe. Florence, South Carolina (where the event was held) was hit by a severe thunderstorm, knocking out the power to the Florence Civic Centre for over an hour during the show. The majority of the matches were contested under emergency lighting until the power was restored in time for the Shawn Michaels vs. British Bulldog main event. Michaels, who was renowned for his petulance, started insulting a female fan who was heckling him mid-match. This caused a ripple effect amongst the crowd until an entire section of fans started booing him. The match itself fell short of expectations and when Michaels' *Sexy Boy* entrance theme malfunctioned, he had a temper tantrum mid-ring. Keep in mind that Shawn was meant to be a virtuous babyface and the company's biggest star at the time. The post-pay-per-view dark match (as in untelevised rather than unlit) featured Owen Hart losing to his old roommate, The Ultimate Warrior.

216

Davey Boy vs. Ahmed Johnson Arm Wrestling Match Stinks Out Building

As told by Ahmed Johnson

Since the day he debuted in the WWF in late 1995, Ahmed Johnson was put in the mix with some of the WWF's biggest stars. After winning literally every single WWF match he wrestled in his first six months, Ahmed found himself on the 8th of April 1996 episode of *RAW* staring across the ring at the British Bulldog (accompanied by Owen Hart), for their first televised arm wrestling match. Both men's personas largely revolved around their incredible strength and the arm wrestling match was contested to see who the strongest man in the WWF was.

All worked arm wrestling matches in pro wrestling follow the exact same script. The heel stalls for minutes on end, complaining about anything and everything before locking hands, then either the babyface loses after the heel cheats or the babyface wins and gets attacked by the smarting heel. This particular arm wrestling contest would be no different, except for Owen being incredibly amusing. Owen whined that: Ahmed was covered in too much oil; that Ahmed's elbow was in the wrong position and that the Bulldog wasn't mentally prepared, before referee Jack Doane (rightly) sent Owen to the back. After several minutes of stalling tactics, Ahmed won the back and forth contest. A petulant Bulldog blindsided Ahmed before throwing the 'Pearl River Powerhouse' through a table, setting up a feud to take on the road for the next couple of months. The arm wrestling angle was pulled off almost flawlessly[1] but the segment still turned out to be a total stinker. Ahmed recalled, "I knew something was up, these two coming against me. They've got something planned. I know they got something planned!"

The reason why the match stunk out the building was thanks to Owen and Davey's pre-match preparations to gain the edge on Ahmed.

"They took a stink bomb[2] and smashed it in [Davey's] hand so it smelled like dog shit coming all the way up to the ring. Then we lock up and I mean it's the stinkiest smell you ever smelled. It smelled like pure dog doo-doo!" Unfortunately for Ahmed, the segment was being recorded live-to-tape for broadcast the following week, so there was no way he could break character and leave the ring to escape the smell. At the end of the post match brawl, Davey Boy went straight up to the nearest camera, struck a pose and yelled, "THAT'S WHAT YOU GET WHEN YOU MESS WITH THE BRITISH BULLDOOOOOOG!"

The reason why Owen and Bulldog went to such lengths to mess with Ahmed that evening was because they found out he had an important appointment after the show. "I had to meet what was going to be my wife's parents that night." Ahmed tried his best to get rid of the smell to no avail and resigned himself to the fact that he simply wasn't going to make the best impression on his future in-laws that evening. "[Owen and Davey are] just laughing their asses off. Then I had to go [meet] my soon-to-be wife's parents and I smelled like pure dog shit. [It was] the first time meeting them and I was like, I dunno what they're gonna say about me now!"

[1]Ahmed Johnson managed to injure his thumb during the encounter. Ahmed's biggest claim to infamy in the WWF was that he was incredibly injury-prone not only to others but to himself. While he didn't miss any ring time over the broken thumb, it was the start of a laundry list of physical trauma he would endure over the next two years as a WWF wrestler. Ahmed received a broken nose and a ruptured kidney in two separate matches during the same *WWF RAW* taping in July '96, which sidelined him for five months. Ahmed also hurt his knee immediately after his big heel turn in '97, aborting a WWF Championship pay-per-view main event and prominent feud with The Undertaker. After several more injuries and returns (including a car crash), Ahmed departed the WWF for good in February 1998. Ahmed reasoned that his injuries were due to his advancing age. "For those of you that didn't know, I was already in my thirties when I went to WWF. I lied. I was not born in 1972, or '69 or whatever the Internet

says. I was born in 1963. I was already on my way to being an old man. So of course I had some injuries."

[2]Stink bombs featured heavily in Owen's day-to-day pranking cycle. Former WWF announcer and writer Kevin Kelly rhapsodised about a particularly memorable incident at a television taping. "Backstage at TV is a madhouse. Crowded hallways fill with talent, television crews, caterers and the like, reflective of a nightclub. Without warning, a skunk-like odour permeates the air. The sulphuric aroma is pungent, yet familiar. Collectively, the crowd taking up space in the hall shout, 'Owen!' Another stink bomb dropped by the master. While no one actually saw the 'accused' drop the bomb that caused the human mass to pull their shirts over their noses, they all knew it was him."

Battle Royal Ribs

As told by Triple H and Jim Duggan

For those unaware, the traditional wrestling 'battle royal'[1] is a multi-person match where the only way to be eliminated is to go over the top rope and land on the floor outside the ring. Battle royals are notoriously unpopular with most wrestlers because it usually means working twice on the same show; and because battle royals are normally late on the card, everybody has to stay behind and fight through traffic along with fans leaving the arena at the same time. The issues of cooling down after the first match, gearing up for a second performance and the eternal dilemma of between-match showering does little to manufacture enthusiasm. Pranksters, however, saw these speciality matches as an opportunity to rib a multitude of lethargic, unsuspecting wrestlers in front of thousands of people while getting paid for it.

A classic example of battle royal-ribbery comes from Jim Duggan, the Big Boss Man and Mr Perfect. Duggan recalled in an interview that he and Boss Man once forced the Ultimate Warrior into a corner and 'worked him over' with chokes and strikes and the like. With the working punches and kicks proving an effective distraction, Boss Man took Warrior's arm and grape-vined it around the top rope in order to restrain him. With his arm incapacitated, Mr Perfect rolled onto the ring apron where he tied Warrior's nylon bicep tassel to the top rope. When the trio broke away from the corner, they watched in amazement as the meat-headed Warrior tried to tear the wet, nylon cord caveman-style by wrenching his arm away from the top rope as hard as he could. This resulted in the Warrior screaming in agony as the tassel painfully constricted around his heavily-muscled bicep. This extraordinary scene was followed by road agent Chief Jay Strongbow bumbling down to the ringside with a pocket knife before climbing onto the ring apron to cut him free. Duggan later said of the incident, "Curt, Boss and I got a free trip up to [WWF headquarters] Stamford, Connecticut for that one [to] talk to the big man a little bit!" With a well known internet meme comparing Ultimate Warrior's arm tassels to a little girl's bike, there were now two good reasons why Warrior should have considered a change in wardrobe.

In one particular battle royal in the mid '90s, Owen put his wrestling skills to misuse as he would go after the aristocratic blue blood, Hunter Hearst Helmsley, with a series of pinning attempts, such as school boys, backslides and sunset flips. The fact that pinfalls don't count in over-the-top battle royals didn't deter The King of Harts from performing the series of false finishes, all while Triple H was, "Laughing so hard and trying not to get caught laughing," at the illogical choice of move set. Owen would nearly always pull his in-ring antics on non-televised house shows, where only the fans in the arena would bear witness to Owen's jolly japes; but not always. During the *Royal Rumble 1996* pay-per-view, Owen can clearly be seen rolling up Helmsley in a pinning manoeuvre, after which Helmsley can briefly be seen laughing on-camera.

Owen would also bring certain tools of the trade with him for these multi-man matches, such as stink bombs to break over someone's head before escaping to another part of the ring. Owen also brought athletic tape with him and, like Mr Perfect before him, would force a wrestler into the corner before wrapping the entire roll of tape around their arm and the top rope, before walking off and leaving them to struggle through the unravelling process. Triple H, with a smile on his face, said of the rib, "Trying to rip athletic tape off when you're in the middle of thirty guys in a battle royal... is just misery."

[1]Battle royals were originally conceived as 'Broughton's Battle Royals' in eighteenth century England by bare-knuckle pugilist John Broughton. These involved eight men fighting in one ring at the same time until an eventual winner was crowned. In the United States, from the days of slavery to as late as the 1950s, battle royals were almost exclusively contested between black boxers for white audiences. Combatants numbering anywhere from four to thirty were often blindfolded and advertised as 'fun for all the family' comic relief at the beginning of boxing/wrestling cards, or as part of amusement fairs or carnival festivities. Sometimes, the participants had one hand tied behind their back, or would be wearing feed bags, or sometimes even barrels. Along

with several future heavyweight boxing champions of their eras such as Jack Johnson, 'The Godfather of Soul' James Brown participated in battle royals during his teenage years. As Loretta Lynn once sang, *We've Come a Long Way, Baby.*

Marc Mero Locker Room Locked Up

As told by Marc Mero

After five years of bouncing around WCW's mid-card as Little Richard rip-off 'Johnny B Badd', Marc Mero (confusingly named after the famous song by Chuck Berry) was suddenly discovered by Vince McMahon. McMahon saw a potential main-eventer in the *Tutti Frutti* impersonator and quickly signed him to the WWF in March 1996. 'Wildman' Marc Mero signed the WWF's first-ever guaranteed contract to the tune of $350,000 per year.[1] His blonde bombshell wife Rena 'Sable' Mero was also signed to be his valet and he received a big push right out of the gate. Owen Hart, who had a proven track record as an effective upper-mid-card to main event player, re-signed shortly after the unproven Mero's WWF debut for significantly less money, which also didn't endear Mero to anyone in the locker room.

In his first year with the WWF, management was determined to get the Wildman over with the fans. Mero was booked to wrestle Hunter Hearst Helmsley practically every night, with Mero unrepentantly beating the future Triple H in nearly every match they ever had. As summer turned to autumn, the powers-that-be gave Mero a break from destroying Helmsley and booked him in several singles matches against both Owen Hart and 'British Bulldog' Davey Boy Smith.

On the 14th of September 1996, the WWF crew were in the midst of yet another European tour, only this time it would be a European tour of Africa: Sun City, South Africa, to be precise. Mero and Bulldog were in a locker room getting changed into their ring gear, going over the planned spots for their match that night and warming up before heading out to the ring. With the match now about to start, the Wildman's angry jungle cat-themed entrance music kicked in over the arena speakers. Mero went to exit the locker room only to find that the door wouldn't budge; somebody had locked the door from the other side. To make matters worse, the show was being filmed in front of over 6,000 fans for a special on South Africa's SuperSport channel.

With panic setting in and Mero's entrance music still playing, both men broke down laughing at the absurdity of the situation and knew exactly who was responsible. Davey Boy turned to Marc and exclaimed, "Wait 'til I get my hands on that guy!" In the nick of time, the door flew open and Owen Hart was grinning on the other side. Even though Owen was as guilty as a dog standing next to a big pile of poo, the Wildman had no time to engage in protracted discourse over the rib he'd just endured. Marc sprinted past Owen towards the entrance curtain before confidently walking out in front of the crowd like nothing had ever happened. What is known is that Owen definitely locked the door. What isn't known is how Owen managed to sneak backstage in the first place, as he'd been sitting ringside for the entire show providing colour commentary with Jim Ross.

In the end, the biggest rib played on Marc Mero during his Federation tenure was the one he played on himself. With the Wildman character not connecting with the fans whatsoever and his buxom, silicon-enhanced wife-turned-valet, Sable, completely overshadowing him, Marc would inadvertently make the call that would put the final bullet in his WWF career. During a storyline breakup angle between the real-life couple, Marc allowed the incredibly popular Sable to hit him with her powerbomb finishing manoeuvre. Not only did Mero become a total joke in the fans' eyes, Stone Cold Steve Austin, upon witnessing Marc's 100lb wife destroy him with ease, cancelled a lucrative main event house show run that Marc and Austin were booked to face each other on. By the end of 1998, the newly-dubbed 'Marvellous' Marc Mero lost a 'loser leaves town' match to lifelong jobber Duane 'Gillberg' Gill and a mixed tag match in London before being taken off WWF television permanently, never to return.

[1]Before this date, McMahon only offered his wrestlers 'opportunities' and a guarantee of ten dates per year at $150 a shot. Obviously, the full-timers made far more than that but wrestlers also wouldn't know what to expect financially until they received their *WrestleMania* cheques, which was the highest paying event in the WWF calendar (and it still is, discounting some of the cheques from the bi-annual WWE-

Saudi Arabia shows). WCW had been handing out guaranteed contracts for years. Sting was famously the highest paid WCW wrestler under contract for several years in the 1990s, earning a flat $750,000 per year. The $750k figure would be referred to by those in the industry as 'Sting money'. With WCW buying up as much talent as possible, McMahon was forced to provide more financial security for his wrestlers and relented on the guaranteed money issue. Only a couple of weeks prior to Mero signing, future three-time WWE Champion Mick Foley inked his WWF deal under the old non-guarantee contract structure for far less money and let his feelings be known in great detail in his 1999 biography *Have a Nice Day: A Tale of Blood and Sweatsocks*.

Ahmed Johnson on Jay Leno

As told by Ahmed Johnson

Back in 1996 and the WWF's biggest pay-per-view event of the year *WrestleMania XII* was being held in Anaheim, California. Bret Hart vs. Shawn Michaels for the WWF Championship would headline the card, The Ultimate Warrior would return from Parts Unknown (AKA Scottsdale, Arizona) after a three and a half year layoff and Ahmed Johnson would make the first of two appearances at 'The Granddaddy of Them All.'[1] All the wrestlers were given a week off before flying to Anaheim several days prior to *WrestleMania* to meet fans, sign autographs and promote the upcoming pay-per-view. As one of the hottest new stars on the WWF roster, opportunities were presenting themselves for Ahmed to go beyond the wrestling bubble and into more accepted media.

A couple of days before *WrestleMania*, Ahmed got the biggest mainstream opportunity of any WWF wrestler in several years. "I'm in my [hotel] room with my brother and the phone rings and it's *The Jay Leno Show,*" said Ahmed. "I'm talking to 'em and giving them the information they need and I was going to be on the next day." If he was going to be making his network television debut as a WWF superstar, Ahmed reasoned that he'd better look the part. "I went out and I spent about $4,000 on a suit and some shoes and a nice chain and everything. I get dressed up; I mean $4,000 [worth of clothes]. I'm decked-out and I'm pimped up from head-to-toe." The *Leno Show* rep told Johnson to be outside his hotel for eight o'clock sharp so the limo could take him to the studio.

Ahmed was outside the hotel early waiting in anticipation when Owen and Davey Boy Smith saw Ahmed togged up to the nines and asked him what the big occasion was. "I told them I had *The Jay Leno Show* and they got pissed off," Ahmed recalled. "They're like, 'We've been here for so-and-so many years and you got *The Jay Leno Show* and we haven't done his talk show or anything?'" The Pearl River Powerhouse was sympathetic to the mischievous brothers-in-law and couldn't fully justify why he was getting more mainstream attention in six months than they had after many years of loyal service. The trio stood and chatted before Ahmed embarked on the one hour trip to Burbank Studios; but before long Ahmed realised something was amiss. "I'm sitting out there, man, in my new clothes, my new watch, my new jewellery and eight o'clock hits: no limo. Owen looks at me and says, 'Ain't your limo supposed to be here at eight o'clock?' I say, 'Yeah!' Then I thought, how the hell did you know my limo was coming at eight o'clock?"

It turned out that nobody from *The Jay Leno Show* had called Ahmed's hotel room the previous night. In fact, no one on Jay Leno's booking staff had probably even heard the name Ahmed Johnson. The voice on the other end of the line claiming to be Leno's rep was actually Owen. On the strength of what a voice over the phone had told him, Ahmed went out and spent $4,000 of his own money on apparel when WWF paycheques weren't as robust as they once were. "I got all dressed up and went outside for nothing and [Owen] and Davey hit the floor laughing and Bret came out [and] fell in the bushes he was laughing so hard. They got me good, man!"

On top of everything else, Owen's story didn't even add up. *The Tonight Show* was not (and still isn't) broadcast live; it's taped earlier in the day, usually five o'clock EST as of this writing. Even if Ahmed Johnson was getting picked up for eight o'clock, by the time he got to the studio, the episode would have already been taped and ready for broadcast. Despite finding himself massively out of pocket and having his dreams of mainstream recognition dashed, Ahmed only has fond memories of his interactions with Owen. "Owen Hart kept morale up. Owen Hart [was] the best, man. I swear to god I used to love coming to work just 'cause Owen was going to be there and you know he's going to be doing something crazy."

[1]Reports at the show indicated that the majority of fans went to *WrestleMania XII* for The Ultimate Warrior's return and not the Bret vs. Shawn sixty-minute Iron Man match main event. Warrior got the biggest reaction of the night by far, even after Michaels zip-lined down to the ring from the rafters during his entrance. It was said that hundreds, if not thousands, of fans left during the main event, which came across far worse live than it did on TV, where the match was hailed as an instant classic.

De-Pantsing on
The Wrestle Vessel

As told by Jim Ross

One of the more innovative ways various pop culture icons have cashed in on their loyal fan base in the past few decades has been through fan-themed cruises.[1] WCW got in on the action in 1991 with the 'Bruise Cruise', featuring: Sting, The Fabulous Freebirds, Scott Steiner, Marc Mero and Jim Ross, among others. WCW quickly keelhauled the Bruise Cruise concept only for the WWF to salvage the wreckage from Davey ~~Boy~~ Jones' Locker in 1996. The WWF called their cruise experience the 'Wrestle Vessel'; a five day odyssey from Key West, Florida to Cozumel, Mexico and back, with many of the WWF's biggest stars aboard for the long haul. There would be signings, photograph opportunities and a volleyball tournament to entertain the fans. Of course, Owen Hart was aboard for the trip, as well as brother Bret and parents Stu and Helen. A lot of wrestlers brought their families and it was a nice way of spending a relaxing week off the road while still getting paid.[2]

On the second day, the cruise liner was traversing the Gulf of Mexico and many of the wrestlers, their families and WWF fans were relaxing and tanning by the pool. Jim Ross, who by this time was a rugged veteran of wrestling-themed cruises thanks to his Bruise Cruise experiences, understood his portly frame was not best suited for the intense heat of the summer sun and spent the majority of his time submerged in the pool. Ross was frolicking in the shallow end in full view of the wrestlers, the wrestlers' wives, the wrestlers' children and numerous fans and cabin crew, when Owen slipped into the pool behind him. Without so much as a warning shot across the bow, Owen broadsided the WWF President of Talent Relations by yanking Jim's trunks right down to his ankles. "Everyone laughed but no one laughed louder than Owen," Ross later recounted. "As *Seinfeld's* George Costanza once bemoaned, there was significant shrinkage!" After the whole ship got a good look at his midshipman and with the wind very much taken out of his sails, Good Ol' JR hoisted his trunks back up and scuttled off in embarrassment.

In a rare occurrence, Owen would receive a measure of comeuppance a year later. In 2018, Dwayne 'The Rock' Johnson posted a brief video clip of him pantsing Owen while the WWF toured Dubai in 1997. Members of the press were taking photographs of the wrestlers out in the desert when a smiling Rock ripped down the unsuspecting Owen's shorts. Owen, who was thankfully wearing underwear, barely flinched and instead just grinned goofily as the press continued to snap away. As of this writing, the four-second de-pantsing video on The Rock's Instagram account has been viewed more than ten million times.

---

[1]Stadium glam rockers and equal-opportunity merchandisers KISS are perhaps most notorious for hosting celebrity themed-cruises for their most die-hard (and wealthy) fans but they're not the only band to rock the high seas. Everyone from Weezer to Def Leppard to Motorhead to a million other classic rockers have played on cruise ships. Cult television shows have got in on the act as well, such as *Star Trek, The Walking Dead* and even *Impractical Jokers*. Wrestling cruises recently made a comeback, with Chris Jericho's 'Rock 'N' Wrestling Rager at Sea' shipping out in 2018, with a further cruise booked for 2020.

[2]Well that was the theory, anyway. As weird as wrestling superfans tend to be (a statement backed up by WWF-shot footage from the 1997 cruise), they were all very respectful and kept their distance from their heroes during non-official meet-and-greets. The problems were caused by the non-WWF guests. "The rest of the folks on board didn't really respect any boundaries while the guys were out with their families," said Prichard. Regular guests would crowd around wrestlers while they were eating dinner with their families. When the cruise liner people took photos of the wrestlers and their families, fans bought up the photos before the wrestlers had the chance to buy them for themselves.

230

Cake Wars: Davey vs. Tammy
A British Bulldog Entry

As told by Tammy Sytch, Sean Waltman and Steve Austin

Tammy Sytch arrived in the World Wrestling Federation with her real-life boyfriend Chris Candido in May 1995. The young couple had previously enjoyed a two year run in Jim Cornette's Smoky Mountain Wrestling with Candido under his birth name and Sytch as Tammy Fytch; a disciple of Hilary Clinton, which got tremendous heat in the deeply Republican, bible belt-based territory. After losing a loser leaves town match to Boo Bradley (Balls Mahoney) at SMW's *Sunday Bloody Sunday II* event that February, Candido and Sytch joined the WWF as 'Skip' and 'Sunny'; a pair of fitness fanatics who got heat by calling fans and other wrestlers 'fat'.[1] Sunny was stunning, full of attitude and quickly became the breakout star, especially among male fans. Her character swiftly switched from a fitness freak to a gold digger. She ditched The Bodydonnas (Skip and Tom 'Zip' Prichard[2]) for the hillbilly Godwinns when they won the WWF Tag Team Titles shortly after *WrestleMania XII*. By the summer of 1996, Sunny had switched allegiances again to The Smoking Gunns after turning on The Godwinns and helping the Gunns win the belts.

SummerSlam 1996 was to see The Smoking Gunns defend their Tag Team Titles against three other teams, but for Tammy, the event would be more memorable for the battle for dominance that occurred backstage. *SummerSlam '96* was held at the brand new Gund Arena in Cleveland, Ohio. The building was state-of-the-art, spacious and enriched with brand new carpeting, not only on the floors but on the walls and the WWF pay-per-view would be the very first show to be held within its virginal confines.

Before show time, Tammy was walking backstage when she noticed Bret Hart staring down at a large sheet cake with an intricate portrait of himself printed on it. Bret said a fan had sent it to him and therefore absolutely refused to eat it, then he walked off. A few minutes later, Tammy walked by the same table, this time with Davey Boy Smith looking down at the cake. "Tammy, smell the nose. It smells like strawberry," invited Davey. Because Davey was as well known as Owen for being a prankster, Tammy knew that if she put her head anywhere near the cake she'd end up wearing it as a hat. As a pre-emptive measure, Tammy grabbed a handful of cake and palmed it in Davey's face. Tammy recalled that Davey was understandably not best pleased. "Oh, Okay, Tammy," he said, as he regained his composure, "shit's on now!"

Davey grabbed the entire cake and chased Tammy across the carpeted hallway until they reached a dead end. Without having time to even turn around, Davey drilled Tammy in the back of the head with a wad of cake. By this time the commotion had caught the ear of several wrestlers and Owen walked out of the locker room to investigate. Dave and Tammy looked at each other, then Davey gave Tammy a wink. With that, Owen found the entire cake being shoved in his face so hard he hit his head on the wall behind him. Owen pealed the sheet cake off his face, then immediately got revenge on the Bulldog by taking what remained of the butter cream confection into the locker room and dumping all of it inside Bulldog's gear bag.

With the entire locker room laughing at his misfortune, Davey, still bestrewn with icing, was scooping out cake remnants from his bag when he saw Tammy laughing at him from the door way. "Tammy, you think that's funny, huh?" he shouted in his thick, Mancunian accent, before giving chase once again. Tammy bolted to the women's locker room where her boyfriend Chris Candido was sitting down, minding his own business. Once again, Davey and Tammy were at an impasse, eyeballing each other with a fistful of cake in each hand, with Candido sat down between them. Once again, Davey winked and both knew exactly what the other was thinking. "At the same time, we turned and our handfuls of cake went flying at Chris' face, exploding all over the carpeted wall behind him."

All the commotion attracted the attention of 'Mr Personality' Tony Garea, the long-time Federation employee whose number of WWWF Tag Title reigns over the years outnumbered the amount of fans who'd ever bought tickets to see him wrestle (five). Garea was one of the agents that evening when he walked into the room and observed the turmoil. "WHAT IS THIS TRAVESTY?" Garea shouted in an admonishing tone. Bulldog and Tammy slunk out of the room, leaving Chris Candido, still smeared in cake, to take the brunt of New Zealander's tongue-lashing.[3]   After establishing the facts, Tony ordered Tammy and Davey to stay behind after the show to clean up the carpeted walls. Garea also fined them $500 apiece. "It was absolutely hilarious as we were scrubbing the walls, still covered from head to toe in cake. It was the best $500 each of us had ever spent."

Tammy was probably hoping to get a measure of revenge on Davey with the cake attack after he ribbed her during a three week tour of Germany that April. Because she was a heel, Tammy rode the heel bus alongside Owen and Davey throughout the tour, guaranteeing some sort of prank would befall her. After a number of days, the tour bus' tiny latrine started smelling particularly ripe. This was despite the fact it was rarely used, as the guys preferred to wazz in a bottle and throw it out the window.

During a particularly lengthy commute across the Vaterland, Tammy decided she couldn't wait for the bus to stop. When she assumed everyone else to be asleep, Tammy braved the trip to the on-board khazi to attend to some much-needed business. After she was done, she tried to open the door to find that it wouldn't budge. She finally managed to prise the door ajar just enough to figure out that somebody had filled the stairwell with every single piece of luggage on board the coach. Tammy, who hadn't ingratiated herself to her co-workers as well as she might have done over the past year, wouldn't be let out of the putrid bathroom until the end of the journey, which would take another two hours. Tammy quickly realised that the perpetrator of the rib had a 'distinct British laugh'. "The culprit was Davey Boy, the British Bulldog. If he and I weren't such good friends, I might have been pissed off but I knew it was all in good fun."

She certainly took that rib better than the next one. After allegedly grousing that some of the crew's tardiness was disrupting her workout schedule, Tammy would find herself in the crosshairs of the Kliq. Chris and Tammy had already generated enough animosity with the WWF crew that they'd taken to hiding their bags in every arena as a pre-emptive measure. One day during that same tour, Kliq member Sean Waltman found Tammy's bag behind a locked chain link fence in the bowels of the arena. Waltman scaled the fence and went to work, interfering with the packed lunch Tammy was saving for that night. "I found the food, I opened it up

233

nice and carefully, I pulled the chicken breast up and I dumped a turd under the chicken breast... and I put it back in place nicely... I can't tell you whose turd it was but it wasn't mine!"

Steve Austin, who had no clue about the prank at that point, recalled his reaction when the bus pulled up to the hotel that night, "When they popped the [luggage] hatches on that damn bus it smelled like someone had taken a big, steaming shit on the sidewalk!" According to Austin, despite the overpowering stench, Tammy and Chris collected their bags and checked in to the hotel apparently oblivious to Tammy's supplemental carry-on. "They went all the way up to the room, put the bags in the room... and still didn't smell a rat [or] in this case a turd! At 3:30-4:00 in the morning, I guess someone got the munchies and went to open [the food container] and there was a big-ass stink-pickle!" Tammy was hysterical, Candido was furious and, curiously, Davey Boy was hopping mad over the rib as well, seeing it as a step too far. Tammy complained to WWF head office and ended up leaving the European tour early, likely bringing even more ill will on herself in the bizarre and often disgusting world of wrestling.

[1]While Candido was a very good worker, he never made it in the WWF as he was undersized for the time, the physical trainer gimmick was uninspired and Chris was completely overshadowed by his girlfriend/valet Tammy. Candido left for ECW in the Autumn of 1996 while Tammy stayed on, becoming AOL Online's most downloaded celebrity of that year (beating *Baywatch* belle Pamela Anderson) before self-destructing on drugs and bad attitude. She was fired in July 1998.

[2]According to former Federation announcer Kevin Kelly, 'Dr' Tom Prichard was one of many victims to receive a phone call from a 'hotel manager' telling him to vacate his room an hour early. Kelly's version follows the familiar pattern of the good Doctor becoming more and more agitated until he stormed into the lobby, where he was greeted by a smirking Owen and Davey Boy. Prichard's version goes exactly like this. "I was getting ready to check out of my hotel and [Owen] called acting like he was the manager hurrying me up. I knew it was Owen right off."

[3]This wouldn't be the only time Candido would be made to look the fool at the hands of Tammy and Davey, as the pair (by Tammy's own admission) had an 'on-and-off' relationship after she'd stopped seeing Shawn Michaels (also behind Chris' back). The list of wrestlers Tammy has admitted to sleeping with over the years is only dwarfed by the list of wrestlers she's been *accused* of sleeping with. "I was the source for a lot of heat," Tammy would admit years after her WWF run.

"Hey, Look!"
Indian Vomit Stop

As told by Bret Hart and Kevin Nash

In February 1996, the WWF embarked on its first-ever trip to India; a five day, whistle-stop tour across the Asian subcontinent. The flight to India was already eventful, as Razor Ramon and Savio Vega had engaged in a Machiavellian battle of wits at 35,000 feet. The opening salvo was Razor giving a sleeping Savio the old shaving cream turban gag before drawing all over his face with pink lipstick. Later on in the flight, Savio avenged the rib by chopping Ramon's ponytail off, as well as Shawn Michaels' for good measure while they were both zonked out. Shortly after the tour began, many of the wrestlers started suffering from Delhi Belly and taking hard bumps in the ring became a life-or-death exercise in bowel control.

The last day of the tour, coincidentally, took place in Delhi on the 6th of February. At the prompting of Owen, his wife Martha and some of the other wrestlers, the promoters of the Delhi show booked a tour bus for Agra to see one of the seven modern wonders of the world; the Taj Mahal. Most of the wrestlers were sick and tired not only with the runs but with the disgusting conditions, the poverty, the death, the heat and the choking pollution that hung heavy in India's sprawling cities. Owen convinced many of the crew to come anyway as it was unlikely they'd ever be in the country again. The four hour drive to Agra was described by Bret as a 'death ride' and the drive back was even worse. "Those Stampede Wrestling black ice hell rides, even the time Smith drove André to the airport,[1] they were a merry-go-round ride compared to this." The bus driver drove even more like a mad man on the return leg, as Delhi was under a curfew and the bus wouldn't be allowed to enter the city if they arrived after 10pm. As India has more fatalities on its roads than any other country in the world, everybody's concerns with the bus driver's lack of due care and attention were well-founded.

Toward the end of the seven hour trip back to the hotel, which saw a dog get run over and various deals with various deities made to survive the journey, the driver pulled into a petrol station to fill up. As the bus crawled onto the forecourt, another bus pulled up beside theirs. The packed bus' doors flung open and several Indians jumped out. The sickly natives commenced puking up all over the floor in unison, probably ailing from the same motion sickness and low-quality cuisine the WWF crew had been suffering from. Because the wrestlers had embarked on the death bus to see some spectacular sights, Owen pointed out the window and called out, "Hey look!" Oblivious WWF agent and former Oklahoma State wrestler, Gerald Brisco, ran over with his camera ready to take a snap for posterity, unaware of the revolting scene that was about to greet him. "It probably made my trip and everyone else's on that lousy bus to watch the ripple effect on Brisco," said Bret. "[Brisco] scrambled down the steps and up-chucked his curried rice!"

[1]The car ride refers to the time eldest Hart kid Smith gave Andre the Giant a ride to the airport in 1979. Andre and NWA Champion Harley Race were the superstar attractions booked for the annual Calgary Stampede festival shows in July. Andre's original flight to Butte, Montana had been cancelled but Smith found a seat on a flight leaving in twenty-two minutes. The problem was that it was a forty minute drive to the airport. Smith, Andre and Bret careened down the highways at breakneck speed before pulling up outside the airport. When they arrived, the trio were promptly detained by the Royal Canadian Mounted Police. Andre never forgave Smith or Stu for letting Smith drive; and Bret got the cold shoulder from 'The Boss' for several years too. The show in Butte also turned out to be a disaster, as Smith forgot to hook up the ring trailer to the van and NWA World Champion Harley Race had to defend his title in front of a sold-out crowd on gym mats.

Roman Candles

As told by Dustin Runnels and Tammy Sytch

Back in January 1996, the entire WWF crew embarked on a two week tour that kicked off in Cornwall, Ontario. While Canadian crowds were usually hot, the Canadian drives were often long and arduous, especially in the winter months. This particular trip was looking to be especially tough as there was a blizzard forecast and there was thick snow and ice on the ground. Tammy Sytch, Chris Candido, Goldust, Marty Jannetty, Al Snow (Sarven), Bart Gunn, Billy Gunn, Davey Boy Smith and Owen Hart all clubbed together to rent a twelve seat Ford minibus for the fourteen day trip. The WWF's explosion in popularity was still a couple of years away and most members of the roster were looking to save a buck anywhere they could.

A couple of days into the tour, Owen decided he didn't want to pay one ninth of the fuel and toll costs and hopped in a different van with one of his regular fans for the rest of the loop. While piloting down a desolate, baron highway towards Montreal, the remaining wrestlers' eyes were drawn to an inviting advertising hoarding: 'FIREWORKS ON SALE HERE!' Fireworks weren't the easiest thing to come by in the States, especially out of season. The minibus pulled into the truck stop and everyone vaulted out to partake in a little late night shopping. After making their purchases, the wrestlers hit the road again where it didn't take long for trouble to start brewing. Whether it was from boredom or recreational goodies or snow blindness or whatever, an impromptu triple threat match between Jannetty, Goldust and Davey Boy broke out in middle of the minibus. They got so raucous that they ended up ripping the seat right out of the floor. Davey soon solved the issue of the detached seating by launching the three berth chair out of the minibus' side door and into the middle of the highway while still travelling eighty miles per hour. While many might consider Davey's actions reckless, keep in mind that it was a twelve-seat vehicle. They could have even thrown one more out and still have one each, plus a bigger space to wrestle in.

During a designated toilet stop for Owen, the fan and the minibus contingent, Davey Boy set to work utilising the first of his firework store purchases. While Owen and his friend were in the public convenience making use of the facilities, Davey Boy lit three smoke bombs and dropped them into the fan's motor. As the wrestlers took off in the minibus, Goldust looked in the rearview mirror and saw, "This green and yellow smoke coming out of the [van]. Smoke is everywhere, Owen is laughing his ass off and his friend is freaking out because he thinks his [van] is on fire."

After order was restored and everybody took their (remaining) seats, Marty, for reasons unknown, wound down the window to let some of the bitter January snow into the minibus. Marty then snapped the window-operating handle clean off. Tammy attempted to explain Marty's actions thusly. "Why did he break it? Because it was there. What were the repercussions? We couldn't close the window in the middle of a blizzard." If Owen and his fan/chauffeur, who were closely following the now nine-seater Ford minibus, thought Davey's high-speed ejecting of furniture was the most perilous act they'd witness all evening, they were seriously wrong.

While Owen and the fan were tootling along behind the rest of the crew, several of the wrestlers poked out of the minibus's windows clutching the rockets and roman candles they'd purchased from the roadside store and declared World War III on the fan's pristine white van. "Upon Davey's orders, we lit them all and shot balls of fire out of the [minibus] directly at Owen behind us," recalled Tammy. The van started speeding up towards the minibus, either because Owen wanted to catch fireballs in the van's grill or because the fan was so upset he was chasing after the minibus, depending on who's telling the story. Either way it wasn't the smartest of moves. "We all died in laughter as the fan's van began filling up with smoke, almost to where you couldn't see their faces through the windows," said Tammy. When Owen and the fan caught up to the minibus, Goldust recalled breaking out the heavy artillery to drive them back. "We're flying down the freeway at around eighty miles per hour still shooting these Roman candles at his hood and we're throwing firecrackers out the windows at them any time they got close."

Owen and the fan briefly gave up the chase and pulled over because they could no longer see or breathe properly. When the van was suitably aerated, they tore off in search of the rest of the WWF crew. Goldust's recollection of events was that he was driving the minibus at this point and in order to fool Owen and the fan, pulled over into a ditch adjacent to the highway and turned the minibus's lights off. After Owen and the fan obliviously drove past the darkened minibus, Goldust, so as to not give away his location, inched out of the ditch with the lights still off before racing to catch up. "So I pull right up on their ass and I'm talking about within a foot of their [van] and I'm just hoping they don't slam on the brakes. So here goes Davey Boy, he lights up another Roman candle and—*voom!*—he starts shooting it at their back window. I turned on the brights and started honking the horn trying to freak them out."

The next morning, the full extent of the damage on the van was revealed. The once shiny, white exterior was now stippled with filthy brown-black burn marks from the fireworks, as well as burn marks to the van's interior carpet where Davey Boy had dropped the smoke bombs. To make matters worse, the fan's van wasn't a rental; it actually belonged to him. Astonishingly, the fan took it well. "He didn't care," remembered Goldust. "He was just a big fan of Owen's, they were friends, so he was like, 'It's cool.' I'll never forget that."

The minibus however *was* a rental and over the course of one trip they'd almost totalled it. None of this worried Davey Boy Smith however as he knew exactly how to handle the situation. He confidently walked up to the rental agency's reception desk and, with faux-indignation in his Mancunian accent, laid the blame squarely on the rental company. "I can't believe you rented me a [minibus] in this condition! The front window is broken, there is no middle seat and it smells of smoke with burns all over the carpet! I had my wife and children in this [minibus]! This is a travesty!" The rental manager was so embarrassed he not only reimbursed Davey the two weeks money on the minibus but gave him a week's free rental by way of apology. When he left the car rental shop, Davey was 'laughing and smiling,' full of pride at his accomplishment. According to Tammy, Davey wasn't entitled to any money at all. "It wasn't rented on his credit card but he got it refunded to him. He turned a profit on the deal!"

Bad Matches:
Owen Hart vs. Marc Mero
and Imaginary Cigarettes

As told by Mick Foley

On the 11th of August 1996, the WWF held a show at the Catholic Youth Centre in Scranton, Pennsylvania where Mick Foley had the pleasure of watching Owen Hart engage in one of his celebrated 'bad' matches for the very first time. Before he was to wrestle The Undertaker later that night as Mankind, Mick walked to a little hallway near the entrance curtain where he could get a good look at Owen take on WWF newcomer and heat magnet Marc Mero. The match was not the crisp and smooth affair it should have been and from Mick's point of view it was the veteran Owen's fault. When Mero landed a flying shoulder tackle, Owen fell down slowly like a felled tree instead of throwing himself to the ground back-first to register the impact. When Mero whipped him into the ropes, instead of running normally, Owen took enormous, arching steps like an ostrich. When Owen took a hip toss, he practically rolled on the floor instead of jumping in the air.

Mick, like every other wrestler, had taken part in more than a few stinkers over the course of his career but the idea of someone having a bad match on purpose was a completely foreign concept to him until that day. "This was Owen Hart, whose matches I'd seen in Stampede and New Japan and WWE, one of the best wrestlers in the business just reeking. Then I heard Davey [Boy Smith] going, 'Look at Owen, ooh! Look at Owen! He's too much, he's too much!' That's when I realised he's doing this to entertain us and I took that as a challenge."

During a short tour of the tiny, Middle East country of Kuwait in April 1997, Owen once again did his best to make everyone else in the match look ridiculous, just to amuse his biggest fan, Davey. Bret Hart, The Undertaker and 'The Stalker' Barry Windham[1] took on Owen, Davey and Mick Foley (as Mankind) in the main event of the show. Windham gurned and scowled at the audience as he clamped Owen in a rear chinlock. Owen reacted to the submission attempt by showing absolutely no emotion whatsoever, before reaching his hand to his mouth to smoke an imaginary cigarette.

At the culmination of the match, Bret had Owen locked into his Sharpshooter submission. Bret had his devastating finisher locked in but Owen looked as if he was feeling no pain. "He rubbed his eyes sleepily and checked his wrist for an imaginary watch," said Mick. "Bret cinched up further and Owen yawned. Finally, Bret rocked back even further and Owen finally yelled out in pain." Bret was legitimately annoyed with Owen, whose antics he felt showed him a lack of respect. Owen couldn't have cared less. "He was an incredible talent," Triple H said, "but he just didn't take things too seriously and I think that there was a bit of animosity between him and Bret because Bret took things *so* seriously."

[1]Billed from 'The Environment' The Stalker, played by former WCW World Champion Barry Windham, was conceived as a militia-type loner, knocking about in the woods, stalking unidentified prey. The Stalker's original storyline feud was rumoured to be against Marc Mero, where The Stalker would 'cut Sable's throat'. Mero flat out refused to allow the angle to go ahead, so The Stalker, with his ominous, axe-murderer entrance theme and camouflage face paint, was introduced as a babyface that literally nobody could get behind.

Marty Jannetty's Pink Singlet

As told by Al Snow

For well over a decade, 'The Best Kept Secret in Professional Wrestling', Al Snow, toiled in ignominy, wrestling for small-time promotions across the States before making appearances for ECW and SMW in 1994. By 1995, Snow, who was a competent in-ring performer, finally developed an on-screen personality as a cocky heel alongside his tag team partner, Mike Unabomb.[1] When Al finally made it to the big-time (WCW didn't pick him up after a try-out match) the brain trust at the WWF turned Al into the Hayabusa rip-off Avatar, a Japanese ninja/Power Ranger who walked to the ring carrying his mask in his hand. Snow would then put his mask on, engage in pre-match katas, get beaten up, lose and then unmask again. When that gimmick obviously didn't work, poor Al was repackaged as the Great Sasuke rip-off Shinobi (also a ninja) with a mission statement to destroy Shawn Michaels. He didn't and was repackaged again after just two matches.

Al Snow's third WWF character in less than a year lasted a little longer but was still a hopeless endeavour. Snow was teamed up with former Midnight Rocker Marty Jannetty to become The New Rockers.[2] Snow was rechristened Leif Cassidy (a portmanteau of seventies heartthrobs Leif Garrett and David Cassidy) and told to act as goofy and as geeky as possible. Jannetty once claimed that The New Rockers were meant to be a straight wrestling act until Jannetty's ex-Rocker tag partner, Shawn Michaels, suggested to Vince McMahon that The New Rockers should be a goofball comedy team.

Because The New Rockers were a bottom-of-the-rung act, the WWF could only be bothered to make two outfits apiece. The first design was a black singlet with luminous green strips and lots of fringe and was passable at best. The second singlet design was hot pink with multicoloured stripes and fringes that even children's TV presenter Timmy Mallett would have felt was a bit too garish. Jannetty's incessant complaining over the neon outfit caught the ears of Owen Hart and Davey Boy Smith, who obviously 'misinterpreted'

Jannetty's grumblings and assumed he wanted to wear the pink singlet for *every* match.

One day, Marty arrived in the locker room to find a giant padlock on the shoulder straps of the preferred black and green singlet, rendering it completely unwearable. The padlock was so heavy duty no one could figure out how to remove it. Snow and Jannetty borrowed a workman's drill to no avail before hanging the singlet and the padlock out of the boot of their car, dragging it along the ground while they drove. "It didn't do a thing to the padlock," said Snow, "but when I had to brake sharply, it swung up and put a big dent in the back of the rental car." Eventually they rented industrial bolt cutters to free the shoulder straps *and* Jannetty from the embarrassment of the hot pink accoutrement.

To get back at Owen and Davey, Marty went on a campaign of retaliatory ribs, including breaking off toothpicks in the key holes of their rental cars, cancelling their flights by simply phoning up the airline and rescinding the tickets, as well as dumping shrimp in brine in their gear bags. The original plan was to release a skunk into Owen and Davey's hotel room, which unfortunately never came to fruition. Snow and Jannetty were travelling to Montreal in the middle of the night when Jannetty spotted a lowly stink badger at the side of the road. At Marty's insistence, he and Al fumbled about in the pitch black Canadian wilderness futilely grasping at the terrified skunk while getting sprayed from its anal scent glands. The New Rockers didn't manage to catch the skunk that night but did manage to stink out their own hotel room. "This was what Owen and Davey could drive you to: two grown men on a grass median at 3am, getting sprayed by a skunk." It turns out that Shawn Michaels may have had a point about booking The Midnight Rockers as a goofball comedy tag team after all.

[1]Glenn Jacobs, who played Unabomb, was soon picked up by the WWF where he portrayed the evil dentist Isaac Yankem DDS and the fake 'Diesel' before his career skyrocketed playing The Undertaker's younger brother Kane. The real Diesel (Kevin Nash) had left the WWF in May 1996 for WCW along with Scott 'Razor Ramon' Hall. By September, *WCW Nitro* was destroying *WWF RAW* in the weekly ratings war, in no small part thanks to Nash and Hall. In an act of desperation, the WWF

announced the return of 'Diesel' and 'Razor'. With speculation running rampant, Jim Ross introduced the obviously counterfeit 'Diesel' and 'Razor' on the live 23rd of September *RAW* to an outraged audience. Hall and Nash, who'd jumped to WCW for more money ($800,000 in year one, $850,000 year two and $950,000 year three) and less dates (around 180 a year instead of 280+), had only signed deal memos with WCW, not hard contracts. Because of the WWF's ridiculous storyline, WCW offered Hall and Nash an extra $800,000 apiece and a nine month extension on their three year contracts to sign hard copies. It's a shame WCW officials hadn't watched *RAW* the week prior, as figurehead WWF President Gorilla Monsoon unequivocally stated, "Kevin Nash and Scott Hall will *not* be appearing, as both of these individuals are currently under contract to another organisation."

[2]Any tag team with the 'new' prefix is destined to die a painful death. The New Rockers, The New Blackjacks, The New Midnight Express, The New Dream Team and The New Fabulous Ones were all flops. Even The New Foundation with Owen Hart and Jim Neidhart only managed one good match on pay-per-view before the WWF binned off Neidhart following the drug test debacle.

246

CHAPTER 8

The Hart Foundation Reunites

1997 would turn out to be the biggest year for Owen creatively since his 1994 career-making storyline where he turned heel on Bret. In a continuation from the previous year, Owen and Davey's on-screen relationship continued to deteriorate. Owen purposely eliminated Bulldog from the Royal Rumble '97 match and then claimed it was an accident. The furious Bulldog yelled, "YOU IDIOT!" before heading back to the locker room. During a singles match between Bulldog and Doug Furnas on the 27th of January edition of *RAW*, Owen accidentally clobbered the Bulldog with his Slammy Award statue. After Bulldog pinned Furnas anyway, he teased breaking up with Owen over his miscalculated interference. At the *In Your House 13: Final Four* pay-per-view on the 16th of February, Bulldog had Phil LaFon hoisted up on his shoulders for his signature powerslam finisher when Owen wandered into the ring and needlessly shellacked LaFon with his Slammy award. Owen and Bulldog once again teased breaking up but Owen eventually raised Davey's arm in triumph and the squabbling twosome left together once again.

On the 22nd of February edition of *WWF Shotgun Saturday Night*[1] the British Bulldog fired his and Owen's manager Clarence Mason. The Bulldog was taking on Mason's other charge, Brian 'Crush' Adams, when

Crush's Nation of Domination teammates came to his aid and helped him pick up the victory. After the match, the Bulldog, who was getting cheered more and more by audiences as of late, fired Mason despite Owen's protestations. In reality, Clarence was probably elated to no longer be associated with Owen and Davey after an incident in Las Vegas a month earlier. On an untelevised house show on the 12th of January, Owen, Davey and John 'Justin Bradshaw' Layfield took on Bart Gunn and The Godwinns in a six-man tag team match. Before the opening bell, Clarence was posing on the ring apron with the WWF Tag belts and Owen's Slammy Award when Bradshaw ran into the ropes and bounced poor Clarence onto the floor. Owen and Davey thought it was funny and ended up engaging in a 'who can prank Clarence more' competition. Owen and Davey ribbed Clarence so badly for the rest of the loop it got to the point that he refused to walk to the ring for fear of further humiliation.

During the same run of tag team matches, Bradshaw recounted one of Owen's preferred methods to get under Davey's skin while Owen was stood on the apron watching him work. "Owen would call out spots to fans while Davey Boy was calling the same spot in the ring. Owen would talk to fans the entire match critiquing Davey Boy's moves." When Owen wasn't nattering with the ringside fans, he would be shouting incredibly unhelpful 'advice' to Davey when he found himself getting out wrestled on the mat. According to Diana, Owen would scream out unorthodox counter holds such as, "Scratch his snatch!" Davey and his opponent would both start laughing before telling Owen to shut up. "There was not one sane moment with those two," laughed Bradshaw. "Davey would just laugh; he thought Owen was hilarious even when Owen was ribbing him."

The big news heading into the nine day tour of Germany was the creation of a brand new singles championship being created by the World Wrestling Federation for the first time since September 1979. The WWF European Title tournament would be contested over several days in various German cities. The finals would be filmed for the 3rd of March *WWF RAW* from Berlin. Davey Boy was the obvious favourite to win as he was one of the Federation's biggest stars over in Europe, especially the UK, as well as being the only European wrestler entered in the tournament. According to Bret Hart, "Vince [McMahon] had made promises to Davey when he signed him [in 1994] but he hadn't lived up to them and was trying to appease Davey by putting the European title on him."

After Bulldog helped Owen defeat his brother Bret in the semi-finals in Hamburg via count-out (in Owen and Bret's last ever one on one match) Owen and Davey squared off in Berlin in the finals. The brothers-in-law and Tag Team Champions put on a match of the year candidate and probably the best TV match in the history of *WWF RAW* up to that point. After an even back and forth affair, Davey Boy reversed a roll-up to pin Owen at the 23:00 mark to become the first-ever European Champion. A perturbed Owen shook Bulldog's hand and the two remained tag team partners. As great as the match was, the Duestchlandhalle arena's lighting was appalling, the sound was murky and the picture was foggy because of the PAL to NTSC conversion. Despite the Owen vs. Bulldog classic, the 3rd of March *RAW*, with its terrible production values and lack of storyline advancement, achieved a 1.91 rating. This would be one of the lowest ratings in *RAW's* history[2]

Like *RAW* from Berlin, *WrestleMania XIII* on the 23rd of March, was a lame-duck show that heavily relied on the Bret Hart vs. Steve Austin 'I Quit match' to lift the pay-per-view out of the realms of mediocrity.[3] Miraculously, Austin and Bret not only saved the show, they arguably fought the best match in the thirty-five year history of *WrestleMania*. Bulldog and the two-time Slammy Award winning Owen (more on that later) took on Mankind and their old Camp Cornette teammate Vader. The match was decent yet forgettable, with the brothers-in-law working as the babyfaces, before the lame count-out finish where Mankind refused to release the Mandible Claw submission on Davey. In spite of the awesome Bret vs. Austin feud heating up, interest in WWF programming was near rock bottom and TV leading up to *WrestleMania 13* was a mess courtesy of Shawn Michaels' abrupt 'retirement'. *WrestleMania 13* remains the only *WrestleMania* not to be the most ordered wrestling pay-per-view of the year. In fact, *WrestleMania 13's* buy rate was so low, five other wrestling pay-per-views outdrew it that year. Broadcast one week prior, *WCW Uncensored* achieved 325,000 buys compared to *WrestleMania's* 237,000.

The next day on *RAW is WAR*,[4] months of miscommunication, bickering and jealousy between the Bulldog and Owen finally came to a head during a tag team encounter with The Headbangers. Referees and officials separated the warring siblings-in-law while the crowd chanted for the Bulldog. Owen grabbed the microphone and officially challenged his brother-in-law to a match for the European Title. "Hey, Bulldog! I'm sick and tired of your crap! I'm sick and tired of carrying this team. I'm the only reason you're the champion that you are and we all know I could've beaten you any time [in Germany] for that European belt because I'm the captain of our team and I'm the best!" Bulldog, who was fast becoming a popular babyface, accepted Owen's challenge for *RAW is WAR* the next week.

On the same show, Bret came to the ring to justify his heel-ish actions over the past few months. Bret had pushed over WWF owner Vince McMahon on *RAW* before launching into a profanity-laced tirade and also attacked Steve Austin after the bell at *WrestleMania 13.*[5] Bret said sorry to his fans in South Africa, Germany, the UK and Canada for his recent actions but refused to apologise to the American fans. While the camera repeatedly cut to Vince McMahon sat at the commentary table, Bret blamed the American fans for cheering 'poor role models' like Shawn Michaels and Steve Austin and blamed the WWF and Vince McMahon for screwing him out of the WWF Title. Solidifying his heel turn, Bret snarled, "It's obvious to me that all you American wrestling fans from coast to coast, you don't respect me. Well the fact is I don't respect you. You don't deserve it. So from here on in, the American wrestling fans coast to coast can kiss my ass!" The still injured Shawn Michaels came out to confront Bret but ended up getting attacked by him. The segment lasted twenty-one minutes and was one of the best promos of a year filled with all-time classic interviews. Like Owen in 1994, Bret went from being mediocre on the microphone as a babyface to becoming one of the best speakers in professional wrestling after turning heel.

On the 31ˢᵗ of March *RAW is WAR*, Owen and Davey squared off again for the European Championship. In what turned out to be another fantastic match between the two. Owen dominated for the most part when he attacked Bulldog before the opening bell. When Davey bumped the referee out of the ring some sixteen minutes into the bout, Owen brought in a steel folding chair to attack the Bulldog with. When Davey managed to grab the chair off Owen, the newly heel Bret Hart bounded down to ringside to put an end to the fighting and bring the family back together.

In an effort to reunite his truculent siblings, Bret reminded Bulldog of their storyline issues back in 1992 and blamed the WWF and the fans for messing with Owen's head in 1994 when he turned heel. Bret brought up a true story of defending Owen from a teacher that was picking on him. "Americans don't understand family," chastised Bret. "They don't give a damn about family. Owen, Davey, I'm asking you for your help because I need you. Owen, look me in the eye. Nobody was there for you more times than I was." Davey and Owen slowly went from calming down to crying uncontrollably as Bret pleaded with them to band together. "I want you to hear me. I want you to hear me loud and clear. I don't care about these people [in the audience], not anymore. Owen, I love ya. I love ya."

With lips quivering and tears in their eyes (or probably just sweat from the match), Owen, Davey and Bret put aside their differences and embraced in the middle of the ring. Bret slowly lifted his head up from this tender moment with a taunting look of both revulsion and satisfaction as the audience vehemently booed all three men. The look on Bret's face was unbelievably great but also a happy accident, as Bret was actually trying not to laugh after Owen spontaneously tousled his and Davey's hair during their reconciliatory embrace. The new and improved Hart Foundation was born and would soon declare war on Steve Austin, Shawn Michaels and the recently returned Legion of Doom. On the road, Owen would face off against Steve Austin, Ahmed Johnson and LOD in singles and tag team action throughout April and May. Tremendous heat was immediately generated from the angle, with Bret reporting that The Hart Foundation was receiving fan vitriol not seen since Sgt Slaughter declared his allegiance to Saddam Hussein during the Gulf War in 1990. "I needed a police escort to get out of town," said Bret. "Even then, I often found myself speeding to outrun fans who chased me, hanging out their car windows, shaking shotguns and half-empty beer bottles while trying to run me off the road."

On the 21st of April *RAW is WAR*, Bret and Austin went at it in a rematch of the rematch of the rematch from *Survivor Series*. Because the bout was a no disqualification Street Fight, Owen and Bulldog jumped Austin from the start. When Shawn Michaels ran off Owen and Bulldog, Austin eventually got the upper hand and went after Bret's knee. Austin injured Bret's knee in storyline, as well as in real life when Austin twisted

Bret into his own Sharpshooter submission. Bret actually injured his knee ducking an Undertaker clothesline while touring Kuwait a week prior but put off surgery to make the *In Your House 14* main event. As Bret was being wheeled out to an ambulance, Owen, in his amusingly overbearing cadance, kept shouting slogans like, "THIS IS A BUNCH OF CRAP!" and "WATCH HIS KNEE, YOU IDIOT!" "I almost cracked up", Bret later admitted. Austin, who was hiding in the driver's seat of the ambulance, then pounced on Bret until Owen and Davey ran him off. The whole angle was equal parts intense, effective and hilarious. "He's gonna pay for this," Owen threatened as the ambulance finally left the arena. "We'll kill 'im!" In the last segment of the show, while Vince McMahon interviewed Austin, Owen and the Bulldog ran in and attacked him. After they were run off by Shawn Michaels once again, Brian Pillman[6] emerged from the crowd and jumped Austin from behind. Pillman officially became the fourth member of the Hart Foundation.

The next week, Owen became a rare dual WWF Champion. While still reigning as Tag Team Champion with the British Bulldog, Owen pinned blue chipper Dwayne 'Rocky Maivia' Johnson (The Rock) for the Intercontinental title. While The Rock is now thought of as one of the most charismatic and entertaining people in the history of wrestling and Hollywood, Rocky Maivia in early 1997 was bland, lacking in confidence and had completely failed to connect with the audience. It also didn't help that Rocky had made powerful enemies behind the scenes purely because he was thought of as a can't miss prospect by management.[7] The Owen vs. Rocky Maivia contest would somehow turn out to be one of the greatest performances of the Bulldog. Davey, who was watching on the stage with his wheelchair-bound brother-in-law Bret, hilariously clapped, cheered and shadow-boxed throughout the bout in support of Owen. When Owen got the clean pinfall on Rocky in 8:00, the Bulldog went crazy, roaring with delight and running on the spot. Bret, whose character was now an embittered, humourless heel who hadn't smiled in months, couldn't stop laughing at Davey's over-the-top, unscripted jubilation. In the Bulldog vs. Undertaker main event, Steve Austin was stalking the crippled Bret when Jim 'The Anvil' Neidhart made his surprise return to rescue him. The Hart Foundation was now at full strength.

Over the course of the next month, Bret and The Hart Foundation came onto *RAW is WAR* to cut rambling, entertaining speeches on how much they loved other countries, especially Canada, before denigrating America and bloodthirsty American wrestling fans. During a loop of Canada in May, The Hart Foundation were cheered like national heroes but in the United States they were treated with genuine, hostile antipathy by patriotic Americans. The WWF took note of the Canadian reaction and added dates in Canadian markets at the expense of international touring for the rest of the year. "You cannot ignore when the crowd is cheering like crazy for your top heels and booing the living shit out of your top babyfaces," said WWE Producer Bruce Prichard.

On the 26th of May live episode of *RAW is WAR*, Owen and Bulldog lost their Tag Team Titles to Steve Austin and the now un-retired Shawn Michaels, in an awesome matchup. In the wider story of the Hart Foundation, Bret Hart vs. Shawn Michaels and Brian Pillman vs. Steve Austin were scheduled for *King of the Ring* and Bulldog was developing a feud with Ken Shamrock. After Shawn Michaels' 'Sunny days' promo on *RAW is WAR* the week prior,[8] Bret legitimately refused to go ahead with the match, citing that his knee still wasn't healed. Instead, Michaels faced off against his tag team partner Steve Austin.

On the 9th of June, after months of trading sly digs and getting too personal on interviews, Bret and Shawn got into an ugly and very real backstage fight hours before *RAW is WAR* was set to broadcast live. Michaels, who had a chunk of hair ripped out of his skull,[9] quit the WWF citing 'unsafe working conditions'. Bret was also sent home, throwing the evening's booking out of whack, not to mention plans for the July pay-per-view emanating from Calgary. Commentators Vince McMahon and Jim Ross refused to divulge the details of the fight on-air, instead saving the juiciest gossip for their premium 900 number in order to make a little extra money.

On the 30th of June *RAW*, one of the most bizarre moments of the year occurred. Owen and Davey had just defeated The Headbangers when Jim Cornette, who hadn't been seen in a managerial capacity since The Undertaker Tombstone Piledrove him on the 5th of January episode of *WWF Superstars*, debuted his new tag team. Cornette cut a brief promo on Owen and Davey then blew on a whistle. On the whistle's shrill toot, out dawdled The Headhunters; two bloated, 400lb identical twins that resembled Abdullah the Butcher in appearance, but could do backflips. Eighteen months after making a one-off appearance at *Royal Rumble 1996* as The Samoan Squat Team, The Headhunters shambled down the entrance ramp to ambush Owen and Davey. Owen and Davey clearly weren't interested in making The Headhunters look good and immediately pummelled and slammed the corpulent clones, before The Headbangers got in the ring and beat The Headhunters up too! The Headhunters eventually got the upper hand on the 'Bangers but their debut was so embarrassing they were never invited back. Following the segment, Cornette was allowed to go back to his backstage producing and ancillary commentary roles, much to his relief.

[1]The WWF debuted *Shotgun Saturday Night* on the 4th of January 1997. The show was originally filmed at several curious New York locations, including nightclubs, a chain restaurant and Pennsylvania Train Station in a misguided effort to mimic ECW's edgier, less refined production values. The concept lasted six weeks before *Shotgun* was filmed directly before *RAW* to save on time and production costs.

[2]The opposing *WCW Nitro* achieved a 3.4 rating, which was among the biggest ratings defeats the WWF endured since the Monday Night Wars began in September 1995. Jim Cornette was one of several dissenting voices over the concept of filming *RAW* in Germany (and potentially Kuwait) in the first place. "They literally had cameras shoot a dark house show and broadcast it for two hours on a Monday night while [WCW] were blowing up fuckin' all the pyro in fuckin' Atlanta." McMahon called an emergency meeting the next day where junior booking team member and *WWF Magazine* editor Vince Russo told McMahon that he knew the Germany show would bomb. For better *and* worse, Russo would soon be given more booking power, eventually becoming the sole writer for all Federation programming. At least the WWF learned their lesson about broadcasting house shows on television... Yeah, right. Just one month later, the 14th of April edition

of *RAW is WAR* consisted mostly of house show footage from South Africa with the same production woes and terrible rating as a result.

[3] *WrestleMania XIII* was supposed to be headlined by the rematch of last year's *WrestleMania*, Bret Hart vs. Shawn Michaels. Bret and Shawn, who were beginning to develop a very real animosity with each other behind the scenes, had been cutting scathing, semi-real promos denigrating each other's character flaws for months leading up to the big event. With almost no prior warning or build up, WWF Champion Michaels relinquished the belt on a live edition of *RAW* on the 13th of February, citing a 'career-ending' knee injury. Vince McMahon, Gorilla Moonson, three blubbing women and several thousand irked fans looked on as a bleary-eyed Michaels slurred his words (supposedly from crying and not from any substances he'd ingested prior) claiming his in-ring career was over. "I'll believe it when I see the scar," said an incredulous Undertaker watching on a monitor backstage. "The little fucker doesn't want to drop the belt." Michaels claimed he'd also 'lost his smile' since becoming Champion and was heading home to San Antonio, Texas to find it. While Michael's knee was really hurt, many wrestling insiders suggested that he exaggerated the injury in order to not lose the belt to Bret at *WrestleMania* (which was the planned finish). That claim was further bolstered when Michaels went to get a second opinion from well-respected orthopaedic surgeon Dr James Andrews. Andrews said the knee didn't even require surgery and Michaels was to be reassessed in four to six weeks. The *WrestleMania* card had to be completely restructured, with Bret now facing Austin and Sid defending the WWF Championship against The Undertaker in the main event. Michaels would return to in-ring action in May.

[4] *RAW* had recently been renamed *RAW is WAR* and expanded from one hour to two to compete with the already two hour *WCW Monday Nitro.* The theme song was updated too. After three weeks of *The Beautiful People* by Marilyn Manson, the *RAW is WAR* theme song switched to the songs *We're All Together Now* and *Thorn in Your Eye* by 'The WWF Superstars & Slam Jam', a heavy metal super group featuring Savatage's Jon Oliva on vocals and Anthrax's Scott Ian on guitar. The Slam Jam

songs originally appeared on the *WWF Full Metal* album in September 1996. A promotional video for *We're All Together Now* was filmed earlier in the year but because it heavily featured the WCW bound Kevin Nash and Scott Hall, the WWF never aired it on their TV shows.

[5]At *WrestleMania 13*, Bret defeated Austin after special guest referee Ken Shamrock called off the match. Austin 'passed out' from blood loss when he refused to give up to Bret's Sharpshooter, earning Austin legions of fans for his toughness in defeat. Conversely, Bret was jeered for attacking Austin post-match before backing away from Ken Shamrock's challenge for a fight. WWE folklore asserts that the double turn of Bret and Austin occurred solely at *WrestleMania 13* but that simply isn't the case. Bret had been receiving progressively more boos since January and a significant portion of the audience still had contempt for Austin for months after their classic *WrestleMania* encounter.

[6]The previous eighteen months had been a wild ride for Brian Pillman. He had morphed into his 'Loose Cannon' persona; a wild-eyed, unpredictable lunatic, both on and off-screen. Pillman wanted to create buzz for himself to advance his career, earn more money and maybe even get a SAG card for health insurance benefits before his crumbling body gave out. While still contracted to WCW, Pillman conspired with Eric Bischoff and Booker Kevin Sullivan to blur the line between fantasy and reality with his character. Worked-shoot promos and confrontations were broadcast on television. A pay-per-view match between Pillman and Sullivan ended abruptly after Pillman exposed Sullivan as WCW's booker and walked out of the arena. After Pillman was allowed to make appearances for ECW while still contracted to WCW, Hulk Hogan, who had full creative control written into his contract, demanded Pillman return so he could beat him on television and kill his momentum. Pillman avoided a Hogan beating by booking throat surgery when he was supposed to lose. Pillman then convinced Bischoff to give him a real-life release from WCW. On the 15th of April 1996, Brian wrecked his Hummer H1 car and destroyed his ankle in the process. Pillman massively downplayed the devastating injury and both

WWF and WCW aggressively sought to sign/re-sign the now free agent. After much soul searching, Pillman signed one of the first WWF guaranteed contracts for between $250,000-400,000 (depending on the source) per year for three years on the 7th of June. Aside from some interviews, commentary and occasional physical angles with Steve Austin, Pillman wouldn't return to the ring until May 1997. Pillman's ankle was still nowhere near ready to wrestle on and the increasing amount of painkillers he ingested in order to compete, mixed with everything else he was taking, drastically cut short Brian's life. Pillman died alone in his hotel room in Bloomington, Minnesota just five months after returning to the ring on the 5th of October 1997.

[7]Best friends and backstage instigators Shawn Michaels and Triple H had recently been sitting in on booking meetings and influencing Federation storylines. They particularly hated Rocky Maivia and had already lobbied for Bret to beat Rocky clean for the Intercontinental Title several weeks earlier. This would not only demote Rocky but also keep Bret out of the WWF Title picture, clearing the way for Shawn to be top dog. The animosity was apparently mutual, as when Dwayne Johnson was thirteen years old, he supposedly witnessed Michaels disrespecting his grandmother Lia Maivia while working Hawaii in 1985. Shortly before *WrestleMania XV* in 1999, Michaels, who had retired the year prior, allegedly lobbied to have The Rock removed from the main event and replaced with... guess who? Triple H! In another incident, Michaels intentionally stiffed The Rock hard with a superkick during an angle. Rocky confronted, then beat up, Michaels after Shawn told him, "If you can't take it, you shouldn't be in this business." Jim Cornette later quipped, "Michaels is 0 for life on any kind of fuckin' real fight!" In 2005, The Rock gave the following cryptic quote to WWE.com. "I was never interested in working with Shawn Michaels to be honest with you. I've known him for a long time... it was just one of those things."

[8]The weeks before the inevitable fight saw Shawn and Bret ramp up the personal attacks on one another. Bret had claimed that Michaels was faking his knee injury and was a bad role model with his long hair,

tattoos, strip show dance routines and Playgirl pictorial. It should be pointed out that Bret also had long hair. Michaels kept referring to Bret facetiously as 'the almighty' and called Bret a mark for himself, believing he took the business too seriously. That's rich, considering how Michaels also took himself, the business and his legacy just as seriously. Michaels also accused Bret of being 'no angel' when he was on the road and away from his family, which was a veiled accusation that he was sleeping around. This was true, as according to Bret's autobiography, he'd engaged in a string of extramarital affairs to combat the loneliness of touring.

On the final segment of the 12th of May *RAW is WAR*, Bret and Shawn were alone in the ring, cutting promos. Bret forgot his time cue and rambled on for so long that *RAW* went off the air before Michaels could superkick him. Michaels felt Bret did this on purpose to undermine him in their feud. The next week, Bret challenged Michaels to a match at *King of the Ring* where he said if he couldn't beat Shawn in ten minutes he'd never wrestle in the United States again. In response, Michaels, who had clearly consumed too many flippy wippys and flying willards, garbled, "Bret, believe me, you couldn't go ten minutes in any situation, if you know what I mean. Even though lately you've had some 'Sunny days,' you still can't get the job done." Michaels was fragrantly accusing Bret on national television of piping Sunny, which was rich coming from Shawn. Not only had Shawn boffed Sunny behind her boyfriend Chris Candido's back, but so had Davey Boy Smith *and*, according to Mark Madden, Brian Pillman as well! Unbelievably, Sunny herself referenced 'Sunny days' in a promo on the 5th of April episode of *Shotgun Saturday Night* when she predicted she herself would become the fourth member of Bret's group.

⁹Jim Cornette, who was backstage during the fracas, would later admit that when he spotted Shawn's chunk of hair on the floor he, "Picked it up and shoved it in a fuckin' paper bag and took the hair home," to provide a morbid visual punch line for when he told the story to his wife that night.

The Slammy Awards

As told by Mick Foley, Clarence Mason and Bruce Prichard

Fun fact: Despite 'winning' his second Slammy Award trophy in 1997 and being announced to the ring as "the two-time Slammy Award-winning Hart," Owen was only ever legitimately a one-time Slammy Award-winner, yet had three awards. Here's why:

Owen won his first Slammy on the 31st of December 1994 episode of *WWF Mania*, hosted by the vomit-inducingly saccharine duo of Todd Pettengill and Stephanie Wiand. Owen won the 'Biggest Rat' award for turning on his brother Bret at the beginning of the year, one of no less than twenty-six 'awards' handed out that morning. In reality, the awards show special was just an excuse to fill Saturday morning airtime over the holidays, with no physical Slammy trophies being handed out and no real mention of them taking place on other WWF programming.

The Slammy Awards made its return proper[1] on the 29th of March 1996 at the Anaheim Marriot, two days before *WrestleMania XII*, hosted once again by Todd Pettengill. Owen's first physical Slammy trophy was for 'Squared-Circle Shocker'. The Slammy was supposed to be awarded to Shawn Michaels because he fainted (in storyline) after Owen gave him his trademark Enzuigiri kick. Instead of announcing Michaels as the winner, guest presenter Hunter Hearst Helmsley announced Owen's name instead. The hilariously overbearing Hart leapt onto the stage, let out a trademark, "WOOO!" and tore the gold award statue out of a model's hands yelling, "GIMME THAT!" He then thanked no one, especially his 'lousy brother, Bret', before celebrating with his Camp Cornette stable mates, which included a genuinely elated Bulldog. Owen carried the trophy around for the entire year, constantly referring to himself as the 'Slammy Award-winning Hart' (and sometimes hitting opponents with it, too). Like a true professional, Owen took what was meant to be a one night joke award and turned it into an incredibly memorable part of his character.

Owen's second Slammy award trophy was even more of a burglary than in 1996. From Chicago's Westin Hotel, two days before *WrestleMania*

259

13, Owen Hart was called onto the stage to present the distinguished 'Best Bowtie' award. Instead of reading out the nominees, he claimed the trophy for himself, yelling, "WOOO! I did it again!" before Todd had even given him the list of nominees to read out. Owen's former manager, Herman 'Clarence Mason' Stevens Jr remembered being somewhat put out by the impromptu acceptance speech. "I was supposed to win... I had my speech and everything ready to go. I was on cue and Owen announced himself as the winner!"

Owen, who wasn't even wearing a bowtie, put the nominees' envelope in his jacket and launched into his acceptance speech, famously uttering the line, "I did it again! I have nobody to thank once again; I did it all by my sweet little self. WOOO! Hey Bulldog, you may have two titles but you don't have two Slammys!" The camera then cut to a shot of Davey Boy Smith who appeared to be actually radiating with joy, as well as his wife Martha, who was similarly beaming at Owen's extraordinary acceptance speech.[2] "Owen took it upon himself to take both Slammys out into the ring and present those damn things as more important than the World Championship," said Bruce Prichard. "If you gave him an inch he would take ten miles and make something out of nothing."

Owen went on to light-heartedly threaten his and Bulldog's *WrestleMania 13* opponents; Mankind and Vader. After Owen finished up on the podium he walked off the stage straight towards Vader to hurl more abuse. While Owen and Vader verbally sparred back and forth, a waiter carrying ten pitchers of iced tea attempted to walk between them. Owen put a hand on the waiter's back and shoved him hard, dumping all ten pitchers of the cold beverage over Vader (and pleasingly, the waiter as well). Seeing that a live televised slaughter might ensue, Owen darted off through the tables to the other end of the banquet hall. The soaking-wet Vader, visibly angry and clenching his fists (but with a giant smile on his face) froze for a second before deciding to give chase.

Vader, at a billed weight of 450lbs, made it two seconds before tripping over a chair and wiping out not only himself but Spanish commentator Carlos Cabrera as well. A defeated Vader got back up and, still smiling, watched Owen on the other side of the room hold aloft his Slammy award in triumph. According to Mick Foley, "[Vader] actually missed a few shows due to injury." The injury was a deep bruise in his knee that he originally suffered at the IYH 13: *Final Four* pay-per-view the month prior. Vader managed to turn up to *WrestleMania* where the two heel teams brawled their way to a lame double count-out, before taking two weeks off to rest the injury.

Executive Producer Bruce Prichard revealed many years later that Vince McMahon himself had set up the prank. This is hardly surprising, as it's well known within Vince's inner circle that his favourite past time was pushing unsuspecting people in his pool, regardless of whether they were a wrestler, a high-ranking WWF employee or an innocent tradesman whom McMahon had never met before.

[1]The original *Slammy Awards* were held on the 1st of March 1986. Broadcast on MTV during the 'Rock 'N' Wrestling' crossover boom period, the awards show was ultimately one long commercial for wrestling theme/novelty record, *The Wrestling Album*, released some five months prior. At the awards show, there were several mimed performances to tracks off the album and five awards handed out; most notably to Nikolai Volkoff taking the coveted 'Most Ignominious' statuette back to Mother Russia. The second *Slammy Awards* ceremony (billed as the 37th) would be held in 1987 to promote *Piledriver: The Wrestling Album II* before the concept was temporarily retired. The clear highlight of the show was an incredibly goofy performance of *Stand Back* from the *Piledriver* album, sung by Vince McMahon himself. While WWF Superstars mimed playing instruments, McMahon strutted his funky stuff with a troop of dancing girls and recited lyrics such as, "If you stand in my way, I promise you will lose." The song was taken by many within the industry as a transparent, saxophone-infused threat to the few remaining wrestling territories still operating.

[2]To highlight the ludicrous nature of wrestling, appearing with Owen's loved ones in the camera shot was the masked 'Sultan', a 350lb Middle-Eastern character played by proud Samoan wrestler Solofa 'Rikishi' Fatu. At the 'prestigious' awards, The Sultan teamed a red tuxedo with

his Ermac-from-*Mortal Kombat*-style facemask that he wore because, thankfully only in storyline, his tongue had been cut out.

Ken Shamrock's Locker

As told by Ken Shamrock

'The World's Most Dangerous Man' Ken Shamrock had just re-entered the world of professional wrestling, jumping from the struggling UFC due to financial difficulties and a campaign to ban the sport by Senator John McCain. After remaining un-ribbed while those around him were being pranked on a continual basis, Kenny believed his reputation had scared his co-workers off from trying anything funny. Seeing how badly Shamrock beat Vader in his WWF in-ring debut when he was co-operating with him, the real thrashing that a still-in-his-prime Shamrock could hand out to anyone in the company was a threat not to be taken lightly.

During a show, Kenny left his gear bag in a locker and headed out to wrestle his match. When he returned to the back, he saw Owen Hart and cohorts (possibly including Steve Blackman) grinning at him. Shamrock was suspicious enough to ask the group, "What're you smiling about?" Sensing a rib in progress, Shamrock also quizzed the group if something was up. Kenny then walked over to his locker to retrieve his gear bag. When he tried to open the locker, Shamrock unwittingly plunged his hand into a mound of slime that was smeared all over the door and handle. With the Owen-led group busting out into laughter, Ken knew he'd been had by Owen and chums. "Tell me that it's not something gross?" begged Shamrock, "tell me it's something like Vaseline!" Luckily for Shamrock (and Owen and Blackman and everybody else in the building, including the arena employees), it was, indeed, Vaseline.

Instead of getting angry and 'snapping' over the relatively mild prank like his TV character would have done, The World's Most Dangerous Man enjoyed the rib, ultimately making him feel accepted by the guys and more comfortable in the locker room.

The Headbangers Too Close for Comfort

As told by Headbanger Thrasher, Ted DiBiase and Vito LoGrasso

Glenn 'Thrasher' Ruth, along with tag team partner Chaz 'Mosh' Warrington, went through a number of off-kilter characterisations such as 'The Flying Nuns' and 'The Sisters of Love' before reverting back to their most famous gimmick of 'The Headbangers', a pair of grimy metalheads who wore skirts, painted black triangles under their eyes and, curiously in 2000, wrestled wearing giant furry cone-shaped braziers. Thrasher had already appeared numerous times on WWF television since 1990 as a TV jobber, sharing a locker room with all-time wrestling mega stars such as Hulk Hogan and Ultimate Warrior... or he would have if they hadn't insisted on private dressing rooms.

When the Headbangers debuted at the beginning of 1997, Owen Hart and the British Bulldog were in the middle their 246 day reign as WWF Tag Team Champions; the longest unbroken run of the 1990s. Owen was aware of Thrasher from his enhancement talent days, which eased his and Mosh's passage into the WWF locker room but certainly didn't give them immunity to being pranked. As Thrasher recalled, "[Chaz and I] travelled together, we stayed together, we did everything." The Headbangers even sat next to each other in the dressing room to change into their gear. After returning to the locker room after their scheduled match, Mosh and Thrasher found Owen conspicuously hovering over their gear bags.

When The Headbangers walked towards where they had left their gear, they found they'd now be a little too close for comfort; *someone* had padlocked their bags together. To make matters worse, a metal folding chair between the two bags was caught up in the same padlock. Thrasher remembered yelling at Owen, shouting, "Oh, hey, what are you doing?" Owen, who surprisingly didn't blame Davey Boy for once, elucidated; 'Oh, your bags are locked together. I don't know who did that, I just came over and saw it!" There was absolutely no doubting who was responsible. "We knew it was Owen," said Thrasher, "because he's sitting there, sitting in the corner and he's just going, 'Hehehe'. He's just laughing to himself." Knowing a little bit about locker room politics, the kayfabe thrash metal aficionados didn't react angrily. Instead, The Headbangers quietly picked up their bags and walked out of the locker room to their rental car with the folding metal chair swinging between them.

When Mosh and Thrasher arrived at the next day's television taping, Owen walked up to them slightly incredulous and enquired, "What, you're not going to saying anything?" Thrasher replied, "No, 'cause if we feed you, you're going to keep doing it to us!" Owen, letting Mosh and Thrasher know that they'd passed the test, said, "Boy, you guys are smart!" As with most backstage pranks, the ribber is hoping to get a rise out of the ribbee one way or another. If the ribbed party downplays the situation, it generally kills off the perpetrator's interest and they move on to another target. If the ribbee outwardly reacts or worse, complains to management, there is a good chance the ribbing will become more frequent and more punitive in nature.

According to 'Million Dollar Man' Ted DiBiase, Owen would perform a slight variation of the bag padlocking prank when he wanted to up the severity. "What Owen would do was he'd take a chain and he'd wrap one part of it around the posts of that bench," said DiBiase. "Then [Owen would] run it through the straps on your travel bag and padlock it." You'd come back from the ring and your gear and all your stuff inside it is secured to the floor. There's no way to set it free unless you tear up your bag or get a pair of bolt cutters. So that was a serious rib."

'Big' Vito LoGrasso claimed Owen would go even further in the wrestler bag-ribbing stakes back in the early '90s when Vito was making sporadic WWF appearances as enhancement talent. "The [rib] that probably stands out is the gravy train. That's when you take a gentleman's bag, fill it with dog food, then fill it with water and shake it up, then you got the gravy train." The aim would appear to be to 'gravy train' the wrestler's bag before they'd had chance to wrestle that night. "To get that stink out of it is pretty bad so when guys gotta go out and work that night, he's gotta wash his gear out and it smells like puppy chow... I'd have to say that's the one rib I remember."

Headbangers Room with Owen and 'King of Carry-On'

As told by Headbanger Thrasher, Martha Hart and Jeff Jarrett

Owen, as anyone who spent time travelling with him can attest, was famous for never checking luggage and packing incredibly light with just t-shirts, socks and undies along with ring gear and gym clothes that he'd wash in the hotel sink. Scott Hall dubbed Owen 'King of Carry-On' in honour of how little he brought with him on the road. Fellow second generation wrestler and good friend Jeff Jarrett saw Owen's luggage philosophy firsthand many times. "When we're making trips with talent and they come out of the airport, nowadays some guys will have a huge carry-on and then their wrestling bag and then a backpack and then a man-purse and I'm like, 'Are you kidding me?' Owen Hart would show up for... a two week run and he would have like one half of his little suitcase would be his wrestling gear and the other half would be his clothes for two weeks!"

Owen's reasoning was that because he had no luggage to check in at airports he wouldn't be wasting time at the baggage carrousel. This would gift him more time to catch connecting flights back home to Calgary so he could spend more time with his family. To further speed up the process, Owen put his bag in the overhead bin nearest the plane door no matter where he was sat on the plane. After the plane had safely landed but while it was still taxiing on the runway, Owen would unbuckle his seatbelt, march to the front of the plane and grab his luggage so he could be first to disembark, much to the dismay of the flight attendants. According to his widow Martha, "[Owen was] so anxious to get home at the end of a road trip, he'd sometimes dash from an arena to the airport in his wrestling gear to catch the last flight of the evening." Sometimes Owen would even bolt from an arena still in his ring attire just to save time. "In those cases, he'd change on the plane without showering," said Martha. "I doubt his fellow passengers appreciated that but I sure did."

In April 1997, Owen would receive one of the biggest pushes of his career when he became a dual WWF Champion, holding the Intercontinental and Tag Team Titles at the same time. From a fan's perspective, being in possession of two of the World Wrestling Federation's premier titles, as well as two Slammy Awards, would be a great boon to a wrestler's career. For Owen, it was most likely a complete nightmare, as workers not only carried their own gear but their championship belts as well. The business is full of stories of wrestlers getting held up at airport security, especially with airport staff with an authority complex, having to explain the belts. Transporting two heavy title belts *and* two Slammy Awards as carry-on would have weighed Owen down significantly.

Shortly after becoming a rare double-champion, the World Wrestling Federation headed down to Texas. Unfortunately for Owen, there were no hotel rooms available in the area and he also needed a ride to the show. Glenn 'Thrasher' Ruth offered Owen a lift to the hotel many of the guys were staying in that night so he could try his luck there. Alas, when they arrived at the hotel there were no rooms available. Owen asked The Headbangers if it was okay if he roomed with them for the night, with Thrasher enthusiastically replying, "Absolutely! You're Owen Hart! We're nobody, you're Owen Hart!"

When the incongruous threesome entered their room, Thrasher offered his bed to the senior wrestler. Owen insisted that because he was 'heeling in' on the room, he would happily sleep on the floor. When Owen went to the bathroom to have a shower, Mosh and Thrasher noticed that Owen's bag was partially open and there were glints of gold glistening through. Because Owen was to be occupied for another few minutes, The Headbangers peaked into Owen's bag to discover his Slammy Awards and championship belts. The Headbangers, who were still 6-year-old children at heart, fan-girled like crazy. They took all of the gold out of Owen's bag and jumped up and down on their beds cheering, "Hey look, we're champions, wooh-hoo!"

After a few minutes of living out their childhood fantasies, Mosh and Thrasher heard the shower shut off. They hurriedly put all of Owen's gold back in the bag and lay on their beds trying to act cool. According to Thrasher, "Owen looks at us, he looks at the belts [then] looks back at us and goes, 'You kids have fun jumping around the bed with the belts?'" "What're you talking about, we wouldn't do that, we wouldn't go in your bag," cried The Headbangers in defence. "Why did you think I left [the bag] open?" came Owen's knowing reply.

Thrasher went on to say that when he brought his kids backstage, Owen would make them feel welcome by playing around and colouring in pictures with them in catering. "That's the kind of guy Owen was; he made you part of the family. I couldn't possibly find one bad thing that Owen ever did or ever said. He was the best guy ever."

Mark Henry's Crutches and Subway Special

As told by Mark Henry, Sean Waltman and Headbanger Thrasher

Billed as the 'World's Strongest Man'[1] former Olympic weightlifter[2] Mark Henry arrived in the WWF with a tonne of fanfare and expectation, making his pay-per-view debut as a guest commentator at *SummerSlam 1996*.[3] The completely unprepared powerlifter had his first match live on pay-per-view against Lawler the next month, before breaking his ankle running the ropes in a training session; it reportedly took four men to carry him back to the locker room. Henry was still required to make certain dates despite the injury and that's where problems began to arise. The WWF felt that Henry was a couldn't miss prospect and not only sponsored his Olympic bid but offered him a $250,000 per year, ten year contract, which put many wrestlers' noses out of joint. A rumour soon spread to industry newsletters that the 25-year-old Henry had a bad attitude, poor locker room etiquette[4] and was incompetent in the ring.

Backstage at an event in late 1996 (possibly the San Antonio press conference announcing *Royal Rumble '97's* location), some of the wrestlers decided to test Henry's temperament to the extreme. With his leg still in a cast, an unknown person (not Owen Hart) stole his crutches. According to Mark himself, when he saw the crutches were missing he went absolutely ballistic and started threatening people, cutting a promo on the entire locker room. "Hey, shit's all fun and games when I've got a cast on my leg but as soon as this cast's off my ankle, all y'all fucking with me are gonna get dealt with and there ain't shit you can do about it!"

The WWF's top babyface and world-class pot stirrer Shawn Michaels stood behind his on-screen rival, the 6'8" muscle-bound 'Sycho' Sid Eudy, for protection and began taunting the World's Strongest Man over the purloined crutches. "Shawn is all in my face, like, 'Aw man, big guy, they hide your crutches?' I was like, 'Man, you think this motherfucker standing in front of you is going to protect you from me? I will rip you off the bone

270

and then I'm gonna put my foot in your ass!'" Mark, who'd come from the world of competitive weightlifting, was unequipped to handle the snake pit-like environment of the WWF locker room and made the cardinal mistake - if you react to the rib, you will be ribbed even harder next time.

In what may well be an apocryphal tale,[5] Mark eventually got his crutches back and made an announcement to everyone within listening range that he was leaving his meatball Subway sandwich on the table and that nothing better happen to it by the time he got back. According to Sean Waltman, an unnamed wrestler took the opportunity to, "Shit on [the sandwich and] put it back together." When Henry returned, he allegedly saw his sandwich intact and tucked right in. Depending on who tells the story, Henry took one bite, tasted the off-menu topping and ran to the bathroom to throw up or, according to Waltman, "Ate the whole thing and licked his fingers afterwards."

Whether the above story is true or not, the cantankerous Henry, who had since found his crutches, returned and sat down in his chair. Once again, his crutches, which Henry had placed behind him, disappeared, this time courtesy of Davey Boy Smith. Headbanger Thrasher, who witnessed the burglary, picks up the story. "So [Davey] steals the crutches without Mark Henry even knowing and then Owen comes up to Mark and says, 'Hey, Vince [McMahon] wants you and he's on the other side of the arena.' So, Mark is looking around and going, 'Oh my god!' and can't find his crutches." The crutch-less Henry, at around 400lbs, didn't want to keep the boss waiting and hopped his way out of the locker room and across the arena where, of course, McMahon was nowhere to be seen. Owen had just made it up.

Sometime after the crutch taking incidents and confrontation with Shawn, Mark actually *was* then summoned to McMahon's office. It turned out that the tough-talking Michaels cried off to the boss, telling Vince that Mark threatened to beat him up. "Vince said, 'Hey man, you can't threaten our top guys! What's wrong with you?' And I was like, 'Look man, I just ain't used to nobody trying me; like if they wanna try me, they gotta be able to accept the consequences.' [Vince said], 'No, dammit! You can't just be beating people up! It's not gonna fix it. They're trying to bring you in but you're pushing them back.'" Mark was sent to Calgary to train at Bret Hart's house with a number of upcoming prospects and established wrestlers whose in-ring skills were lacking.[6] A year later, Mark returned to the main roster, where he endured years of hazing, injuries and humiliating storylines seemingly designed to force him to quit. Henry not only stuck out the whole of his ten year contract, he was re-signed in 2006. He remained with the WWE for another twelve years before retiring and being inducted into the WWE Hall of Fame in 2018.

In what may be the single most touching compliment anyone has bestowed upon their fellow man, Sean Waltman expressed his fondness for The World's Strongest Man thus: "I love Mark Henry... He's a wonderful guy and I never would ever shit in his fucking food."

[1]Many pro wrestlers have been billed as world's strongest men including: Ken Patera, Jeep Swenson, Bill Kazmaier, 'The Great' Antonio Barichievich and probably dozens more.

[2]While he wasn't expected to win an Olympic medal, Henry had set several powerlifting records and was the largest Olympian in history. He received an enormous amount of publicity in the run up to the Games, appearing on network talk shows and in dozens of magazines, as well as being named captain of the USA Olympic weightlifting team. Unfortunately, fate wasn't on his side as Mark injured his back during a lift and finished in 14th place.

[3]After coming to the attention of the WWF in 1994, Mark Henry made his first appearance on *WWF RAW* in March 1996 where he press slammed Jerry Lawler. At *SummerSlam '96*, Henry commentated on the Jerry Lawler vs. Jake Roberts grudge match. Lawler ruthlessly mocked Jake's struggles with alcoholism in a three and a half minute comedy routine that Henry, who was meant to be supporting the babyface Jake, couldn't stop laughing along with.

[4]Locker room etiquette refers to the archaic, almost Masonic practice of shaking everybody's hand the wrestler comes into contact with, as well as keeping their mouth shut and their ears open (especially if they're a rookie).

[5]Mark Henry has denied that his food was defecated in but did claim that his Nation of Domination teammate Dwayne 'The Rock' Johnson was once ribbed in a similar manner. "I saw it happen and people were like, 'Shh, don't tell. Come on, the rib is on him.' No, you crazy? You putting shit in somebody's food. Ask [The Rock] about it, he'll tell you."

[6]Wrestlers Bret trained at his house include Adam 'Edge' Copeland, Jay 'Christian' Reso, Robert 'Kurrgan' Maillet, Andrew 'Test' Martin, Ken Shamrock and others.

Jamie Dundee Ribs

As told by Jamie Dundee

Jamie Dundee (James Cruickshanks) is the son of Memphis area legend and frequent partner and rival of Jerry Lawler, 'Superstar' Bill Dundee. While Bill is best known as the cute wrestler from Australia whose working punches were stiffer than most peoples' actual punches, self-described 'low life' Jamie found his greatest success as part of PG-13. For years Dundee, with his tag partner Kelly 'Wolfie D' Wolfe, played the part of Vanilla Ice-style whack rappers crossed with the whitest of white trash in the USWA territory. In 1996, PG-13 became the leaders of the original Nation of Domination group, which consisted almost entirely of WWF rejects and future WWF rejects. By November of that year, the Nation of Domination concept was brought to the WWF. Rather than being leaders of the WWF's version of the Nation, PG-13 acted as MCs, rapping (occasionally in time with the music) as new leader Faarooq and the gang made their grand entrances.

At January '97's *Royal Rumble* pay-per-view from San Antonio, Texas, PG-13 were booked to rap the Nation of Domination theme in front of 60,000 fans before Faarooq's grudge match against the returning Ahmed Johnson, but nearly didn't make it out of the locker room thanks to Owen. In a sort of 'greatest hits' compilation of pranks, Owen pilfered the boots of: Dundee, Wolfie D, The Undertaker, Davey Boy Smith, Vader and a couple of other huge wrestlers. He then superglued them to the floor of what Dundee described as a 'closet', cranked up the thermostat as high as it would go and then snapped off the controls so the heating couldn't be turned down.

When the resentful wrestlers foolishly walked into the tiny locker room to wrench their boots up off the floor, the door was shut behind them and locked. "The Undertaker and them were kicking the fuck out of [the door and] it wouldn't open," said Dundee. "It was like a steel door and [Owen's] going, 'I'll get someone to get some help. Hang on, brothers, I love you!'" Being stuck in a tiny room with a half dozen enormous wrestlers, Jamie started panicking, then hyperventilating. "There was like so many of us packed in... and I'm like, 'You're taking up all my oxygen!'" Eventually the door was opened, nobody died of claustrophobia or heat stroke and everybody made it to the ring in plenty of time. "That to me is my greatest rib," smiled Dundee.

The young Dundee was pranked again several months after the *Royal Rumble* locker room sauna episode. Jamie was sat with The Hart Foundation in an airport terminal waiting to catch a flight to the next show. The last thing Jamie remembered before falling asleep was being sat next to Bret, who had his leg stretched out across him due to a recent knee injury. "I didn't go to sleep for ten minutes [before] I woke up." While Dundee was zonked out, Owen and Davey sprayed a giant cone of shaving cream on top of his head. Jamie quickly rallied round, grabbed his cases and started walking across the terminal oblivious that he was wearing a creamy white dunce cap, until someone eventually stopped him and pointed it out. "As soon as I [touched my head] everybody pops... Owen and Davey were fuckin' ribbers from way back, man."

Cocaine Doughnut

As told by Jim Ross

As a forty-five year veteran of the professional wrestling business both on-camera and behind the scenes, Jim Ross is best remembered as being arguably the greatest wrestling commentator in the history of the business. Famed for wearing his black Stetson cowboy hat, 'Good Ol' JR' also wore many hats of a metaphorical nature during his twenty-six year on-and-off tenure with WWE,[1] becoming an integral cog in the company's day-to-day operations. In 1996, Ross took over JJ Dillon's role as Executive Vice President of Talent Relations, which was arguably the toughest job in the company. In simple terms, Ross' duties consisted of hiring and dealing with talent, keeping up with his legendary workaholic boss Vince McMahon and a thousand other tasks, all while performing as the lead commentator for *RAW is WAR* and pay-per-view broadcasts.

Whoever took the Talent Relations job became unpopular overnight as the assignment also included reprimanding and firing talent when required. As respected as he was for his knowledge of the business, the Norman, Oklahoma native was not immune to gaining enemies and having ribs pulled at his expense, including the time an unnamed thief stole his car keys. According to Bruce Prichard, he and other WWF staff laughed at Ross as he fruitlessly searched around for them before giving up. Laughter then turned to consternation when Ross got in his car and drove off. It turned out he kept a spare set of keys under the sun visor. A lot of people in the company still liked and respected Good Ol' JR however, including Owen Hart. Over the years, Owen and Ross had developed a peculiar way of greeting each other. "Owen and I used to do this thing where we'd meet each other down the hallway and lock up... sometimes we'd not say a word; we'd lock up and then he'd continue going his way and I'd go my way. People were looking around [saying], 'What the hell are those guys doing?'"

As Talent Relations head, JR would be present at television tapings to deal with wrestlers' grievances in person, usually revolving around money, injuries, time off or, in this instance, suspected drug abuse. During one

276

particular taping, Ross and an unnamed wrestler had been talking behind closed doors for a remarkably long time. "I was having a long day in my makeshift office at an arena when I was in charge of the talent roster at WWE. I had an extended conversation with someone that was having substance abuse issues; that was our suspicion."[2]

The lengthy showdown hadn't gone unnoticed to many in the locker room, including Owen, who knew the unnamed wrestler was receiving a lambasting over what WWE simplistically insists on referring to as 'demons.' Eventually, the informal counselling/last chance saloon-ing session wrapped up and Ross left his temporary office to head to the ringside to call the night's matches. Immediately after he walked out the door, he was confronted by Owen, who had seemingly developed some 'demons' of his own.

"I see him coming down the hall and he's staggering," Ross said, "he's doing a really poor job of playing a drunk. They had doughnuts at catering - these powdered doughnuts. So [Owen] gets the powdered sugar off the doughnuts and puts it all over his nose like he's been doing cocaine. He's so unversed in cocaine, not knowing that it takes you the other way; it doesn't bring you down, it takes you the other direction. He don't know, he just knows that I've been in this [endless] meeting drug counselling somebody, so he's just gonna have some fun with it [so I'd think], 'Oh no, not another one!'"

Ross, who was apparently better acquainted to the ways of the world than Owen was, let him know that he wasn't falling for the ruse. "I said, 'Look, it ain't gonna work. First of all, you've got powdered sugar on your nose and secondly if you're doing anything like that you'll be going the other direction,' and so we started laughing and *then* we locked up. Then he went on his way and I went on mine!"

[1]Jim Ross would suffer through several involuntary sabbaticals through his WWF/WWE career due to various attacks of Bell's palsy. Ross would be fired just two weeks after suffering his first bout of the affliction in 1994. He left once again for several months in 2005 and 2006 due to severe colon issues and was forcibly retired (i.e. fired again) in 2013, this time for apparently standing too near a drunk Ric Flair

telling ribald stories during a *WWE 2K14* roster announcement panel. WWE felt Flair overstepped the mark as regards to acceptable conversational boundaries and reacted by canning event moderator Ross for not controlling the situation; and for allegedly also being drunk. The 2K people (who hosted the event, not WWE) actually enjoyed Ric Flair's performance and were pleased with the event in general.

[2]The World Wrestling Federation had good reason to suspect wrestlers of using drugs in the late 1990s. The various drug policies that were implemented in the late '80s/early '90s were mostly phased out by the late '90s. The original tests, which the WWF touted as a superior system to the Olympics' testing protocols, looked for steroids, marijuana and cocaine but not prescription uppers and downers that would ultimately prove far more fatal in the wrestling business than steroids ever would.

Jim Cornette on Owen's Constant Ribs

As told by Jim Cornette and Kevin Kelly

Jim Cornette, the fast-talking, southern 'mama's boy' manager with the disconcerting fashion sense, finally landed in the World Wrestling Federation in 1993. Most well known for managing The Midnight Express tag team, Cornette enjoyed success in Memphis, Mid-South and the Carolinas, before quitting WCW in late 1990 over clashes with Vice President and former Pizza Hut executive Jim Herd.[1] He wouldn't return to the big leagues for nearly three years. During his final, miserable days in WCW, Cornette began mapping out his future, which eventually morphed into Smoky Mountain Wrestling; a small-time, regional promotion based in Kentucky, which focused on keeping the magic of old school territorial wrestling alive, financially backed by music producer impresario Rick Rubin.[2]

In 1993, Cornette returned to WCW for a storyline where he and Smoky Mountain Wrestling were invading the promotion. When that storyline was almost immediately cancelled (believed to be on the orders of incoming WCW VP Eric Bischoff), SMW linked up with the WWF for a talent trade agreement.[3] Cornette's first on-screen WWF roles were managing his SMW team, The Heavenly Bodies and becoming the 'American spokesman' (i.e. the manager) for monosyllabic, superheavyweight WWF Champion Yokozuna. Yoko's original manager Mr Fuji stuck around but as he was not a particularly accomplished talker, Cornette cut all the promos. "They were great, I loved them," said Cornette. "I liked Yokozuna and I liked Mr Fuji but when I first went up there and started managing [Yoko], those matches were just so bloody, fucking awful, except for Yokozuna and Undertaker... Undertaker could get a great match out of Yokozuna, nobody else could."

When Yoko returned to be Owen's *WrestleMania XI* mystery partner, Cornette ended up becoming the *de facto* manager of Owen as well, referring to the team as Camp Cornette. When Davey Boy Smith turned heel in August of 1995, Cornette became his manager too. "When I got a chance to work with Owen and Bulldog then at least we got back into some fucking matches. I mean, I wouldn't work up a sweat a lot of times with Yoko because, fuck, he was slow!" After SMW folded in December 1995, Jimmy joined the World Wrestling Federation on a full-time basis, appearing as a manager on television and pay-per-view and working in the office in a producer role. This was when Cornette would begin to fully appreciate the brothers-in-law's talents for high jinks.

During promotional interview sessions,[4] Owen and Bulldog would ratchet up the pranks on Cornette and each other. "Owen and Bulldog were always ribbing each other, always fucking with each other," said Jim. "We'd do the promos and Owen would have the squirt bottle of water they used for the fake sweat. While we're standing there waiting to get the shot blocked, he'd spray the crotch of my pants and I didn't know about it. It looked like I'd pissed myself."

On the 15th of July 1996 edition of *WWF RAW* Jim, Owen, Davey and newest member of the team, Leon 'Vader' White, were preparing to cut a promo when Owen decided to cut the cheese, dropping a library sound effect-worthy bum trumpet that broke everyone up and caused the whole shot to have to be reset. Former manager and legal advisor to Camp Cornette, Clarence Mason, also brought up Owen's penchant for 'treading on a duck' and squeezing out a 'tripey ronk' while in packed locker rooms. "Everybody got ribbed by Owen. Whether it was if he was in the locker room and he let out a major gasser and we just told him, 'Man, you light a flame and that thing would've probably blew up the entire locker room.' That wasn't pleasant but that was just who he was."

Another time, Cornette was preparing to launch into one of his trademark rapid fire monologues on behalf of Owen and Davey when all of a sudden he found himself dwarfed by his charges. "We'd look around and Owen was standing on a roll of duct tape so he'd be the tallest one of the bunch of us, 'cause all three of us are [vaguely] the same height. Then Davey would stand up on his tip toes. Then Owen would get a fuckin' block of wood. Then all of a sudden I'd look like [midget wrestler] Cowboy Lang; Just endless!"

According to former WWF announcer Kevin Kelly, Owen decided to test Cornette's reflexes during a tedious television taping. Corny's most famous moment in his career came when he volunteered to take the fall in the *NWA Starrcade '86* 'Scaffold match'.[5] The original plan was for Cornette's bodyguard Big Bubba Rogers to catch him, as Dusty Rhodes theorised, "Like they catch the girls at the football game." What actually happened was Jim hurtled some twelve feet into the ring landing feet first, blowing out his knee, while Bubba stood and watched. Ten years later, Jim's knee still caused him issues. Interested to know how far Corny's recovery had come along, Owen grabbed Jim's ubiquitous tennis racket prop and whacked him right in the knee. As Cornette hopped in obvious discomfort around the backstage area, a disingenuous Owen asked aloud if he had 'accidently' grazed his knee.

Thankfully for Jim, he understood that he was getting away lightly compared to some who travelled on the road day in and day out. "I was only there for TVs and I guess also because I was an office member they didn't want to go too far, so they kinda took it easy on me because it could've been brutal. Their best ribs were at house shows and on the road; I didn't spend a lot of time on the road with the guys, thankfully. I may have ended up duct-taped to a tree with my pants around my fuckin' ankles or whatever! You always had to be on your toes even at TV tapings."

[1]Years later, Cornette, who is legendary for holding onto a grudge, discussed his continuing hatred for Jim Herd. "I can't wait for the day he fucking dies! I'm going to drive to St. Louis, I'm going to dance on his grave and I'm going to have a fuckin' Emo's Pizza in celebration... I hope he dies a horrible death to this day, painfully, in front of his family, because he not only fucked up The Midnight Express... he gave Vince [McMahon] an eight year head start. The three years that [Herd] was there, [WCW] were so far in the hole that Vince had taken off and left 'em and even Vince being indicted by the Federal Government couldn't fuckin' turn the tide because of Herd's mismanagement. He's the reason the WWF-style cartoon wrestling instead of NWA-style southern, believable wrestling, won the war – because of Jim Herd, single-handedly."

²Shortly before *WrestleMania X,* Owen made a single appearance for Smoky Mountain Wrestling. He teamed with Well Dunn in a losing effort to Brian, Scott and Steve Armstrong on the 10ᵗʰ of March 1994.

³Jim Cornette, along with The Midnight Express, first discussed business with Vince McMahon all the way back in 1986. Instead of offering The Midnights monetary guarantees, potential storylines or future opponents, McMahon's attempts to lure the Midnights to the WWF focused on unspecified royalty cheques from the WWF's new line of LJN wrestling dolls. As heels, The Midnights didn't understand why fans would want to buy their merchandise. "We didn't know there was gonna be $80,000 fuckin' cheques over fuckin' dolls!" Jim quipped. The Midnight Express passed on the WWF as they were the incumbent NWA Tag Team Champions at the time, making nearly $200,000 a year each and it wasn't worth the risk.

⁴For years, common practice in wrestling at TV tapings was for talent to cut the exact same interview many times over for individual markets, changing only the relevant place names and dates.

⁵A Scaffold match involves a platform being erected high above the ring supported by scaffolding. Both parties start at the top and fight it out until someone is thrown off the platform. Aside from Cornette's Midnight Express vs. The Road Warriors and a few others, most Scaffold matches were huge let downs and had been mostly phased out by the '90s. Cornette was paid $10,000 for his *Starrcade '86* appearance but after paying a medical insurance deductible of $1,500 for the knee operation and the $7,000 wages he lost staying home recuperating for two weeks, he ended up being only $1,500 up on the deal. Cornette also received two permanently damaged knees: one from the initial fall and the other one from leaning all his weight on it, overcompensating for the injured knee.

Car Rides with Owen:
Brian Christopher Rental Car

As told by Brian Christopher Lawler

After months of speculation from insider newsletters, Brian Christopher Lawler arrived in the World Wrestling Federation on the 16th of June 1997. Brian had been a headliner for his father Jerry 'The King' Lawler's USWA promotion from 1991 through to its dying days in 1997 under the name Brian Christopher. Brian, who was well built and around 5'8", was brought in to bolster the WWF's revived lightweight division but instead made his WWF debut against ECW's Chris Candido in an historic ECW vs. USWA inter-promotional match that practically no one is aware of today. Brian's WWF debut match was treated as an afterthought thanks to a staged ringside confrontation between Jerry Lawler and guest commentator, ECW owner Paul Heyman. Heyman had revealed on commentary that Christopher's real last name was Lawler and he was Jerry's son. This had been a tightly kept secret during his entire USWA tenure as, allegedly, Jerry didn't want his fans thinking he was old enough to have an adult son. With everything else going on, Brian would have to wait a full week to receive his official welcome to the WWF roster.

After touching down at Detroit Metropolitan Airport for that evening's live *RAW*, Brian was waiting to pick up his luggage from baggage claim when Owen Hart sidled up next to him. The two first met in 1993 when the WWF sent some of their talent down to the USWA, with Owen even working a brief programme with his father, Jerry. Owen enquired as to who Brian was travelling to the arena with that night. Brian, who'd only been on the road for a week and hadn't had time to strike up many personal relationships, informed Owen he was travelling on his own. Being the affable type, Owen offered to be his travel buddy for the evening. In regards to their ride for the day, Owen gave Brian incredibly exact instructions to go to Hertz car rental and get a specific model of car (speculated to be a Chevrolet Monte Carlo, although this titbit of information is lost to time).

Owen suggested that Brian drive the first leg of the trip and he'd drive the second leg back to the airport (kicking his leg out from under his leg, so to speak).[1] When they got onto an estimated mile and a half, arrow-straight road, Owen egged Christopher to drive faster. "Come on, let's see what this thing will do!" Christopher hit the gas, getting the car up to eighty-five but Owen kept encouraging Brian. "Oh come on, man, go, GO!"

With his foot pushed down hard on the accelerator, Brian got the car up to almost one hundred miles per hour. That's when Owen decided it was the perfect time to pull the emergency hand brake as hard as he could. The car started spinning out of control down the carriageway for what seemed like an eternity before the car came to a stop, with both passengers mercifully unharmed. It transpired that Owen asked him to pick that particular car because he knew the handbrake was easily accessible from the passenger side. Brian said of the incident many years later, "I thought I was going to die, it was great!"

It should also be mentioned that shortly after the handbrake stunt, Owen once again welcomed Brian to the fold by sewing his trouser legs shut.

[1] 'The Heartbreak Kid' Shawn Michaels has accidentally cut several interviews in a similar vein to Owen's classic *Rumble* '94 gaffe. During one promo shortly after *Survivor Series 1997*, HBK bragged about being responsible for running Bret Hart out of the WWF, stating that, "The World Wrestling Federation was not big enough for the Heartbreak Kid and Shawn Michaels." Shawn also once threatened to kick his own teeth down Steve Austin's throat during their heated rivalry in 1997.

The Honeymooners and
Relationships with Fans

As told by Kevin Nash, Martha Hart, Jerry Lawler, etc.

Everyone who knew Owen was aware that he was possibly the cheapest wrestler in history. One of his money saving tips was to blatantly befriend fans, then have them pay for his meal, rental car, or even stay at their house so he could save a few dollars on a hotel room. Over the years he assembled an entire network of admirers that he relied on to help him save money. Every one of them was a wrestling fanatic, many of who were total misfits and oddballs. Many times, Owen would attempt to get other wrestlers involved in his curious money saving system. "[Owen and I would] land at the airport," related Scot Hall. "I'd go, 'Owen, who're you riding with? Do you want me to get a rental car? You gonna get the car? You wanna ride together?' [Owen] would go, 'Oh no, I got some friend to meet me here.' So I thought well cool... can I come? Then we'd be there and they'd just be really die-hard fans." Jim Ross, similarly sceptical of Owen's choice of travel companions, postulated the worst case scenario of staying with an un-vetted super fan. "What if you woke up in the middle of the night and the whole family is kind of semi-circled around the bed watching you sleep. But that was Owen; he made friends with people, he trusted people."

This wasn't just localised to meeting fans opportunistically during his travels. According to his wife Martha, "[Owen] figured that if someone had taken the time to write to him, he owed it to them to read their letter." He read every fan letter he received and if he liked the sound of someone, he'd write back and build a rapport, eventually assimilating them into his travelling network. It was a win-win as Owen would save money and the fan would get to hang out with their hero. According to Jerry Lawler, the wrestler-fan relationship wasn't just a one way street. "I guarantee you he always made the fan feel that they got their money's worth, no matter what they spent on him, no matter how far they took him. Owen was such an entertaining guy and such a really cool guy that I'm sure they were always happy." Aside from giving his time, Owen would hook fans up with prime ringside tickets and backstage passes to shows, as well as take a genuine interest in the fan personally.

Mick Foley, who similarly had a network of fans to ferry him around (including some of Owen's), informed Owen that one particular fan had probably cost him more money than he'd saved in the long run. "He really embraced these people," Mick said. "It wasn't like he was using them because I remember one time he missed a loop, including [Madison Square] Garden, in order to go to the wedding of this friend on the road. I did the maths for him - 'Over the course of time he's probably saved you X number of dollars. He just cost you The Garden, Philadelphia and Boston. He cost you five times what he saved you over those years'. Owen laughed and said, 'Probably'. Loyalty was big for him." It would be this same fan whose wedding day he attended, at great personal expense, whose honeymoon he would go on to purposely ruin.

Owen gave the newlyweds a hotel suite for the weekend as a wedding gift. Owen then booked himself in the room next to the honeymooners, which benefitted from having connecting doors. Not long after the newlyweds had settled into their suite, they received a visit from the local constabulary. The policeman informed the honeymooners that they received a report that the room was being occupied illegally. Confounded and hoping for an explanation, the fan knocked on the adjoining door to Owen's room. When the fan informed Owen that the police were outside, the King of Pranks feigned panic at the thought of the policeman knocking on *his* door next. Owen started routing around his room before returning with a large bag of dubious white powder. He thrust it into the fan's hands and told him to take care of it for him. As Kevin Nash recalled, "The guy of course dumps it in the toilet and flushes it, thinking he's saving Owen. And it's basically a re-enactment of *Goodfellas*... 'Karen, where's the stuff? That's $3,500!'"

Of course, no phone call to the police had been placed; Owen had befriended the policeman in the hotel lobby and put him up to the jape. The suspicious bag of white powder was not in fact a controlled substance but some baking powder in a clear plastic bag that Owen had pre-prepared, probably hoping it would be found by the policeman in the fan's possession. Nash said, "[Owen] stayed on it for like two days just to drive the guy insane and then finally he said, 'No man, it's just a joke, it was all set up.'" Nash would go on to describe Owen as, "The greatest ribber of all time. A lot of guys would do a rib but he'll actually rib himself… just to torture the guy. He's that kind of guy." Little did the honeymooning fans realise they would receive the ultimate wedding gift: a classic rib from the best there ever was.

CHAPTER 9

Owen 3:16 and the Montreal Screwjob

♥ ♥

In Your House 16: Canadian Stampede on the 6th of July was booked to be the big homecoming for The Hart Foundation but the pay-per-view main event was shaping up to be a total catastrophe in the weeks leading up to the big show. The original plan was for the entire Hart Foundation to face off against Stone Cold Steve Austin, Shawn Michaels, Sycho Sid and the Legion of Doom but Shawn had quit after his backstage fracas with Bret on the 9th of June and Sid was injured in a car crash on the 15th.[1] It turned out the WWF needn't have worried, as over 12,000 rabid fans gathered in the sold out Calgary Saddledome to witness The Hart Foundation take on Austin, the Legion of Doom, Ken Shamrock and Goldust in one of the greatest and most memorable main events in the history of the business. In a little known fact, the ten men actually had a kind of dress rehearsal six days beforehand after the 30th of June *RAW is WAR* taping. In the dark match main event, Austin pinned Owen after hitting the Stone Cold Stunner.

Coinciding with the annual Calgary Stampede festival,[2] The Hart Foundation arrived in town early to take part in the parade. Diana Hart won the Miss Calgary competition and a reported 8,000 fans created a mile long line to grab autographs from Bret, Owen and Davey. Amazingly, every single fan received an autograph. As hated as they were in America, The Hart Foundation were beloved in their home country of Canada.[3] At the pay-per-view, the usually reserved Canadian crowd lost their collective minds as each Foundation member was introduced one by one. Bret came out last to an ovation so thunderous only a handful of wrestlers will ever get to experience it. Everyone on the opposing team, including Steve Austin, who was the now the Federation's most popular wrestler, were booed out of the building.

After twenty-four minutes of intense, fast-paced action in front of a red hot crowd, Austin attacked Owen on the outside in front of Stu Hart, Helen Hart, various Hart brothers and other family members. When Austin threw Owen back in the ring, Bruce Hart stood up and chucked his drink over Austin's back. The salty Austin turned around and grabbed a very frail Stu by the lapels up off his chair, with Bruce and fourth Hart kid Wayne jumping the guardrail to intervene before Austin could strike their Father. Bruce, upset at a stiff punch Austin landed on him earlier in the match, gave him a receipt in the form of a very hard forearm to Austin's lower back. Bret threw the dazed Austin back in the ring and Owen schoolboyed Austin for the clean win. The crowd went ballistic and the entire extended Hart family celebrated in the middle of the ring in one of the most emotional moments in WWE history. After the festivities had died down, Owen and Bret dressed down Bruce backstage for drawing the attention away from Owen's pinfall by engaging in an unscripted brawl with Road Warrior Hawk. The unscheduled mêlée with Hawk, as well as the bruised kidney he'd given Steve Austin, put paid to the notion of Bruce becoming the sixth member of The Hart Foundation.

The WWF travelled to San Antonio, Texas for the live *RAW is WAR* on the 14th of July, where The Hart Foundation set out the stipulations they'd agreed to for their respective *SummerSlam '97* matchups. In the spectre of a fan-made sign that read 'Bret Hart Humps Cows', Owen announced that Steve Austin had agreed to kiss his backside in the middle of the ring (the wrestling ring that is) if Owen defeated him.[4] On the same show, Owen and Bulldog, who'd recently won a tag team tournament to become number one contenders, lost their WWF Tag Title match against Steve Austin and his new partner, Mick 'Dude Love' Foley.

In an interview shortly before the big *SummerSlam* showdown, Owen didn't give his opponent much of a chance of winning. "I was the man who beat Stone Cold Steve Austin. I was the man who pinned his shoulders to the mat, one, two, three. The odds are I can beat Stone Cold Steve Austin. I beat him twice before and with my Intercontinental Title on the line I can guarantee ya I can beat him again." *SummerSlam '97* had been a somewhat lacklustre event and the 20,000 strong New Jersey crowd weren't very lively other than when Ken Shamrock 'snapped' and suplexed numerous WWF officials after losing to the British Bulldog.

In the semi-main event, Austin and Owen were easily putting on the best match of the night, with the crowd going hysterical with Austin's every move. "The crowd was right where we wanted them," recalled Owen. "Everything was perfect, I could do no wrong and my opponent Austin was perfect." Fifteen minutes into the match, Owen reversed a tilt-a-whirl-type manoeuvre and picked up Austin in a reverse piledriver position (which for you *Karma Sutra* fans out there is basically a standing sixty-nine). Owen and Steve had discussed the piledriver spot in the dressing room prior to the match. Owen insisted on dropping posterior first to the mat and Austin was insistent Owen drop to his knees like The Undertaker did for his patented Tombstone Piledriver. After telling Owen twice, Austin assumed Owen had got the message and thought no more about it.

After reviewing the footage multiple times, Austin estimated that his head was 'six or eight inches' too low for the move. When Owen jumped off his feet and landed in a sitting position, he spiked Steve's head into the mat for real. Scott Steiner had been doing a version of the sit-out piledriver for years and had never hurt anyone badly with it. The Steiner Screwdriver started from a standing vertical suplex position and was unbelievably dangerous looking. The difference was that Steiner was far bigger and far stronger than Owen and could control his opponent's position better. "As soon as my head hit that mat, I was thinking Christopher Reeve," Austin explained. "I thought I was never gonna walk again, ever. I couldn't feel anything from my neck down."

Owen, who was one of the best and safest workers in the business, had catastrophically miscalculated the move. "There was a little bit of a push and an impact on my thighs," said Owen, "and his neck is so vulnerable, it just kinked and just went numb." Some people questioned why Owen would even attempt the manoeuvre as nobody could recall Owen ever trying it before. Theories abound as to why Owen didn't drop to his knees instead, which was a far less risky landing and would allow Austin to tuck his head in. Did Owen have a lapse in concentration? Was Owen trying to avoid 'gimmick infringement' by not directly copying The Undertaker's finishing move? Whatever the reason, Austin suffered a serious stinger from blunt force trauma to the top of his skull. Steve couldn't move his limbs and was in terrible trouble. "It went from utopia to hell in a second," recalled a remorseful Owen.

In a state of transient quadriplegia, Austin told referee Earl Hebner, "Tell [Owen] not to fucking touch me, I can't move." Owen immediately knew he'd hurt Austin badly and, wearing a mask of confusion on his face, began taunting the crowd to buy Steve some time. Mercifully, Austin started regaining movement (and pain) back in his arms and rolled over to his front. Steve looked up at Earl Hebner and said, "Tell Owen Hart, 'Roll up for the win'." While Owen hit a bicep pose facing away from his opponent, Austin crawled towards him on his forearms and a less-than-convincing schoolboy pin for the win. "I roll Owen up with the worst cradle in the history of the business," Austin said. "Davey Boy Smith was livid because I'd exposed the business but I just wanted out of the match." Owen kicked out just after three in order not to look too weak but the force of the kick out hurt Austin's neck further. As ridiculous as it sounds today, Steve refused to lose the contest because of the 'kiss my ass' stipulation in effect. Personal pride also played a part on wanting to finish the match. "There was no way I was gonna lay there and let some ambulance and a bunch of paramedics carry me out of that ring."

When Steve Austin was announced as the new Intercontinental Champion, a lot of the audience still cheered like crazy, failing to grasp the severity of the situation. As unbelievable as it was that Austin had summoned up the strength to move at all, it was more unbelievable that the WWF had no protocol for this type of incident. The WWF let Austin move with a neck injury unaided, then sent out a couple of referees to help carry him to the back. After being practically dragged backstage, Austin was sat on an industrial storage case in the Continental Airlines Arena and looked over by medical personnel. "I am in a world of shit," said Austin, recalling his state of mind at that moment. "I am confused. I am in pain. I just damn near got paralysed for the rest of my life and I escaped it and I am highly emotional."

Owen was very concerned and followed Steve through the backstage area after the match before an ambulance took Austin to be x-rayed. Despite the axial load he'd just endured, Austin was discharged from the hospital that night. After failing to send out EMTs to tend to Austin as soon as he was dropped on his head, the WWF also failed to have anyone from the office accompany him to the hospital. Austin ended up hitching a ride from three female fans that had followed the ambulance from the arena. In true Stone Cold style, Austin asked the girls to buy him a twelve pack of Budweiser on the way back to the hotel!

The next night on *RAW is WAR*, Owen explained away the phony looking pinfall loss by blaming it on himself. "You were a crippled freak, you could barely move and the only reason you beat me is because I had compassion and I beat myself." The badly hurt Austin, who had driven himself the 110 miles to Bethlehem, Pennsylvania, emerged from the back and promised he'd get revenge on Owen later that night. In the main event, Austin, who by rights shouldn't have been allowed out of a hospital bed, interfered in the main event when he clonked Owen over the head with his own Slammy Award, allowing Dude Love to get the pin.[5]

Austin took a few weeks off the road, with his absence making fans clamour for him even more. On his return to the ring, Austin was forced to drastically alter his wrestling style from high impact scientific wrestling to a brawling style with less hard bumps. Austin's haste to return to the ring was great for his career in the short-term but his neck was living on borrowed time. Austin had neck fusion surgery in late 1999 that kept him out the ring for almost a year and ultimately cut short his wrestling career. According to Steve, he still suffers negative effects from the piledriver more than twenty years after the fact. "My left side was impacted more so than my right. To this day, my left hand is atrophied [and] when it gets cold that left foot starts dragging behind me."

Even though they weren't close friends, Owen and Steve's relationship fell apart that day. According to Owen's widow Martha, Owen had a personal dislike of Steve, stating that he believed his own hype and 'just wasn't a very nice person'.[6] Owen called Steve at the hospital that night to check up then never called him again, which greatly offended Austin. "That incident really bugged him on so many different levels," WWE Chairman Vince McMahon recalled. Bret kept telling Owen to call Steve to check up on him but he never did, presumably because of embarrassment, shame or even denial. "I don't think [Owen] handled it very well," said Bret. "It did change the relationship Steve had with Owen."

According to multiple people in the business, Owen privately expressed sorrow and regret for the incident to them but never to Steve himself. Owen even talked about his guilt over the piledriver incident in a 1998 interview. "I knew that Steve had a bad neck prior to us going in the ring... I felt terrible that it did happen. I'm glad that he's back in the ring and successful as he's been." The two remained cordial, greeting each other if they passed in the hallway but that's as far as the personal relationship went. "It was never the same between us," said Austin. "I didn't think he was as funny as I used to think he was."

Austin returned at *In Your House 17: Ground Zero* on the 7th of September to forfeit the WWF Tag Team Titles with Dude Love and drop Jim Ross with a Stone Cold Stunner for good measure. The next night on *RAW is WAR*, Sgt Slaughter placed Austin on storyline medical suspension and stripped him of the Intercontinental Title, too. A tournament to crown a new IC Champion was also announced, with Owen declared as one of the participants. Making the best of a bad situation, Owen continued to brag about being the man who put Stone Cold out of action. It's around this time that language restrictions on WWF TV were being relaxed and Owen relished in finally being able to say he was going to kick Austin's 'ass' rather than his 'butt' in interviews. The next week, Austin was handed a restraining order claiming he wasn't allowed within 100 feet of Owen. Austin promptly walked right up to Owen and tore up the legal document.

On the 20th of September, the WWF held their first-ever UK exclusive pay-per-view, *One Night Only*, at the Birmingham NEC. Unlike previous years, the WWF hadn't visited Europe all year and this would be the only test of whether The Hart Foundation were truly babyfaces in Europe. The British Bulldog vs. Shawn Michaels for the European Title was the main event of the show, with Bret vs. Undertaker and Owen vs. Vader on the undercard. Davey, who was told he'd be going over, gave interviews to tabloid newspapers promising he would win the match for the UK and his cancer-stricken sister Tracey, who would be sitting ringside.

Despite cutting promos throughout the show sucking up to the UK contingent, Owen and Bret still only received a 50-50 response from the audience, proving that their anti-American shtick had only been a complete success in Canada. When the Bulldog walked out however, the fans were fully in support of their countryman. Shawn Michaels, who made his entrance first, was still cheered by a lot of the girls but was now a fully fledged heel after weeks of highly obnoxious and contemptuous interviews. Over the past few months, Michaels had also developed a curious habit of constantly glancing at himself on the giant *RAW is WAR* video screen while he talked. He even once cut a promo wearing spandex hot pants with a roll of gauze stuck down the front, for which Shawn was fined $10,000 by Vince McMahon. In a promo several weeks after *One Night Only*, Michaels said that Stu Hart was dead but he was still walking around Calgary because his brain hadn't figured it out yet, which genuinely offended Bret.

On his way down to the ring in the Birmingham NEC, Michaels grabbed a young boy's British Bulldog action figure, dropped it down the front of his tights, pulled it out and threw it back to him. Partway through the match, Hunter Hearst Helmsley, Chyna and Michaels' 'insurance policy' Rick Rude[7] arrived at ringside in support of Michaels. Despite liberal interference from Michaels' seconds, Bulldog regained the upper hand when he clotheslined Michaels to the outside. Davey scooped Michaels up on his shoulders for his running powerslam finisher when his foot slipped off the raised platform at the edge of the ring mat, causing Davey to 'injure' his knee. Michaels threw Bulldog back in the ring, applied a figure-four leg lock and refused to let go. Like Steve Austin before him, the valiant babyface Bulldog refused to give up to the submission for several minutes before 'passing out'.

After being announced as the new European Champion, Michaels got on the microphone and verbally abused the increasingly hostile audience, who responded by showering Shawn in a hail of bottles and other detritus. Michaels then taunted Davey's wife Diana who was sat at ringside, before putting the boots to Davey once again. Diana jumped in the ring to put a stop to the four on one attack, eventually followed by Owen and Bret.

Despite the show being held in Davey's home country, the booking was designed to make only Shawn look good and The Hart Foundation look like complete idiots for not coming to Bulldog's rescue much earlier. Even though Michaels, Helmsley, Chyna and Rude hadn't settled on a name for their group, this would be the singular moment D-Generation X was officially born. Earlier in the day, Michaels and Triple H supposedly pulled a power play behind the scenes and got the finish changed from Davey winning clean to Michaels winning the belt. Shawn had already let it be known to his fellow workers that he was not willing to do jobs, earning himself even more animosity behind the scenes.

Jim Cornette, who was on the booking committee at the time said, "If I'd have been Davey, 'cause Davey was more than capable of doing it, I would've just knocked [Shawn] the fuck out and just fuckin' won [the match] and said fuck all y'all on my way out!" Fellow booking committee member Bruce Prichard denied that the booking decision was influenced by Michaels and Triple H. "It's not a big conspiracy theory, it's not an, 'Oh my God, they fucked Bulldog'. It was for heat, it was for a story." Davey was told that the loss would lead to a rematch in his home city of Manchester down the road where he'd regain the belt. While a nice idea in theory, there was very little chance of Michaels doing a clean job for the Bulldog. Either way, Davey was devastated at having to lose after promising everybody he'd win, as was his terminally ill Sister, who still believed wrestling was real. After a year of backstage politics and unnecessary stress, Bret claimed that losing to Shawn in Birmingham was the beginning of Davey's downward spiral. "I saw the light die in Davey's eyes that day, darkness seeping into a heart that was giving out."

At the 22nd of September *RAW is WAR* from Madison Square Garden, Owen was scheduled to face Brian Pillman in the semi-finals of the Intercontinental Title tournament. Pillman, who had branched off into feuding with Goldust, pretended to have a broken arm to get out of the match. The two Hart Foundation comrades then proceeded to have a 'fake' match. After Pillman's valet Marlena[8] interfered, Owen and Pillman started wrestling 'for real' until Goldust ran in, giving Owen a disqualification win. Austin then ran in and destroyed Owen to continue their feud and set up their eventual rematch. The next week, Owen was flanked by two helmeted security guards wearing an 'Owen 3:16 Says I Just Broke Your Neck' t-shirt, in mockery of the wildly popular 'Austin 3:16' tee, which was selling by the millions. Austin himself personally wasn't a fan of the Owen 3:16 parody t-shirt. "That was pretty damn cheesy. If I was going to get any royalties off that one, maybe I would have liked it better but if he's going to put the money in his pocket for messing my life up, I wasn't real fond of that." When Owen was asked about the shirt a year later, he confirmed he received the royalties. "[It] wasn't my idea, somebody else came up with the marketing of the shirt and I just reaped the benefits [in my] bank account." This being wrestling, Austin revealed himself to be one of the disguised security guards and hit Owen with another hit-and-run Stunner to a tremendous ovation.

On the afternoon of *In Your House 18: Badd Blood*, Hart Foundation member Brian Pillman was found dead in his hotel room in Bloomington, Minnesota. Pillman had a congenital heart defect that had been responsible for the early deaths of several of his family members, including his father. With Pillman self-medicating to cope with the pain of his shattered ankle, as well as various amounts of body enhancing and recreational drugs added to the concoction, it was a matter of sooner rather than later before Brian's heart gave out. In what must have seemed a blur to everyone in the company, especially the Harts and Pillman's good friend Steve Austin, it was quickly business as usual backstage and no one was given time to process their grief. Owen defeated Faarooq in the Intercontinental tournament finals after Austin hit Faarooq with the Title belt behind the referee's back.[9]

The post-*Badd Blood RAW is WAR* is infamous for one of the most disgraceful ratings ploys the World Wrestling Federation has ever perpetrated (and consider how much ground *that* covers). Vince McMahon interviewed Brian Pillman's devastated widow Melanie live on *RAW* a little more than twenty-four hours after his body was discovered. If that wasn't bad enough, the WWF scheduled the interview late in the show in order to hype the segment throughout *RAW* to steal some extra viewers from *WCW Nitro*. Through her debilitating grief, Melanie made a sobering plea to wrestlers who were overindulging on painkillers, uppers, downers and anything else, to take note of her husband's untimely death and alter their self-destructive habits. No one did.

The next month saw Stone Cold Steve Austin reinstated as an in-ring wrestler and booked to face Owen at *Survivor Series '97* for their inevitable Intercontinental Title rematch. Throughout the weeks, Austin continually interfered in Owen's Title defences so Owen remained champion come the 9th of November in Montreal. The main storyline heading into *Survivor Series* was the big rematch between Bret Hart and Shawn Michaels for the WWF Championship. More words have been dedicated to the *Survivor Series '97* match and the issues surrounding it than any other event in professional wrestling history. Unfortunately, there's no getting around the story, so the following is an overview of what would come to be known as the Montreal Screwjob.

While Bret was still on sabbatical from the WWF in 1996, WCW VP Eric Bischoff offered Bret $2.8 million a year for three years and less dates (180) to leave the Federation. With the WWF haemorrhaging money, McMahon counter-offered with an unprecedented twenty year contract worth $10.5 million in total, 180 dates a year and a promise to push Bret as the top star in the company. Bret would receive $1.5 million for three years as a wrestler, $500,000 for seven years as a senior advisor then $250,000 for ten years as a standby to make the occasional goodwill appearance. Loyalty won out and Bret signed the unparalleled WWF contract in October 1996.

While always competitive with each other, the personal problems between Bret and Shawn escalated upon Bret's return. Shawn wanted the top spot in the company and was unhappy earning less than Bret (a 'paltry' $750,000 per year). Shawn also felt that Bret didn't give him the respect he deserved when he was the Champion. According to Bret, he disliked enough about Shawn personally that he refused to endorse him to the rest of the boys. Ever since his own WWF Title run in 1996 hadn't generated the expected uptick in business, Shawn had become more obnoxious and volatile behind the scenes, while continuing to abuse prescription drugs. Over the next nine months, numerous on-screen interviews between Shawn and Bret had gotten too personal, feelings were hurt, punches were thrown and hair was ripped out.

On the 2nd of June 1997, McMahon, who was suffering from buyer's remorse, tried to restructure Bret's contract, citing the 'financial peril' the company was in at the time. Bret turned the request down flat. McMahon tried to slash Bret's pay by more than 50% once again on the 8th of September and was once again told no.

Bret, as well as Owen and Davey, had become increasingly uncomfortable with the recent direction of the WWF. In what was still designed to be a product aimed at children: racially sensitive storylines, increased swearing and blatant sexual content featuring Sunny, Sable and Marlena, as well as Michaels' striptease routines, had all featured on WWF programming over the past year. When Michaels returned to the WWF on the 14th of July after McMahon threatened to stop paying him, he and Bret were more cordial with one another. After the Michaels-Helmsley power play at the UK pay-per-view, tensions once again escalated. A few weeks later Michaels and Helmsley, who were still sitting in on booking meetings, convinced a reticent Bret to call them 'homos' on a live interview. Bret did, then immediately regretted it.

On the 22nd of September before *RAW* at Madison Square Garden, Vince told Bret he was breaking their contract, urging him to call Eric Bischoff to see if he could get his old deal with WCW. McMahon's financial situation was so desperate[10] he was considering downsizing from a national promotion back to a North-Eastern promotion again and asserted that he was going to be firing a lot of people. Shortly afterwards, Bret confided to Owen that Vince was probably going to shaft him over his contract one way or another.

On the same night as the Owen Hart-Dude Love San Jose popcorn fiasco on the 12th of October (more on that later), Bret told Shawn he'd have no problem dropping the WWF Championship to him at *Survivor Series*. According to Bret, a recalcitrant Michaels replied, "I appreciate that but I want you to know that I'm not willing to do the same thing for you." According to Michaels, he said this because, "Someone started spreading rumours that I was refusing to lose to people. So I started walking around the locker room bragging that I wouldn't do jobs. I was teasing and egging them on. It was my method of getting back at them." At the *RAW* taping on the 21st of October, McMahon held a meeting with Bret and Shawn where he declared that Shawn would win the WWF Title back from Bret at *Survivor Series*. Bret, who took the business and himself very seriously, steadfastly refused to lose to Shawn after his comments in San Jose. Bret offered to drop the WWF Title to anybody else in the company but wanted to leave *Survivor Series*, which was to be held in Montreal, Canada, as WWF Champion. Because Bret had 'reasonable creative control' for the last thirty days of his WWF career written into his contract, he had the right to refuse to lose to Shawn at *Survivor Series*.

Jim Cornette described booking meetings getting interrupted over stalled negotiations between Shawn and Bret regarding the *Survivor Series* finish. "We would have to sit and wait while Vince would have these phone calls. First it was Shawn. Then it was Bret. Then with someone else weighing in with their fuckin' opinion, whatever the fuck it was." Over the next few weeks, every conceivable scenario was discussed with Bret, including having the rest of The Hart Foundation turn on Bret and cost him the belt. Bret turned all of the proposals down. Shortly before the pay-per-view, Cornette reached the end of his tether. "I said, 'Vince, there's got to be something we can do. It's your company and it's your belt.' Vince looks at me and says, 'Well how would you do it, pal?' Well now it's a fuckin' challenge. Once again I'm going through every finish I can think of... where nobody wanted to do a job and I said, 'God damn, double-cross him.'"[11]

On the 27th of October episode of *RAW is War*, Bret Hart cut a promo that eerily foreshadowed the events of Montreal. "I'm right back to where I was a long time ago; complaining about Shawn Michaels. The fact of the matter is after the *Survivor Series* I won't have to worry about [Shawn] anymore, 'cause I know in that one single match that no matter what happens, I'll finally get my hands around his little scrawny neck and that truly is gonna be the end once and for all."

After several weeks' worth of negotiations with Eric Bischoff, Bret was offered $2.5 million per year for three years, special dispensation to turn up late to shows, comprehensive health insurance and 125 dates a year; down from 180 from the previous offer and less than half of the 280 or so dates the WWF required of him for most of his career. After a last minute phone call with Vince, Bret signed the WCW contract on the 1st of November and faxed it back to WCW's Atlanta office. Four days before the pay-per-view, word of Bret signing with WCW had leaked. McMahon felt it imperative to get the WWF Title off him before Bischoff could announce on *WCW Monday Nitro* that he'd signed his World Champion. Come *Survivor Series*, Bret and

McMahon agreed that the match would end in a disqualification with Bret retaining. They also agreed that with the permission of Bischoff, Bret would stay on with the WWF an extra week (while WCW paid him) to drop the Title to Michaels in a four person match also featuring Ken Shamrock and The Undertaker at the Springfield, Massachusetts pay-per-view on the 7th of December. Bret would then give a farewell speech the next night on *RAW* before heading off to WCW.

In a secretly taped conversation on the afternoon of *Survivor Series*, the WWF Chairman told Bret, "I can't tell you how appreciative I will always be for everything you've done for this company; and like I said in our previous conversations I'd just be damned even though it's Ted Turner's money and... all that kind of shit, that's no reason for two people who have spent as much time as we have spent together through the years and have worked as closely as we have had through the years, it's no reason to have any problems." At another point during this private conversation, Bret reiterated that he'd like to simply forfeit the WWF Title and give a farewell address the day after *Survivor Series* in Ottawa. "I made my thoughts known to Vince," Cornette said regarding Bret's somewhat self-serving suggestion. "I said why don't you just lay down there and let [Bret] piss in your mouth while he does that!"

The *Survivor Series* showdown between Bret and Shawn, which was eighteen months in the making, started off incredibly hot. The rivals brawled all around the ring and up the entrance way while surrounded by WWF officials, including Jerry Brisco, Sgt Slaughter and McMahon himself. Bret and Shawn eventually made their way back to the ring and Vince and his comrades remained at ringside, which was strange to say the least. After twenty excellent minutes of fierce wrestling and brawling, Bret allowed Shawn to tie him up in his own Sharpshooter leglock submission, as had been agreed to backstage. The pre-arranged sequence was for Bret to somehow escape his own hold and battle Shawn for a few more minutes before D-Generation X ran in for the disqualification.

The following is what actually occurred: Shawn applied the Sharpshooter on Bret. Earl Hebner flapped his arms around for a couple of seconds before shouting, "RING THE BELL!" Earl then legged it out of the ring, jumped into waiting a car driven by his twin brother Dave and sped out of the arena. Earl, who'd sworn on his children that he wouldn't screw Bret the day before, was gripped by McMahon on his way to the ring and was told to comply 'or else'. When the bell didn't ring, McMahon politely but firmly, requested timekeeper, Mark Yeaton to, "RING THE FUCKING BELL!" Cornette, who had inadvertently come up with the Screwjob finish but had no idea it would be implemented, remembered his reaction vividly. "[When] I was sitting there at the monitor [backstage and] I saw them going into the spot, that's when I shit myself." Like nearly everybody else close to the situation, fellow booking committee member and McMahon confidant Bruce Prichard, was kept in the dark regarding the Screwjob. "Oh god! I was pissed off that I wasn't smartened up as to what they were doing. I was pissed off because I was left in the back alone in [Gorilla] position where everyone thought they knew I was involved and I wasn't. I felt very alone and I felt very betrayed."

Owen, Davey and Jim Neidhart, who were stood at Gorilla position waiting for their cue to chase DX off, were left wondering what the heck just happened. When reality dawned on Bret, he stood up, saw Vince glaring up at him from ringside and spat right in his face. Michaels, who was acting like he was confused and angry at Vince, was quickly ushered to the dressing room by Jerry Brisco. Bret then went on to smash up some expensive television monitors and paint the letters 'WCW' in the air with his finger for all the fans to see. When Bret finally arrived in the locker room, Shawn swore to god that he wasn't in on the plan. Even at the time, Owen wasn't buying Shawn's act. "I don't doubt for a second [Shawn] was in on the whole thing. His emotional temper tantrum at the end of the match was merely as close as he can come to good acting. His crying and weeping like a baby in the dressing room while he was in the corner biting his nails were much the same. He's a dirty, lying cheat." Shawn would publicly deny any knowledge of the Screwjob until he admitted his involvement in a WWE-produced piece in May 2002.

As much as it looked like a perfectly executed wrestling angle to the untrained eye, McMahon had legitimately screwed Bret out of the WWF Title and a fourteen year relationship was down the drain. Although never corroborated, there had been rumours circulated by an unnamed WWF official that the plan had been to get rid of Bret to placate Shawn since the 9th of June, when the pair had their pre-*RAW* backstage brawl. Many things happened backstage immediately after the Screwjob but the most salient event was when Vince went to the locker room with his son and his aging entourage to confront Bret at The Undertaker's insistence. Bret, who was in the shower, told Vince he was going to punch him out if he was still in the locker room when he was done. When McMahon refused to leave, Bret got dressed, walked over to Vince and gave his now former boss a knuckle supper. Bret and Vince locked up like it was a wrestling match before Bret damn near uppercutted Vince's head off. McMahon was knocked out cold and for good measure rolled his ankle as he crumpled to the locker room floor. Michaels later claimed that Vince took a dive, then told Bret, "I owed you that." In early 1998, Owen's emotions were still raw when the Screwjob was brought up. "[Bret] wasn't like an Ultimate Warrior that walked in and took whatever he could get and then left. When Warrior left, he left for his own selfish reasons. He didn't train or help the younger guys and Bret Hart was a guy who'd do that. His absence is noticeable, by me especially."

Nearly every wrestler in the locker room was outraged that McMahon screwed Bret and threatened to boycott the next evenings' live *RAW is WAR* telecast. By the next day, the only wrestlers who'd gone home were: Bret, Owen, Davey Boy, Jim Neidhart and Mick Foley. At Bret's insistence Foley, who prided himself on his strong moral compass, returned for the *RAW* taping the day after. Rick Rude and Brian 'Crush' Adams left the Federation for WCW shortly after, citing the Montreal Screwjob and distrust for McMahon as a major factor in their leaving. To mess with the WWF, Rude, who was working for McMahon on a per-appearance basis, turned up on a live *WCW Nitro* with a moustache at the same time he appeared on a pre-taped *RAW is WAR* with a beard.

In October 1996, Vince McMahon said, "WCW would never know what to do with a Bret Hart." He was right. WCW waited five weeks to debut Bret, then inexplicably booked him as a special guest referee for a match between Larry Zbyszko (a retired wrestler) and Eric Bischoff (a non-wrestler) for control of *WCW Nitro*. It was a complete waste of a debut. Bret then briefly feuded with Ric Flair but thanks to locker room politicking, both were quickly taken off TV and their entertaining feud was killed stone dead. The rest of Bret's tenure would be characterised by either doing nothing noteworthy or being booked badly on purpose, before an errant kick from Bill Goldberg at *Starrcade '99* ended his in-ring career. "[WCW] never had a clue," said Bret. "I think there was a lot of sabotage in all of that. I think it's safe to say now that [Hulk] Hogan and Bischoff basically brought me there to sit me on the bench.... for the rest of my career." Bret has publicly accused Hogan of subverting his position in WCW and has described Bischoff in even more unfavourable terms. "There have been few more clueless idiots in the wrestling business than Eric Bischoff just for... straight up knowledge of what to do and what not to do in a wrestling ring. He's pretty close to an imbecile."[12]

Davey Boy had grown sick of the behind-the-scenes politics and desperately wanted to get out of his contract and follow Bret to WCW. Davey quickly scheduled knee surgery so the WWF couldn't force him to wrestle, claiming he'd reinjured it during the post-Screwjob locker room fracas. McMahon told Davey he'd have to pay a $150,000 fine to break his five year contract thirty-two months early, which was negotiated down to $100,000. Davey soon signed a three-year deal with WCW for $333,000 for the first year, $383,000 in the second and $433,000 in the third. WCW also paid half of Davey's fine for getting out of his WWF contract early. Davey quickly went from being a very good worker in the WWF to a very bad worker in WCW. Without the personal attention he received in the WWF, Davey seemingly completely lost interest in wrestling and sank deeper into his personal problems.

Jim Neidhart went back to the WWF after a few days and on the 24th of November *RAW* was introduced by Shawn Michaels and Triple H as the newest member of D-Generation X. DX then immediately double-crossed and attacked Neidhart (in storyline this time). Neidhart and Triple H squared off on *RAW is WAR* the next week, which of course, Neidhart lost. After wrestling a few more matches on Federation house shows, Neidhart had been offered contracts from both WWF and WCW. Neidhart chose WCW because they offered more money and also for creative reasons, as he'd been buried on WWF TV the past two weeks by DX. The Anvil lasted six months in WCW before he was taken off the road. Like Davey, Neidhart went off the rails and struggled to wrestle even passable matches during his tenure.

Owen didn't show up at the next two *RAW* tapings but curiously did wrestle a tag team match with Jim Neidhart in Ontario, Canada three days after Montreal, in a losing effort to Steve Austin and Dude Love. Owen was understandably upset and was also sick of the string of adult-oriented storylines the Federation had been presenting over the past year. Owen asked the WWF for an unconditional release, which was refused. According to former Federation Head Writer Vince Russo, a devastated Owen rang him shortly after the Montreal Screwjob saying that Bret was going to disown him if he continued working for the WWF. When Bret called Russo to discuss Owen's future with the company, he received a phone call from Vince McMahon immediately afterwards. McMahon curtly told Bret, "If you say another word to Owen I'll sue you so fast you won't know what hit you."

Caught between a rock and a hard place, Owen was still viewed as a valuable asset to the WWF and McMahon wanted to keep him around. Although his Federation agreement was iron-clad, McMahon offered Owen a new contract with a handsome raise; $400,000 plus an estimated $50,000 in royalties per year. To sweeten the deal further, McMahon offered to backdate the pay rise to the beginning of the contract year. This was a big break as, according to Bret, Bischoff had seen nothing in Owen and offered him less money than he was making on his old WWF contract. "Eric Bischoff didn't think my brother Owen was good enough, which shows you how much Eric Bischoff knows about wrestling. He picked up Davey Boy and Jim Neidhart like that but passed on Owen."

After much soul-searching, Owen re-signed with the WWF. "Our agreement has got to be based on trust now," said Owen with regards to his re-signing. "If I walk around thinking I can't trust [Vince], it isn't going to work. I have trust and I have good feelings." Despite Montreal, Owen was still generally happy working for the company and had lots of friends. He also recognised that Bret could be difficult to deal with and considered his brother's issues with Vince a separate matter. Owen made his on-screen return to the World Wrestling Federation on the 7th of December. A month after Montreal, Bret went from supposedly 'threatening to disown' his younger brother for staying with the WWF even though he had little recourse, to accepting his decision to remain with the company, "I love

[Owen] very much, I wish him all the best and I hope someday we can sit out on his boat and go fishing and talk about how crazy life got back in 1997."

[1]Sid was driving a rented Lincoln Continental from Toronto to Montreal with Doug Furnas, Phil LaFon and Charles 'Flash Funk' Skaggs along for the ride. Speeding down the highway at 100mph, Sid lost control of the car while he was fiddling with the sun roof. "[Sid] hit the soft shoulder and rolled about four or five times," said Phil LaFon. "I'm saying four or five times but I woke up in a hospital." Miraculously, nobody aside from Doug Furnas, who received a broken shoulder, was seriously hurt. Sid claimed he received a concussion and his back injury was re-aggravated and was removed from future cards. Sid had once again proved he was a liability; he was already becoming difficult to work with and had no-showed bookings. Aside from a very brief appearance on the 14th of July 1997 *RAW is WAR*, the WWF wouldn't book Sid again until 2012, where he defeated comedy heel Heath Slater on *WWE RAW*.

[2]The Calgary Stampede is an annual ten day festival featuring the rodeo, exhibitions, the circus, concerts and more. Now attracting around a million visitors every year, the festival traces its roots back to the 1880s. Stampede Wrestling held shows at the festival every year.

[3]The Canadian fans graciously overlooked the fact that the Bulldog was, unsurprisingly, British, and Jim Neidhart and Brian Pillman were both American. Also, Bret and Owen were dual Canadian-American citizens as their mother Helen was born in New York.

[4]The other members of The Hart Foundation also agreed to wagers if they lost at what Bret consistently referred to as '*The SummerSlam*'. Bret claimed he would never wrestle in the United States again if he failed to win the WWF Title from The Undertaker. Bulldog agreed to eat dog food if he couldn't beat Ken Shamrock. Brian Pillman agreed to wear a dress if he didn't beat Goldust (and insulted his father Dusty Rhodes while he was at it). Jim Neidhart agreed to shave his trademark goatee off if any Hart Foundation member lost at *SummerSlam*. Pillman

lost his match to Goldust and wore a succession of gold dresses (and for some reason, make up) on *RAW* but Neidhart didn't shave the beard. In fact, Jim was nowhere to be found. The WWF had just discovered that Neidhart had signed an exclusive contract with Ultimate (or Universal, depending on the source) Championship Wrestling, a small independent promotion based in New York. Neidhart was quietly and temporarily let go by the WWF before *SummerSlam* and brought back when the contractual matter was resolved. By the time Neidhart returned in September, everyone forgot about the beard shaving angle. Bruce Hart, who happened to be UCW's booker, was given his walking papers when the owners assumed he had something to do with Neidhart's WWF defection.

[5]Steve Austin would take a month off before returning at *In Your House 17: Ground Zero* on the 7th of September. While not wrestling, Austin started getting involved in semi-physical angles. He Stunned announcers, figurehead WWF President Sgt Slaughter and eventually Vince McMahon himself, kicking off the legendary Austin vs. McMahon feud that would erupt in 1998. "Steve, I think when he got injured, was able to then show his range as a performer," said Triple H in 2011. Austin, who was becoming more popular by the week, was rushed back to the ring in late October, taking part in tag team matches and short singles matches to ease him back into active duty.

[6]Owen's widow Martha claimed in her book that Owen insisted he had executed the piledriver properly and Austin may have faked the neck injury to get time off the road. Anyone with working vision can see this is patently ridiculous. Owen's own words, both public and privately to his co-workers, also contradicts Martha's assertion.

[7]'Ravishing' Rick Rude hadn't wrestled since a back injury in 1994 forced him onto the sidelines. After three years away from the business, Rude made sporadic, non-wrestling appearances for ECW in 1997. Rude couldn't take any bumps after claiming on his Lloyd's of London health insurance policy. Many wrestlers including: Road Warrior Animal, Curt Hennig, Nikita Koloff, Diamond Dallas Page, Vader, Ted

DiBiase, Bret Hart and more purchased similar insurance policies in the early 1990s when the risks of pro wrestling were less understood. Some wrestlers claimed 'career-ending injuries' (usually back related as they're harder to disprove) and declared themselves permanently disabled so as to claim large cash payouts. Some, like Bret, genuinely suffered career-ending injuries but others like Hennig and Animal returned to the ring when the WWF and WCW started handing out large, guaranteed contracts. Joe 'Animal' Laurinaitis negotiated a stipulation with Lloyd's where he could work tag team matches and still receive payouts; so half the work and twice the pay! Rude was training hard for an in-ring comeback before he died on the 20th of April 1999 aged 40.

[8]Pillman had 'won' Goldust's valet and real-life wife Terri 'Marlena' Runnels' services for thirty days at *In Your House 17*. This basically meant Marlena was forced to be Pillman's sex slave in storyline. Pillman once dated Terri in real life back in WCW before Dustin had met her, which made Dustin deeply uncomfortable with the storyline. Had Pillman not have passed, the booking direction was to have Marlena turn on Goldust and stay with Pillman as his valet, culminating in a wedding live on *RAW*.

[9]Rocky Maivia was originally slated to meet Owen in the IC tournament final. Rocky had recently torn some nerves and a tendon in his hand on an exposed nail, which required minor surgery. Maivia's Nation of Domination teammate Faarooq took his place.

[10]It begs the question that if the WWF was in such financial peril, why did they run a contest for a lucky fan to win $1 million at *SummerSlam '97*? The WWF broadcast several weeks' worth of abstract videos then gave out a 'clue' at the end. After all the clues were broadcast, fans had to decipher the answer, which was a number from 1-100. A correspondingly numbered key would then be picked to try to unlock the million dollar coffin (obviously) and win the money. Two fans were called live on the *SummerSlam* broadcast... well, actually four. The first fan's phone was disconnected and the second number rang out. Two fans who'd won tickets to the show also picked keys and attempted to

unlock the coffin unsuccessfully. Nobody won anything except the fans at home who won an opportunity to put the kettle on. Even with the benefit of hindsight, none of the clues seemed to hint towards any particular number whatsoever. The correct key was key 3.

[11]Cornette was speaking out of frustration when he suggested screwing Bret out of the belt. Cornette also suggested booking former UFC Champion Ken Shamrock against Bret to win the WWF Title on the theory that Shamrock would hurt Bret legitimately if he didn't cooperate. Fellow WWF booking team member (and Cornette's mortal enemy) Vince Russo has also claimed that he came up with the idea to double-cross Bret. In response, Cornette said, "It wasn't fuckin' Vince Russo's [idea but] Russo's taken credit for it. When I said double-cross in jest about the Shamrock thing, Russo's eyes got even buggier than normal. He didn't know what a double-cross was." In another interview Cornette said, "Vince Russo is the biggest liar in professional wrestling and imagine the territory that takes in!"

[12]Perhaps Bret had a point with regards to Eric Bischoff's competence. With the arrival of Bret in late 1997, WCW had the greatest array of talent ever assembled under one promotion. Despite the incredible amount of box office attractions under contract, WCW was already crumbling from within thanks to: bad and/or repetitive booking, lack of clean finishes, disgruntled employees and politicking by key WCW talent. In September 1999, Eric Bischoff was fired from his Vice Presidential role after sagging ratings and years of unsatisfactory storylines (even though WCW consistently beat the WWF in the ratings up until April 1998). The next time Bischoff was put in a position of power was in 2010 when he took on an Executive Producer role for the TNA promotion along with Hulk Hogan in a major shakeup. Despite a great roster of superstars and hungry young talent, TNA was completely mismanaged and viewership dropped during Bischoff' and Hogan's three year tenure. On the 27th of June 2019, Eric Bischoff was announced as the Executive Director of *WWE Smackdown!* in anticipation of the show's move to FOX on the 4th of October. Bischoff was appointed due to his history in wrestling, his history of dealing with

television executives and his name value to WWE stockholders. Bischoff was fired on the 15th of October, with wrestling journalist Dave Meltzer claiming that the sum total of Bischoff's creative contributions were occasionally being spotted in catering. "[Eric] was a bad hire. He [was] not up to date on the current product and the business has changed."

Davey Boy's
Sumo Suit Nightmare
As told by Triple H

In the 1990s during intermission on house shows, the WWF would allow fans to get into the ring and participate in sumo wrestling matches while wearing giant, padded comedy suits. The suits themselves were a bit of a tight squeeze to get into and greatly restricted the motion of the wearer, forcing the pugilists to battle gravity as well as their opponent in a bid to amuse the fans during half-time. On an untelevised house show in Niagara Falls, New York, Owen saw the suits laid out in the backstage area in preparation for the half-time entertainment and began plotting. In short order, Owen had devised one of his finest pranks; all he had to do was seduce his brother-in-law and tag team partner Davey Boy Smith, into wearing the sumo outfit.

Owen started needling Bulldog, accusing him of being 'too fat' to fit inside the suit. In reality, Smith, who had been using steroids since the early '80s, was obscenely well-muscled to the point that road agent Chief Jay Strongbow gave him the nickname 'Robot.' While Davey's physique looked fantastic on television, his colossal frame hampered his natural range of movement and thus resembled Johnny 5 of *Short Circuit* fame in his mechanical, rigid mannerisms.

"They got into this argument that Owen masterfully set up for like an hour about Davey not being able to fit in the suit, where Davey now is gonna show Owen, 'Of course I can fit in the stupid suit!'" recalled Triple H. "As dumb as that argument sounds, Owen could manipulate you and he manipulated Davey into getting in this suit." Eventually, the Bulldog finally had enough of Owen's teasing and decided to prove him wrong; unaware he had just fallen into the trap Owen had been engineering all this time.

With Owen's help, Davey stuffed himself into the sumo suit with Owen, ever the doting brother-in-law, zipping him up from the back. Davey had, in his own mind, shown Owen up in front of their peers but was now

310

practically immobile with his arms sticking out in a 'T' formation and his legs unable to bend. Taking advantage of Davey's sudden susceptibility, Owen forcibly grabbed his brother-in-law and ushered him across the backstage area to the Gorilla position, then through the dividing curtain, through the entrance way, down the aisle way and towards the ring; all while the show was in full swing and a wrestling match was in progress.

The crowd's attention quickly diverted from the in-ring action to the entrance way, where a giant, pink spheroid with the British Bulldog's head on top paraded towards the ring. With the crowd cat-calling and laughing hysterically at the extraordinary, unscheduled run-in, Owen continued to frog march his hapless brother-in-law down the walkway towards the ring.

Sensing the rib was coming to a close, the magnanimous Owen apparently decided three-quarters of the way to the ring was enough humiliation for poor Davey Boy. At that point Owen promptly left him in the aisle surrounded by baying fans and jogged back towards the dividing curtain on his lonesome. Triple H, who witnessed the incident, said that, "Davey had to turn around... swearing the whole time, trying to manipulate his way to the locker room area." In what must have felt like an ice age, the Mancunian strongman pivoted his legs back and forth, moving roughly at the speed of continental drift, before eventually getting back through the entrance curtain; humbled but stoically upright until the end.

Using the Facilities

As told by Ahmed Johnson and Jim Neidhart

It's been a classic prank for many decades to the point that it's become a cliché but when you gotta go you gotta go. In what would be a fairly regular (if you'll pardon the pun) escapade, Owen would procure (or possibly steal) someone else's room key so he could use their facilities instead of his own. If he couldn't snatch a hotel key, Owen would simply go to the hotel check-in desk and pretend he'd lost his key, before purposely giving a different room number for the replacement. Once inside the wrestler's room, Owen would make himself at home by delivering an unwanted offering to the porcelain throne and then conveniently 'forgetting' to flush. To add insult to injury, Owen would then crank up the thermostat to its highest setting so that the bowl full of bum slugs would smell extra ripe, festooning the entire room with the stench by the time the rightful occupant retired for the evening.

While it isn't known how he acquired his room key, Ahmed Johnson, one of Owen's numerous victims in this regard, was worried Owen was hazing him because he disliked him until Owen's brother set him straight. "Bret told me one day, he said, 'Look man, Owen doesn't rib people he don't like. If he's ribbing you it's because he likes you.' He was just a good dude, man. I mean, I know people said that [about Owen] all the time. They said Jeffrey Dahmer was a good dude! But Owen? Really genuine." The King of Pranks was less kind to Ahmed during an AOL chat from 1996. While in character, Owen mocked Ahmed's unique cadence, claiming he, "Sounds like he's got a mouth full of marbles," and that the Pearl River Powerhouse had "a million dollar body and a two cent brain."

Jim 'The Anvil' Neidhart also found himself getting pranked by Owen when it came to room keys. The brothers-in-law would often travel together, with Owen acting as a sort of babysitter to keep Anvil on the straight and narrow as much as possible. They also roomed together many times, like so many wrestlers did to save a little money on the road. One evening, Neidhart asked Owen for their room number and key. Owen handed the key over and the former shot-putter headed to the room to do

313

whatever it was he needed to do. When Jim walked through the door, he was confronted by a complete stranger in bed trying to sleep. Both men got a shock and the startled Anvil ran off to get some answers from Owen. When Anvil was asked to describe Owen in an interview years later, the response was unequivocal; "Probably the biggest ribber of all time."

Harley Race Chilli Cook-Off

As told by Harley Race, Terri Runnels and Steve Austin

Wrestling legend among legends 'Handsome' Harley Race once described his range of talents thus, "There's two things I can do in life; wrestle and cook." The eight-time NWA World Heavyweight Champion was one of the legitimately tough men of his era. Respected and feared by his contemporaries in equal measure, Harley looked tough and was even tougher and was the consummate professional throughout his thirty year in-ring career. "Harley Race was as good at one time as anybody in the business," said Jim Cornette. "To be the travelling World Champion and be fucked up in all those [car] wrecks and still be able to perform at a high level for twenty years and be a street fighter that could knock you the fuck out in sixteen ways... Harley for a considerable period of time was one of the best in the business." When 'Nature Boy' Ric Flair had to defend the NWA Title in Japan, Harley Race alone was sent with him as backup in case some of the tough Japanese wrestlers tried to pull a fast one on Naitch. They never did.

As far as cooking goes, many wrestlers looked forward to working Kansas City because Harley would put on a big barbecue for WWF personnel. "Harley could cook his ass off," said wrestling legend Stone Cold Steve Austin. [Harley] and his wife BJ, who is no longer with us, she would make all these desserts. She was awesome and could cook great. So we'd go over there and just load up, eat like pigs and then we'd eat dessert and you got all the boys working Kansas City that night."

Even at these friendly barbecues, the long-retired 'Handsome' one could still put what Mick Foley would term 'the fear of Harley' into the wrestlers. Describing one such exchange, Steve Austin continued, "So we're all laying on the floor [napping]... you don't wanna just get up and leave, like eat and run. So we're all kinda hanging around and all the boys are tired 'cause we've been on the road and kinda halfway asleep and everybody's starting to kick out of their naps now. So you don't know when it's time to leave, to kinda start making that segue to go back to the hotel to go to the show [that night]. Finally, Harley would come in and go, 'Alright, everybody get out!' That was like Okay, now we can leave. We didn't want to offend Harley Race!"

When the WWF held a show at Kemper Arena in Kansas City, Missouri on the 6th of October 1997, some of the wrestlers and staff made their usual pilgrimage to the Race household for another barbecue, a game of pool in the basement and a nap before heading to the *RAW is WAR* taping that evening. That day, Terri 'Marlena' Runnels and her real-life husband Dustin 'Goldust' Runnels were present, as well as Mick 'Mankind/Dude Love/Cactus Jack' Foley and of course Owen Hart. The main feature of Harley's barbecues was a giant bowl of chilli that he took enormous pride in making, even winning prizes at local chilli cook-offs for his culinary skills. None of these commendations mattered to Owen, who brought what Harley identified as a bottle of 'Insanity Hot Sauce' with him to the party. When Owen thought no one was looking, he edged towards the blue ribbon vat of chilli and dumped the entire bottle of hot sauce in the bowl, ruining the whole lot. Shortly after, Mick Foley unwittingly scooped a plate of the contaminated cuisine and golloped it down before choking on the intense heat. Afterwards, Owen swore up and down to Terri that he, "Intended to put a few drops in but the lid came off and everything went in," an explanation that strains credulity.

The next day, the WWF was taping another episode of *RAW* some sixty miles away in Topeka, Kansas. Over the course of the previous twenty-four hours, Harley had satisfied himself that it was Owen who'd spiked his chilli and ballsed up his barbecue. The Handsome one decided to head down to the Landon Arena to get Owen's side of the story and perhaps extend the olive branch of peace. Unfortunately for Owen, Harley was fresh out of olive branches, so he took his high voltage stun gun with him instead and made the one hour drive to Topeka. "Harley was famous for and took great pride in his chilli," remembered Terri. "As we all know, Harley Race is a very prideful man. You don't take away from what he has done."

When he arrived at the site of that evening's *RAW is WAR* taping, Harley began the hunt for the King of Harts all over the arena, before finding a stark-naked Owen as he was getting changed in a locker room. While Owen had his back side turned to the door, Harley strode in with stun gun in hand. With Owen's guard (and trousers) down, Harley decided it was time to show the chilli contaminating Hart his gratitude. "I inserted [the stun gun] in his butt and squeezed it off and all he could do is just shimmy and jerk until I released the trigger," said Harley in his usual gruff, understated way. Goldust was in the locker room at the time. "You should've seen Owen, I mean he was going crazy, it was the funniest thing you ever seen!" Terri Runnels confirmed the altercation. "He used his stun gun on Owen until tears were coming out of Owen's eyes!"

It didn't matter to Owen if it was his family, his boss or even a wrestling legend, no one was off-limits to getting ribbed. Since there are no further reports of Owen getting tasered in the posterior while in the nip, it's a safe bet that Harley Race's food remained un-tampered with at future barbecues.

Michael Cola

As told by Michael Cole

By the late 1990s, ubiquitous World Wrestling Federation presenter Todd Pettengill had been working as both a full-time radio disk jockey for WPLJ in New York and hosting various WWF programmes for four years. Todd was hired in 1993 by (at the time) the Federation's clueless Head of Human Resources Lisa Wolf, who along with Executive Producer Kevin Dunn, were big fans of 'real' celebrities from outside the wrestling bubble and were willing to overpay to hire them. According to Jim Cornette, Pettengill was paid, "Three-hundred grand a year to work part-time" and who "the wrestling fans universally panned because it was obvious he didn't know anything about wrestling." Cornette also added that Todd was, in fact, very talented as an on-screen personality.

By the summer of 1997, Pettengill made the choice to let his WWF contract run out and commit fully to radio, leaving wrestling behind for good.[1] His parting gift to the world of Sports Entertainment (if it can be described as such) was to put forth a recommendation for his replacement. The replacement turned out to be diminutive former CBS broadcast journalist, Sean Michael Coulthard. Coulthard would be rechristened Michael Cole, bunged into an ill-fitting suit and tasked with interviewing World Wrestling Federation superstars. Cole, who had reported on-site during the Waco siege and the Yugoslavian civil war, was visibly nervous during his WWF debut on the 30th of June 1997 episode of *RAW is WAR* but his official welcome to the business would occur five weeks later.

At the *In Your House: Ground Zero* pay-per-view, Cole's only job for the night would be to interview the World Wrestling Federation Champion Bret 'Hitman' Hart before his big title defence against 'The Patriot' Del Wilkes. With microphone in hand and bedecked in a tuxedo he had no business wearing, Cole would later admit he was still nervous doing live television and that 'his hands were shaking' right before he was due to go on air. Michael must have looked visibly flustered, so with just one minute left

318

to go before the interview, Bret's Hart Foundation comrades Owen and Davey Boy poured out some Coca-Cola to cool down the junior announcer.

Unfortunately for Michael, the brothers-in-law didn't pour the carbonated soft-drink into a glass and hand it to him. Rather, they yanked open Cole's trouser waistband and poured the entire one litre bottle of Cola down the back of his tuxedo trousers and walked off laughing. With less than a minute to go, Cole had no time to change and he couldn't very well conduct the interview trouser-less. His only option was to stand there like an idiot with his underpants soaked in high fructose corn syrup and cola dribbling down the back of his legs. When the camera went live for the backstage interview, Michael hurriedly yelped out his scripted lines to set up Bret's monologue about how he was going to 'kick the crap' out of The Patriot, before Cole, who by this point was looking particularly forlorn, threw back to the commentary team with an abrupt, "That's the champion, Bret Hart, back to ringside."

Shortly after this incident, Michael Cole (or Michael Cola as he would be known as for a time) would go on to become the butt of practical jokes on-screen as well. Over the course of the next few months, D-Generation X would collectively give him wet willies, push him over in-ring and give him a shower while he was still in his suit. If they only knew that Cole would go on to assault the ears of loyal WWE fans for twenty years (and counting) as a subpar commentator,[2] Owen, Davey and D-Generation X would have probably tried harder to run him out of the company while they still had the chance.

[1]Pettengill made the correct decision to stick with radio, as he would remain as WPLJ's breakfast host for a staggering twenty-seven years, winning Billboard Magazine's Major Market Air personality of the year six times, before finishing up on the 31st of May 2019. The Todd-ster made one more appearance for the WWE, hosting *The Best of In Your House* three-disc DVD compilation set in 2013.

[2]Michael Cole was groomed early on to become the WWF's lead commentator, despite the fact that he had no sports commentary experience and simply wasn't very good. Over the years, more qualified

wrestling commentators such as Kevin Kelly and Joey Styles were overlooked and Jim Ross, arguably the greatest play-by-play man in the history of the business, was consistently pushed aside in favour of Cole.

D'Lo Brown's 40 Foot Bag

As told by D'Lo Brown and Scott Hall

Accie Conner, fresh from stints in Smoky Mountain Wrestling and World Wrestling Council in Puerto Rico under the name D'Lo Brown, was brought in to the WWF fold at the beginning of 1997 to be a nameless, bow tie wearing punching bag for the heel Nation of Domination faction. The Nation was originally conceived as a pastiche of the Nation of Islam. Its mission was to wage war with popular black, babyface Ahmed Johnson because the Nation's leader Ron 'Faarooq Asaad' Simmons accused Johnson of selling out and bending to the will of the white man.

For all the group's strengths, the original iteration of NoD was not without its flaws; visually, there was a disconnect with the group's presentation. Instead of Nation of Islam-style flowing robes, Faarooq and team wore a curious mix of pan-African coloured stripes sewn onto black spandex, aside from Brian 'Crush' Adams, who opted for a neo-Nazi denim biker look, possibly inspired by his recent incarceration for possession of steroids and an illegal hand gun. Also, a black power gang with no less than three white guys and Puerto Rican wrestler, Savio Vega, sent out a surprisingly tolerant and inclusive message to the WWF audience.

While D'Lo was just another body in a suit on television, he was wrestling on the untelevised house show circuit to gain experience. It was after one of these matches that D'Lo encountered Owen Hart and Davey Boy Smith as he entered the locker room. They were huddled together, snickering and giggling; a sure sign that a rib was being perpetrated on some poor unfortunate. D'Lo walked to his chair to take his gear off, grab a towel and hit the showers but his bag wasn't where he'd left it. Initially thinking he'd sat down in the wrong part of the locker room, D'Lo got up and walked up and down to try to discover where he'd left his bag. While D'Lo looked around in vain for his lost luggage, Davey and Owen walked out of the locker room. Shortly after making their exit, the Bulldog, in his thick Mancunian-ish accent, wailed at the top of his lungs, "OH MY GOD, LOOK AT THIS!"

D'Lo, who still hadn't located his property's whereabouts, ran out of the locker room and craned his head up to see his bag swinging an estimated forty feet in the air and padlocked to the chain that operated one of the arena's giant metal shutters. To add insult to injury, Owen and Davey had also padlocked the chain together so the only way to retrieve the bag was to find some bolt cutters and a thirty-five foot ladder. It is unknown if he ever got his bag back but what is known is D'Lo Brown got one heck of a welcome to the WWF.

D'Lo's gym bag wouldn't be the first to be hoisted high into the air; another wrestler's bag to receive the Jolly Roger treatment was the four-foot Mini Me to Doink the Clown,[1] Claude 'Dink' Giroux. Dink's short stature made him an obvious target for locker room bullies. Scott 'Bam Bam' Bigelow, who really hated both Doink and Dink (possibly because he was stuck in a programme with them), would leave Dink's bag in high up and hard-to-reach places and once also glued the zips of his bag shut. Kliq members Sean Waltman and Scott Hall also got in on the action by putting Dink's bag up on high shelves and laughed as the poor little guy struggled to get it back down again.

Dink eventually went to WWF management to complain about the hazing, claiming he'd quit if the boys didn't cut it out. He also remarked to Jacques Rougeau that there was, "Too much bullshit, [I] never bullshit the boys." Dink then waddled his way into the dressing room to announce that he'd spoken with booker Pat Patterson and the bullying was to stop. "That just set Owen off!" laughed Hall. At the next town, Dink's bag went missing again. Owen had somehow chained it to the beams at the very top of the arena. Shortly after Owen had won the gear bag elevation challenge, Dink found himself in the crosshairs of Davey Boy Smith during a tour of the Far East. At the Indoor Stadium in Kallang, Singapore in May 1995, Savio Vega witnessed Davey Boy forcibly tie Dink to a chair, cover his entire head and face in shaving cream[2] and leave him out in the hall of the arena. Dink sat squirming for several minutes before someone felt sorry enough to come to his rescue.

Complaining to the office made Dink public enemy number one in the locker room and there was nothing Patterson could do about it. There was also nothing Patterson could do to stop fans chanting 'kill the clown' whenever Doink and Dink appeared in arenas towards the end of their run. The Doink character was already being phased out by 1995 and Dink was axed from the company right after the Singapore shaving cream incident. For everyone's sake, the Doink character was also mercifully killed off in January 1996 after being on life support since '93.

[1]As inane as the gimmick looked on paper, the original, evil incarnation of Doink the Clown was superbly portrayed by Matt Borne. The character came about in 1992 after Road Warrior Hawk pointed at the slovenly Borne slouched on a bench and dubbed him 'Krusty the Clown' in front of Vince McMahon. McMahon loved the moniker so much he turned Borne into a literal wrestling clown, despite never having seen *The Simpsons,* nor understanding the Krusty reference. The character's intrigue immediately died a death when Doink turned babyface and Borne was fired for repeated narcotic-based infractions in September 1993. With a revolving cast of wrestlers donning the face paint and green wig, Doink would soon be gifted (by Father Christmas no less) a four foot clone called Dink to the delight of no one, save for the very youngest and very dimmest WWF fans.

[2]According to 'Dirty White Boy' Tony Anthony, a typical Owen rib would involve filling someone's shaving kit full of foam. Owen would then rib himself by filling his own shaving kit with foam in an effort to make himself look innocent. In a similar vein, Matt Borne used to pull the old standby rib of tying knots into people's shirt sleeves and trouser legs really tightly. Borne would then proceed to tie looser knots in his own clothes so he looked like a prank victim but could still wear his clothes without cutting off the knots. 'Nasty Boy' Brian Knobbs was known for shaving off sleeping wrestlers' eyebrows on long plane rides before shaving his own off to deflect unwanted accusations; dedication of the highest magnitude.

Bad Matches:
Owen & Bulldog vs.
The Godwinns

As told by Dennis Knight

Because apparently one pig-farmin' bumpkin from Bitters, Arkansas was deemed insufficient for the World Wrestling Federation audience, Dennis Knight was brought in to portray Mark 'Henry O Godwinn' Canterbury's on-screen cousin Phineas I Godwinn in January 1996. H.O.G. and P.I.G. (WWF creativity at peak performance) were accompanied to the ring by James 'Hillbilly Jim' Morris (so make that three country bumpkins) along with real-life pigs, goats, buckets of slop and rollicking bluegrass banjo-pickin' entrance music.[1]

When Owen Hart and the British Bulldog became WWF Tag Team Champions in September 1996, The Godwinns would become their main adversaries on the untelevised house show circuit. With the Federation's two most notorious pranksters staring at them from across the ring, The Godwinns knew they'd end up getting pranked sooner rather than later. Five days after Owen and Bulldog won the belts, they faced off against the storyline cousins from Bitters, Arkansas at the Joe Louis Arena in Detroit, Michigan. IBA Superheavyweight Champion boxer Eric 'Butterbean' Esch was booked to accompany The Godwinns to the ring that night and keep an eye out for shenanigans from the Champions.

The point of hiring a celebrity enforcer is to build up suspense for the match's crescendo where said celebrity interferes in the bout and gets a rise from the crowd. Before the match, Owen and Davey decided that they didn't want to work physically with Butterbean in any capacity. "When they didn't want to work they became a total nightmare," said Phineas. As the match progressed, The Godwinns had Owen rocking and reeling and went to perform their favourite double-team manoeuvre in a bid to win the match. Henry would often slam his opponent to the ground, then pick up and bodyslam the 300lb Phineas on top of his prostrate opponent. This time in Detroit, Henry bodyslammed Owen to the ground, but when Henry turned around to scoop up Phineas, Owen got right up off the mat. When Henry turned around carrying the enormous Phineas upside down in his arms, he was confronted with the sight of Owen Hart stood upright and grinning at him. After a couple of seconds of contemplating his options, Henry had no choice but to slam his own cousin to the mat and look like a complete doofus in the process.

The similarly 300lb, 6'4" Henry O was absolutely furious with Owen and took out his frustrations after the match. "[Henry] tore up a bathroom in anger," recalled Phineas. Because Owen and Davey were so much higher up the WWF food chain than The Godwinns, Henry couldn't do anything that wouldn't result in punitive measures being taken against him. At least Henry's on-screen cousin Phineas took the jape better than he did. "I never took most of their stuff seriously. I miss both of them very much."

¹The banjo-pickin' entrance music is entitled *Don't Go Messin' With a Country Boy*. The song was originally commissioned by the WWF for Hillbilly Jim in 1985. Primarily written by Doc Pomus and Marshal Chapman, the song was performed by Eric Weissberg, who played the solo on *Duelling Banjos* from *Deliverance*. *Don't Go Messin' With a Country Boy* is incredibly catchy, which makes it a damn shame WWE won't pay for the rights to use it anymore. In the hundreds of instances the song is appears on archived shows on the WWE Network, WWE has opted to dub the song over with an awful library music approximation.

Owen Hart Meets Master Impressionist Jason Sensation

As told by Jason Sensation

Gifted impressionist Jason 'Sensation' Tavares was a Canadian WWF superfan desperate to ingratiate himself to the company any way he could. With no physical gifts to speak of, Jason was never going to be an in-ring competitor but was encouraged to take up a broadcasting course and attempt to get hired by the Federation as an announcer. While exploring that avenue, Jason went to every WWF show he could, even appearing on *RAW is WAR* in 1997 singing *O Canada* in an airport after Bret Hart regained the WWF Championship at that year's *SummerSlam* pay-per-view.

During a house show in Ottawa in 1997, Jason would come face-to-face with some of his heroes for the first time. Jason's girlfriend had bought him a VIP ticket as a gift, which granted him access to the wrestler meet-and-greet signing before the event. The wrestlers booked to be met-and-gret that day happened to be 'British Bulldog' Davey Boy Smith and Owen Hart. Jason lost his mind with excitement and pushed past everyone in the queue to get to Owen and Davey's table. "Guys, I can do voices! Guys, I can do any voice you want!'" insisted Jason. Owen's wheels started turning and he asked him to do an impression of the Bulldog. After spoofing Davey eating a bowl of dog food,[1] Jason was challenged by Davey to impersonate Owen. After giving a pitch-perfect rendition of the Slammy Award winner, Owen buttered Jason up by saying he could get a contract with the WWF. "I'm gonna get you in the dressing room and who knows, if they like you, you might be on the road with us!'"

After Jason basked in his personal Shangri-La of the WWF backstage area, Owen put him to work. First up for imitation was Goldust and Triple H. At first, Jason was relatively well received. "Dustin [Runnels] was really nice about the Goldust impression and Triple H was like, 'Hey, that's good, that's good.' He seemed to like it." Owen dragged Jason round the locker room introducing him to various wrestlers before telling Jason to 'do them' but the wrestlers' reactions were lukewarm at best. "I'm doing all these wrestlers' voices right to their faces now and the only one laughing really is Owen!"

Owen and Jason eventually made their way to Ahmed Johnson, the 6'2", 300lb black powerhouse who was almost unintelligible when he spoke. "I'd never even tried it before but Owen was like, 'Just give it to him.'" Jason plucked up the courage to give it a shot, launching into a cross between ebonics and a man with a sock in his mouth. "So I'm like, 'AHHM AHMED JOHNSON AND AHHM A GANG MEMBAH, BEHBEH! I'M GON' KILL DA NATION! I was basically mumbling my speech through it, man. [Ahmed] didn't look impressed at all but he just nodded to Owen like [he knew] it was Owen messing around again."

Finally, the big punch line Owen had been setting up all this time was about to be dropped on Jason, when Owen asked him if he could do an impression of curmudgeonly WWF agent George 'The Animal' Steele. The best-remembered incarnation of The Animal was as the simplistic, yet loveable brute that would act like a caveman, tear up turnbuckles and roar like a wild beast. "Can you do George?" asked Owen. "George loves impressions, he's a huge fan of imitations! Nobody can do George, you give him your best George, I'm not even gonna introduce you. Just run up to him and do your best George!" Looking back on it now, Jason knew he should have realised something was up. "I guess this was Owen's big plan from the get-go; to annoy the agent at the time, George 'The Animal' Steele." Without objecting, Jason ran up to the busy Steele and started imitating his trademark 'YEURRRGH' moan, complete with wild arm motions, then awaited The Animal's response.

"GET HIM THE EFF OUTTA HERE! SOMEONE MOVE, GET THIS GODDAMN KID THE EFF OUT!" screamed George, who was unamused to say the least. Jason tried to explain to the exasperated agent he'd been sent to do the impression by Owen but when Jason turned around to get his confirmation, Owen had already run away and was nowhere to be seen. "They just throw me out of the dressing room!" said Jason. I guess [Owen had] done his part and given me my dream."

Owen had actually done more than that, as he'd introduced Jason to WWF President of Canadian Operations, Carl De Marco. The next year, D-

Generation X was doing a spoof of The Nation of Domination faction, with the DX members impersonating the Nation members and they needed an Owen Hart. Jason got his fifteen seconds of fame[2] and ended up stealing the show as Owen and was invited back to appear on WWF programming several more times over the course of 1998. However, Owen wasn't done with putting Jason in hot water with the wrestlers. When Jason was booked to make a television appearance to perform as Owen, the real Owen would crank call wrestlers in the middle of the night without disguising his voice and cut promos on them. When Owen was confronted by the angry wrestlers the next day, he'd deflect the blame, claiming, "That damn Jason Sensation did it!"

[1]Davey had recently fought Ken Shamrock in a 'Dog Food match' at the *SummerSlam 1997* pay-per-view, with the loser having to eat a tin of dog food, naturally. Neither ended up chowing down on the chum, as Bulldog slapped dog food in Shamrock's face, prompting Shamrock to go crazy and smash the dog food tin across the back of Bulldog's head, leading to a disqualification loss for 'The World's Most Dangerous Man.'

[2]Jason Sensation wound up getting an additional couple of minutes of infamy in 2018 when he tweeted that he'd snuck a gun into Toronto's ScotiaBank Arena and was going to kill himself live on WWE television. Despite briefly living out his dream, Jason found that his appearances on for the WWF were ultimately destructive to his wellbeing. "I suffer from depression and some mental issues... I have some issues with wrestling and I have some issues with how my career went."

Pervert Filming
Chyna's Boobies

As told by Mick Foley

Joanie 'Chyna' Laurer made a big impression on World Wrestling Federation fans upon her debut in February 1997 as a plant in the audience. She attacked Goldust's valet Marlena after the twosome distracted the Hunter Hearst Helmsley, causing him to lose to Rocky Maivia. Chyna would soon align herself with Helmsley as his bodyguard/ringside enforcer, replacing transitory bodyguard Mr Hughes. Helmsley and Chyna started dating in real life shortly after her debut. They had a lot in common; they were both bodybuilders, both were teetotal[1] and both attended the same wrestling school run by Walter 'Killer' Kowalski.

The double act caught on in a big way, permanently dragging Helmsley out of the career pothole he'd found himself in for the majority of 1996.[2] There had been no woman like Chyna in the history of the WWF. Randy Savage's valet and real-life wife Miss Elizabeth brought beauty and elegance to the WWF in the mid '80s. Sunny brought sex appeal and a venomous persona to the role of the valet in the mid '90s. Chyna was the first woman to be booked as a brute and a physical threat to the WWF's male wrestlers, thanks to her bodybuilder physique and stern demeanour.[3] For most of 1997, Helmsley and Chyna were feuding with Goldust and Marlena, as well as Dude Love in featured spots on the card.

At the height of the 1997 pro-Canadian Hart Foundation storyline, the WWF made a multitude of trips north of the border, including rare shows booked for the far-reaching eastern provinces of Newfoundland and Nova Scotia. When the WWF crew touched down at St John's International Airport, Newfoundland on the 19th of July 1997, the wrestlers were greeted by hoards of WWF fans at baggage claim who weren't used to wrestlers travelling to their neck of the woods. While Mick Foley was walking around some of the fans, he noticed one particularly shifty-looking individual with a camcorder zooming in on Chyna's breasts, long before everyone and their

330

mother had seen them in Playboy.[4] Mick, who described the fan as looking like 'a sheep molester' was outraged and demanded that the slime ball rewind the tape and record over the Chyna-centric footage.

While the Hardcore Legend was giving the randy rascal an earful, Owen popped over to lend a hand. "Hey, you two, how about I get some footage of you two together?" Owen said in his usual overbearing way. Mick was boiling over with anger and told Owen to butt out but he could already see where the encounter was headed. "Oh, come on, [Cactus] Jack. Come on, he's a big fan. Let's get some footage. Maybe you can put your arm around him, Jack." Mick argued with Owen, trying not to lose his temper in public, before he finally gave in. The defeated Foley ended up allowing Owen to film Mick with his arm around the sheep fondler's shoulders like they were the best of friends. As a bonus, the filthy miscreant also got to keep his Chyna footage to watch in the privacy of his subterranean bunker. Although Mick was fuming at the time, he saw the funny side of the meeting by the time he wrote his first book. "He could drive you crazy and tick you off but I find myself laughing out loud when I think of Owen now."

[1]Without going into forensic detail, Joanie would drop her sobriety after leaving the WWF in 2001. Levesque began publicly dating Vince McMahon's daughter Stephanie in 2000, which had a devastating personal effect on Joanie. In a move her sister Kathy claimed was one of her great regrets, Joanie left the WWF in 2001 after turning down a $400,000 a year contract that would have likely seen her make $800,000+ after bonuses and merchandise revenue was accounted for. Joanie demanded a $1 million base salary, which WWF Head of Talent relations Jim Ross called, "An outrageous demand that wasn't even realistic."

[2]Known as the 'Curtain Call', real-life best friends and Kliq members Helmsley, Shawn Michaels, Kevin 'Diesel' Nash and Scott 'Razor Ramon' Hall controversially hugged in the middle of the ring at the conclusion of the house show's main event at Madison Square Garden on the 19th of May 1996. It was Diesel and Razor's last night in the WWF before jumping to WCW to perform under their birth names of

Kevin Nash and Scott Hall and the Kliq wanted one last hurrah. The controversy stemmed from the fact that Michaels and Razor were babyfaces and Diesel and Helmsley were heels, therefore breaking kayfabe. Because Michaels was the champion and Diesel and Razor were leaving, that left only Helmsley for McMahon to spank. The 1996 *King of the Ring* tournament, which Helmsley was slated to win, instead went to Steve Austin and the Connecticut blue blood was booked to lose nearly every match that year, mostly to newcomer Marc Mero. The Kliq's fifth member, Sean '1-2-3 Kid' Waltman, wasn't present at the show, having been taken off the road at the end of April to enter rehab. Waltman would soon be let out of his WWF contract to join Nash and Hall over in WCW that September.

[3]Chyna claimed on *The Howard Stern Show* she could bench press 365 pounds.

[4]After numerous plastic surgeries to enlarge her cup size, as well as reconstructive surgery to alter what has been unflatteringly described as her Antonio Inoki-like jaw line, Chyna posed nude for Playboy in their November 2000 issue, shifting over a million copies. In 2004, she and then-fiancée Sean Waltman released a sex tape. In later years, Chyna starred in several, mostly bizarrely-themed porn videos for Vivid Entertainment, before passing away in 2016 aged 46.

Bad Matches:
Owen Hart vs. Dude Love

As told by Mick Foley, Dave Meltzer and Steve Austin

With Steve Austin out indefinitely as a result of Owen's botched piledriver at *SummerSlam '97*, Austin's tag team partner Mick 'Dude Love' Foley[1] was booked as Austin's replacement on the house show circuit through the autumn. By the time of the character's debut, Mick purposely set Dude Love apart from the intense, masochistic Mankind persona, not just visually but in mentality. "Gone was the aggression and tenacity, to be replaced instead by some of the worst-looking offence this side of Baron Sikluna", Mick recalled. "Weak chops replaced stiff forearms and on the speaking side of things, Mankind's deranged philosophical shriekings yielded to worn-out seventies clichés."

In mid September, the Dude and Owen were booked on numerous untelevised house show matches where they endeavoured to put on the most ridiculous, phony-looking bouts possible. Back rakes, fake-looking headbutts, kicks up the 'arris and *Austin Powers*-style judo chops (with obligatory 'hi-yah' battle cry) were thrown around with gay abandon but the most farcical manoeuvre implemented during these purposeful abortions was the Dude's finisher. With his opponent down on the mat, the Dude would go to the corner and stomp one foot on the mat à la Shawn Michaels setting up for his Sweet Chin Music crescent kick. When the Dude's prone opponent made it back to their feet, Dude waddled up to meet them and toe-bunged his adversary in the lower leg, before hitting Cactus Jack's old double-arm DDT finisher for the win. Mick called the move 'Sweet *Shin* Music' and it never failed to get a rise from the crowd.

A couple of months following the piledriver incident, Steve Austin, who had been making regular appearances on WWF television, returned to the house show circuit in a non-wrestling capacity. "I was still coming back from a neck injury," said Steve, "so I would be ringside to make an appearance." Austin was in Dude Love's corner to counteract interference from Owen's corner man the British Bulldog in a series of Street Fight matches.[2]   With Austin back on the road, Owen and Mick challenged themselves to put on a match so woeful as to make the 'Texas Rattlesnake' break character and laugh.   They'd already developed some ridiculous routines from their previous stinkathons, including the 'microphone sell spot'.   Dude would address the fans over the house mic when Owen would Pearl Harbour him.   With the microphone still near his lips, Dude would launch into an appalling acting job of pretending to be in pain.   "Oh God! No, please! Oh, it hurts! Oh, the pain, the pain, please stop! Oh, God! You're killing me!" Mick would then get the upper hand and choke Owen with the microphone cord.   In a voice reminiscent of Butt-Head of *Beavis & Butt-Head* fame, Owen would gasp into the mic, "I, huh, huh, can't, huh, huh, breathe." On the 11th of October, Owen and Mick almost succeeded in breaking Austin in the Arrowhead Pond in Anaheim, California via the use of a devastating sack full of plastic soft drink container lids raining down on the prone opponent.

The next day, the WWF were in San Jose; the home of venerated wrestling journalist Dave Meltzer. Meltzer would be in the crowd reviewing the matches for his *Wrestling Observer* industry newsletter and Mick was concerned about receiving a negative write-up for the match. After he asked Owen to perform a normal, non-wretched performance, Mick felt like such a mark that he went back to Owen and asked him to disregard his previous statement.   Mick and Owen agreed to construct a match so preposterous they'd earn a negative star match in next week's *Observer* newsletter.

Come match time, Mick and Owen embarked on another Street Fight that resembled anything but, with the Dude attacking Owen with a piece of carpet, before reaching in the mini dumpster he'd wheeled to ringside to retrieve the crown jewel of nonsensical weapons.   Before the match, Mrs Foley's baby boy had gone to Owen to ask him for permission to use a weapon he thought may be pushing the boundaries of acceptability. "Would you mind if I hit you with a bag of popcorn?" asked Mick. "Sure, Jack," replied Owen, "just not too hard."

Dude Love hoisted the clear sack full of dried corn kernels aloft, reared back and hammered Owen on top of the head with an earth-shattering 'pffffthhff. After several more unanswered blows to the skull, Owen dropped to the ground like he'd been shot by a howitzer, then writhed around on the canvas as Dude Love emptied the salty snack sack all over his prone body. When the Dude turned his attention away from Owen to do his celebratory Charleston 'bees knees' dance for the crowd, Owen sprang back to life and dropped the 'Loved One' into the popcorn debris. As Owen laid in some light kicks, the downed-Dude flapped his arms and legs around in even, windscreen wiper-like motions. When Owen picked Dude Love up off the ground, everyone in the arena observed that the Dude had left a perfect popcorn angel on the canvas.

Had Owen and Mick done enough to get Steve Austin to break character? "I looked at Austin," Mick recalled. "He was trying to cover his face but I could see his stomach shaking and tears rolling down his face. 'You two are the shits,' was all he could manage to say." Steve Austin later recalled breaking character while observing the sorry display. "I've got my head on the apron with my… face down because I'm bald-headed and I can't use my hair to cover my face and I'm laughing my ass off!"

At the time, Dave Meltzer described the contest in his *Wrestling Observer* newsletter as 'pretty bad' but rated it a one star match. Not only did Mick and Owen fail to receive the negative star rating they so desired, Meltzer had rated the Dude Love-Owen Hart catastrophe more favourably than no less than *four* matches on that evening's card! Ever since Mick Foley's book 'Have a Nice Day' came out, Meltzer has revised his view of the titanic battle to reflect wider opinion. "It really wasn't what I would call a bad [match]," said Meltzer in 2019. "It was like watching two guys do a comedy match but they're talented guys. It really wasn't anything resembling a negative star, horrible match. It was just a comedy match that got over with the crowd."

In the end, Austin didn't even need to be in San Jose that day to counteract Davey Boy's presence, as the Bulldog had the weekend off due to a weightlifting injury.

¹In the spring of '97, weekly snippets of Jim Ross interviewing Mick Foley (as Mankind) aired on *RAW is WAR*. The interview blurred fiction and reality and weaved in personal camcorder footage of Mick as a young man, as well as footage from ECW and Japanese IWA Death

matches. Part two of the interview concerned Dude Love; the chick magnet wrestling persona Mick created for himself when he was still an awkward teenager in high school. The Dude Love concept proved so popular with fans watching, that Mick ended up becoming the character on television, helping Steve Austin defeat Owen Hart and the British Bulldog for the WWF Tag Team Titles six weeks later.

[2]Street Fights are no disqualification matches with weapons allowed. Other terms used for no DQ matches include: no holds barred, anything goes, lights out, hardcore, non-sanctioned, extreme rules, Raven's rules, etc and are all basically the same. Death matches differ from no DQ only in the amount of genuine risk that they carry. Commonplace weapons in Death Matches include: real glass, barb wire, drawing pins, staplers, explosives and fire and are still fairly common in smaller, outer-fringe wrestling organisations.

Prank Phone Calls: Mark Henry's Manager Terry Todd

As told by Mark Henry

Despite Mark Henry being one of Owen's favourite rib victims, the two got along famously and travelled together on a number of occasions between towns, along with Owen's tag partner Jeff Jarrett. By the late 1990s, the wrestling world had finally cottoned on to the idea of mobile phones, meaning Owen no longer had to wait to get to the hotel to annoy people from the lobby's pay phone. One evening while driving down the highway, Henry suggested Owen prank call his long time manager and mentor Terry Todd. Todd had taken Henry under his wing when he was a wayward 16-year-old and trained him in the sport of powerlifting.[1]

Todd recently purchased a ranch and had complained to Mark that he was having trouble with his fencing, with cows escaping onto neighbouring properties. The World's Strongest Man let Owen in on the details, before calling his mentor on the phone, then handing it over to Owen. Owen, pretending to be a disgruntled neighbour, let loose on the 60-year-old former powerlifter. "All these damn cows are over here and I'm fixing to come over there and kick your ass," threatened Owen. "I'm going to go out there and start shooting them!" Todd was very apologetic and fully intended to come and retrieve his cows but the discontented neighbour was having none of it. "No, it's too late. I'm going to come over there and kick your ass!"

Proving that the 60-year-old still had some fire in his belly, the normally peace-loving ex-strongman dropped the pleasantries and let loose a tirade of threats and profanity that had Mark Henry, who was covertly listening to Todd on the phone's speaker, stunned. "I've known Terry Todd since I was sixteen years old," Henry smiled, "and I had never heard him cuss before."

[1]Terry Todd also coached three-time World's Strongest Man and lumbering pro wrestler Bill Kazmaier. Todd was instrumental in bringing World's Strongest Man events into the mainstream and was also the creator and director of the Arnold Strongman Classic. He passed away on the 8th of July 2018 aged 80.

CHAPTER 10

Time 4 A Change

Owen made his on-screen return to the WWF at the *In Your House 19: D-Generation X* pay-per-view on the 7th of December. Shawn Michaels, Triple H and Chyna were triple-teaming Ken Shamrock after the main event when Owen, dressed in a black hoodie and jeans, pushed Michaels off the ring apron and through the Spanish announce table. Owen pounced on Michaels, landing some stiff-looking punches to his forehead and bloodying up his nose before Triple H ran him off. To create the illusion that he was ripping into Shawn's nose and eyes, Owen sliced open his own fingers just before he went out to the ring and pawed away at Michaels' face. The live audience reaction wasn't huge, possibly because the attack was so quick that many hadn't figured out the identity of the assailant.

The next night on *RAW is WAR*, Michaels described The Hart Foundation as a 'big, huge, smelly, stinky turd' that needed to be flushed and Owen was the 'small, chunky, little nugget' that refused to disappear down the U-bend. The insult was inspired by a particularly troubling bowel movement Vince McMahon recently had and McMahon suggested it for Shawn's promo. Later in the show, Owen once again leapt out of the crowd to attack Michaels, who by this time was in the ring in just his boxer shorts after engaging in an impromptu game of strip poker with his DX cohorts... obviously.

On the 15th of December edition of *RAW is WAR*,[1] Vince McMahon, who in the wake of Montreal had transitioned from a goofy commentator into an evil on-screen version of himself, ordered Owen to, 'appear in this ring right now'. A bedraggled-looking Owen arrived at ringside through the crowd sporting a scruffy beard and shades, accompanied by chants of 'OWEN, OWEN'. Boss and independent contractor met in the middle of the ring, where McMahon talked down to Owen like a little child. In reply to McMahon's chastising, Owen said, "You think I owe you a god damn apology? I don't owe you a god damn thing. I'm sick and tired of trying to please everybody else around here. The bullshit stops right here. My brother Bret and Neidhart and Bulldog, they did what they had to do and now it's time for me to do what I have to do and that is to remain right here in the World Wrestling Federation."

While jabbing his finger into Vince's chest, Owen finished his diatribe with an obvious inference to McMahon and Montreal. "Nobody, and I mean *nobody*, is gonna run me out of this company and you know exactly who I'm talking about." Owen declared he would make Shawn Michaels' life 'a living hell' before rather unfortunately stating that he was indeed the 'little nugget' that would float back up to haunt Michaels. After McMahon made a match between Owen and Michaels for an unspecified date, Owen grabbed McMahon by the lapels before being ushered out the ring by uniformed police. The segment, which if executed perfectly could have set Owen up as a main event player, didn't work for several reasons. The 5'9"-ish Owen appeared tiny compared to the 6'1", middle-aged, bodybuilding WWF Chairman. Unlike his recent interactions with Steve Austin, McMahon talked down to Owen in a condescending manner throughout the interview and even refused to act scared when Owen put his hands on him. The 'nugget' comments were just the brown icing on the cake that seemed to permanently reduce Owen's stock before he'd even returned to the ring.

Later in the broadcast, Michaels and Triple H played rock-paper-scissors to see who would get to beat up Owen. Triple H won and the Owen vs. Michaels feud shifted over to Helmsley before Owen had even wrestled

Michaels. This was reportedly another power play by Michaels behind the scenes who, for whatever reason, didn't want to work with Owen, further trivialising Owen's push and the very real Montreal Screwjob.

The next week, Shawn Michaels dropped the 'coveted' European Championship to his best friend Triple H in yet another 'fake' wrestling match that further tarnished the image of the European Title less than a year after its creation. The Black Hart, as Owen had started to refer to himself, finally got his hands on Michaels in their last-ever televised match on the 29th of December live *RAW is WAR*. Why wasn't this big-time match that had been building for weeks held on pay-per-view you ask? And why wasn't Owen facing Helmsley as the rock-paper-scissors game had stipulated? Because Owen was actually scheduled to take on and defeat Triple H for the European Title that night but Helmsley had legitimately dislocated his kneecap and partially torn his meniscus the evening before in Hamilton, Ontario. Michaels ended up taking Helmsley's place at the last minute. Owen got the visual win on Michaels when he locked him into the Sharpshooter, only for Triple H to bash Owen over the head with his wooden crutch for the disqualification... eventually. The first time Triple H swung, the crutch got caught up in the ropes and missed Owen's head by several feet.

The next couple of weeks saw Triple H undermine Owen when he failed to act scared by his threats, then Owen jumped the crippled Triple H while he was alone in a limo, which of course DX got the better of. At the *Royal Rumble* pay-per-view, Owen was attacked in the aisle way by none other than... Jim Cornette and NWA North American Champion Jeff Jarrett,[2] who had no on-screen relationship with Owen whatsoever. Owen returned to eliminate Jeff from the Rumble match twenty minutes later, before Helmsley and Chyna attacked Owen with crutches and eliminated him. After Triple H and Chyna made good their escape, Owen ran after them down the aisle and up a small ramp. Owen then took a misstep and fell over, disappearing through the curtain not unlike Dr Drake Ramoray falling down an elevator shaft. This unfortunate tumble would have mostly gone unnoticed by the viewing audience had commentator Jerry Lawler not pointed out Owen's impromptu nose-dive while cackling uncontrollably.

The big news coming from the *Rumble* pay-per-view was the severe back injury Shawn Michaels sustained while defending the WWF Championship against The Undertaker in a 'Casket match'. Unfortunately for Owen, the schedules of the upcoming Vancouver and Toronto house shows had to be changed from Owen vs. Michaels in the main event to Owen vs. Goldust lower on the card. Despite a severely damaged vertebral disc in his back, Michaels returned to begrudgingly drop the WWF Championship to Steve Austin at *WrestleMania XIV* on the 29th of March before retiring from the ring. Michaels would make sporadic appearances in non-wrestling roles over the next four years before returning to the newly renamed WWE in the summer of 2002 as an in-ring participant.

On the 26th of January edition of *RAW*, Owen defeated 'Triple H' for the European Title. It wasn't actually Triple H but The Artist Formerly Known as Goldust dressed as Triple H, complete with big fake nose and his new valet, Gertrude 'Luna' Vachon, playing the role of Chyna. After Owen submitted 'Hunter-Dust', Commissioner Slaughter ruled that Goldust was a legal substitute and awarded Owen the European Championship, further devaluing the Title and allowing Triple H to drop the belt without getting pinned. Owen started aligning himself with his former enemy Steve Austin (which made absolutely no sense storyline-wise), as well as Mick 'Cactus Jack' Foley and Terry Funk to take on D-Generation X and their new associates the New Age Outlaws. Owen also defeated Jeff Jarrett on the 16th of February *RAW is WAR*, wrapping up their feud which consisted almost entirely of that one match.

Since late January, there had been talk regarding Owen Hart winning the WWF Intercontinental Title from The Rock while still holding the European Title. Thankfully cooler heads prevailed, as The Rock was fast becoming one of the most entertaining performers in the industry and would be fast-tracked to the WWF Heavyweight Title before the year's end. Owen would have his weekly European Title defences suffer interference from Chyna, while still retaining the belt. The European Title defence on the 9th of March *RAW* against Barry Windham became notable when Owen injured himself in a freak accident. "I stepped onto [Windham's] boot and rolled my ankle and ripped [and] tore the ligament on the right side," recalled Owen several days after the injury. The next week on *RAW*, Triple H, who had just recovered from a leg injury of his own, baited Owen Hart into a European Title defence right then and there, despite Owen's right leg being in an air cast. Chyna sneak-attacked Owen's hurt ankle with a baseball bat, allowing Triple H to earn a referee stoppage win in 0:52 to regain the European Title. The timing of the cheap title switch was pretty curious considering the two were scheduled to meet for the European Title at *WrestleMania XIV* twelve days later. The entire segment made Owen, the babyface, look like a complete moron for accepting Helmsley's challenge. In a wrestling tale as old as time, audiences will always reject a stupid babyface, which was how Owen was now being booked.

Owen's first match back was at *WrestleMania XIV* after taking nearly four weeks off rehabbing his ankle. Owen had only taken his cast off earlier that day and was clearly not 100%, with Triple H not fairing that much better with his dodgy knee. Despite their physical limitations, the rivals put on a pretty decent in-ring showing. Chyna was handcuffed to Commissioner Slaughter out on the floor to prevent her interfering. Chyna then interfered by throwing powder into Slaughter's eyes and hit a low blow on Owen to give Helmsley the victory. Owen was once again outsmarted by the bad guys. The next evening's *RAW* was possibly the most momentous post-*WrestleMania* episode in the show's history. New WWF Champion Steve Austin Stunned Vince McMahon once again to ignite their legendary feud. Triple H officially fired Shawn Michaels from DX and brought in the New Age Outlaws and the returning Sean 'X-Pac' Waltman as official members. X-Pac cut a revolutionary promo[3] burying WCW's Hulk Hogan and Eric Bischoff, as well as claim Kevin Nash and Scott Hall were being 'held hostage' by their WCW contracts. Also, the first of the hilariously filthy vignettes touting the debut of wrestling porn actor Val Venis was broadcast. Owen was not on the show.

The next month saw Owen align himself with the returning Legion of Doom, now known as LOD 2000, with their new manager Sunny[4] to combat D-Generation X. On the house show circuit, Owen continued to face off against various members of the Nation of Domination as he had been doing for most of the year, many times with tag team partner Ken Shamrock. At the *Unforgiven: In Your House* pay-per-view on the 26th of April, Chyna would be locked in a cage and raised high above the ring so she couldn't interfere in the Owen vs. Triple H rematch. Of course, Chyna escaped and distracted several referees long enough for X-Pac to bonk Owen over the head with a fire extinguisher, once again handing Triple H the cheap win. Owen would then be dropped further down the pecking order to squabble with his old pranking partner X-Pac in another example of being shunted down the card to feud with a lesser member of D-Generation X.

On the *RAW* after *Unforgiven*, Owen teamed with Ken Shamrock to take on Nation of Domination members Mark Henry and The Rock. In an effort to shake up Owen's character and write the injured Shamrock off TV, Owen turned heel by kicking Shamrock in The World's Most Dangerous testicles and Pilmanizing Ken's ankle[6] before officially joining the Nation of Domination as its co-leader. Yes, the very Caucasian Owen Hart joined a black power, Nation of Islam-inspired wrestling group as their co-leader. Other than the obvious racial barrier, Owen joining The Nation made some sense, as NoD were feuding with DX and The Rock was entering into a programme with Triple H. Owen's babyface run had also been a flop, partially owing to lacklustre creative and backstage politicking and also because Owen was just so much better as a bad guy. Commentators hinted that Owen was looking for a surrogate family after the rest of The Hart Foundation had 'abandoned' him after Montreal. Also, thanks to their recent sophomoric high jinks and on-location skits,[5] D-Generation X were fast becoming one of the most beloved acts in the company and there was no way Owen was going to be cheered feuding with them for much longer. When a fan asked if he preferred being a babyface or a heel, Owen replied, "A heel for sure. [There's] a lot of anxiety off you, stress-release of telling people to shut up. You can tell it like it is, where as a good guy, you have to smile. If a fan mouths off to you, you have to pretend like you didn't hear it."

DX and the now-abbreviated Nation battled it out week after week, with Owen breaking out his latest heel tactic; biting people's ears. If cutting one's forehead wasn't barbarous enough, Owen's victims would blade themselves behind the ear to draw real blood for added gruesomeness. Despite being billed as The Nation's co-leader, Owen, along with everyone else in the heel junta, was being overshadowed by The Rock's tremendous charisma. While continuing his issues with DX, Owen faced off against

NWA Champion Dan 'The Beast' Severn[7] on the 25th of May episode of *RAW*, which ended in a DQ after The Nation interfered. The next week, Owen and Triple H were the last two participants in a six-man elimination match when the returning Ken Shamrock destroyed Owen, leading to a pier six brawl between The Nation, Shamrock and Shamrock's real-life UFC rival Severn.

Over the next few weeks, a curious sort of 'shoot fighter' sub-division emerged in the WWF, featuring: Owen, former UFC Champions Shamrock and Severn and martial artist Steve Blackman. The end game was for Severn and Shamrock to eventually face off on pay-per-view in a marquee matchup, since they'd fought twice in the UFC, winning one apiece. In a match almost no one remembers, the future UFC Hall of Famers would in fact wrestle one singles match on *RAW* in August, which ended after two minutes when Owen interfered and attacked Shamrock. The next few weeks saw Severn and Shamrock attack Owen, Owen attack Severn and Shamrock, then Severn attack Shamrock to team with Owen while Steve Blackman teamed up with Shamrock. Shamrock and Blackman eventually started feuding, too.

On the 6th of July *RAW is WAR*, one of the most memorable skits in wrestling history took place when D-Generation X came out to parody The Nation. Triple H, Road Dogg, Billy Gunn and X-Pac imitated The Rock, D'Lo Brown, The Godfather and Mark Henry respectively. The audience went crazy at Triple H's suggestion that everyone could smell what The Rock was cooking when he dropped the kids off at the pool, accompanied by Road Dogg's head bobbing with 'B-Lo' written across his chest protector. The microphone was then handed over to an unidentified skinny little white boy sporting yellow 'caution' tape, a blonde wig and a big, fake, warty nose. It was Owen's old Toronto-based impressionist buddy Jason Sensation, who the WWF had kept on file for such an occasion. The rest of DX stood well back and watched in awe as Jason put on the performance of a life time. Jason buried Owen's new attire; "I look like a damn road sign," and Owen's prominent proboscis; "If anybody smells what The Rock is cookin' it's me, look how big my damn nose is!" Owen's kayfabe disdain for being called a 'nugget' was also raised. Shawn Michaels' original nugget comments, which had been mostly forgotten by the viewing audience, immediately became the fans' new favourite insult thanks to Jason's performance.[8]

The next week on *RAW is WAR*, Jason was invited back as himself to be interviewed and provide impressions of various WWF Superstars. Owen Hart, standing in the back with the rest of The Nation, threatened to 'slap the piss' out of Jason if he imitated him once more. At the behest of Jerry Lawler, Jason duplicated the promo Owen had just cut on him, leading to The Black Hart coming out and slapping the piss out of Jason as promised, before putting him in the Sharpshooter. The segment garnered tremendous heel heat for Owen and immediately afterwards saw Owen's stock rise as far as fan reaction was concerned. Owen was all over WWF programming through June and July, not only battling DX but interfering in Ken Shamrock's matches, too. The Hart vs. Shamrock feud escalated to a special one-on-one, pay-per-view encounter on the 26th of July at the *Fully Loaded* pay-per-view, which was actually taped several days beforehand. Owen and Shamrock faced off in a submission-only match in the basement of Hart House, otherwise known as The Dungeon.

For the vast majority of fans, this would be the first glimpse of the fabled Dungeon that had been referenced on Federation programming since in the 1980s in a trend started by commentator Jesse 'The Body' Ventura. In what must have been a disappointment to many, The Dungeon was revealed to be a dingy, wood-panelled basement with a rotten green mat on the floor, dirty piping overhead and a window into blackness. "It was fun to watch that take place and be able to get the legendary Stu Hart dungeon on pay-per-view," said Bruce Prichard. It's a good thing smell-o-vision was never invented, as according to Keith Hart, the mat was, "Pretty stiff and starchy from cat piss and dog piss and all the animals Stu had around." Owen and Shamrock put on a good, hard-hitting affair, which was particularly difficult when they didn't have a live crowd to feed off of. Both men used the unique surroundings, including ramming each others' heads into the walls and ceiling and Owen powerbombing Ken onto the hard, widdle-soaked floor. The finish came after Shamrock inadvertently kicked guest referee Dan Severn in the head and Owen dropped Shamrock with a gimmicked dumbbell. With Shamrock 'knocked out', Owen manipulated Kenny's arm into tapping out, with a groggy Severn declaring the youngest Hart the winner. "In over fifty years we didn't do damage to the walls or ceilings," recalled Owen in a Prodigy Chat. "In that one match I put Shamrock's head through the ceiling and cracked the walls. It was a rough, hard fought match and Shamrock's gotta pay for that dumbbell he dented with his head!"

The next night on *RAW is WAR*, Owen, who was almost drowned out by 'nugget' chants, declared himself the most dangerous man in the World Wrestling Federation and most assuredly *not* a nugget. Owen issued an open challenge to anyone in the back, which was quickly answered by Jason Sensation dressed up as Owen, who led the audience to chant 'nugget, nugget, nugget'. Emerging between Owen and Jason in his trademark double-breasted suit jacket and '90s tie came Dan Severn, who accepted Owen's challenge. The two squared off until Shamrock ran in to attack Owen, at which time Severn, for some reason, started choking out Shamrock and aligned himself with Owen. This was one of WWF Head Writer Vince Russo's trademarks; have nothing make sense and have everyone double-cross everyone else every week until brains liquify and logic is rendered meaningless. Russo would perfect this anencephalic style of storyline construction in 1999 when he jumped to WCW.

Owen and The Rock continued their TV tag team partnership throughout the summer while Shamrock mostly destroyed Owen in singles competition on house shows. Owen, Shamrock and Severn had a three-way match on the 17th of August *RAW* which amounted to little more than a two-on-one beating on The World's Most Dangerous Man. When 'Lethal Weapon' Steve Blackman came to Shamrock's aid, Blackman received a Dragon Sleeper from Severn for his efforts. Shamrock, whose character was becoming ever more volatile by the week, started tearing up the backstage area in a wild fury. In an unintentional bit of comedy, the stone-faced Blackman just sort of shrugged his shoulders and joined in on the destruction by upturning a stretcher and throwing barrels around. It was then announced by Michael Cole that Severn would be Owen Hart's trainer for the upcoming 'Lion's Den match' with Shamrock at *SummerSlam '98*, which sent The World's Most Dangerous Man further into beast mode. Even in storyline, Severn training Owen shouldn't have been a big deal as the pay-per-view was only thirteen days away. How much Shamrock-trouncing wisdom could Owen absorb in less than two weeks?

The Lion's Den cage was a take-off of the UFC's patented octagon cage design, with an inverted cone-shaped layout with chain link walls and a small, unforgiving mat. Because there was so little floor-surface area, referee Jack Doan was forced to watch on from scaffolding above the cage. The cage itself was too big to fit into the main arena of Madison Square Garden, so the Den was instead erected in the amphitheatre within the MSG complex. An extra 2,500 fans (with a 4,500 capacity) cheered on Ken Shamrock to destroy Owen once and for all. Owen had spent the majority of the year overcoming injuries and strange match stipulations to put on very good performances and this was no exception. Owen and Shamrock pounded away on each other and used the taut cage walls to great effect. The finish came when Shamrock reversed Owen's new Dragon Sleeper finisher and locked in his ankle lock submission. After what was no doubt an intense thirteen day training regime with Severn, Owen had no answer for the ankle lock and tapped out. Severn apparently had no answer for it either, as he immediately sauntered off as soon as Shamrock had the hold applied.

Owen took a well-deserved couple of weeks off the road to nurse a groin pull before returning to unsuccessfully challenge Triple H for his newly won Intercontinental Championship on the live *RAW is WAR* on the 14th of September.[9] Owen lost (again) after being distracted by Chyna (again). Helmsley celebrated pinning his old foe yet again by motioning for women in the audience to flash their breasts. Owen continued to lose to Shamrock with Oklahoma wrestling legend Danny Hodge in his corner on the house show circuit.

Owen finally faced off against his wayward Lion's Den coach Dan Severn in a Submission match on the 28th of September live *RAW is WAR*. The story of the match would revolve around Owen 'accidentally' injuring Severn with the same reverse sit-out piledriver that he had legitimately injured Steve Austin with one year ago. The match started off with heavy slams and suplexes by Severn, including a running powerslam, which was famously the British Bulldog's finisher. Since it wasn't the Bulldog slamming him, Owen completely no-sold the move and dropped The Beast with a spinning wheel kick instead.

After a couple of minutes, Owen reversed Severn's Dragon Sleeper into the reverse piledriver position as pre-arranged. After a couple of seconds getting Dan into position, Owen dropped to his posterior, seemingly dropping The Beast right on his head. In a scene reminiscent of the Steve

Austin episode from last year's *SummerSlam*, Owen immediately backed off while referee Tim White talked openly with Severn, who could be clearly heard saying that he couldn't move his arms. After returning from an abrupt commercial break, Severn was still in the ring being assisted by EMTs while Owen shook his head mournfully, then followed Severn as he was being stretchered into an ambulance. The angle was given a significant amount of airtime to breathe but not many people were convinced. The piledriver angle seemed to ape a real-life injury scare Tomas 'Villano IV' Mendoza experienced after a mistimed powerbomb on *WCW Nitro* the week before. To his great credit, Scott 'Raven' Levy the powerbomb had gone wrong, promptly broke character and stabilised the head and neck of his opponent. Villano IV made a full recovery and, as of 2019, still wrestlers in Mexico.

While not as effective as WWF officials had hoped, the piledriver injury angle and subsequent stretcher job went off without a hitch, except for one thing. "He literally did drop me on my head," Severn said. "Owen always put a little bit of baby oil on his chest... it might be a combination of that. Maybe he didn't realise how heavy I am. All I know is I shifted a little too far south so when he went down I hit the top of my head and I did have a stinger that ran right down my leg; the whole nine yards. As I laid there I realised very subtly that I could move my feet and I think I'm okay." When Severn was telling the referee he couldn't move, that was for real. When Owen realised that The Beast may not have been acting, he subtly checked on his wellbeing. "[The incident] freaked Owen out to where he knelt down and grabbed my hand for a second and said in a low voice, 'Squeeze my hand if you're okay.' I did not squeeze his hand."

Owen, who was still regarded as one of the absolute best, safest workers in the business, had nearly caused a second catastrophic injury to a fellow wrestler with the exact same manoeuvre that damn-near paralysed Steve Austin just one year earlier. Thankfully, by the time Severn had reached the ambulance he'd regained feeling in his extremities. When the cameras shut off, Severn got up off the stretcher and angrily confronted an apologetic Owen. The Beast let The Black Hart know in no uncertain terms how upset he was that Owen put his health in jeopardy, while reminding him of the fury he could easily bring down on Owen should he wish to get more real the next time they met in the ring. "The number one rule in professional

349

wrestling is you take care of me and I take care of you."[10] Reacting to the angle in Rolling Stone Magazine, Steve Austin said, "On one hand, you would think maybe they would think a little bit more about how you feel about it before they do it. But on the other hand, it's a business where they try to take advantage of a lot of things you wouldn't expect them to take advantage of and this just happens to be one of those instances." Vince McMahon also defended the angle saying, "If something like that is an opportunity for us to capitalize on it, we will unabashedly capitalize on it. I don't believe any subject matter is sacred. It is the American way."

On the WWF's new B-show *Sunday Night HeAT*, a disconsolate Owen, with thoughts of Severn on his mind, was defeated by X-Pac. The next week on *RAW*, Owen strolled out in his street clothes to a shower of boos, grabbed a microphone and spoke to the crowd. "I've been in the wrestling business for thirteen years now and the wrestling business has been my whole life; but last week after I did what I did to Dan Severn and I looked into his eyes I saw my wife and my two children." The promo itself was, for whatever reason, heavily edited before broadcast. Owen actually walked out and spoke to the audience twice that evening. He was reported as saying he'd never return to wrestling and then later specifically said he'd never return to the WWF. Owen continued, "I never really meant for anyone to really get hurt and I am so sorry for what I did." With his lower lip quivering, Owen dropped the microphone and walked out of the arena. When Michael Cole attempted to get an interview with the departing Hart, all Owen would say was, "It's over, I'm done." It appeared that after thirteen years, Owen had finally had enough of the wrestling business.

On a lighter note, Owen and his no good, lousy brother Bret reunited on-screen around this time to film an episode of the third-rate sitcom version of *Honey I Shrunk the Kids*.[11]

[1]This episode of *RAW* would become infamous for one of the strangest segments in the show's long, storied history. In a pre-recorded monologue, McMahon talked to the audience directly, announcing that the World Wrestling Federation was officially gearing towards more adult-oriented programming. McMahon described pro wrestling as

having more in common with *The Jerry Springer Show, Days of Our Lives* and *King of the Hill* than with real sports and mapped out the future creative direction of the WWF. "We in the WWF think that you, the audience, are quite frankly tired of having your intelligence insulted. We also think that you're tired of the same old simplistic theory of 'good guys vs. bad guys.' Surely the era of the superhero urging you to, 'Say your prayers and take your vitamins,' is definitely passé. Therefore, we've embarked upon a far more innovative and contemporary creative campaign that is far more invigorating and extemporaneous than ever before." In practical terms this meant that, under Vince Russo's vision, WWF programming would feature less actual wrestling in favour of sex, profanity and outrageous stunts, which young audiences demanded at the time. During this period, Russo actually wrote some of the most intelligence-insulting storylines in the history of the company, but with the WWF riding a wave of momentum thanks to: Steve Austin, DX, Mick Foley, The Undertaker, Kane, The Rock and the new evil Mr McMahon character, the World Wrestling Federation went from losing $6,505,000 in the 1996-97 fiscal year to making $56,030,000 profit in the 1998-99 fiscal year.

[2]In late '97, Jim Cornette buried WCW's woeful Hulk Hogan vs. Roddy Piper 'Age in the Cage' main event from *WCW Halloween Havoc* on WWF's incipient internet show *Byte This.* Cornette's comments drew a huge online response and Vince McMahon asked Jim to cut 'shoot' promos on *RAW is WAR* on whatever was making him mad in the world of wrestling that week. After several of these promos aired, Cornette, at the behest of head writer Vince Russo, parlayed the weekly promos into a storyline where Corny claimed he was going to bring back 'real' wrestling in the form of the National Wrestling Alliance. The NWA, once a powerful network of wrestling territories, had been pretty much dead for a decade at that point. In order to allow anything NWA-related onto WWF programming, NWA President Howard Brody was forced to sign an open-ended contract that would give the WWF the rights to use NWA's intellectual property. "Basically, that means that for the last twenty years and conceivably for evermore, the WWE has

had... the rights to advertise and use the NWA name and belt and history and whatever the fuck else they want to use of the NWA anytime they wanted to do it," Jim Cornette presupposed. *Smashing Pumpkins* front man Billy Corgan bought the rights and trademarks to the NWA in 2017, possibly without knowing of the WWE's potential ownership claim. Howard Brody said shortly after Corgan's purchase of the NWA, "If [the WWE] can't find their copy [of the NWA contract], I know I've still got a copy 'cause I don't throw shit out!"

[3]Okay, so X-Pac's promo wasn't *that* revolutionary. When Jeff Jarrett returned to the WWF (the second time) in October 1997, he criticised Eric Bischoff as well as Vince McMahon on *RAW is WAR*. Unfortunately, Jarrett's dreary eight minute 'worked-shoot' promo was so whiney and desperate the whole segment came off as embarrassing.

[4]LOD 2000 was the WWF's latest failed attempt at reinvigorating the once beloved Legion of Doom. In June 1992, LOD were handed (i.e. had foisted upon them) a ventriloquist dummy mascot called 'Freckles' to accompany them to the ring to 'inspire' them. The dummy only inspired every single man, woman and child to roll their eyes or turn the channel, except for Vince McMahon, who loved it. The dummy, quickly renamed 'Rocco', drove Mike 'Hawk' Hegstrand particularly crazy, causing him to go AWOL before quitting the Federation after August's *SummerSlam* pay-per-view in London, England. Joe 'Animal' Laurinaitis later confessed, "That doll never made it back from London, I'll tell you that much!" Animal left the WWF two months after Hawk and then sat at home claiming on his Lloyd's of London insurance policy for four years. LOD returned to the WWF in February 1997 but were no longer booked as the dominant duo. Hawk in particular struggled to work as a babyface in peril and the team were broken up in February 1998, only to be repackaged one month later. At *WrestleMania XIV* they were rechristened LOD 2000 with new ring gear, music and new manager Sunny. The new look failed to galvanise the team and Sunny was removed on the 5th of June after coming to the ring in MSG 'Soma'd up' and slashing herself across the cheek on Animal's spiked shoulder pads. Hawk was then re-booked as an on-

screen drug addict who would stumble to the ring, fall over and cost LOD matches. Darren 'Puke' Drozdov (don't ask) temporarily replaced Hawk, with the storyline eventually revealing that Droz was supplying Hawk with drugs in an effort to kill him so he could become Animal's full-time tag partner. This pathetic melodrama culminated in Hawk climbing the twenty-two foot high scaffolding that framed the giant *RAW is WAR* video screen without safety equipment. Droz followed him up, then 'accidentally' pushed Hawk off the scaffolding, with a dummy (possibly Rocco but probably not) substituting for Hawk. While Hawk survived, interest in the Road Warriors was killed off for good. Hawk's television persona sadly mirrored his off-screen habits at the time. Despite overcoming his addictions months before, Hegstrand would die of a massive heart attack in October 2003, aged 46.

5DX's most famous skit saw the faction drive to the Norfolk Scope, the site of that evening's *WCW Monday Nitro*, in an army jeep with a large artillery gun. While it was a revolutionary sketch, nothing much happened. DX got WCW fans to say that WCW and Eric Bischoff sucked, DX requested the release of Scott Hall and Kevin Nash and DX talked about WCW giving away tickets (a practice both the WWF and WCW adhered to, known as 'papering'). Among shots of fans chanting 'DX', footage of the Scope's digital marquee reading 'FREE ADMISSION, FOR INFO CALL: 683-2312' was inserted in the vignette. The WWF was clearly implying that WCW was giving away tickets on the day of the show. The problem was that *WCW Nitro* that evening was a legit sell-out. WCW filed a $2 million lawsuit over the vignette on the 18th of May. "Titan [Sports, Inc.] wilfully and maliciously represented falsely that WCW was offering free tickets to its *Nitro* event in Norfolk. In the professional wrestling business, the giving away of free tickets to an event on the day of the show is a response to a failure to sell out a venue and it reflects badly on a promotion, suggesting that an insufficient number of fans are willing to pay to see the show." The same suit also complained about on-air name calling by Jim Cornette and Sean Waltman, as well as the *Billionaire*

Ted skits that the WWF aired back in 1996, which parodied Ted Turner, Hulk Hogan, Randy Savage and Gene Okerlund.

[6]Shortly before he appeared in Pete Williams' corner (in a wheelchair to sell his ankle injury) at *UFC 17*, Shamrock gave an interview to UFC concerning his WWF career. To Shamrock's credit, he said pro wrestling was far tougher on his body than mixed martial arts, as well as hinting that Owen Hart 'went against the script' and hurt his ankle for real. In one of the biggest upsets in UFC history, Williams defeated Mark Coleman via head kick KO in 0:37. The bout is one of five individual fights inducted into the UFC Hall of Fame as of this writing.

[7]Like so many mixed martial artists at the time, Dan 'The Beast' Severn turned to pro wrestling to supplement his income while actively fighting in UFC, Japan and elsewhere. As reigning NWA Champion, 'The Beast' was brought in as part of the failed NWA invasion of the WWF by Jim Cornette in March 1998. Unlike nearly every other wrestler, Dan was only contracted to wrestle around sixty WWF dates per year while being allowed to fulfil his NWA commitments. Dan also competed in no less than eight MMA bouts during his eleven-month WWF run, winning seven and drawing one against fellow UFC Hall of Famer Pat Miletich.

[8]Jason's scene-stealing monologue was followed by X-Pac as 'Mizark', parodying Mark Henry - mizark being carny code for 'mark'. X-Pac, who blacked up far more than the other DX members, portrayed Henry as a Fat Albert-type character and said, "I don't know what y'all cookin. Smells like shit but I think I'll eat some anyway!" X-Pac was referring to the rumour that Henry once bit into a sandwich that someone had... ahem, befouled, a couple of years prior. Henry denied this ever happened but also at some point confronted X-Pac over his comments. X-Pac claimed he'd merely heard the rumour while he was in WCW.

[9]The day before, tragedy struck for Davey Boy Smith in WCW. Davey and Neidhart were wrestling on the *Fall Brawl* pay-per-view. The Ultimate Warrior had just debuted in the promotion, now apparently with the power to teleport. To create Warrior's vanishing act, a trap

door was built into the ring. Alex Wright inadvertently slammed Smith onto the door, crushing his C-9 and C-10 vertebrae and fracturing four more. Davey somehow managed to keep wrestling for another five weeks before coming off the road, with his pre-existing painkiller addiction escalating as a result of the injury. On the 5th of April 1999, Davey was in intensive care, bedridden and in a full body cast with a severe infection in his spine. While looking at the business end of a *second* spinal tap, WCW FedExed Davey his marching papers. After the heartless firing was made public, WCW VP Eric Bischoff backtracked and kept Davey on the payroll. He recovered well enough to return to the WWF in September '99 but a combination of his injury-ravaged body and personal demons saw his initial push, then his WWF contract, terminated in short order. Davey's last years were dogged by drugs, marriage issues and a near-fatal motorcycle accident in 2001. In his final days, Bulldog had cleaned up, was living with Bruce Hart's wife Andrea and had made two in-ring appearances tagging with his 17-year-old son Harry. Davey died one week later on the 18th of May 2002 aged 39. Harry Smith currently performs as 'Davey Boy Smith Jr' in honour of his father.

[10]Despite the temporary stinger, Severn was fine. He took three and a half months off from WWF television to sell the injury while wrestling for various independents. He'd turn up in a neck brace, accept the challenge of a heel wrestler 'against doctor's orders' and retain his NWA World Championship. The WWF had a very legitimate neck injury occur on *RAW* in June when, in his main roster debut, Edge broke the neck of Jose Estrada Jr with a flip dive over the top rope onto the floor. Because this particular neck break was unscheduled, the WWF quickly wheeled Estrada out of the arena and forgot about him forever. Also around this time, New Japan's Masahiro Chono announced he was vacating the IWGP Heavyweight Championship to get surgery on a herniated disc. Ironically, Chono's neck had been bothering him ever since he was dropped on his head in 1992 from an errant piledriver from none other than Steve Austin. After returning to WWF rings in January 1999, Severn ran foul of scriptwriters when he refused to be

booked as the satanic Ministry of Darkness' latest disciple due to its religiously sensitive nature. The plan was for The Beast to literally have 666 (the number of the beast) etched onto his forehead while doing The Undertaker's evil bidding. When Dan refused, WWF officials threatened to have him lose all of his future matches. Severn reminded the unnamed officials that he only allowed wrestlers to beat him at his own discretion. Severn parted ways with the WWF for good the next month.

[11]Ed Ferarra, who was involved in the development of the sitcom, would soon join the World Wrestling Federation as Vince Russo's co-writer.

"Two Points!"

As told by Brian Christopher Lawler

In 2017, Brian Christopher Lawler, best remembered as one half of Too Cool with Scott 'Scotty 2 Hotty' Garland, described the following as the greatest rib he ever saw.

Noted shooter, former UFC Superfight Champion and two-time UFC tournament winner Dan 'The Beast' Severn's eleven month run in the WWF can be described as unremarkable at best and a complete waste of talent at worst. While Dan was imposing, unique and had a wealth of amateur credentials, he struggled to acclimatise to the WWF 'Sports Entertainment' style during his tenure. When Mick Foley asked Owen how a match had gone with 'The Beast' during a May 1998 *RAW is WAR* taping, Owen replied, "He really is a nice guy."

One of the WWF's all-but-forgotten shows during the golden age of the 'Attitude Era'[1] was called *Super Astros*; a *lucha libre* show exclusively shot for the Spanish-speaking market that would be recorded before *RAW*. The show featured undercard Federation wrestlers, high-flying imports from Japan and masked *luchadores* from Mexico. Smelling an opportunity, Owen procured one of the Mexican wrestlers' bags and put on their wrestling attire, including iconic *lucha libre*-style mask.

Television taping days were much longer than regular untelevised house show matches. Wrestlers were required to turn up early to: film pre-taped segments; to go over particular storylines for the evening; to talk to Vince McMahon and to complain to Jim Ross about a paycheque, amongst various other reasons. Severn, in an exercise to kill time during one of these protracted taping days, was resting on the floor of the dressing room with his eyes closed. Before anyone in the locker room, including Severn, knew what happened, a masked Mexican assailant dove onto the two-time all American from Arizona State, rolled him over and cried, "TWO POINTS!" before jumping off and showing Severn a clean pair of heels. 'The Beast', who was irate over what just transpired, leapt up and screamed, "WHERE IS THAT MEXICAN MOTHERFUCKER?" According to Lawler's version of events,

Severn hunted around the arena before eventually discovering the Mexican motherfucker in catering, where a smack across the head and a severe tongue lashing greeted the no doubt confounded *luchador*. The poor kid had no idea why he was being admonished in front of his peers and to compound the confusion, probably didn't even speak much (if any) English, so no one could explain to him that he'd been the unwitting victim of a classic Owen Hart rib.

When Severn himself was apprised of the story, Dan explained that he'd 'lived the life of six men' and doesn't have the best recollection of his wrestling career but was happy to concede that the prank probably occurred, except for the last part. "I'm okay with all of [the story] until the severe tongue lashing part because that's not in my character. I enjoy a good sense of humour... I very, very, rarely ever curse, period!"

The Beast has spoken.

[1]Depending on who you talk to, the Attitude Era is very loosely defined as some time in 1996-1997 until *WrestleMania X-Seven* in April 2001, where at his own insistence, Stone Cold Steve Austin turned heel and aligned himself with his arch-rival Mr McMahon. The fans hated the storyline and the WWF's business started trending downwards. Austin's heel turn, coupled with the disastrously handled WCW invasion angle later that year and the brand extension, ran off a third of the viewing audience by the summer of 2002. As of 2019, the WWE has never been able to come close to its peak popularity years of 1998-2001.

DX's Face Paint

As told by Sean Waltman and Brian James

Current WWE producer and former *Smackdown!* writer Brian 'Road Dogg' James, most famous today for lecturing his Twitter follows why wins and losses don't matter in professional wrestling (when they clearly do), was an in-ring stalwart of the World Wrestling Federation from 1994 to 2000. He slogged his way through several unsuccessful gimmicks, languishing at the bottom of every card before achieving worldwide fame as one half of the wildly popular New Age Outlaws tag team.

Back in his early WWF days scraping the bottom of the barrel performing as Jeff Jarrett's bump-taking lacky 'The Roadie', Owen would find creative ways to get under his skin. On a number of occasions, Owen would drive from town to town with the on-screen pair. The trio would often head to a restaurant to fill up on calories on the way to the next destination. Before leaving, Owen would make sure to get to the exit first, before loudly and embarrassingly announcing to everybody within ear shot, "Ladies and gentleman, Jeff Jarrett and The Roadie!" before diving back into the rental car.

When Road Dogg returned to the WWF in September 1996,[1] Owen Hart was there to welcome him back in the form of purposely ruining his matches even when he was nowhere near the ring at the time. On his return, The Roadie was repackaged 'The Real Double J' Jessie James. Togged up like the Midnight Cowboy with sleeveless, fringed western shirt and ten gallon hat, James body-popped his way to the ring while singing along with his entrance theme before every match. After the song and dance routine, James would, more often than not, end up on his back with his opponent pinning him for the three count.

Before The Real Double J started to wrestle, he would hand over the aforementioned ten gallon hat to a ringside attendant, who would dutifully carry the Stetson to the backstage area for safekeeping. During one untelevised house show match, James saw the cowboy hat make an unscheduled run-in thanks to Owen. "You'd be having your match and

[Owen] would send out... a guy to run my hat back down to ringside and try to give me my hat while I was in the middle of a match. I'd just know that's god-dern Owen back there doing something!"

By the time the 1990s rolled around, Davey Boy Smith was no longer the mean-spirited bully that followed the lead of his cousin, Dynamite Kid Tom Billington. While Davey was mostly reformed, not all of the bad habits he'd picked up from his more nefarious cousin had gone away completely. "Davey Boy 'Halcion'd' me one time and I blacked out at the bar," Road Dogg chuckled. In other words, Road Dogg left his drink unattended and Davey plopped the powerful (and addictive) sleeping drug Halcion in his drink for a joke. While Owen would never spike someone's drink for a rib, he was certainly not above taking advantage of the situation once the damage had been done.

When the Dogg awoke from his sleeping pill-induced stupor, he staggered his way to the bathroom to check on himself. When he looked into the bathroom mirror, the image staring back at him was a 6'4", red-headed transvestite courtesy of Owen painting his face with heavy makeup, including eye shadow and lipstick. "I saw in the mirror and I looked like a friggin' clown!" Road Dogg chortled, "[but] it's good-hearted stuff, you know what I mean. It makes me laugh now."

Fellow D-Generation X alumni Sean 'X-Pac' Waltman added that Owen had played amateur beautician with him too. Instead of Davey Boy dropping an 'H-bomb' in his beer, X-Pac, for reasons few will ever understand, Haclion'd *himself* and passed out at the bar. Going through the same process as his fellow D-Generation X member, Waltman awoke from the self-induced coma, headed for the bathroom and saw an ugly, bearded chick staring back at him. After washing all the make-up off his face, (and presumably cursing Owen while he did it) X-Pac headed back to his room to get some sleep before his flight. The next day he drove to the airport, flew home, undressed and climbed into bed with his wife. It was only then X-Pac and his wife discovered at the same time that Owen had painted his toenails pink as well.

[1]Double J and The Roadie legitimately double-crossed the World Wrestling Federation at the *In Your House 2* pay-per-view some fifteen

months prior to Roadie's return. The plan following his loss to Shawn Michaels was for Jarrett and The Roadie to break up and start a feud with one another. Instead of going through with the post-match split, Jarrett simply got up and left the arena, convincing The Roadie to leave with him. More cynically-minded types have advanced the theory that Jarrett's real motivation for leaving the WWF was that, after working with the likes of Razor Ramon, Shawn Michaels and Diesel throughout 1995 as WWF Intercontinental Champion, losing the belt just to feud with his punching bag lackey over who really sang *With My Baby Tonight* was a huge demotion. Double J convincing The Roadie to leave with him that night could have scuppered Roadie's chances of making it big in the World Wrestling Federation, which it thankfully didn't. Brian James would eventually become the Road Dogg and, at the height of his popularity, earn seven figures in a single year.

362

Prank Phone Calls: Mick Foley

As told by Mick Foley

On the 28th of June 1998, Mick endured the most brutal match of his (or practically anyone's) wrestling career. Mick had just fought The Undertaker in a 'Hell in a Cell match' at the *King of the Ring* pay-per-view. The highlights of the match included: The Undertaker hurling Mick off, then through the sixteen foot Cell, being slammed onto thousands of drawing pins twice and numerous unprotected chair shots to the head. Mick could have legitimately died during several points of the match but 'only' suffered: a dislocated shoulder, a dislocated jaw, bruised ribs, a bruised kidney, numerous puncture wounds and cuts, broken teeth, a severe concussion and memory loss.[1]

That night, Mick had his dislodged tooth wired back in his head and was released under his own recognisance after a four hour hospital visit. Still in a concussed fog, Mick arrived at The Red Roof Inn at 3am, dragging himself to his room unaided and prepared to have the most well-earned sleep in the history of mankind (the human collective, as well as the wrestler).[2] Some ten minutes after settling in, Mick's room phone rang. The Hardcore Legend had already endured an upsetting phone call earlier that night from his hysterical wife and children, who scolded him over putting his health at risk. The person calling his room at this time wasn't his wife, but the suddenly inquisitive Scottish check-in clerk, who decided that this was the perfect time to air his misgivings of Foley's profession. "I hear this voice going, 'You can level with me, that wrestling, it be a little fake, huh?'" said Mick. "It just caught me off-guard. I'd spent hours in the hospital and here I am dealing with the fake issue from the guy at the front desk."

After ten or so minutes of what he described as a 'spirited' phone conversation, Mick, who was the nicest, most amiable person in real life, was readying himself to get dressed and head down to the check-in desk to give the mouthy Jock a little more than a piece of his mind. At that point, Owen dropped the Scottish accent and started chuckling down the phone. "That's usually how all the Owen Hart hotel stories end; with a laugh and you go, 'Argh! You got me!' He would just push your buttons until things were about to get ugly, then he would kind of let you know you'd been pranked, zoinked, had, whatever the case may be. Then you'd have a good laugh then try and get some sleep."

[1]Why would Foley knowingly put himself through such torture? He'd portrayed three separate characters (Mankind, Dude Love and Cactus Jack) over the past year and was one of the WWF's biggest stars. Mick had switched numerous times between them and burned the audience out of all three acts. When he returned as the heel Mankind a couple of weeks prior, the audience let out a collective fart. The stunts in Hell in a Cell, which were insane even by Foley's reckless standards, were to give both the match and his career a much-needed shot in the arm. In the two months after *King of the Ring*, live audiences were still apathetic towards the Mankind character, rendering his sacrifices almost pointless. It was only when Foley started cutting funnier, snappier promos, formed a comedic father/son-like duo with Vince McMahon and wore a sock puppet on his hand, did Mick finally achieve the status of bona fide main event superstar – none of which carried any physical risk.

[2]He would need all the sleep he could get, as after the vicious Cell match, Mick had his shoulder put back in the socket and was shoved right back through the curtain to interfere in the Steve Austin vs. Kane main event. If you think that was callous, Mick was booked to wrestle The Undertaker and Kane just two days later, which saw the still-concussed Mankind take another chair shot to the head, which thankfully barely grazed him. Mick was only given another ten days off the road before returning to full-time in-ring action.

Bad Matches:
Edge & Christian Part 1

As told by Adam Copeland and Jimmy Korderas

After Owen Hart and Jeff Jarrett lost the WWF Tag Team Titles to Kane and X-Pac on the 30th of March 1999, the team stuck together for the most part, occasionally splitting off into singles action but mostly taking on other top teams in the Federation, such as the New Age Outlaws, The Acolytes and their newest prank victims, Edge and Christian. Adam 'Edge' Copeland, Jay 'Christian' Reso and their vampire-like leader David 'Gangrel' Heath, formed The Brood; a non-promo cutting undercard faction that dressed up in frilly blouses and adhered to what commentator Jim Ross referred to as 'the gothic lifestyle'. Edge, Christian and Gangrel all rotated as tag team partners throughout their year-long association but the on-screen duo and off-screen best friends Edge and Christian were the clear cut premier combination.

It would indeed be the future Tag Team Championship combination of Edge and Christian that would face off against Owen Hart and Jeff Jarrett more than a dozen times in April and May of 1999. Every match between the two teams seemed to bring with it a host of new pranks, starting with their very first two-on-two encounter in Oberhausen, Germany on April Fool's Day 1999. After a few minutes of back and forth action, the dastardly Owen cut the ring off, isolating Edge from his tag team partner. With the WWF Tag Team Titles up for grabs, Owen, behind the referee's back, reached into his singlet for a foreign object. Owen wrapped the mystery object around his hand and blasted Edge right in the jaw, before returning the object from whence it came. Edge took the punch like he'd been hit with knuckle dusters and looked to be down and out on the canvas. Owen took advantage of his prone opponent by climbing onto the bottom rope (not a typo) and hitting a big body splash... onto Edge's legs. Owen then lay on top of his legs for an ineffective pin attempt. Edge, who was still reacting from the foreign object shot, barely kicked out before the three count. Owen then went for another, more off-colour pinning attempt. "He stuck his crotch in my face," said Edge, "forcing me to kick out before three. All the while he laughed like a hyena."

Referee Jimmy Korderas, whose job it was to act like he was incompetent, kept checking Owen for the concealed weapon but could never find it. "We're doing the old back and forth and he's passing [the foreign object] to Jeff and I'm checking and Christian's complaining and Edge is selling like he's getting hit with brass knuckles," said Korderas. After the foreign object had been surreptitiously used on several occasions, the referee felt the time was right to call Owen out for cheating. Owen had purposely made the mistake of letting Korderas see him conceal the object under his arm and Korderas walked over to confront him.

In reality, Edge, Christian and Korderas had zero idea what Owen was using as a weapon as they didn't discuss its usage over in the locker room prior to the match. Korderas, who was as intrigued as everyone in the audience to find out what The King of Pranks had been utilising to dominate Edge, threatened Owen with disqualification unless he raised his arm right there and then. After some mild protesting, Owen, in front of 7,000 baying German fans, lifted his arms to reveal that the device of annihilation he'd been killing Edge with was in fact... a red napkin. As the napkin floated harmlessly to the ground, everybody in the ring broke character. "I looked at Jeff, then I looked at Christian and Edge and it became a laugh-fest," recalled Korderas. "I usually pride myself on the fact that I am very good at not cracking up in the ring. That night I didn't have a prayer."

"What's the Time, Gangrel?"

As told by Jay Reso

Back in the middle of 1998, the World Wrestling Federation enjoyed an influx of young, fresh talent in an effort to help market the company as the hip, youthful brand of wrestling to counteract WCW's roster of middle-aged former WWF stars. New wrestlers debuted almost every month with edgy and fresh new characters, including long-time journeyman David Heath. Heath already had over ten years experience wrestling in territories and independent promotions across North America, as well as for All Japan Pro Wrestling as one half of The Blackhearts. In the mid 1990s, Heath developed the 'Vampire Warrior' character, an occult gimmick inspired by classic vampire films such as *The Lost Boys*, which saw Heath install permanent fang-like incisors in his mouth and screech 'HEEEEEE' like an itchy poltergeist during his interviews. When Heath was finally picked up by the Federation in 1998, Vampire Warrior transformed into Gangrel, which was essentially the same character with a frilly 'Interview with a Vampire' style shirt and a super sweet ring entrance.

The influx of new talent not only created exciting new characters and match-ups for fans to revel in, it also meant that Owen Hart had a lot of fresh meat to play pranks on. Shortly after Gangrel's main roster debut,[1] the World Wrestling Federation tour arrived in Philadelphia, Pennsylvania. That evening in the locker room, Gangrel was getting dressed after wrestling a match when he went to retrieve his watch from the specific place in his gym bag where he always left it. When the watch wasn't there, he began to panic. While Gangrel was frantically searching for his wristwatch, Owen sidled up to him and asked him if he knew what time it was. Instead of seeing through the obvious set up line, Gangrel explained that he didn't know the time as he'd lost his watch. Owen, who most likely had the watch in his possession waiting to give it back, instead 'helped' Gangrel look for the misplaced timepiece for about an hour before the pair gave up.

A couple of months of touring across North America passed before the WWF arrived at the same Philadelphia arena for the next show. Gangrel, whose lost watch was a distant memory, returned to the locker room after his match to find the watch in his bag in the exact same place he'd left it before it went missing two months prior. As Gangrel stared in disbelief at the reappearing chronometer, unable to make head-nor-tail of the situation, Owen sidled up to him again and asked if he knew what time it was, just as he had done months before.

[1]Like so many before him, David Heath first appeared on World Wrestling Federation as enhancement talent from 1994 to '95. Heath primarily competed in the WWF under a mask as 'The Black Phantom'. He also made an appearance on a 1998 edition of *WCW Worldwide*, losing to Meng and The Barbarian.

"Could You Sign 250 of These, Mr Venis?"

As told by Sean Morley

In May 1998, former CMLL Champion[1] Sean Morley made his much anticipated World Wrestling Federation debut as adult film star 'Val Venis'.[2] The Val Venis character was the apex of the WWF's foray into sex and sleaze that the young audience demanded at the time. Weeks of introductory vignettes were broadcast before Venis' debut, featuring the wrestler-cum-porn star hanging out with starlets on set, in convertibles and in the shower. The most memorable of these introduction videos took place in WWF Producer Bruce Prichard's back garden. Claiming to be on the set of his latest movie, *Soldier of Love*, Venis emerged from the bushes with real-life porn star Jenna Jameson,[3] who was naked except for two bandoleers covering her enormous, fake breasts, with tiny penises replacing the bullets. Val Venis was an immediate hit with the fans and became somewhat of a household name thanks to the explosion in popularity that wrestling was experiencing.

Early one morning in 1999, Val and the rest of the WWF crew flew into St Louis, Missouri for one of the WWF's quarterly shows at the 18,000+ seat Kiel Centre that evening. After collecting baggage and hiring cars, the crew headed for the Marriott Hotel adjacent to the airport where WWF employees received a favourable corporate rate. Val's itinerary for that day was much the same as everyone else's; get some sleep, hit the gym and eat before heading to the show. Because it was well known that the wrestlers stayed at that specific Marriot, Val and his travelling companions were greeted by hundreds of mostly young wrestling fans congregating in the hotel lobby, hoping to get autographs and pictures with their heroes. Because he'd arrived later than a number of other wrestlers, there was plenty of time for Val to interact with fans while standing in line to check in.

Between the hoards of children getting autographs from the storyline porn star, a gross-looking, long-haired, Comic Book Guy-type walked up to Val and asked if he could sign some 8x10s for him. "This one guy comes up

369

to me with a stack of about two-hundred and fifty Val Venis pictures and says, 'Hey, brother, can you sign these?' I look at him and I say, 'No, I can't sign all those!' Like he expects I'm going to stand there and sign all 250 pictures for him." Venis told the scumbag to get lost then carried on signing autographs and taking photos with the real fans.

After checking in, Val headed off to his room to settle in and get some sleep after the flight. Just as he was about to drift off to 'the land of nod', the hotel room telephone rang. Val didn't recognise the voice on the other line but the guy on the phone certainly knew Val. "So I pick up the phone and I go, 'Hello' and the voice on the other end says, 'Hey man, you promised me you'd come down and sign these pictures. You'd better come down and sign 'em and keep your promises.' I went 'WHOA, WHAT? I didn't promise you anything, I'm not signing your damn pictures [and] I don't appreciate you calling my room.' Boom, I hung up the phone. Just as I go lay back down to bed it rings again, so I pick up the phone and just as I put it to my ear he goes, 'I'm a big man, you won't get by me! You better come down here and sign those pictures!' So I go, 'STAY RIGHT THERE!'"

Val threw on whatever clothes were legally required for him to wear out in public before running down the stairs to confront the opportunistic autograph hunter. When Val arrived in the lobby, it was completely empty. All the wrestlers had checked into their rooms and the fans had already gone home. The only people still hanging around were Owen Hart and Jeff Jarrett who were sat at the hotel bar, which was closed. "I'm looking around and I say, 'Hey, Jeff, Owen, did you guys see a long, scraggly, dark-haired guy with a stack of pictures?' [Owen] goes, 'I saw a guy with greasy long hair run out the front door.' So I run out the front door and I'm looking for this guy, I can't find him anywhere." After looking high and low, Val eventually gave up the search and headed back to bed. The adrenaline from the phantom confrontation coursed through his veins. "It took me an hour and a half to get back to sleep after that."

A number of months later, Val Venis and fellow Ontarian Edge were making a promotional appearance on the Canadian sports talk show *Off the Record with Michael Landsberg*. While the pair were just off camera waiting for the presenter to welcome them into the live studio, Edge turned to Val and said, "Hey Val, you remember St Louis airport where you wanted to kill that guy that wanted you to sign that stack of pictures?' I went, 'Yeah?' He goes, 'That was Owen!' I guess Owen had text [Edge] saying tell him now. Now we're just getting ready to go on air and I'm seething!" It turned out that Owen was stood behind Val in the hotel lobby when the 8x10-wielding weirdo was abruptly turned away. Always the opportunist, Owen crafted another finely tuned rib to fool one of the smartest wrestlers on the WWF roster.

[1]Morley won the CMLL Heavyweight Champion as the masked robot like character 'Steele', wrestling for the Mexican promotion from 1997 to 1998. Even when he was firmly established as Val Venis, the WWF allowed Morley to return to CMLL for a number of shows under his former moniker.

[2]Contrary to his character, Sean Morley is in fact a serious, well-educated man who is heavily into politics and Libertarianism. WWF Head Writer Vince Russo envisioned the Val Venis character during their initial one-on-one meeting. "I spent a little time with Sean and the guy was so heavy into politics," Russo recalled. "I can't write a political character for Sean Morley, I [wouldn't] know what I'm doing. The more and more time I spend with him [and] I'm looking at him, I just come to the realisation that this guy just looks like... a sleazy porn star." Russo pitched the idea to Vince McMahon who was so enthusiastic about the gimmick that he called Morley up on the spot to offer him the role.

[3]Several more vignettes with Jenna Jameson were filmed, including footage of Venis and Jameson totally naked in Bruce Prichard's hot tub. WWF owner Vince McMahon saw the promotional clips and axed the lot, believing that Jameson, who was the most famous porn star of her time, was 'too ugly' to be on his television show!

Prank Phone Calls:
The World's Strongest Mom

As told by Mark Henry

As established in a previous entry, Mark Henry wasn't above pranking his trainer, mentor and surrogate father figure, Terry Todd. It turned out that Henry wasn't above getting Owen to crank call his beloved mother either. "The best Owen Hart story I can think of was me and him calling and pranking my Mom," said Henry. "Nobody was exempt!"

In the late 1990s, Mark asked Owen to wind her up by pretending to be the taxman. "We called my Mom and Owen said, 'Excuse me, is this Ms Barbara Jean?' She said yes. 'I'm with the IRS and you haven't paid taxes in the last five years and we're gonna have to come and take your house." Barbara dropped her polite demeanour and immediately lost her mind. "I never in my life heard my Mom use the m-f'er word; never in my life! She was like, 'You can come on if you want to!' and she went off and she was cussing and everything! This was the woman who went to church... if there's anyone who's gonna sit to the left hand next to god, it's her."

After letting 'The World's Strongest Mother' fly off the handle for a suitable amount of time, her doting son finally intervened. "Man, she was cussing like a sailor. I finally got to the point where I could breathe again and I said, 'Mom, Mom, Mom! Stop! Stop! It's me and Owen!' She was like, 'I'm gonna whoop yo ass when you get home!' She threatened to whoop a grown man. Oh man, it was funny!"

Bad Matches:
Edge & Christian Part 2

As told by Adam Copeland

After six weeks and numerous matches contested between the two teams, Edge and Christian once again faced off with Owen and Jarrett on the 13th of May 1999 in Hershey Pennsylvania. Not only were Owen and Jeff one step ahead of their more youthful rivals in the grappling stakes (they'd go on to win every match they fought) but the second generation wrestlers were always two steps ahead in the in-ring pranking department as well.

The beginning of the match in Hershey kicked off rather unusually, in that it was basically shenanigans-free. Further into the contest when the match broke down and all four participants were in the ring at the same time, Edge and Christian gained the upper hand and forced Owen and Jeff into opposite corners. With their rivals ripe for the picking, Edge and Christian stood on the second ropes and rained down the dreaded ten punches of doom onto their opponents' heads in unison, with the crowd counting along with every strike. Instead of lolling in the corner helplessly and rocking their heads to register every blow, Owen and Jeff seemed strangely pre-occupied. "I noticed that Owen's head was kind of buried into my crotch. I was like that's... that's weird. That's an odd way to sell this," said Edge. "I was punching him on the top of the head and I [connected with] a couple and I'm sure it hurt his head."

After the ten punches were executed, both Edge and Christian climbed down off the ropes in order to whip Owen and Jeff into each other for the spot's crescendo. When Edge and Christian looked their opponents in the face, they realised why their opponents had their heads down during the punches; they were now wearing big red clown noses that they'd stashed in their tights. "I came down, looked at [Owen] and I had to bite the sides of my cheeks," said Edge. While doing their best not to laugh, Edge and Christian proceeded with the pre-planned spot and whipped Owen and Jeff into each other. "As they bumped, the clown noses flew straight up into the air and landed on them," chuckled Edge. "We laughed, they were in a heap laughing hysterically and the crowd couldn't help but laugh, too."

Owen Ribs the Boss AGAIN

As told by Matt Hardy and Terri Runnels

Along with brother Jeff, Matt Hardy had been making appearances as enhancement talent since 1994 when Matt was 18 and Jeff was '18' (really 16). Matt and Jeff had worked their way from rolling around on their trampoline as kids to working local independents under a variety of nom de plumes, including Matt's character 'High Voltage'.[1] The brothers, while green, were very talented and were finally signed to full-time WWF contracts in 1998. Long before the brothers were on the road full-time, they had become fully aware of Owen's reputation. *"Even when we were first starting on TV as part-time workers, Owen was always constantly up to different jokes,"* said Matt.

In the late 1990s wrestling boom, Owen would take great delight in pranking the new, young guys joining the company but he would also enlist naive rookies to do his bidding, assisting him on larger-scale pranks. To pull this particular rib off, Owen needed to keep all the WWF bigwigs, including Vince and the producers, in their meeting room. *"Probably the greatest rib I've ever been involved in happened at a pay-per-view event where Owen used me as one of the guys to stand guard and make sure that Vince McMahon and the office guys didn't leave the building,"* recounted Matt. While the pre-show production meeting was in session, Owen barged in and fabricated a story that there was some type of emergency going on in the building and that they all had to stay in the room. Why anybody would believe Owen at this point is still a mystery but that's why Matt, along with another accomplice, was stationed outside the room to make sure everybody stayed put.

Because WWF talent was required to turn up early on taping days, Owen and the rest of the roster arrived at the arena before the decorative stage hoardings had been put up. With McMahon and the producers unwittingly incarcerated, Owen went to work uprooting the unattended adornments and found a new home for them. "[Owen] rushed all of the hoardings that they bought for the set into Vince's office and they crashed and ruined it," said Matt. At the very least, unlike farm animals, signs and decorations do not defecate, leaving Vince's office in a more useable state than when it became a pigpen courtesy of Owen in 1995. To this day, it remains the favourite prank Matt ever found himself involved in. "[It] was pretty hilarious and also pretty gutsy on Owens part to rib the boss like that."

Another Vince McMahon-based rib Owen would like to pull would be to convince a gullible wrestler that Vince wanted to see them while he was in a production meeting. McMahon's interminably long production sessions were (and still are) very private, sacred affairs. Even when ESPN was invited to film a pre WWE pay-per-view meeting in the late 2000s, the cameras were ejected as soon as storylines were being discussed. A major no-no for the WWF crew was to interrupt these meetings, especially when that person didn't have the proper clearance. According to former valet Terri Runnels, when the wrestler would rightfully refuse to believe him, Owen would exploit the chump's inexperience by replying, 'Fine but he's sitting there waiting for you. If you don't want to go in that's fine but I told you." The wrestler's paranoia would eventually get the better of them and blunder into the production meeting in-progress, where the tempestuous Vince would react by blowing a gasket and throwing them out the room. "Just stuff like that was classic Owen," said Terri. "It was one of his fun and endearing qualities."

[1]If you associate the name 'High Voltage' to the undercard tag team from WCW, here's the reason why: Matt sent a video of himself as High Voltage to the WCW office when they ran an 'amateur challenge' contest. According to Chris Kanyon, the tape was viewed multiple times at WCW's Power Plant training facility. The WCW decision makers didn't give Matt a second look but liked the High Voltage name so much they blatantly stole it.

"I Am the Soma King!"

As told by Adam Copeland and Jay Reso

1998 is inarguably one of the most exciting years in the history of the World Wrestling Federation. The controversy of The Montreal Screwjob the year prior created an enormous buzz in the wrestling world. Stone Cold Steve Austin, with the help of Mike Tyson, reached mainstream celebrity status. WWF programming became sexier and edgier and new characters were appearing on television almost every week. A number of wrestlers debuting around this time included a Canada heavy contingent including: Don 'Jackyl' Callis, Robert 'Kurrgan' Maillet, Sean 'Val Venis' Morley, Andrew 'Test' Martin and the 'brother'[1] tag team of Adam 'Edge' Copeland and Jay 'Christian' Reso. The irony was that Bret, who had been personally responsible for giving a lot of Canadian grapplers their WWF break, had been ousted from the company the previous November.

In the last year of his life, Owen spent a lot of time in and out of the ring with Edge and Christian. According to Edge, Owen was the leader of what they referred to as the 'Canadian Mafia.' Edge and Christian still lived in Toronto at the time and Owen would fly to Toronto Pearson International Airport to catch the connecting flight to Calgary. On this particular day Owen had a long layover before his connecting flight to Calgary departed, so he decided to amuse himself by attempting to clear Toronto airport security while wearing a Mexican *lucha libre* mask. While being questioned by airport security, Edge laughingly recalled that, "[Owen] said... his *luchador* name was the 'Soma King'!"[2] As Edge fondly remembered, he and Christian would witness Owen rib himself so they would have something to laugh about for the two days that they were off. "Nowadays that would not fly but it was really funny that he tried to go through customs with a *luchador* mask on."

[1]While not real-life brothers, Edge and Christian are life-long friends who attended the same high school, trained at the same wrestling gym

378

(although at different times) and were brought into the WWF within months of each other in 1998.

[2]For those who don't know, Somas are addictive muscle relaxers that numerous wrestlers used and abused in great quantities in the '80s, '90s and '00s, which contributed to a high number of premature deaths in the business, making it all the more amusing that the straight-laced, drug-free Hart would give himself such a nom de plume. Soma King was also a spoof on the famous *luchador* Silver King, who was appearing on WCW programming at the time.

Al Snow
Gimmick Infringement

As told by Mick Foley

Before its documentation in Mick Foley's seminal biography *Have a Nice Day: A Tale of Blood and Sweatsocks,* the Dude Love-Owen Hart popcorn match had gone down in folklore in the World Wrestling Federation locker room. A little over a year after the series of untelevised, weapons-grade stinkers between Mick and Owen had blighted the eyes of fans and wounded the soul of Dave Meltzer, Mick (as Mankind) was awarded the brand new WWF Hardcore Title by Mr McMahon on the 2nd of November 1998 edition of *RAW is WAR.* The Hardcore Title was to be defended exclusively under no disqualification, no count-out, pinfalls count anywhere rules. The first year of the Championship's division was characterised by hard hitting, dynamic matches filled with crazy weapons and bizarre locales.

Arguably, the most prominent rivalry for the Hardcore Championship in the division's nascent months was between Al Snow and Bob 'Hardcore Holly' Howard. The two adversaries battled to outdo each other in every Hardcore match they fought in, going from all over ringside, to all over the arena, to outside the arena, to production trucks, to dumpsters and even in the Mississippi River.

During an untelevised live event in Las Vegas, Nevada on the 13th of March 1999, Al Snow was still chasing the champion Holly around the country to capture his first WWF singles title. Hard chair shots, crashes through tables and slams on the cold, unforgiving arena floor were all utilized to create another entertaining matchup for the audience. Then, in what Mick Foley would term as 'gimmick infringement', Snow produced a refuse bag full of popcorn and savagely beat the curmudgeonly Holly in front of over 12,000 entertained Nevada fans.

Mick and Owen, who were watching the contest from the backstage area, interpreted Al's popcorn spot as blatant thievery of their intellectual property. They walked over to the boss' son Shane McMahon to lodge a complaint. Gimmick infringement was genuinely taken seriously in the Federation locker room. It was an unwritten rule that you do not use other wrestlers' identifiable moves, interview style, costumes, props, or anything else fans would see as belonging to someone else without the owner's consent.[1]

After the match, Al walked through the curtain with a swollen eye, bloodied nose and bruised chest from the legitimate beating Holly had dished out. Al was pleased with the match and proud of himself until Shane asked to speak to him in private. From across the staging area, Mick and Owen watched Al's body language change from prideful to dejected, as Shane firmly told him that the popcorn spot belonged to Mick and Owen and he was not to use it again without their permission. When Al nodded in agreement and walked away crestfallen, Shane called him back to speak to him again. "Wait, Al, come back here, you know I'm kidding, don't you?" "Mick," was all Al said in response, knowing exactly who'd put Shane up to the jape. Al walked over to Mick and Owen and told them he knew he should have known he was being zoinked the second he saw the two of them huddled together. "I took that as a huge compliment," said Mick when recalling the rib.

[1]The unspoken rule only applied to other wrestlers in the same promotion. Wrestlers in any other promotion were fair game to steal from and occurred very often, as evidenced by how many WCW wrestlers used Steve Austin's 'Stone Cold Stunner' finisher. Steve Austin himself stole the move from its innovator Mikey Whipwreck when the two briefly shared a locker room in ECW.

Autographs and Meet and Greets

As told by Debra Marshall and Mick Foley

After a surprisingly decent two year run in WCW as the valet of her real-life husband and ex-Chicago Bear-turned-wrestler Steve 'Mongo' McMichael, Debra McMichael resurfaced in the WWF in October 1998 after a year lost in the wrestling wilderness. She'd been calling the WWF offices for weeks on end looking for a job before being given the role of Jeff Jarrett's valet; a semi-continuation of her final WCW angle where Debra ditched Mongo for Jarrett.[1] The former beauty queen was a great addition for the colourless Jarrett, who'd been working a tough guy gimmick despite being only 5'10", looking deeply unthreatening and working 'Memphis-style' i.e. very light. Debra, whose incredible body was stuffed into the shortest skirts imaginable, had her character changed from gold digger (playing off her legitimate divorce from husband Steve[2]) to nymphomaniac and compulsive stripper in a matter of weeks.

Debra immediately became the focal point of every Jarrett match and when the similarly directionless Owen was teamed up with Jarrett, Debra took the focus off Owen, too. While Debra didn't travel with Owen and Jeff between shows, the trio spent a lot of time getting better acquainted with the second generation stars during autograph sessions. "I just remember we were in Chicago the night before [*Over the Edge*] and I just remember he was acting a fool," recalled Debra. "We would go take pictures before or after the show with fans. Then Owen would always grab the camera and then he'd be like, 'Oh, the camera's not working,' so he'd make me stand there with somebody with their arm all wrapped completely around me like for ten minutes."

After a show in Florida, Owen managed to pull off the ol' Tennessee switcharoo with Debra's sunglasses. "We were doing our autograph session and I went to put on my sunglasses to leave and Owen had switched them and they were some raggedy, hideous-looking pair and I didn't even notice when I put them back on. We were leaving with the crowd of people [and I didn't notice] until I got into the car."

When at a sit down meet-and-greet with the fans, one of Owen's classic manoeuvres would be to reach over a little too far and draw all over the hand of his lucky autograph session buddy for the day. Either that or write 'let's be friends' on the 8x10 photo his fellow WWF performer had just signed their name on, as Mick Foley once attested to.

While not strictly a rib, Mick suffered a great indignity during an autograph session in Owen Hart's presence in Fresno, California on the 26th of July 1998. A week earlier, Mick and blonde bombshell Sable were booked to do an autograph signing in Fall River, Massachusetts. Almost all the spotty teenage boys in attendance made a beeline for Sable and her enormous, silicon-enhanced knockers, leaving Mick's ego in tatters.[3] However, the Fresno autograph session was packed with eager fans and Mick and Owen were signing pictures as quickly as possible so no one was left out. That was until the line stopped, then dispersed. It turned out that all the fans were there to see the 'real stars', Steve Austin and Ken Shamrock, who had just arrived. While Mick had no idea, Owen was fully aware that they were the also-rans for that particular signing. "I felt my heart drop down to somewhere in the vicinity of my left ball," recalled the Hardcore Legend. "'You mean we have to wait here until then?' Owen seemed to take cruel pleasure in seeing my feelings shattered as he chuckled, 'I hope you brought a book.'"

[1]Excluding her last couple of weeks in WCW where Debra accompanied 'Das Wunderkind' Alex Wright to the ring.

[2]Married wrestlers who brought their wives into the business all but guaranteed themselves an ugly divorce shortly afterwards. Steve McMichael, Randy Savage, Kurt Angle, Kevin Sullivan, The Undertaker, Jake 'The Snake' Roberts, Goldust and Stone Cold Steve Austin (who also married and divorced Debra) can all attest to this fact.

[3]Much like Owen, Mick had concerns that the wrestling business was passing him by and his career was faltering as a result, despite his death-defying Hell in a Cell massacre the previous month.

Prank Phone Call:
Test Cancels Chicago

As told by Andrew Martin

One of the many of young Canadian wrestlers to filter into the World Wrestling Federation roster in the late 1990s was Andrew 'Test' Martin. Billed at 6'6" and ripped to shreds, looks alone mandated the World Wrestling Federation would offer him a job sooner or later. It turned out to be sooner, as less than two years after a chance encounter with Bret Hart at Toronto's Planet Hollywood restaurant franchise, Test made his WWF television debut on the 25th of October 1998 episode of *Sunday Night HeAT*... as Motley Crüe's microphone-testing roadie.[1] Test's debut proper came on the 14th of December live *RAW is WAR*, running in during the WWF Championship main event match between The Rock and Triple H. Test interfered on behalf of The Rock, helping him retain the title and joined Vince McMahon's Corporation faction in one fell swoop, giving the hitherto unseen rookie instant credibility.

Because he was a wide-eyed 23-year-old with little life experience, Test was one of many incoming rookies ripe for the pranking, courtesy of the Owen Hart welcome wagon. On the 6th of March 1999, when Test had been part of the main roster for less than four months, the World Wrestling Federation wrestlers flew into Chicago for a weekend double shot (two shows in one day). On that morning, the weather in Chicago was sub zero and it was snowing heavily. Because the first of the two events was a relatively small-scale show at Notre Dame University, it was cancelled outright. All the wrestlers were then told to go back to the hotel, relax and wait for news of the second show at the sold-out Rosemont Horizon.

While hanging around his hotel room awaiting news of the event, Test received a phone call. "I picked it up and the guy on the other end said he was the head man running the stadium and [wanted to know] if we were doing the show that night. He was told that I was the man to talk to whether we were gonna go ahead with the show." Why the arena manager decided to ask a mid-card rookie wrestler what the WWF's plan was anyone's guess, so Test politely informed the manager he was *not* the man to be talking to. According to the manager, all the other wrestlers had supposedly already cancelled their appearances and Test was one of the last holdouts. "[He] said I was the last guy to talk to [and asked] what did I think? After a few times of telling him I didn't think too much of it and I told him that, again, I wasn't the man to talk to... the last words he said were, 'Well, I'll tell them Test said to cancel the show!'"

Test protested his innocence, telling the arena manager it wasn't his responsibility to be cancelling anything. Unfortunately, the message didn't get through to the manager as he abruptly hung up on him. It turned out that, despite the harsh weather, the show wasn't cancelled after all and 18,046 rabid Chi-Town fans got to witness fellow Canadian Edge pin Test in the second match of the night. Long after the show, the phone call stuck in Test's mind as it had been a bewildering encounter, of which he never got closure. That was until the 24th of May; the day after Owen's passing. During preparations for the *RAW is Owen* tribute episode, someone thought it'd be funny to clue in Test that it was actually Owen pretending to be the arena manager all along. Test's video tribute to Owen that evening would be the re-telling of this story, which would prove to be a fitting tribute to the King of Pranks. Even after his passing, Owen's crank calls were still making his colleagues smile. As Mick Foley once described Owen, "He was the undisputed king of the prank phone calls."

---

[1]Roadies usually have a certain type of... look, and none in music history have ever looked as jacked up as Test, who also acted as a bodyguard when he removed a 'fan' from the stage during Motley's set on *HeAT*. The moniker Test literally came from the roadie's calling card of saying 'test... test... test...' into the microphones before a gig, although many figured it was also a thinly-veiled reference to testosterone. A fun fact about Test; he named his dog 'Jobber.'

Bad Matches:
Edge & Christian Part 3
Owen's Last Ever Match

As told by Adam Copeland and Jay Reso

Owen Hart's last match took place in front of 18,000 fans at the sold-out Rosemont Horizon in Chicago on the 22^n of May 1999. Once again, Owen would team up with Jeff Jarrett to face the up-and-coming tag team of Edge and Christian. On having the distinction of participating in Owen's last match, Edge said, "It's a distinction I'd rather not have; I wish no one had it." Like their titanic battles of the past, Owen once again had some tricks up his sleeve. As Edge and Christian stood in the ring looking towards the stage, the opening twangs of Jarrett's country music-tinged theme song played and Jarrett, Debra and Owen walked through the curtain into the packed arena.

Jeff and Debra were wearing their usual performance garb; Jarrett wore his silver shorts and carried a guitar and Debra wore her impossibly skimpy business suit. Owen then strolled out wearing a bizarre mishmash of gimmicks past. Owen was wearing his new black, silver and red 'OH' singlet along with The Blue Blazer's baby blue boots, which resulted in quite the clash of colours. He also had on his black and yellow 'Time 4 A Change' t-shirt and the black and white chequered headband from his High Energy days. To complete the look, Owen gelled his hair to stick out in all directions so as to look like he'd gone insane; possibly due to the constant stream of unsavoury storylines Vince Russo and Ed Ferrara had written for him that Owen had recently turned down.

When he got in the ring, Owen uncharacteristically jumped on the second rope and started hitting muscle poses for the 18,000 fans in attendance. When the match began, Owen ran through a greatest hits rendition of all the ridiculous things he'd inflicted on others in matches past. "I remember he would lock up and he would go, 'Bllmphhrrmmphh!'" said

386

Christian. "He'd be like calling a spot to you but he'd be mumbling it and you'd be like, 'What? What?' [Then] he'd throw you off the ropes and be like, 'Just do it!'"

After Christian tagged out, Owen and Edge faced off in the ring and things took a turn for the more curious. "We got into the match and I had [Owen] in an armbar," recalled Edge. "He kipped up and he wound up and gave me a big judo chop with a 'HI-YAH!' and chopped me down." When Christian got tagged back in, Owen set him up for another manoeuvre off the ropes. Unlike his unintelligible mumbling from before, this time Owen was crystal clear in what he was going to hit Christian with. Instead of one of any number of conventional moves expected to be performed on a running opponent (clotheslines, backbody drops, etc), Owen whispered into his opponent's ear, "Watch the Cobra Clutch!" The Cobra Clutch, helpfully defined by Wikipedia, is an 'arm-trap half nelson sleeper' and is as complicated as it sounds to apply, especially to a 230lb wrestler running towards you at full pelt. "[Owen] throws me off the ropes and he somehow got me in a Cobra Clutch," recalled Christian. "I was coming off the ropes and he goes, 'Reverse it', and I go, 'Owen, I don't know how to reverse a Cobra Clutch!'"

The silliness didn't end there. Owen, with his and Jeff's winning streak against the on-screen brothers on the line, decided to bend the rules to regain the upper hand. Debra was at ringside for the match and watched as Owen lifted the ring apron to retrieve that evening's weapon of choice. "I... remember that night because he drug out a bunch of coat hangers from under the ring and he was beating up [Edge and Christian] with a coat hanger. I just remember laughing, it was fun." Owen was no stranger to arming himself with the stupidest weapons imaginable. "He would take popcorn and hit 'em and guys would sell it or he would use a cup; the more ridiculous, the better!" claimed Bruce Prichard. "He used foam fingers 'n' shit; anything that would be ridiculous just to have fun [and] to crack the boys up from time to time."

At the end of the match, Edge and Christian ran wild on Owen and Jeff, with Owen's selling looking just as farcical as his offensive arsenal. "I have a picture of Jay and me shooting Owen into the ropes doing his classic, old school high step, sound effects and all," said Edge. "During the comeback that night he ended up tangled in the ropes upside down on his head, his hair a mess and his eyes crossed as Jeff drawled in his southern accent, "My God! Look at Owen, he's unbelievable!"

When all was said and done, Owen and Jeff squeaked out another win against Edge and Christian, closing the chapter on their tag team rivalry and sadly, Owen's wrestling career. At the age of 34, this would be the last match Owen Hart would ever compete in. "It's nice to be able to look back on things like that," said Edge. "He made us all laugh and he's sorely missed."

CHAPTER 11

The Blazer Returns and Final Storylines

♥ ♥

A week after Owen Hart's rather sudden retirement, the original[1] Blue Blazer returned to the World Wrestling Federation on the live *RAW is WAR* on the 12th of October 1998. The Blazer sneak-attacked Ken Shamrock and Steve Blackman during an Intercontinental Title Tournament match and then jogged back up the entrance ramp with arms *and* cape outstretched. The next week, the Blazer once again attacked Blackman during his match against Jeff Jarrett before escaping once again. There seemed to be an understanding between Jarrett and the now not-so-mysterious masked man as they double-teamed Blackman to deafening chants of 'nugget, nugget, nugget!' The apparently partially-deaf heel commentator Jerry Lawler insisted the fans were actually chanting 'Blazer'. This match would also see the debut of Debra McMichael as Jarrett's valet.

Owen, as The Blue Blazer, would jump Blackman for the next few weeks before turning up as himself on the 2nd of November *RAW*. To the audience's cat calls, Owen apologised again to Dan Severn and confirmed he was no longer on the WWF roster. Severn came out in a neck collar and rejected Owen's apology before accusing him of being the Blazer. After Severn referred to Owen as 'nothing but scum', Owen could take no more and attacked Severn until Steve Blackman came to the rescue. Severn returned on the 28th of December to distract Owen during a tag team match, allowing Blackman to get the pin. In a truly stupid turn of events, Owen defeated Blackman in a Lion's Den match a couple of weeks later on *Sunday Night HeAT* when, for storyline reasons that defy all known rationale, Severn attacked Blackman and aligned himself with Owen. After losing to Blackman on every show in the interim, Servern teamed with Owen and Jarrett to defeat Blackman, The Godfather and Val Venis on the 21st of February before vanishing from the WWF for good, wrapping up one of the most nonsensical storylines of the Attitude Era.

Owen's return on the 2nd of November was meant to be his first televised appearance as himself in a month but a massive blooper occurred at the *Judgment Day* pay-per-view two weeks earlier. Following the conclusion of the main event, Vince McMahon 'fired' special guest referee Stone Cold Steve Austin for declaring himself the winner of the vacant WWF Championship. Austin went on a tirade backstage looking for McMahon. He barged into several rooms until opening a random office door to find Owen, dressed in a hideous blue and red shell suit, talking on a phone. This was completely unplanned and Owen was never meant to be on-screen. According to Vince Russo, "We flew [Owen] in a day early to the pay-per-view so we could talk to him about where we planned on going to next day." Austin improvised and yelled, "Where's Vince at?" Without missing a beat Owen replied, "I dunno... I'm retired!" Lawler similarly improvised, saying on commentary, "That was The Blue Blazer!" eliminating any mystery of the Blazer's identity for the pay-per-view audience.

On the 9th of November *RAW*, Owen Hart *and* The Blue Blazer jumped Steve Blackman, 'proving' that Owen was telling the truth. On the *Survivor Series '98*[2] pre-show, Blackman was recoiling after a loss to Gangrel when The Blue Blazer (definitely Owen Hart this time) slowly descended from the rafters towards the aisle way, flapping his arms like a kestrel. As the crowd chanted 'nugget', the cable Owen was attached to 'accidentally' lowered too far, dragging the Blazer across the ground before suspending him several feet in the air. The Blazer was a sitting duck (or chicken, if the white feathers on his cape were anything to go by) for Blackman. The Lethal Weapon slapped, chopped and kicked Owen like a spangled blue piñata before the cable operators raised Owen back up to the ceiling. It was a really fun little segment designed to spoof WCW's Sting, who was famous for abseiling into the ring to fend off Hulk Hogan's New World Order group. Unfortunately, it would also serve as the inspiration for Owen's fatal *Over the Edge* stunt six months later.

The day after *Survivor Series*, Blackman and Goldust faced off against Jarrett and The Blue Blazer. Blackman pinned Blazer with ease but when The Lethal Weapon was about to reveal the masked man's true identity, Owen ran from the back and jumped him. This time, the Blazer was played by Dr Tom Prichard who was a WWF agent, trainer and website contributor after retiring from full-time wrestling in 1996. The next month would see the Blackman/Blazer/Owen angle continue while commentator Michael Cole[3] would insist that Owen was the Blazer, despite ample evidence to the contrary.

The Blue Blazer also participated in his share of ribs. By 1998, Owen had long since stopped caring about keeping up the pretence of wrestling being real and shared cars with his on-screen rival Blackman. When driving, Owen would purposely get lost and then cajole Blackman into wearing his Blazer mask while he asked strangers for directions. "Owen was the type of guy who'd give a cop the finger just to get you pulled over," former colleague Al Snow quipped. Blackman also picked up a bit of in-ring ribbery from working with Owen. To prank less experienced wrestlers, Owen would have them running back and forth in the ring until they were completely exhausted. "I have seen Owen run 'em off the ropes and they would duck an elbow, duck a clothesline, he'll leap[frog] them, he'll drop down," said Blackman. "[Owen would] keep doing that 'til they were so gassed they couldn't move and they wouldn't pick up on what he's doing. There was always somebody for him to rib... always." On the 7th of December *RAW*, locker room heat magnet Tiger Ali Singh was pitted against Blackman in the hopes that the Shotokan karate black belt would rough him up on live television. Blackman apparently didn't quite understand what the WWF office expected of him and he instead exhausted Singh up by having him incessantly criss-cross the ring like Owen would have probably also done to the Hindu rookie.

On the fateful day of the *Over the Edge* pay-per-view, numerous wrestlers were in catering when Owen, wearing the Blazer mask with his normal clothes, introduced himself to the wrestlers as if he'd never met them before. He walked over to Bob Holly and The Blue Meanie and stuck his hand out. "Hello, I'm the Blue Blazer. Oh yes, Bob Holly, nice to finally meet you. *Blue* Meanie, eh? We may have to do something about that name." "Hey, have you guys seen Owen Hart? I'm supposed to be doing something with him tonight. I've heard some good things about him." Owen's antics proved to be a much needed distraction after Blackman and John 'Bradshaw' Layfield ended up having a fist fight at the airport earlier that morning.[4] "When he put that Blue Blazer outfit on, it was like someone gave him a licence to be the most mischievous one ever," said Dan Severn. "You could see he really enjoyed being that character."

At the *Rock Bottom* pay-per-view on the 13th of December, Owen took on Blackman in front of nearly 18,000 Canadian fans in Vancouver, British Colombia. Despite wrestling as a heel, Owen was cheered like crazy by the crowd. That was until he refused to wrestle anymore and simply walked off to the back as scripted. Three months earlier, the WWF had Owen wear a CFL *Toronto Argonauts* jersey at the *Breakdown* pay-per-view in Hamilton, Ontario just so he would be booed out the building. It's unknown why the WWF booked Owen like this in his home country. While Owen was a heel, he was also the only genuine Canadian star[5] the WWF had on the roster. Booked properly, Owen was still a draw north of the border as evidenced by the huge amount of tickets sold in February for the planned Owen vs. Shawn Michaels grudge matches. Also at *Rock Bottom*, The Blue Blazer ruined the party after Jeff Jarrett lost a match to Goldust where the stipulation was Debra had to take off her clothes if Jarrett lost. Part way through the striptease (complete with *Stripper* by David Rose musical accompaniment) Debra decided she liked the idea of being nude and got into the performance, only for the Blazer to cover her up with his cape.

The next night on *RAW*, Blackman vowed to prove that the Blazer was in fact 'that filthy little nugget' once and for all and then amazingly did just that. After Jarrett interfered in the Blazer vs. Goldust contest, Blackman came down, cleaned house and ripped Owen's mask off to a tremendous reaction from the crowd. With a look of consternation, Owen screamed in abject terror while looking around the arena so the entire audience could see his face. Jarrett put his vest over Owen's head but Owen managed to arrange it so only the vest strap covered his face, adding to the hilarity. The segment was absolutely brilliant and even made it into the end of year montage broadcast two weeks later. On the same episode, Owen, in a completely different hideous blue and red shell suit, bashed Blackman over the head with a guitar.

The storyline wasn't quite finished as a week after the de-masking, Blackman took on The Blue Blazer again, this time with Owen on commentary. Owen claimed that the footage from last week's *RAW* had been doctored to make it look like it was he who was him under the hood. When Michael Cole correctly pointed out that particular episode of *RAW* was in fact a live broadcast, Owen thought about it and then responded with, "It's not me, I don't care!" Blackman managed to rip the mask off of the Blazer again to reveal Jeff Jarrett. As an attempt to conceal Jarrett's identity, Owen pulled the Blazer cape over Jeff's head and shouted, "WHO IS THAT MASKED MAN?" before peaking under the cape and saying, "I don't know who it is!" Owen was great.

On the 21ˢᵗ of December Bret Hart's long-awaited documentary *Hitman: Wrestling with Shadows* was released. Featuring Owen, the film covered the lead up to the Montreal Screwjob and provided the most in-depth look at professional wrestling behind the curtain at that point. Critics raved about the doc and no less an authority than Psychological Professor Jordan B. Peterson called *Wrestling with Shadows*, "One of the best documentaries about anything ever," during one of his YouTube lectures in 2017. While most people who watched the film loved it, Vince McMahon was not one of them. Apart from his disdain for pulling back the curtain to reveal the inner workings of the business at that time, McMahon was reportedly angry that footage was included of him staggering out of the locker room right after Bret punched him out. The WWF Chairman was also furious that Bret and director Paul Jay had secretly recorded a conversation where Bret and Vince agreed to the *Survivor Series* main event ending in a disqualification, disproving some of McMahon's public claims in the preceding thirteen months.

While the Blazer would still pop up from time to time over the coming months, the storyline was pretty much done for the time being. For years there had been speculation that Owen was being punished by being booked in the angle but all evidence points to the fact that, while not doing much for his career as far as upward mobility is concerned, Owen quite enjoyed portraying The Blue Blazer character. The angle was good, clean, wholesome fun, was well orchestrated and the fans got into the storyline as it developed. It also kept Owen out of angles that he felt were inappropriate for his children to watch, which seemingly made up 75% of World Wrestling Federation programming at the time.[6]

When asked in December 1998 if the WWF had gone too far, Owen replied, "Well a lot of people feel it has. There's pros and cons to that: the ratings are unbelievable, wrestling is hotter than it's ever been in its history, sell-out crowds everywhere... there's definite success." As far as his own views on the WWF creative direction, Owen said, "It's getting violent, it's getting a little cruder than I'd personally like for my own children... I just don't allow them to watch [WWF programming] but everyone's got their own freedom of democracy to do whatever they want. Personally, anything I do, I'm proud to say I can let my children watch or any other fans, they might not agree with the dirty tactics that I do but I make sure what I do as a professional athlete in and outside the ring is acceptable to my family [and] my friends and I want to uphold the Hart reputation as being a true professional."

Real-life friends Owen and Jeff Jarrett would become a full-time tag team in January, defeating The Brood and The New Age Outlaws before taking on the Tag Team Champions Ken Shamrock and the Big Boss Man on the 25th of January *RAW*. Owen and Jeff had been picking up wins thanks to Debra's own silicon tag team distracting their opponents. A skit earlier in the evening saw the Tag Team Champions drink saltpetre (the powder supposedly given to soldiers to retard sexual arousal during the war) to immune them from Debra's advances. When Debra climbed on the ring apron in just her bra, The World's Least Aroused Man ignored her prodigious shirt potatoes and cinched Owen in the ankle lock. With the referee distracted (which happened constantly during this time period) The Blue Blazer ran from the back and smashed Shamrock over the head with a guitar. This Blazer looked a little... different to the others. This evening for one night only, the Blazer was played by Owen's former High Energy tag team partner Koko B Ware. Koko, for those who don't know, is black. While Owen pinned Shamrock surrounded by guitar fragments to win the

Tag Team Titles, The Black Blazer stumbled back up the ramp, never to appear again. In fact, it was never mentioned on television that Koko was under the mask, begging the question why the WWF went out of their way to book him in the first place. The new Tag Team Champions were interviewed on the entrance ramp by Kevin Kelly where Owen cheered, "I've finally been vindicated! I said all along I'm not The Blue Blazer and now tonight it proves beyond a shadow of a doubt that I am *not* The Blue Blazer!"

In the run up to *WrestleMania*, Owen and Jarrett struck up a rivalry with the newly dubbed 'Sexual Chocolate' Mark Henry and D'Lo Brown after they took offence to Henry's advances towards Debra. To distract Mark from Debra, D'Lo brought in Ivory (Lisa Moretti who played Tina Ferrari in the original GLOW) to be some sort of undefined sex slave. With Ivory now in Henry and Brown's corner, both tag teams became inconsequential to the inevitable crowd-pleasing cat fight that would ensue, which happened every week in various forms. Jarrett, who was a bland heel, had benefited greatly from Debra's presence since her introduction in October but Owen just seemed to be dragged down to a distant third in the three-person act, although the crowd still delighted in chanting 'nugget' whenever Owen got in the ring.

On the 7th of March edition of *Sunday Night HeAT*, Owen tried to interfere in a match between Road Dogg and Jeff Jarrett when The Blue Blazer ran in. Like always, Debra was causing a distraction with her heaving busties when Owen ascended the top rope. The Blazer blocked Owen's path and shouted, "Woo!" Owen, being a great idiot heel, gave the masked man a big thumbs up before finding himself being crotched on the top rope. This time, D'Lo donned the blue mask, bringing the total number of people who were known to have played the Blazer in the WWF over the past few months to at least six (Steve Blackman had also once portrayed the Blazer to sneak-attack Owen). The Federation seamstresses surely had their work cut out for them making all those extra outfits.

On television and house shows, Owen and Jeff defeated every single team they came up against. With no clear number one contenders to their Tag Team Titles, a battle royal was held on the *WrestleMania XV* pre-show. The last two wrestlers remaining would challenge Owen and Jarrett on the *WrestleMania* pay-per-view, which ended up being won by D'Lo Brown and newcomer Test. Owen and Jarrett were performing guest commentary during the twenty-one man mêlée. Owen was on fire, making snide or ridiculous remarks throughout. When asked who he thought might win, Owen claimed it didn't matter because he and Jeff were, "In a world of [their] own." When Tiger Ali Singh, who nobody in the audience or the locker room liked because he was terrible, was thrown out of the ring, Owen dryly observed that, "The popular Hindu performer has been eliminated!" Owen called his old foe Steve Blackman 'Steve Blackburn' before declaring that "fatigue is settling in right now; these guys are tired, they've been going twenty minutes," when in actuality it had been only four. Needless to say when Brown and Test challenged Owen and Jarrett for the belts, Debra and Ivory got into an argument that distracted the referee and all the fans, allowing Owen and Jarrett to pick up another win.

On the 5th of April *RAW is WAR*, Owen and Jarrett lost the Tag Titles to the makeshift tag team of X-Pac and Kane. Ever since his dealings with Vince McMahon's Corporation faction, Kane had become one of the Federations most popular acts. X-Pac was riding a wave of momentum ever since Triple H turned on him at *WrestleMania XV* and began acting as a sort of storyline life coach, helping the disturbed monster Kane relate to his fellow man. Kane teased turning on X-Pac but instead slammed him onto Jarrett for the win to the enormous delight of the audience. At the 17th of April house show in the Calgary Saddledome, Bret walked into a WWF locker room for the first time since Montreal nearly eighteen months earlier. Owen had insisted Bret turn up and Bret's boss Eric Bischoff had been enthusiastic about Bret being seen in a WWF locker room, as he had recently 'quit' WCW in a storyline involving Bill Goldberg.[7]

While Owen and Jarrett entered into a brief rivalry with the New Age Outlaws for a return match against the new champs, a two hour special called *WWF Smackdown!* debuted on UPN on the 29th of April. The very first match of the very first *Smackdown!* was scheduled to be Val Venis vs. Owen Hart. In the back, Jarrett and Debra couldn't find Owen anywhere. The camera then cut to a shot of The Blue Blazer's cape as he ran down the hallway. "The WWF *needs* a superhero," cheered the Blazer, "and I'm here to bring 'em one! Woo!" In an interesting piece of trivia, Owen picked up the very first victory on the very first *Smackdown!* in history, with the aid of Debra and Jarrett, of course.

You may be asking why Owen reverted back to The Blue Blazer character in late 1998 and April 1999 after his triple act with Jarrett and Debra was going so well? Owen had recently turned down several storylines and ideas from writers Vince Russo and Ed Ferrara, including getting his crotch fondled by androgynous weirdo Goldust. Owen also turned down getting felt up by Terri Runnels, who was playing the part of yet another sex-crazed, fake-boobied saucepot running around the World Wrestling Federation for no particular reason. "[Wrestling] had turned so raunchy," recalled Martha. "There was going to be a blow-up eventually because Owen couldn't keep saying, 'No I can't do this, no I can't do that'. Everything they wanted him to do was 'no' because everything was so dirty and filthy and raunchy and corrupt." One of the more innocent suggestions Owen turned down was becoming the latest victim of 'Mr Socko', Mankind's sock puppet, which Mankind would wear on his hand while applying the dreaded 'Mandible Claw'. The Mandible Claw was developed by Dr Sam Sheppard, who the film *The Fugitive* was based on and in storyline was meant to paralyse the sufferer. Owen objected to the Socko Claw on account of the sock being kept down the front of Mankind's tights before it was slipped on. "He thought it held sexual connotations," claimed Martha. Or maybe it was just that Owen placed more value on hygiene than the rest of his colleagues.

The kicker for Owen was when he was written into a storyline where he was to fall in love with Debra and feud with a jealous Jarrett. Martha was even asked to participate in the angle somewhat by giving a kayfabe interview to *WWF Magazine* addressing Owen's storyline infidelity. Smith Hart once gave his two cents on Vince Russo's booking philosophy in regards to women. "[Russo] seems to like that kinky stuff, where somebody's wearing a diaper or someone is seen naked or something. He was a distributor of videos, maybe he got into too much pornography?" While it might have been a fun idea for a TV angle, Owen was absolutely dead set against it, not wanting to upset his family who barely saw him as it was. Russo told Owen, "No problem, we'll do something else." Shortly thereafter, Owen became The Blue Blazer again. While it wasn't the ideal scenario, Owen went along with the return of the Blazer, as well as the rappel stunt at *Over the Edge* because he'd turned down so many proposed storylines in the past few months. Owen was paying for Oje and Athena's private education and with a big house being built and a potential third child planned, he didn't want to jeopardise his financial situation by being overly difficult to WWF management.

When the Blazer character returned in late April, Owen added the character trait of being what Jim Ross described on commentary as a 'nerdy do-gooder' who told fans to say their prayers, eat their vitamins and drink their milk; just like Hulk Hogan did in his 1980s heyday. Owen's only request to Russo was that he win the Intercontinental Championship to give the Blazer some much-needed credibility.[8] There have been suggestions from people close to the situation that the third Blazer stint was just a stopgap before reconfiguring Owen's character once again. After the Blazer gimmick had run its course, Owen was going go gimmick-free and just be himself; a second-generation wrestler who beat his opponents in the middle of the ring by out-wrestling them. This is what he had wanted ever since re-signing with the World Wrestling Federation in late 1997. According to Triple H, 'The Game' moniker, which Helmsley took on himself shortly after turning heel (supposedly as a tribute) was originally going to be given to Owen. With the upcoming debuts of super talented smaller wrestlers like Eddie Guerrero, Dean Malenko and his old friend Chris Benoit just a few months away, Owen would have had plenty of intriguing matchups and rivalries lined up for him in the year 2000 and beyond.

On the 10th of May, Owen Hart pinned Olympic freestyle wrestling gold medallist Kurt Angle in a pre-*RAW* dark match. The WWF had big things planned for Angle since he signed with the company the previous year.[9] After their match, Owen told WWF officials that Angle had the makings of a future World Champion, which was a big compliment coming from somebody as respected as Owen. As well known as Owen was for being a prankster and the life and soul of the locker room, he was also just as appreciated for his kindness in a cutthroat business.

A few months earlier, veteran women's wrestler Luna Vachon was given the unenviable task of leading Sable through a singles match live at the *Royal Rumble* '99 pay-per-view. Thanks almost entirely to Luna, the untrained, untalented Sable came across like a five year veteran. When they returned to the back, Champaign corks were popped and everyone congratulated Sable on what a fantastic job she'd done. Luna, who'd led her by the hand through the match, was completely ignored. Owen specifically sought her out, told her what a great job she'd done and hugged her while she cried on his shoulder. When the beloved, all-time great manager and commentator Bobby Heenan left the WWF in 1993, Owen, who barely knew him, was one of the very few people to walk up to him, shake his hand and thank him for all he'd done for the profession. Many wrestlers have talked about benefiting from Owen's wisdom over the years, from how to survive on the road through to career advice. So many of Owen's peers talk of tales of his pranks but just as many talk about his kindness, his giving nature and his love for his family.

As Jarrett and Debra segued into a feud with Val Venis, Owen began an issue with the WWF's resident pimp and new Intercontinental Champion, The Godfather. Owen snatched Debra to the back after she seemingly accepted The Godfather's invitation to be his latest employee on the 26th of April *RAW*. Somehow, this act of not letting his friend become Godfather's latest labourer in sexual servitude led to Owen being announced as the number one contender to his Intercontinental Title. On the 17th of May episode of *RAW*, Owen once again dressed as The Blue Blazer and teamed with Jarrett to take on their mutual rivals The Godfather and Val Venis. If Debra's presence wasn't distracting enough already, the fun-loving pimp from Las Vegas turned up with no less than five restaurant-quality beauties corralled from a local strip joint to act as his 'ho's' for the evening. Owen had modified his wrestling style to incorporate more high flying moves straight out of the 1980s playbook, including the once crowd pleasing top rope crossbody attack. After a couple of minutes of wrestling action, The Godfather beat the number one contender to the IC Title clean in the middle of the ring.

This was Owen's last televised wrestling match.

[1]**The word 'original' needs to be applied as Mexican promotion CMLL saw the debut of 'The Blue Blazer II' a couple of months earlier. Former WWF and All Japan wrestler Phil LaFon assumed the gimmick**

(possibly without permission) to take part in a number of trios (three-person) tag team matches throughout August and September before disappearing again. LaFon's *lucha* mask was nothing like the original Blazer's and neither were his tights, which were unmistakeably the same ones LaFon donned while wrestling in the WWF less than a year earlier.

[2]One year after the Montreal Screwjob, The Rock and Mankind met in the main event of *Survivor Series '98*. With Vince McMahon at ringside, the recently turned babyface Rock put McMahon's corporate puppet Mankind in the Sharpshooter. Without Mankind yielding to the submission, McMahon once again instructed timekeeper Mark Yeaton to, "RING THE DAMN BELL," allowing The Rock to win the WWF Title, turn heel and align himself with the evil McMahon family. The real-life Screwjob ended up being repurposed as one of the most creative finishes of 1998. The Bret vs. Shawn Sharpshoot finish would be ripped off and parodied countless times over the years with far less success. Two weeks before *Survivor Series '98*, former wrestler Jesse 'The Body' Ventura shocked the world by becoming Governor of Minnesota as an independent. In response, NBC quickly knocked up a made-for-TV movie of Ventura's life. Broadcast in May 1999, *The Jesse Ventura Story* would be a biography in the very loosest of terms as practically nothing shown in the film bore any resemblance to his life. This included Jesse becoming disgusted with wrestling after 'Chaney' (an allegory for McMahon) screwed 'Captain Nice' (who never existed) after WCW wrestler Raven (?) locked him in the Sharpshooter at a WCW event. Despite the fact Ventura hadn't had anything to do with wrestling for several years at that time, the writers added the Screwjob-esque narrative because... well, nobody has figured that one out as of yet.

[3]Junior announcer Michael Cole replaced Jim Ross as lead commentator for several months in 1998 and 1999. Ross suffered a second bout of Bell's palsy in the middle of the UK-exclusive *Capital Combat* pay-per-view on the 6th of December. The attack came one day after Ross received the devastating news that his mother had died of a sudden heart attack while he was flying to London. Upon his on-screen return several

months later, Good Ol' JR was scripted as bitter about Cole taking over his place in the commentary booth and made reference to unnamed WWF officials (most likely including Executive Producer Kevin Dunn) not wanting him on television because he was too old, southern and ugly, especially after the Bell's palsy paralysed half his face. What WWF decision makers hadn't counted on was that Jim Ross was easily one of the greatest announcers in wrestling history and beloved by the fans and Michael Cole absolutely wasn't. If it were not for Steve Austin and The Rock insisting he call their *WrestleMania XV* main event match, Ross might never have made it back to the WWF commentary booth at all. "I was going through a tough time," said Ross, who was still dealing with the physical and mental effects of his latest Bell's palsy attack. "I was producing announce talent and I was happy to do it. But I really believed that *WrestleMania* was my last one and I appreciated the fact that Vince [McMahon] decided to go with me in the main event because he knew that we'd signed two potentially all-time greats."

[4]"[John 'Bradshaw' Layfield] got on [Steve] Blackman's nerves a little too much," Sean 'X-Pac' Waltman explained. "Blackman is... not one to fuck with to put it mildly. JBL pushed him a little too far and Blackman snapped and he went to punch John and he got his foot caught in the straps of a fuckin' duffle bag sitting on the ground. This is all happening at baggage claim [and] we're waiting for our bags. So as he goes to punch him he gets his foot caught in the strap and can't get the punch off and... John tee'd him; hit him about two or three times boom boom boom and [other wrestlers] broke it up. No one got hurt or anything but it was fucked up for Steve 'cause that's not how, ya know, Steve wanted that to go down. But that was how that fuckin' day started off!"

[5]There were plenty of wrestlers on the roster from Canada but Owen was the only wrestler whose Canadian heritage was an intrinsic part of his character ever since Bret had been forced out of the company the year before.

[6]Recently with: DX telling everyone to suck it, porn stars, pimps, sex addicts and scantily clad ladies everywhere, the renewed use of weapons and blood, Terri Runnels claiming she suffered a miscarriage when she was never pregnant and a fat woman deep-throating a giant sausage (yes, that happened), *RAW* was getting harder to justify as a show marketed towards children, which made up a significant portion of the viewing audience. Back in 1995, Owen replied to a fan asking about wrestlers taking shortcuts by using weapons. "I don't like the violence. I like to do what I think the people would like to watch. I think if you can be hated just by using your personality and not a frying pan than you can make it far."

[7]Bret's in-ring career would end at the hands of an errant Goldberg kick on the 19th of December WCW pay-per-view *Starrcade '99*. Bret suffered a concussion so severe that, when he finally got it checked out three weeks later, the doctor barred him from: wrestling, flying, working out or even watching television. In October 2000, WCW curtly fired him citing his 'ongoing incapacity'. This was only the start of Bret's health problems. On the 24th of June 2002, Bret fell off his bicycle after hitting a pothole. After hitting the ground, Bret suffered a stroke, from which he would take several years to properly recover. In 2006, Bret accepted a WWE Hall of Fame induction, then in 2010, he returned to WWE as an in-ring participant, albeit without taking any bumps or shots to the head, against Vince McMahon at *WrestleMania XXVI*. While the build up to the match made for excellent television, the match itself was terrible and seemingly never ending. All of the Hart siblings had reunited for the event after a decade of turmoil to act as outside enforcers, while Bruce Hart was announced as the special guest referee. Bret ended up participating in another ten matches for the WWE, with his last occurring on the 12th of September 2011 at the age of 54.

[8]The Intercontinental Championship was fast losing credibility due to all the recent Title changes. Between February and April 1999, the belt changed hands four times.

[9]The WWF actually had big things planned for Angle back in 1996. Around the same time McMahon offered Olympic weightlifter Mark Henry a ten year contract, he also offered Angle the same deal. Angle told McMahon that he'd be willing to sign but as an Olympic gold medallist he couldn't lose. "He looked at me like I was crazy," Angle said. "I took the contract home and waited for Vince to call me and he never called me. He thought, 'This kid doesn't get it.'" After Angle became more familiar with the product, he was given a tryout with the Federation in 1998.

Epilogue

In 1997, Owen revealed his post-wrestling retirement plans. "I'd probably be a full-time fireman in Calgary or a schoolteacher. I would teach history or English if I could. And I would also coach football and wrestling. I plan to coach both in a few years when I am done wrestling." Martha recalled that he liked the idea of running a bike shop after his in-ring days were over. Owen had no desire to be treated as a celebrity after his exit from the spotlight. "I would like to kind of just disappear from wrestling fans and stuff. I don't want to forget the fans and what they've done... I don't want to be hanging on like one of these wrestlers who's sixty years old saying, 'Hey, I'm a wrestler.' Let it go. Make your money out of it and get on. I really want to devote a lot of time to my family."

Owen himself confirmed he may not leave wrestling totally behind after his WWF contract ended in 2001. "I might do ten weeks a year in Japan. Something just to motivate me to keep in shape, keep involved a little bit but not have to deal with the politics." Owen was also mindful of not getting trapped in the occupation's vice-like grip many wrestlers find themselves caught in, whether it's the money or the inability to leave the spotlight behind. "I'd like to get out of wrestling totally when I'm done. I say that now but I'll probably end up being involved with it until I'm Ric Flair's age (who was pushing 50 at the time)." In another interview, Owen elaborated further. "This business is very addictive. I've seen many people say I'm quitting or I'm getting out of it and just can't."

Most of all, Owen wanted to be able to return to his wife and children every night and enjoy what he craved most; a 'normal' life. When asked by a fan, Owen described his home life on a rare day off the road. "Every second that I'm home I spend doing something. Taking my son to hockey practice, my daughter to swimming, ballet or music, little Gymboree classes. My son's into piano. So, between all that, just taking them out and playing in the yard or tobogganing." After signing one of the WWF's first guaranteed contracts back in 1996, Owen and Martha had started planning their dream house. Shortly after McMahon re-signed him to the tune of approximately $450,000 per year, Owen purchased two acres of land on a lake in Calgary for CA$800,000, with construction beginning in 1998. Owen, Martha, Oje and Athena were scheduled to move into their new house a few days after *Over the Edge*.

Career-wise, Owen continually expressed his desire to stick with the World Wrestling Federation, even after Montreal. When asked (as he often was) about the possibility of going to WCW, Owen replied, "I have no desire to go down there, I'm very happy with the WWF. There's been a lot of speculation about it and I know all my family went down there and I had an opportunity to go down there. I talked to Vince McMahon about a year ago and he was a man of his word and he fulfilled all his commitments that he promised me. I have no desire to go down there. I have my friends in the WWF." Wrestling-wise, Owen wished to one day reunite with Bret, Davey Boy and Jim Neidhart "I wish my family would come back to the WWF because truly that's where The Hart Foundation belongs is right back in the WWF. We'll get it back together and reunite one day, I hope."

Bruce Hart postulated that the World Wrestling Federation didn't treat Owen as well as he deserved to be treated. "I honestly never felt he was allowed to approach his true potential down there, which is too damned bad." Bruce went on to speculate why Owen never received a sustained main event push. "I suspect his disdain for all the political machinations, the rampant ass-kissing, stooging, backstabbing and behind the scenes crap was one of the main reasons he never got the really strong push he should have. He loved the wrestling end of the business but disdained all the insidious dressing room bullshit which had become so pervasive within the business."

Since his passing, there has been much debate on whether Owen would have ever become World Wrestling Federation Champion. During Owen's initial heel run with Bret, Vince McMahon seriously considered having Owen win the Title, as confirmed by WWE Producer Bruce Prichard. "There was a time, right after *WrestleMania X* during that whole run with Bret, that (Owen winning the title) was brought up." Current WWE Executive Vice President Paul 'Triple H' Levesque believed that Owen becoming WWF/WWE Champion was unlikely. "Owen saw this [business] as a career where he could make some money [and] take care of his family. Then he was done with it." Levesque continued, "Being a top guy requires a lot more commitment time-wise [and] responsibility-wise. You know, it's a lot more than they just give you [the WWE Championship] and say, 'Just do what you've been doing.' There's a lot more to it. It requires more work. It requires more time. It requires more effort and I don't know that Owen was willing to do that, but it doesn't change the fact that he's one of the best guys I've ever been in the ring with. Owen was an incredible performer."

The issue of Owen potentially being inducted into the WWE Hall of Fame has been hotly debated over the years, not just by fans but by family members. Over the years, Martha has been obstinately against letting WWE 'exploit Owen's image for commercial gain', which includes WWE inducting him into their Hall of Fame. As Martha still holds WWE and Vince McMahon responsible for Owen's death, this is a perfectly understandable reaction. Some view Martha's stance as her attempt to erase Owen's wrestling legacy. Bret Hart, who reconciled with McMahon in the mid 2000s, wrote on his Facebook page, "For Martha to want to rewrite history, to refuse to acknowledge or recognize his great wrestling career, to brush off what he, myself and my father did as, 'that fake stuff,' is wrong." Both points of view have their merits. Hall of Fame-wise, Owen's World Wrestling Federation career speaks for itself, easily surpassing a number of existing inductees who didn't accomplish anywhere near as much as he did, or enjoyed their greatest success in other promotions. In 2018, Owen Hart was posthumously inducted into the George Tragos/Lou Thesz Professional Wrestling Hall of Fame.

When asked how he'd like to be remembered by the fans, Owen said, "It's kind of an art to going out and performing. I'd like fans to remember me as a guy who would go out and entertain them, give them quality matches and not just the same old garbage every week." At the end of his life, Owen was thoroughly fed up with what wrestling had become; *The Jerry Springer Show* in tights. The last time his parents saw their youngest son wasn't the most pleasant of exchanges. Shortly after his passing, Owen's mother Helen revealed, "The last time [Owen] was here [at Hart House] he said, 'Dad, you know what? I don't want to talk about wrestling. I just can't stand talking about it. I'm so sick of it.' A few minutes after that, he had to go. That was the last time we saw him."

On the 15th of June 1999, Martha announced her intention to sue: the World Wrestling Federation's parent company Titan Sports, Inc., Vince McMahon and twelve other defendants, the makers of the harness and the snap shackle and the City of Kansas City, Missouri. The lawsuit tore apart the Hart family, who were split between family members supporting Martha, family members who were quick to publicly exonerate McMahon and the WWF for their own financial gain and family members who were stuck in between. In November 2000, the World Wrestling Federation settled with Martha for an estimated $18 million: $10 million for Martha, $3 million each for his two children and $2 million for Owen's parents. With her share of the settlement, Martha set up The Owen Hart Foundation to provide university scholarships and a home owner's programme for low income families in the Calgary area.

The Blue Blazer and The Godfather were scheduled to meet at the *Over the Edge* pay-per-view on the 23rd of May 1999, where Owen was booked to win the Intercontinental Championship for the third time. The following promo aired right before the match was scheduled to take place.

Kevin Kelly, "Well, Blue Blazer, you've got a big match tonight, going after the Intercontinental Championship taking on The Godfather.

Owen Hart: "Ooh! The Godfather, just saying his name makes my blue blood boil! Ooh! The Godfather, my arch-nemesis. He represents everything that's wrong with the WWF. But fear not, because I, The Blue Blazer, will always triumph over evil doers and do you know why? Because I always take my vitamins, say my prayers and drink my milk! Wooo!"

The End

References

Television

Every episode of *WWF RAW* from January 1993 to May 1999, every WWF pay-per-view from November 1988 to May 1999, various episodes of *WWF Superstars, Wrestling Challenge, Shotgun Saturday Night, Sunday Night Heat, The Slammy Awards,* the debut episode of *WWF Smackdown!* and an episode of *Saturday Night's Main Event.* Shows and clips that feature Owen from the following promotions were also viewed and referenced: WCW, CWA, NJPW, World of Sport, TWA, Stampede, USWA and WAR.

The John Gallagher Show (1998). TSN, December 9th 1998
Hitman Hart: Wrestling with Shadows (1998). High Road Productions Inc. and National Film Board of Canada, December 20th 1998.
Biography: The Life and Death of Owen Hart (1999). A&E, November 16 1999.
Dark Side of the Ring S01E02 – The Montreal Screwjob (2018). Viceland, 17 April 2019.
WWE Confidential (2002). WWE/USA Network, May 25 2002.

DVD/VHS

Warrior Workout 1 (1995) [VHS], 1995.
Jake 'The Snake' Roberts – Pick Your Poison (2004) [DVD], WWE
The Self-Destruction of The Ultimate Warrior (2005) [DVD], WWE, 2005
WWE Hall of Fame 2006 (2006) [DVD], WWE
Stone Cold Steve Austin: The Bottom Line on the Most Popular Superstar of All Time (2011) [DVD], WWE
Owen Hart: Hart of Gold (2013) [DVD], WWE
Jim Cornette – Live in London (2014) [DVD], WrestleTalk TV, 2014
The Resurrection of Jake The Snake (2015) [DVD], Steve Yu, Slamdance
Shoot Interview with Ahmed Johnson [DVD] Highspots
Highspots - Shoot Interview with Mr. Hughes [DVD] Highspots
Back to the Territories: Amarillo with Jim Cornette and Terry Funk (2015) [DVD] Kayfabe Commentaries
Back to the Territories: Houston with Jim Cornette and Bruce Prichard (2018) [DVD] Kayfabe Commentaries

Breaking Kayfabe with Lanny Poffo (2012) [DVD] Kayfabe Commentaries

Breaking Kayfabe with Troy Martin (2013) [DVD] Kayfabe Commentaries

Guest Booker with Kevin Nash (2015) [DVD] Kayfabe Commentaries

Timeline History of ECW 1992-93 with Tod Gordon (2016) [DVD] Kayfabe Commentaries

Timeline History of WCW 1991 with Barry Windham (2013) [DVD] Kayfabe Commentaries

Timeline History of WWE 1986 with George "The Animal" Steele (2012) [DVD] Kayfabe Commentaries

Timeline History of WWE 1987 with Honky Tonk Man (2009) [DVD] Kayfabe Commentaries

Timeline History of WWE 1988 with Hacksaw Jim Duggan (2009) [DVD] Kayfabe Commentaries

Timeline History of WWE 1992 with Bret Hart (2014) [DVD] Kayfabe Commentaries

Timeline History of WWE 1994 with Sean Waltman (2014) [DVD] Kayfabe Commentaries

Timeline History of WWE 1995 with Kevin Nash (2012) [DVD] Kayfabe Commentaries

Timeline History of WWE 1997 with Jim Cornette (2011) [DVD] Kayfabe Commentaries

Timeline History of WWE 1998 with Vince Russo (2015) [DVD] Kayfabe Commentaries

Timeline History of WWE 1999 with Sean Morley (2012) [DVD] Kayfabe Commentaries

Vince Russo's Attitude with Terri Runnels (2018) [DVD] Kayfabe Commentaries

YouShoot with Honky Tonk Man (2007) [DVD] Kayfabe Commentaries

YouShoot with Jamie Dundee (2008) [DVD] Kayfabe Commentaries

YouShoot with Jim Cornette (2010) [DVD] Kayfabe Commentaries

YouShoot with Scott Hall (2015) [DVD] Kayfabe Commentaries

YouShoot with Sean Waltman (2010) [DVD] Kayfabe Commentaries

YouShoot with Shane Douglas (2012) [DVD] Kayfabe Commentaries

YouShoot with Tammy Sytch (2012) [DVD] Kayfabe Commentaries

YouShoot with Tony Atlas (2011) [DVD] Kayfabe Commentaries

Tony Atlas: Vices (2018) [DVD] MWF

Mabel/Viscera Shoot Interview (2009) [DVD] Pro Wrestling Diaries

Bad News Allen Shoot Interview [DVD] RF Video

Charles Wright Shoot Interview [DVD] RF Video

D'Lo Brown Shoot Interview [DVD] RF Video

Harley Race Shoot Interview [DVD] RF Video

Jim 'The Anvil' Neidhart Shoot Interview [DVD] RF Video

Konnan Shoot Interview [DVD] RF Video

Missy Hyatt & Tammy Sytch Shoot Interview [DVD] RF Video

Mr Fuji Shoot Interview [DVD] RF Video

Road Warriors Shoot Interview [DVD] RF Video

Steve Blackman Shoot Interview [DVD] RF Video

Terry Taylor Shoot Interview [DVD] RF Video

ROH Straight Shootin' Series with Percy Pringle [DVD] Ring of Honor

Online Videos

Alicia Atout – AMBY Interviews (2017) *Jake "The Snake" Roberts interview.* Available at: https://www.youtube.com/watch?v=YjlR-Agw8tk

Jordan B. Peterson YouTube channel (2017) *2017 Maps of Meaning 03: Marionettes and Individuals (Part 2).* Available at: https://www.youtube.com/watch?v=Us979jCjHu8

MrHollywood TV (2016) *Dan Severn Talks UFC, WWE, Undertaker, Owen Hart and Ken Shamrock.* Available at: https://www.youtube.com/watch?v=YKoEC1ifGTM

ESPN films WWE production meeting (2014). Available at: https://www.youtube.com/watch?v=_P5GoNCsJ3E

ECW wrestlers talk about the KLIQ (2009, original footage 1997). Available at: https://www.youtube.com/watch?v=U_7v8nMGPOQ

Peter Rosenberg (2009) *Peter Rosenberg Interviews Triple H Days before Wrestlemania.* Available at: https://www.youtube.com/watch?v=l0sj-i4U2tc

Kalle Beck (2018) *Bill Kazmaier – Remembering Terry Todd - July 30th, 2018.* Available at: https://www.youtube.com/watch?v=lj8cUyWy87w

American Journal Chuck Austin news piece (2016, originally mid-1990s) Available at: https://www.youtube.com/watch?v=zb02_HEdEFM

Peter Rosenberg (2011) *Wrestling with Rosenberg: Mick Foley.* Available at: https://www.youtube.com/watch?v=-DPwPn7TtRk&t=312s

1WrestlingVideo (2013) *HOWARD "THE FINK" FINKEL TALKS BOSS VINCE, CAREER & MORE @THE APTER CHAT.* Available at: https://www.youtube.com/watch?v=MmR694lIc_Y

Pro Wrestling Stories (2015, original date unknown) *Savio Vega on Owen Hart.* Available at: https://www.youtube.com/watch?v=zjhQUVuU5mw

Team Davey Boy Smith (2015) *Former WCW & WWE Superstar Marc Mero.* Available at: https://www.youtube.com/watch?v=GE5IS5BQnO4

The Hannibal TV (2019) *B. Brian Blair on Dynamite Kid & Outback Jack.* Available at: https://www.youtube.com/watch?v=PTNAY8VoT9k

The Hannibal TV (2016) *Bruce Hart Full Shoot Interview! (Bret Hart's Brother).* Available at: https://www.youtube.com/watch?v=Z28ru-QkyUk

The Hannibal TV (2018) *David Schultz on Stampede Wrestling & The Bulldogs!* Available at: https://www.youtube.com/watch?v=PjAKL7bksrg

The Hannibal TV (2018) *Diana Hart Smith Full Shoot Interview.* Available at: https://www.youtube.com/watch?v=uPBL6rYHdQs

The Hannibal TV (2014) *GEORGE CHUVALO ON OWEN HART KO.* Available at: https://www.youtube.com/watch?v=xQSoudVoOic

The Hannibal TV (2019) Greg *Valentine on Brutal Ribs to Outback Jack.* Available at: https://www.youtube.com/watch?v=5iFipWcHEbs

The Hannibal TV (2018) *Jason Sensation on Suicide Threat at Raw in Toronto.* Available at: https://www.youtube.com/watch?v=EXICZr-Di3U&feature=emb_title

The Hannibal TV (2018) *Keith Hart on Owen Hart, Stampede Wrestling & more!* Available at: https://www.youtube.com/watch?v=0il7kjnAVjE

The Hannibal TV (2017) *Larry Zbyszko on Ken Patera Incident.* Available at: https://www.youtube.com/watch?v=Q_HjJeojkgI

The Hannibal TV (2019) *Marty Jannetty on Chuck Austin Paralyzation Incident.* Available at: https://www.youtube.com/watch?v=ktQjaMdIOZ8

The Hannibal TV (2017) *Psycho Sid on Brian Pillman Squeegee Incident.* Available at: https://www.youtube.com/watch?v=poLZyZ6cPtk

The Hannibal TV (2016) *Ray Rougeau on Boxing Owen Hart.* Available at: https://www.youtube.com/watch?v=tEwyJskobCs

The Hannibal TV (2017) *Road Warrior Animal on "Rocco" LOD Puppet.* Available at: https://www.youtube.com/watch?v=rdOD8yPZ3mI

The Hannibal TV (2017) *Road Warrior Animal on Sunny.* Available at: https://www.youtube.com/watch?v=l9qMBj3o1yM

The Hannibal TV (2017) *Rocky Johnson on Shawn Michaels Incident.* Available at: https://www.youtube.com/watch?v=5tMvnOUk6JA

The Hannibal TV (2015) *Smith Hart on Owen Hart WWE Settlement.* Available at: https://www.youtube.com/watch?v=VCN_ElNVACY

The Hannibal TV (2016) *Tiger Jackson AKA Dink Full Shoot Interview.* Available at: https://www.youtube.com/watch?v=fXo2huOV6hk

Thisis50 (2015) *WWE Legend Mark Henry Tells Untold OWEN HART Story; Top 10 Wrestlers, Wrestling Since 1996.* Available at: https://www.youtube.com/watch?v=VyyAirdLP_k

Tyler Daschuk (2014) *Scott Hall Shoots on Randy Savage, Owen Hart, Hall of Fame, Mania 9 & 10.* Available at: https://www.youtube.com/watch?v=-LV0cNWRcCM

Vince Russo (2016) *Jason Sensation (WWE/WWF) - Shoot Interview w/ Vince Russo - Swerve*

Archive. Available at: https://www.youtube.com/watch?v=Dzp1tEh2du0

WGRZ-TV (2017) *Lex Luger Interview: Part 1.* Available at: https://www.youtube.com/watch?v=k7zxcx69Fyc

WWE.com (1997) *Experience WWE fandom on the Wrestle Vessel.* Available at: https://www.wwe.com/videos/experience-wwe-fandom-on-the-wrestle-vessel

X-Pac interview (2015) original source unknown. Available at: https://www.youtube.com/watch?v=Q3owtzRMYD0&t=104s

WWE.com (2018) *Meet WWE's longest-tenured referee: Making WWE.* Available at https://www.wwe.com/videos/meet-wwes-longest-tenured-referee-making-wwe

Podcasts/Radio Shows

Sean Waltman (2019) *X-Pac 12360 – Remembering Owen Hart & Double or Nothing preview* [Podcast]. Available at (http://apple.com/itunes/)

Sean Waltman (2017) *X-Pac 12360 – Road Dogg Sits Down With X-Pac #40* [Podcast]. Available at (http://apple.com/itunes/)

False Count Radio (2010) *False Count Radio: Owen Hart Tribute Show* [Podcast]. Available at (https://falsecountradio.libsyn.com/)

Jim Ross (2019) *Grilling JR - The Night We Lost Owen* [Podcast]. Available at (http://apple.com/itunes/)

MLW Radio (2018) *Why It Ended... with Robbie E #7 - D'Lo Brown* [Podcast]. Available at (https://audioboom.com/posts/6826520-d-lo-brown)

Gerweck Report Hotline (2005) *Gerweck Report Hotline with Luna Vachon transcript* [Podcast]. Available at (https://wrestlingfigs.com/wrestlingnews/luna-vachon-interview-highlights/)

Kayfabe Wrestling Radio (2013) *Kayfabe Wrestling Radio - Headbanger Thrasher* [Podcast]. Available at (https://www.wrestlinginc.com/news/2013/01/former-wwe-tag-champion-talks-wrestlemania-559996/)

MVP (2017) *VIP Lounge with MVP #83: Mark Henry* [Podcast]. Available at (http://www.mlwradio.com/vip-lounge-with-mvp.html)

Interactive Wrestling Radio (2009) *Interactive Wrestling Radio with 'The Birdman' Koko B. Ware* [Podcast]. Available at (http://www.wrestlingepicenter.com/shows/KoKoBWare/kokoshow.mp3)

Adam Copeland and Jay Reso (2018) *E&C's Pod of Awesomeness - 205 Live GM, Drake Maverick* [Podcast]. Available at (http://apple.com/itunes/)

P3 Radio (2018) *P3radio with Brian Christopher* [Podcast]. Available at

(https://soundcloud.com/user-529928808/p3-radio-interview-with-brian-christopher)

P3 Radio (2018) *P3 Radio Interview with Headbanger Thrasher* [Podcast]. Available at (https://soundcloud.com/user-529928808/p3-radio-interview-with-headbanger-thrasher)

Jim Valley and Fumi Saito (2019) *Pacific Rim: Owen Hart's Japanese Legacy* [Podcast]. Available at (https://www.f4wonline.com/pacific-rim-pro-wrestling-podcast/pacific-rim-owen-harts-japanese-wrestling-legacy-284511)

Rowdy Roddy Piper (2014) *Piper's Pit Podcast #6 Jake 'The Snake' Roberts*[Podcast]. Available at (http://apple.com/itunes/)

Rowdy Roddy Piper (2015) *Piper's Pit Podcast #51 - Jake 'The Snake' Roberts* [Podcast]. Available at (http://apple.com/itunes/)

Rowdy Roddy Piper (2015) *Piper's Pit Podcast #52 - Jake 'The Snake' Roberts* [Podcast]. Available at (http://apple.com/itunes/)

Sean Mooney (2018) *Prime Time with Sean Mooney - Jimmy Korderas* [Podcast]. Available at (http://apple.com/itunes/)

Bruce Prichard and Conrad Thompson (2016) *Something to Wrestle with Bruce Prichard #9 – WrestleMania VII* [Podcast]. Available at (http://apple.com/itunes/)

Bruce Prichard and Conrad Thompson (2017) *Something to Wrestle with Bruce Prichard #39 - Undertaker (1993-1994)* [Podcast]. Available at (http://apple.com/itunes/)

Bruce Prichard and Conrad Thompson (2017) *Something to Wrestle with Bruce Prichard #40 - Owen Hart* [Podcast]. Available at (http://apple.com/itunes/)

Bruce Prichard and Conrad Thompson (2017) *Something to Wrestle with Bruce Prichard #65 - Jeff Jarrett* [Podcast]. Available at (http://apple.com/itunes/)

Bruce Prichard and Conrad Thompson (2019) *Something to Wrestle with Bruce Prichard #147 - WrestleMania X* [Podcast]. Available at (http://apple.com/itunes/)

Bruce Prichard and Conrad Thompson (2019) *Something to Wrestle with Bruce Prichard #164 - Fully Loaded 1999* [Podcast]. Available at (http://apple.com/itunes/)

Chris Jericho (2013) *Talk is Jericho with Adam 'Edge' Copeland* [Podcast]. Available at (http://apple.com/itunes/)

Chris Jericho (2015) *Talk is Jericho with Mark Henry* [Podcast]. Available at (http://apple.com/itunes/)

Chris Jericho (2015) *Talk is Jericho with TJ Wilson and Nattie Neidhart* [Podcast]. Available at (http://apple.com/itunes/)

Chris Jericho (2015) *Talk is Jericho with William Regal* [Podcast]. Available at (http://apple.com/itunes/)

Chris Jericho (2016) *Talk is Jericho with Jeff Jarrett* [Podcast]. Available at (http://apple.com/itunes/)

Chris Jericho (2017) *Talk is Jericho with Jim Cornette and Kenny Bolin* [Podcast]. Available at (http://apple.com/itunes/)

Chris Jericho (2017) *Talk is Jericho with Ross Hart* [Podcast]. Available at (http://apple.com/itunes/)

Chris Jericho (2018) *Talk is Jericho with Dave Meltzer* [Podcast]. Available at (http://apple.com/itunes/)

Chris Jericho (2018) *Talk is Jericho – EP157 – Tyson Kidd & Nattie Neidhart* [Podcast]. Available at (http://apple.com/itunes/)

Ric Flair (2016) *The Ric Flair Show #5 - Ken Patera* [Podcast]. Available at (http://apple.com/itunes/)

Jim Ross (2016) *The Ross Report with Bret Hart* [Podcast]. Available at (https://mmapodcast.com/wrestling/ross-report/)

Jim Ross (2017) *The Ross Report with Marc Mero* [Podcast]. Available at (https://mmapodcast.com/wrestling/ross-report/)

Steve Austin (2018) *The Steve Austin Show - The Stone Cold Photo Album* [Podcast]. Available at (http://apple.com/itunes/)

Steve Austin (2018) *The Steve Austin Show with Billy Gunn* [Podcast]. Available at (http://apple.com/itunes/)

Steve Austin (2013) *The Steve Austin Show with Dave Meltzer* [Podcast]. Available at (http://apple.com/itunes/)

Steve Austin (2014) *The Steve Austin Show with Jim Cornette* [Podcast]. Available at (http://apple.com/itunes/)

Steve Austin (2019) *The Steve Austin Show with Mark Henry* [Podcast]. Available at (http://apple.com/itunes/)

Steve Austin (2016) *The Steve Austin Show with Sean "X-Pac" Waltman* [Podcast]. Available at (http://apple.com/itunes/)

Steve Austin (2017) *The Steve Austin Show with Shane McMahon* [Podcast]. Available at (http://apple.com/itunes/)

Steve Austin (2016) The *Steve Austin Show with William Regal* [Podcast]. Available at (http://apple.com/itunes/)

Steve Austin (2014) *The Steve Austin Show - Answering Fan's Questions* [Podcast]. Available at (http://apple.com/itunes/)

Scott 'Raven' Levy (2017) *The Raven Effect – Doink the Clow Bizarre Rib* [Podcast]. Original episode unknown

Scott 'Raven' Levy (2017) *The Raven Effect - Raven on Abdullah the Butcher* [Podcast]. Original episode unknown

Scott 'Raven' Levy (2017) *The Raven Effect - Raven Winning Belts as Punishment* [Podcast]. Original episode unknown

Two Man Power Trip of Wrestling (2017) *Two Man Power Trip of Wrestling with Hillbilly Jim* [Podcast]. Available at (https://www.podomatic.com/podcasts/tmptow/episodes/2017-03-28T04_15_22-07_00)

Under the Mat Radio (2014*) Under the Mat Radio – Ken Shamrock* [Podcast]. Available at (https://www.blogtalkradio.com/pwkgw/2013/12/31/under-the-mat-episode-13-ken-shamrock)

Joel Ross (2006) *SunSport: WrestleTalk with Randy Orton 2006* [Podcast]. Available at (http://apple.com/itunes/)

Dave Meltzer, Bryan Alvarez (2019) *Wrestling Observer Radio October 15th 2019* [Podcast]. Available at (https://www.f4wonline.com/wrestling-observer-radio/wor-raw-draft-new-japan-wwe-presser-notes-more-294891)

The Jim Cornette Experience via Jim Cornette's Talking Sense YouTube Channel

Jim Cornette (2015) *Jim Cornette on His Famous RAW Shoot Promos* [Online]. Author's collection

Jim Cornette (2016) *Jim Cornette on Harley Race* [Online]. Author's collection

Jim Cornette (2016) *Jim Cornette on Scaffold Match Knee Injury* [Online]. Author's collection

Jim Cornette (2016) *Jim Cornette on Todd Pettengill* [Online]. Author's collection

Jim Cornette (2016) *Jim Cornette on Chyna's Dentist Trip* [Online]. Author's collection

Jim Cornette (2016) *Jim Cornette on Being Ribbed by Owen and Davey* [Online]. Author's collection

Jim Cornette (2016) *Jim Cornette on Wrestlers Sleeping On the Job* [Online]. Author's collection

Jim Cornette (2017) *Jim Cornette on WWE Owning the NWA Since 1998 with Howard Brody* [Online]. Author's collection

Jim Cornette (2018) *Jim Cornette on George 'Daddy Said Sell' Gulas* [Online]. Author's collection

Jim Cornette (2018) *Jim Cornette on How Vince McMahon Screwed Stu Hart* [Online]. Author's collection

Jim Cornette (2018) *Jim Cornette on Shawn Stasiak Secretly Recording Wrestlers' Conversations* [Online]. Author's collection

Jim Cornette (2018) *Jim Cornette on Abdullah the Butcher's Secret Wallet Pocket* [Online]. Author's collection

Books

Snow, A., & Williams, R.O. (2019). *Self Help.* ECW Press

Hart, B. (2011). *Bruce Hart - Straight From the Hart.* ECW Press

Hart, B. (2007). *Hitman: My Real Life in the Cartoon World of Wrestling.* Ebury Press

O'Rourke, L. (2017). *Crazy Like A Fox: The Definitive Chronicle of Brian Pillman 20 Years Later.* CreateSpace Independent Publishing Platform; 1st edition

Hornbaker, T. (2018). *Death of the Territories: Expansion, Betrayal and the War That Changed Pro Wrestling Forever.* ECW Press

Grasso, John (2014). *Historical Dictionary of Wrestling.* Roman and Littlefield

Hart, D., & McLellan, K. (2001). *Under the Mat.* Fenn Pub

Runnels, D., & Vancil, M (2011). *Cross Rhodes: Goldust, Out of the Darkness.* World Wrestling Entertainment

Billington, T., & Coleman, A. (2001). *Dynamite Kid - Pure Dynamite: The Price You Pay for Wrestling Stardom.* Winding Stair Press paperback edition (originally published 1999)

Copeland, A. (2004). *Adam Copeland on Edge.* Simon & Schuster

Steele, G., & Evans, Jim (2013). *George 'The Animal' Steele – Animal.* Triumph Books

Duggan, J., & Williams, Scott (2016). *Hacksaw: The Jim Duggan Story.* Triumph Books, reprint edition

Lauer, B., & Teal, S. (2008). *Harvey Wippleman - Wrestling with the Truth - Bruno Lauer.* Crowbar Press 1st edition

Ross, J. (2003). *J.R.'s Cookbook: True Ringside Tales, BBQ and Down Home Recipes.* World Wrestling Entertainment

Korderas, J. (2013). *The Three Count: My Life in Stripes as a WWE Referee.* ECW Press

Hart, M., & Francis, E. (2004). *Broken Harts: The Life and Death of Owen Hart.* M. Evans & Company

Foley, M. (2002). *Foley is Good.* HarperEntertainment, reprint edition

Foley, M. (2000). *Have a Nice Day: A Tell of Blood and Sweatsocks.* HarperEntertainment, reprint edition

McCoy, H. (2007). *Pain & Passion: The History of Stampede Wrestling.* ECW Press, Revised edition

Olver, G., & Johnson, S. (2005). *Pro Wrestling Hall of Fame: The Tag Teams.* ECW Press

Olver, G., & Johnson, S. (2007). *Pro Wrestling Hall of Fame: The Heels.* ECW Press

Reynolds, R.D., & Alvarez, B. (2014). *The Death of WCW 10th Anniversary if the Bestselling Classic – Revised and Expanded*. ECW Press

Robinson, J. (2010). *Rumble Road: Untold Stories from Outside the Ring*. Simon & Schuster

Michaels, S., & Feigenbaum, A. (2006). *Heartbreak & Triumph: The Shawn Michaels Story*. World Wrestling Entertainment new edition

Austin, S., Ross, J., & Bryant, D. (2004). *The Stone Cold Truth*. World Wrestling Entertainment

O'Brien, D. (2014). *Classical Masculinity and the Spectacular Body on Film*. Palgrave Macmillan, 2014 edition

Sytch, T. (2016). *A Star Shattered: The Rise & Fall & Rise of Wrestling Diva*. Riverdale Avenue Books

Hardy, M., Hardy, J., & Krugman , M. (2003). *The Hardy Boyz: Exist 2 Inspire*. World Wrestling Entertainment

Rock, T., & Layden, J. (2000) *The Rock Says....* HarperEntertainment; first edition

Dixon, J. (2014). *Titan Sinking: The Decline of the WWF in 1995*. Lulu.com

Russo, V. (2005). *Forgiven: One Man's Journey from Self-Glorification to Sanctification*. ECW Press

Russo, V. (2010). *Rope Opera: How WCW Killed Vince Russo*. ECW Press

Solomon, B. (2006). *WWE Legends*. Gallery Books

Newspaper

Dufresne, Chris. (1996). *'He Might Not Be the Best, but Henry Is Definitely the Most'*, Los Angeles Times, July 30th 1996

Hart, B. (1999). *'Reflections of a big brother'*, Calgary Sun, May 31st 1999

Hart, B. (2001). *'Stu deserves huge honour'*, Calgary Sun, February 24th, 2001

'Pro Wrestlers Patera, Saito Found Guilty, Sent to Prison' (1985). Schenectady Gazette, June 15th 1985

Superstar Billy Graham quote (2011). Toronto Sun, April 8th 2011

Magazine

Fishman, S. (2016, February). Triple H interview. American Way Magazine.

Unknown author (1998, December 24th – January 7th). Stone Cold Steve Austin interview. Rolling Stone Magazine

WWF Private Eye. (1998, April) Funkin' Dojo profile. WWF Magazine April 1998 – Funkin' Dojo profile. WWF Magazine

418

Kelly, K. (1999) *Owen Hart – A Celebration of His Life.* WWF Tribute Magazine

McGee, J.T. (1969, January). *'Would you send this boy to college?'* Black Belt Magazine

Todd, T. (1998). *'Mark Henry's Dilemma – Reflections on Drugs at the Olympics.* Iron Game History, Volume 5, Number 1

Muchnick, I. (1988, October) *Born-Again Bashing.* Penthouse

Specific Newsletters Sited

Just a few examples of hundreds of Newsletters read for this book

Figure Four Weekly Newsletter, October 23rd 2000

Figure Four Weekly Newsletter, March 17th 2009

Wrestling Observer Newsletter, November 25th 1991

Wrestling Observer Newsletter, December 14th 1992

Wrestling Observer Newsletter, January 24th 1994

Wrestling Observer Newsletter, January 31st 1994

Wrestling Observer Newsletter, May 22nd 1995

Wrestling Observer Newsletter, August 19th 1996

Wrestling Observer Newsletter, May 31st 1999

Wrestling Observer Newsletter, October 20th 1999

Wrestling Observer Newsletter, October 30th 2000

Wrestling Observer Newsletter, January 1st 2001

Wrestling Observer Newsletter, March 23rd 2009

Wrestling Observer Newsletter, February 27th 2017

Wrestling Observer Newsletter, August 12th 2019

Wrestling Observer Newsletter, November 1st 2019

Reference Websites

WWE Network – wwenetwork.com

Wrestling Observer Newsletter – f4wonline.com

Figure Four Weekly Newsletter – f4wonline.com

Cage Match - Cagematch.net

The History of WWE - thehistoryofwwe.com

Wikipedia – Title belt histories

Websites - Reference

5 Most Hilarious Owen Hart Wrestling Ribs - 2. Matilda The Dog Has Bowel Problems On Live TV. Retrieved from http://whatculture.com/wwe/5-most-hilarious-owen-hart-wrestling-ribs?page=5

Joey Haverford (2019) *10 Strange Themed Cruises That Actually Happened And Rocked.* Retrieved from https://www.thetravel.com/10-strange-themed-cruises-that-actually-happened-and-rocked/

Bob Colling Jr (2017) *The Rise And Fall Of Ahmed Johnson.* Retrieved from https://wrestlingrecaps.com/2017/02/26/the-rise-and-fall-of-ahmed-johnson/

The History of Atlantic City. Retrieved from https://www.gamblingsites.org/casino/destinations/history-of-atlantic-city/

Negro Battle Royal (2014). Retrieved from https://www.ferris.edu/HTMLS/news/jimcrow/question/2014/may.htm

Brian Pillman vs. Sid Vicious (2016). Retrieved from http://www.armpit-wrestling.com/brian-pillman-vs-sid-vicious/

Calgary Stampede homepage. Retrieved from www.calgarystampede.com

CWA Catch Wrestling results (1990). Retrieved from https://wwfoldschool.com/cwa-catch-wrestling-association-1990/

Christian. Retrieved from http://slam.canoe.com/Slam/Wrestling/Bios/christian.html

Professional Wrestling holds 2.13.2. Cobra Clutch. Retrieved from https://en.wikipedia.org/wiki/Professional_wrestling_holds

About Dan "THE BEAST" Severn. Retrieved from http://dansevern.com/about/

Don't Go Messin' With a Country Boy writing credits - https://www.discogs.com/composition/6c0edc68-4b8a-48ae-b499-ec3a8a71ae8d-Dont-Go-Messin-With-A-Country-Boy

Welcome to the World's Largest Dinosaur. Retrieved from https://www.worldslargestdinosaur.com/

Andrew Lutzke (2013) *Kayfabe, Lies and Alibis: Dynamite Kid – A Matter of Price.* Retrieved from http://culturecrossfire.com/wrestling/dynamite-kid-a-matter-of-pride/

Zach Linder (2013) *Fire on the mountain: The oral history of Smoky Mountain Wrestling.* Retrieved from https://www.wwe.com/classics/oral-history-of-smoky-mountain-wrestling

National Wrestling Alliance World Heavyweight Title (2019). Retrieved from http://www.wrestling-titles.com/nwa/world/nwa-h.html

Farmer's Almanac (2019). Retrieved from https://www.farmersalmanac.com/

Paul Boesch Wikipedia entry. Retrieved from https://en.wikipedia.org/wiki/Paul_Boesch

Ajith Athrady (2018) *India tops world in deaths due to road mishaps: WHO.* Retrieved from https://www.deccanherald.com/national/india-tops-world-deaths-due-707066.html

Jamie Greer (2019) *Jacques Rougeau Sr. Passes Away at 89.* Retrieved from https://lastwordonprowrestling.com/2019/07/03/jacques-rougeau-sr-passes-away-at-89/

Enterprise Center Wikipedia entry. Retrieved from https://en.wikipedia.org/wiki/Enterprise_Center

WWE.com Luther Lindsay bio. Retrieved from https://www.wwe.com/superstars/luther-lindsay

Richard Whittaker (2008) *Olympian, Pro Wrestler, All-Around Nice Guy: Standing on the shoulders of Mark Henry.* Retrieved from https://www.austinchronicle.com/sports/2008-07-18/645907/

Marty Jannetty firings (2006). Retrieved from https://www.wrestlingnewssource.com/news/169/Breaking_News_Marty_Jannetty_fired_for_the_8th_time/

Might Chang bio (2014). Retrieved from http://www.onlineworldofwrestling.com/bios/m/mighty-chang/

The World staff (2016) *Mr Fuji, a prankster in and out of the ring, dies at age 82.* Retrieved from https://www.pri.org/stories/2016-08-29/mr-fuji-prankster-and-out-ring-dies-age-82

Member of the Order of Canada (CM) (2019). Retrieved from https://www.canada.ca/en/department-national-defence/services/medals/medals-chart-index/member-order-canada-cm.html

JP Zarka. *Owen Hart – The King of Ribs | Stories of Heart, Humor, and Humility.* Retrieved from https://prowrestlingstories.com/pro-wrestling-stories/owen-hart-ribs/

JP Zarka. *Ribs and Practical Jokes in Professional Wrestling – The Best Stories.* Retrieved from https://prowrestlingstories.com/pro-wrestling-stories/ribs-and-practical-jokes-in-professional-wrestling-the-best-stories/

Biography of Reg Park. Retrieved from www.regpark.net/biography

bdamage1 (2019*) Remembering The Short Lived Ultimate Warrior's Wrestling School* (Warrior University). Retrieved from https://ringthedamnbell.wordpress.com/2019/02/01/remembering-the-short-lived-ultimate-warriors-wrestling-school-warrior-university/

Off the Record with Michael Landsberg, March 30, 2001 review. Retrieved from http://evie163.tripod.com/articles/id38.html

David Mikkelson (2001) *Saltpeter in the Military.* Retrieved from https://www.snopes.com/fact-check/the-saltpeter-principle/

Mr. Stewart Edward Hart, C.M. profile. Retrieved from

https://www.gg.ca/en/honours/recipients/146-15161

Greg Oliver. *Stu Hart, the wrestler, circa 1946.* Retrieved from
http://slam.canoe.com/Slam/Wrestling/2003/10/16/228025.html

Obituary: Terry Todd, Ph.D. January 1, 1938-July 7, 2018. Retrieved from
https://www.powerlifting.sport/fileadmin/ipf/data/downloads/terrytodd-obit.pdf

Brian Ashcraft (2011) *The DS Game, Japan Will Forgive. The Sexy Orgy, It Won't.* Retrieved
from https://www.kotaku.com.au/2011/10/the-ds-game-japan-will-forgive-the-sexy-orgy-it-
wont/

Jason King (2016) *The Great Fall of Chyna: How WWE's Greatest Female Wrestler Disappeared.*
Retrieved from https://thelab.bleacherreport.com/the-great-fall-of-chyna/

The Jesse Ventura Story IMDb Entry - https://www.imdb.com/title/tt0198573/

David Bixenspan (2016) *The last wrestling hotline still worth calling.* Retrieved from
https://kernelmag.dailydot.com/issue-sections/features-issue-sections/16651/wrestling-
hotlines-history/

NYCgo.com Staff (2019) *TV Show Tapings.* Retrieved from
https://www.nycgo.com/articles/tv-show-tapings

Mike Mooneyham (2001) *Third Time Charm for Bischoff?* Retrieved from
http://www.mikemooneyham.com/2001/01/21/third-time-charm-for-bischoff/

Jeremy Tepper (2017) *After more than 30 years, Troy Martin, aka Shane Douglas, continues love
of pro wrestling.* Retrieved from https://www.timesonline.com/e166680c-e769-11e6-95b0-
2fadb9e82d43.html

JP Zarka. *Title Belt Maker Dave Millican on His Piece of History.* Retrieved from
https://prowrestlingstories.com/pro-wrestling-stories/title-belt-history/

Jeremy Lambert (2019) *Todd Pettengill Closes Out WPLJ Radio Show In New York.* Retrieved
from https://411mania.com/wrestling/todd-pettengill-wplj-new-york/

WWE.com Joseph 'Toots' Mondt profile. Retrieved from
https://www.wwe.com/superstars/joseph-toots-mondt

Stefano Mocella (2015) *Top 15 Funniest Owen Hart Prank Stories.* Retrieved from
https://www.thesportster.com/wrestling/top-15-funniest-owen-hart-prank-stories/

John-Paul Volino (2014) *Tragedy in The Hart-Land.* Retrieved from
https://www.prowrestlinghistoricalsociety.com/articles-0077.html

UFC Hall of Fame - https://www.ufc.com/ufc-hall-fame

The Chyna Sex Tapes. Retrieved from https://www.vivid.com/celebs/chyna/Chyna.html

WCW lawsuit – *World Championship Wrestling v. Titan Sports, Inc., 46 F. Supp. 2d 118 (D.
Conn. 1999).* Retrieved from https://law.justia.com/cases/federal/district-

courts/FSupp2/46/118/2488082/

Michael Sidgwick (2018) *Why Mark Henry Was NEARLY WWE's Biggest Ever Flop* - https://whatculture.com/wwe/why-mark-henry-was-nearly-wwes-biggest-ever-flop

Joshua A. Shuart, Ph.D. & Peter A. Maresco, Ph.D. (2006) *World Wrestling Entertainment: Achieving Continued Growth and Market Penetration through International Expansion.* Retrieved from http://thesportjournal.org/article/world-wrestling-entertainment-achieving-continued-growth-and-market-penetration-through-international-expansion/

Wrestlecrap - http://wrestlecrap.com/inductions/past-inductions/

Art O Donnell (2018) *BRET & OWEN ON HONEY, I SHRUNK THE KIDS – THE HARTS TEAM WITH THE KIDSHRINKERS.* Retrieved from http://wrestlecrap.com/inductions/honey-i-shrunk-the-kids/

RD Reynolds. *WrestleCrap – The Jesse Ventura Story: Never Let the Truth Get In the Way of a Good Story.* Link unavailable

RD Reynolds. Wrestlecrap - *Workout War! Chyna! The Warrior! And Richard Simmons!* Link unavailable

Sheldon Kane III (2004) *WrestleMania XIV Review.* Retrieved from http://www.thehistoryofwwe.com/mania14review.htm

Dawn Walton (2000) *Wrestler widow, WWF settle.* Retrieved from https://www.theglobeandmail.com/news/national/wrestler-widow-wwf-settle/article4168593/

WWE Anthology Personnel. Retrieved from https://en.wikipedia.org/wiki/WWE_Anthology

Emma Kelly (2018) *WWE star Jason Sensation threatens to shoot himself at RAW event in apparent Twitter hoax.* Retrieved from https://metro.co.uk/2018/08/28/wwe-star-jason-sensation-threatens-to-shoot-himself-at-raw-event-in-apparent-twitter-hoax-7888814/

WWE.com Staff (2012) *Whatever happened to the In Your House house?* Retrieved from https://www.wwe.com/article/wwe-in-your-house-winner-interview

WWE.com Staff (2013) *Jim Ross to retire.* Retrieved from https://www.wwe.com/inside/jim-ross-to-retire

Websites – Interviews

Adam Harrison (2014) *Interview: From nWo to Magic Mike: An Interview with Kevin Nash.* Retrieved from https://aestheticmagazinetoronto.com/2014/06/05/interview-from-nwo-to-magic-mike-an-interview-with-kevin-nash/

Keith Elliot Greenberg (2013) *After Addiction and Tragedy, The Iron Sheik Gets Back Up off the Mat.* Retrieved from https://bleacherreport.com/articles/1732808-after-addiction-and-tragedy-the-iron-sheik-gets-back-up-off-the-mat

Kris Eazay (2013) *Ahmed Johnson Clears the Air and Kills a Few Rumors.* Retrieved from https://bleacherreport.com/articles/1727303-ahmed-johnson-clears-the-air-and-kills-a-few-rumors

Evan Ginzburg. *An Interview with Bruce Hart: How He Revolutionized Pro Wrestling.* Retrieved from https://prowrestlingstories.com/pro-wrestling-stories/bruce-hart-interview/

Joshua Gagnon (2016) *Bret Hart On Wrestling Kurt Angle In His Dreams, Losing Movement In Fingers, Owen Hart.* Retrieved from https://www.wrestlinginc.com/news/2016/12/bret-hart-on-wrestling-kurt-angle-in-his-dreams-620428/

Keith Elliot Greenberg (2014) *Bret Hart, Jeff Jarrett and More Reminisce on Owen Hart 15 Years After His Death.* Retrieved from https://bleacherreport.com/articles/2072366-bret-hart-jeff-jarrett-and-more-reminisce-on-owen-hart-15-years-after-his-death

Bruce Hart (2000) *Remembering my brother: Bruce Hart reflects back on the life of his brother Owen on his 35th birthday.* Retrieved from http://www.angelfire.com/ny2/RayNRon/misc/bruceowentrib.html

Bill Hanstock (2017*) Debra McMichael Shares Tips For Staying Awake On The Road And Her Memories Of Owen Hart.* Retrieved from https://uproxx.com/prowrestling/debra-mcmichael-interview-wcw-pepe-the-dog-owen-hart/4/

Danny Stone (2016) *Royal Ramblings Meets Diana Hart-Smith.* Retrieved from https://www.huffingtonpost.co.uk/danny-stone/diana-hart-smith_b_7649338.html

Greg Oliver (2012) *Doug Furnas dies in his sleep.* Retrieved from http://slam.canoe.com/Slam/Wrestling/2012/03/04/19457996.html

Mark Suleymanov (2015) *Exclusive: Val Venis Talks Attitude Era, Owen Hart and Medical Marijuana.* Retrieved from https://www.inquisitr.com/2151309/exclusive-val-venis-talks-attitude-era-owen-hart-and-medical-marijuana/

Josh Barnett (2017) *From mat to ring, WWE's amateur and pro wrestling.* Retrieved from https://eu.usatoday.com/story/sports/2017/05/02/wwe-olympic-wrestling-ncaa-kurt-angle-brock-lesnar-chad-gable-jason-jordan/100825750/

John Gleeson (1999) *Hart was 'sweetest guy you'd ever meet.* Retrieved from http://www.angelfire.com/oh/sacstuff/owen.html

Interactive Wrestling Radio Interview – 'Bastion Booger' Mike Shawn transcript. Retrieved from http://www.wrestlingepicenter.com/IWR/interviews/MikeShaw2804.html

Alan J. Wojcik (2004) Interview with Mideon AKA Dennis Knight transcript. Retrieved from https://www.twnpnews.com/messages2/10000/10892.shtml

Daniel Pena (2014) *Jim Cornette Speaks Out On Triple H, Vince Russo, The State Of TNA, Owen Hart & British Bulldog.* Retrieved from https://www.wrestlinginc.com/wi/news/2014/0122/569457/jim-cornette-speaks-out-on-triple-h/index-2.shtml

Justin Barrasso (2016) *Week in WrestlingL Is Roman Reigns ready?; Ken Shamrock looks back.* Retrieved from https://www.si.com/extra-mustard/2016/02/24/week-wrestling-roman-reigns-joey-ryan-triple-h-ken-shamrock

Brock Allen (2018) *Throwback Tribute: Jim "The Anvil" Neidhart.* Retrieved from https://www.wrestlingdvdnetwork.com/throwback-tribute-jim-the-anvil-neidhart/158686/

Tim Fiorvanti (2017*) Jim Ross reflects on his time with, and the future of, wrestling commentary.* Retrieved from https://www.espn.co.uk/wwe/story/_/id/20981392/wwe-jim-ross-reflects-changing-wrestling-commentary-landscape

Joshua Caudill (2014) *WWE Wrestler Mark Henry: One-On-One Interview.* Retrieved from https://www.mandatory.com/culture/772913-wwe-wrestler-mark-henry-one-one-interview

SLAM! Wrestling Staff. *Never rib a midget and other fun tales.* Retrieved from http://slam.canoe.com/Slam/Wrestling/2016/02/09/22602024.html

Brad Dykens (2011) *A Tribute to the King of Harts* (Owen Hart). Retrieved from http://www.onlineworldofwrestling.com/a-tribute-to-the-king-of-harts-owen-hart

Tommy Messano (2018) *Owen Hart's widow, Martha, responds to Bret Hart's WWE Hall of Fame claims.* Retrieved from https://www.cagesideseats.com/wwe/2018/7/12/17565668/owen-hart-widow-martha-hart-responds-bret-harts-wwe-hall-of-fame

Kenai Andrews. *Reno Riggins: Getting the job done.* Retrieved from http://slam.canoe.com/Slam/Wrestling/2007/06/21/4280344.html

Danny Stone (2014) *Royal Ramblings Meets Matt Hardy.* Retrieved from https://www.huffingtonpost.co.uk/danny-stone/matt-hardy-wrestling_b_5846114.html

Savio Vega Reddit AMA (2015) *I am Savio Vega aka TNT, Kwang, The Caribbean Kid and El Hombre Dinamita. Ask Me Anything!* Retrieved from https://www.reddit.com/r/SquaredCircle/comments/3ndppc/i_am_savio_vega_aka_tnt_kwang_the_caribbean_kid/

Eric Gargiulo (2011) Shane Douglas Interview Transcript. Retrieved from https://prowrestlingradio.com/shane-douglas-interview-transcript/

Rob Leigh (2016) *WWE announcing legend Jim Ross believes he was fired by Vince MCMahon to 'save face'.* Retrieved from https://talksport.com/sport/wwe/47097/wwe-announcing-legend-jim-ross-believes-he-was-fired-vince-mcmahon-save-face-160302186846/

Adam Proteau (2017) *Talking Wrestling and Comedy with 'Million Dollar Man' Ted DiBiase.* Retrieved from https://www.vulture.com/2017/04/talking-wrestling-and-comedy-with-million-dollar-man-ted-dibiase.html

Terri Runnels Reddit AMA (2014) *I am former WWE/WCW Diva Terri Runnels/Marlena/Alexandra York, here to answer your questions, so go ahead AMA).* Retrieved from https://www.reddit.com/r/IAmA/comments/24th69/i_am_former_wwewcw_diva_terri/

Raj Girl (2014) *Terri Runnels Talks Owen Memories, Pillman Angle, Goldust, Which Angle She Shot Down, WWE Career.* Retrieved from https://www.wrestlinginc.com/news/2014/07/terri-runnels-talks-owen-memories-577830/

Brian Ellion. *Val Venis talks wrestling again and politics.* Retrieved from http://slam.canoe.com/Slam/Wrestling/2009/08/26/10615476.html

Claudia Reiff (email). *The WWF Wrestle Vessel.* Retrieved from www.ddtdigest.com/features/vessel.htm

RD Reynolds. *Wrestlecrap - Curt Hennig Was Right - Rap IS Crap! + Bonus Interview with Oscar* (link unavailable)

Jon Robinson (2009) *WWE Legends: Bret Hart Interview.* Retrieved from https://www.espn.co.uk/espn/thelife/videogames/news/story?id=3965096

Phil Speer and Seth Mates (2003) *WWE Superstars Remember Owen Hart.* Retrieved from http://www.angelfire.com/ny2/RayNRon/misc/remember.html

Bobby Melok (2012) *Where Are They Now? Tod Pettengill.* Retrieved from https://www.wwe.com/classics/wherearetheynow/where-are-they-now-todd-pettengill

WWE.com interview with The Rock (2005). Link unavailable

Facebook

Bret Hart (2018, July 19th) *Bret replies to Martha* [Facebook post]. Retrieved from https://www.facebook.com/hitmanbrethart/posts/10156642506929443

Brian 'Blue Meanie' Heffron (2013, May 23rd) *The Meanie Message: Remembering Owen Hart* [Facebook post]. Retrieved from https://shitloadsofwrestling.tumblr.com/post/145159961734/the-meanie-message-remembering-owen-hart-by-the

John Layfield. Retrieved from https://www.facebook.com/John-Layfield-194176253533/

Mick Foley. Retrieved from from https://www.facebook.com/RealMickFoley

Online Interviews

Hart, Owen. (1998) *Interviewed by Mike Mooneyham for www.mikemooneyham.com* | Available at http://www.mikemooneyham.com/1998/01/18/owen-keeps-job-family-separate/ (January 18th 1998)

Hart, Owen. (1995) AOL interview transcript | Available at http://www.hack-man.com/Wrestling/Interviews/wres-news-owen-hart-interview-2.html (December 1995)

Hart, Owen. (1996) AOL interview transcript | Available at http://www.hack-man.com/Wrestling/Interviews/wres-news-owen-hart-interview-1.html (March 1996)

Hart, Owen. (1996) Interviews by Bill Banks for AOL, AOL interview transcript | Available at http://wrestlingarchive.yolasite.com/interviews/interview-with-owen-hart-1996 (May 1996)

Hart, Owen. (1998) 'Owen Hart talks to SLAM! Wrestling', Interviewed by Greg Oliver for SLAM! Wrestling | Available at http://slam.canoe.com/Slam/Wrestling/Bios2/2011/06/22/18319021.html (March 6th 1998)

Hart, Owen. (1998) Interviewed by John Powell | Available at http://www.angelfire.com/ut/owenhart/interview898.html (1st August 1998)

Hart, Owen. (1998) 'Owen Hart interview concluded', interviewed by Greg Oliver for SLAM! Wrestling | Available at http://slam.canoe.com/Slam/Wrestling/Bios2/2011/06/22/18319086.html (December 1998)

Hart, Bret. (1997) Prodigy Chat interview transcript | Available at http://paullfc2.tripod.com/bret.html (December 7th 1997)

James Romero is a YouTuber, property developer and
noted raconteur living in Cheshire, England.
This is his first (and probably last) book.

Photograph taken in Da Nang, Vietnam.

Made in the USA
Coppell, TX
29 December 2019